KEEPING THE FAITH: STILL RUNNING

DELLA LOREDO

*"I have finished the race, I have kept the faith.
Finally, there is laid up for me the crown of righteousness,
which the Lord, the righteous Judge, will give to me on that Day."
2 Timothy 4:7, 8, NKJV*

*"Don't stop running,
for until the war with Stan is over,
you must remain strong to withstand his attacks."
- Crown Prince Joshua Damour*

TEACH Services, Inc.
P U B L I S H I N G
www.TEACHServices.com • (800) 367-1844

Copyright © 2015 TEACH Services, Inc.
ISBN-13: 978-1-4796-0540-8 (Paperback)
ISBN-13: 978-1-4796-0541-5 (ePub)
ISBN-13: 978-1-4796-0542-2 (Mobi)
Library of Congress Control Number: 2015908747

Published by

TEACH Services, Inc.
PUBLISHING
www.TEACHServices.com • (800) 367-1844

DEDICATION

To José, my favorite husband
(Okay, my only husband—but still my favorite!)

Acknowledgments

Thank you to my family—my husband, **José Loredo**; my children, **David** and **Ariel**; my parents, **Finn and Margie Santala**. Thank you all for your forbearance and flexibility.

A big thanks to each of those who took the time to evaluate the early drafts of this tale: **Sonia Brock; Celia and Catalina Gil, Robert Lingle; Celia Romero, Peggy Mishele Sneed; Dennis, Jenae,** and **Elise Williams**. Your insights, encouragements, and criticisms were invaluable in helping me whip this story into something akin to a book.

A special thanks to **Chris Dolph** and **Matt Stevens** of the Division of Clinical Anatomy at Stanford University for your helpfulness in showing me around and your patience in answering one or two (hundred) questions.

Thank you (again!) to **Youth With a Mission (YWAM)** in Creel, Mexico, and translators **Josué Pérez Moreno** and **Domingo González Garcia** for your help with the Tarahumara translations.

Thank you to the members of the National City branch of the San Diego Christian Writers Guild who helped me polish this manuscript: **Felicia Alvarez, Gail Bones, Candy Rizzardini, Marta Wingler,** and **James Wyatt**.

Most of all, a big thank you to our gracious God for this glimpse into Your awesome love. Truly, "In Your presence is fullness of joy; At Your right hand are pleasures forevermore" (Psalms 16:11, NKJV).

CONTENTS

Author's Note

This novel is an allegory—a long, drawn-out parable. Though based on a metaphor from the Bible, it, like any parable, has limits beyond which it breaks down and is unable to represent truth. It's simply impossible to adequately represent the infinite with the finite, so trying to do so will necessarily create some challenges.

In this book, all of the physical properties assigned to supernatural beings will suffer from this limitation. For example, although the Bible clearly speaks of the Holy Spirit as "He," it became necessary to represent Him as a woman for the purposes of this fictional narrative. This is not to imply that I believe God is a woman; I don't. It's simply a literary device that allows me to use a physical being to represent—though imperfectly—One whose nature is beyond human comprehension.

Another example is in the representation of angelic beings. The Bible tells us little of their nature and society, so putting together a cohesive story required filling in the gaps where our knowledge is lacking. If this sounds like a fancy way of saying that I made stuff up, that's because it is. Please recognize these filled-in gaps for exactly what they are—my inventions. They are not truths about the real world and should never be used to corroborate or inspire nonbiblical ideas.

Despite their limitations, parables do have the distinct advantage of being able to speak to many different individuals in widely varying circumstances. Perhaps that's why Christ used them so often. It's my hope that this story will provide you with a fresh perspective and some thought-provoking insights regarding your relationship with God. However, be sure to evaluate any ideas it spawns in light of the only sure authority—the Bible.

To help you with this, you can find a list of the scriptural references alluded to in this book, as well as links to some excellent Bible studies, at my website: www.DellaLoredo.com. You'll find other fun stuff there, including deleted scenes and behind-the-scenes commentary. Oh—and it's the only place on earth where you can learn to speak Paradisian!

Cast of Characters

[Paradisian spelling/pronunciation in brackets where applicable; Paradisians generally use these terms among themselves.]

@management.com: The division of Moden Industries dedicated to overthrowing the Damours through "company management" (the manipulation of groups) and "entity management" (the manipulation of individuals). Code names used in these e-mails include:

    #1offspring: Stanley Moden Jr.

    A- or **MA-(any number):** various agents (A-) or master agents (MA-)

    bestagent: Adlai Menod; agent assigned to Chris Strider

    companymaster: Stanley L. Moden Sr.

    Dictator: Doug Damour

    entitymaster: Camille L. Desmon

    KK: Kids' Klub

Adlai Menod: Stan's research assistant; Moden Industries' best agent; holds PhDs in physiology and biochemistry

Aedan McElroy: pacesetter at the RAB in Stanford; brother to **Sean McElroy**. Wife: **Julie**; two daughters, including **Hannah**

Benjamin Strider Sr.: Chris's late father; envisioned the Kids' Klub

Benjamin Strider Jr. (Benny): Chris's eldest brother; a gardener. Wife: **Marie**; Sons: **Kevin**, **Adrian**, and **Harry**

Camille L. Desmon: Stan's sister; Moden Industries' junior partner; holds a PhD (psychology) and MBA. [**Kamíl** *(kah-MEEL)* **Lanáj** *(lah-NAZH)* **Desmón** *(days-MOAN)*; nickname: **Kami** *(KAH-mee)*]

Christian Strider: Susana's husband; medical student (later pediatrician)

Debora Damour: Queen of Paradise Island [**Debora** *(day-BORE-ah)* **Deón** *(day-OWN)* **Damoúr** *(dah-moe-OOR)*]

Doug Damour: King of Paradise Island, president of Damour Enterprises, world's richest man [**Doúg** *(doe-OOG)* **Deón** *(day-OWN)* **Damoúr** *(dah-moe-OOR)*]

Efraím Suarez: Chris's classmate (later medical partner)

Gabriel *[ga-BREE-el]* **Lanáj** *[lah-NAZH]*: the general in command of the Paradisian army

Garrick Sondem: Stan's closest friend; director of security for Moden Industries; holds an MD, PhD (physics), two MAs (pharmacology and psychology), and MBA. [**Garike** *(gah-REE-kay)* **Lok** *(loke)* **Sondem** *(SONE-dame)*]

George Strong: Chris's classmate (later a pediatrician). Wife: **Vanessa**

Iona: Camille's executive secretary

Jané *[zhah-NAY]* **Lanáj** *[lah-NAZH]*: a colonel in the Royal Guard; assigned to Susana

Joshua Damour: Crown Prince of Paradise Island; world's most renowned running coach [**Joshua** *(joe-SHOO-ah)* **Deón** *(day-OWN)* **Damoúr** *(dah-moe-OOR)*]

Juan Misi: Chris's great-grandfather; responsible for the scar on Stan's cheek

Lanse *[LAN-say]* **Meshon** *[MAY-shone]*: lieutenant general in command of the Paradisian Royal Guard.

Lester Stretch: Chris's classmate (later a neonatologist)

Madelyn: Stan's executive secretary

Maurice Pim: the company physician for Moden Industries; holds an MD and PhD in physiology

Mike Strider: Chris's second oldest brother; a gardener. Wife: **Michelle**; four sons, including **Roman**

Patric: Camille's assistant and most trusted staff member

Ray Mendez: Chris's maternal uncle; a carpenter. Wife: deceased; two daughters and a son

Rose Strider Moore: Chris's twin sister; Stan/Camille's egg donor. Husband: **Ivan**; three sons

Sadira L. Moden: Stan and Camille's youngest child and only daughter

Saxon L. Moden: Stan and Camille's second son

Serji *[SAHR-zhee]* **Meshon** *[MAY-shone]*: a major in the Royal Guard; assigned to Susana

Sheridan L. Moden: Stan and Camille's third son

Stanley L. Moden Sr.: Camille's brother; senior partner of Moden Industries; America's richest man; holds a JD, PhD (sociology), DSc (biochemistry), and MBA. [**Lustanli** *(loo-STAN-lee)* **Lanáj** *(lah-NAZH)* **Modén** *(moe-DANE)*; nickname: **Lusu** *(LOO-soo)*]

Stanley L. Moden Jr.: Stan and Camille's eldest son

Steve Strider: Chris's third oldest brother; a gardener. Wife: **Jeannie**; three sons

Susana López Strider: Chris's wife; PT doctoral student (later pediatric physical therapist)

Taylor Menod: accountant and entity management agent with Moden Industries. Brother: **Adlai**

Vanessa Strong: Susana's best friend; husband: **George**

Vanti *[VAHN-tee]* **Lok** *[loke]*: a captain in the Royal Guard; assigned to Chris Strider

Viktor *[VEEK-tor]* **Lok** *[loke]*: a major in the Royal Guard; assigned to Chris Strider

PROLOGUE

Camille L. Desmon, PhD, slipped her rented Bentley into a parking spot far from the hotel's front door, stole up the back stairwell, and carefully scanned the hallway before dashing to her hotel suite. It was all rather indecorous behavior for one of her stature, and she wondered briefly what the media would say should they learn that the "most powerful woman in the hemisphere" was engaging in behavior that could only be termed "skulking."

Still, some prey merited special attention. And, although meeting this couple here in Big Sur was sheer chance, she could not allow the opportunity to pass unexploited.

She approached her bedroom window obliquely to stay out of view and surveyed the surrounding redwoods. When she spied the couple stretching in the shade of a tree not far away, the tension in her chest abated. They had obviously not sighted her as she'd driven past. If they had, they'd not be chatting and laughing in such a carefree manner now.

The two set off together, their strides easy, and she murmured crossly, "Still running."

It didn't surprise her, not from those two. Yet it would have made her life so much easier if they had grown lax after finishing Damour's big race. Although Damour himself warned his runners to remain vigilant and fit, her agents had a remarkably easy time convincing many that they "deserved" a break after his grueling 6,000-mile racecourse.

But, of course, Christian and Susana Strider *would* be an exception. They would probably even maintain peak conditioning by participating in Damour's yearly ultramarathons, exactly as he advised.

She heaved a frustrated sigh. The couple had already evaded several of her agents' plots against them. Yet she dare not admit defeat. Paradise Island's royal family had already exiled her and her brother, world-renown mogul Stan Moden, from their homeland, denying them access to the life-sustaining Viv fruit that was their birthright. Now King Doúg Damoúr, Queen Debora, and Crown Prince Joshua intended to destroy all that she and Stan had spent six long millennia building. And they intended to use this couple in their wretched plan.

Still these two—mere humans—had not the perspective granted her by virtue of her long life and superior intelligence. Nor had they virtually unlimited financial resources, ruthless determination, and centuries of experience in fighting Damour's supporters. Not that any of this would be worth a jot against them if they truly trusted Damour's wisdom. Yet her brother had largely reconditioned the human race; most now relied on their own wisdom rather than Damour's.

She stepped to the dresser and withdrew the plain ironwood box nestled beneath her undergarments. She had long required herself to be ever prepared to meet the enemy, wherever she may find him. Today that meticulous preparation would be rewarded.

Opening the box, she examined the collection of vials that rested in carefully padded cells until she found the poison she sought. Then she selected one of the small plastic pouches secured to the lid and held it up to the light to confirm the presence of a tiny dart within.

Yes, she had all she needed.

PART I

CHANGE

As the trail grew steeper, Susana Strider's sides heaved painfully, her breathing labored. Something was wrong—her gait felt off, slow and awkward. If she didn't reach the finish line soon, she wouldn't be able to complete this race.

Her feet hit a paved surface as she rounded a corner. Cheers erupted from the spectators lining the home stretch, and a surge of adrenaline reenergized her. She could see the finish line now—just there, halfway up the golden street.

Wait—the what? Was she on Paradise Island? How had she gotten here?

The crowd's energy swelled as she drew near her goal, and a short, bald man stepped out from the crowd. "Mind if I join you?"

"Of course not," she said and then gave him another look. "Excuse me, but what's your name? I feel like I should know you."

"I'm Paul of Tarsus. Prince Joshua asked me to watch for you."

She caught her breath. "You're Paul? You spread running—"

"Pardon me," he said, holding up a hand. "But please say nothing of my life as you know it, for much of it is yet to be. You see, this time is still in the future for me—as it is for this great cloud of witnesses."

As his hand swept the crowd, she realized that she must be dreaming. She couldn't be on Paradise Island. And she couldn't be talking to Paul—he was dead.

"For you, however, it's the present," he continued. "And you're needed inside—urgently."

His gaze fell to her hands, and his expression turned to one of sympathy, almost pity. She looked down to see a stunningly beautiful bouquet in her arms. She had never seen such vibrant colors, such full blossoms. But as the delightful fragrance wafted upward, the implausibility hit her: Why was she trying to carry a bouquet while running?

Yes, definitely a dream.

Paul leaned toward her confidentially. "Do you mind some advice from an old runner?"

"No, I'd appreciate your coaching."

"This probably seems like a dream to you, but it isn't."

A chill crawled up Susana's back at this echo of her thoughts.

"So don't let anything interfere with running. Not here, and not back home. Throw off everything that hinders you, and run the race with perseverance."

Did he mean she should throw away this gorgeous bouquet? Was he nuts?

Besides, she suddenly remembered that she was supposed to take it some-where. She didn't remember where exactly, but she was supposed to deliver the flowers safely to—well, someone.

"Oh, these flowers are easy to carry," she said brightly. "Besides, the end is right here."

"End? No, this is merely the beginning."

She must have heard him wrong—they crossed the finish line as he spoke, and a fresh round of cheers drowned out his voice. Besides, the words she thought she heard didn't make sense.

Breathing much harder than usual, she slowed first to a jog and then to a walk as she cooled down. Paul matched her pace as he led the way to a handsome building at the end of the street. Itsun Ekanu *was printed over the entrance—"Army Headquarters." Opening the door, Paul motioned her into a large, crowded room.*

"Who are all these people?" she asked.

"They're forecasters. This is the Forecasters' Observation Room," he added. "But you're needed elsewhere—as a participant. I'll show you the way."

He guided her toward the room's opposite side. Something there held the group's attention, but she was too short to see through them. Suddenly several people cried out: "Isaiah, look!" "Oh, no, only an hour!" "Daniel, if he gets in now, will there still be enough time?"

"What's going on, Paul?" she asked.

The last of the crowd parted before them, and Susana stood before a long wall with a door in the middle. Above the door, the red numbers of a digital clock read 23:01:02, with the seconds clicking forward as she watched.

Extending outward from either side of the door, a window ran the entire length of the wall. Through this window she could see into three different rooms: on her far left, a courtroom with a trial in progress; in the middle, some kind of control room, buzzing with military personnel; on her right, a hallway ending at a door that led into the control room.

One person stood at the door in that hallway: Chris Strider, the man she had just married. Obviously flustered, he was desperately searching through his pockets and muttering, "What did I do with it? It must be here somewhere."

"Chris," she called with a wave.

"He can't see or hear you," Paul said. "The windows are one-way mirrors."

"Oh. What's he's looking for?"

"The access badge that will grant him admittance to the War Room."

She stifled a gasp. War Room? She didn't like the sound of that at all. Once Chris went in, they would no doubt ask him to do something dangerous, probably on a front line somewhere. And, knowing Chris, he'd do anything their sponsor, King Doug Damour, asked. But she didn't want him doing something risky. Surely there was somebody else in this great big world who could do the job instead. Why did Doug need to involve Chris?

Aloud she said, "I don't remember seeing such a badge among his things."

"No," Paul agreed. "He hasn't received it yet, but he doesn't know that, and we can't take it to him." Stepping toward the door that led into the War Room, he added hopefully, "But now that you're here …"

Susana followed him warily. War Room?

Approaching the Royal Guard who stood at attention beside the door, Paul said, "She's here."

With a warm smile for Susana, the guard said, "That's excellent news, Paul. Thank you." He tapped his head behind his right ear and said, "She's arrived, Your Majesty … Yes, sir."

He opened the door and beckoned Susana to enter. Everyone within stopped their work, and a wave of relieved murmurs rustled through the room. She recognized only one person—General Gabriel Lanáj, the commander of the Paradisian army.

A door connecting the War Room to the courtroom on the left opened, and she heard the Damours' archenemy, Stan Moden, railing against a man who cowered near the judge's bench. As Stan's booming voice enumerated several accusations, something tightened painfully in Susana's stomach. Less than three months before, she had stood by helplessly while he mercilessly prosecuted her husband—then fiancé—in the same way. Stan had even gotten him sentenced to death. Only the intervention of Doug's son, Prince Joshua, had saved Chris's life.

Yet this seemed to be a different kind of trial. She got the idea that a guilty verdict here would result in something far worse than death. What's more, the charges—selfishness, love of ease, vanity—were things she could also be accused of.

It was again Josh, now sitting as judge, who saved the poor wretch at the bench. Raising his voice over Stan's tirade, he thundered, "I reject all your accusations, Stan! I've plucked this brand from the fire!"

Authority resounded in the prince's voice, evincing a raw power and majesty that made even Susana tremble a little, although he was her friend. It certainly was not lost on Stan. The beefy strongman quailed and fell immediately silent.

Turning to the two bailiffs, Josh softened his tone. "Take off his filthy clothes." As the men pulled a hopelessly stained robe over the defendant's head, Josh told the man, "Don't worry—I'll give you a rich robe instead. I've taken away all your kanuf." (Paradisian: sin)

He motioned to the men who had taken the dirty robe, and they put beautiful, clean clothes on the defendant. Josh went on to promise him many wonderful things that made his face light up.

While Josh spoke, another man standing at the one-way mirror to Susana's left scribbled frantically. When the prince finished, Paul asked, "Did you get it all, Zechariah?"

"Every last word," Zechariah replied in a husky voice, obviously moved.

Josh stepped down from the bench and kissed the newly acquitted man on the forehead. Then, removing his judge's robe, he passed through the door into the War Room and called amiably, "Come in, Susana. We've been waiting for you."

Susana's heart leaped at his greeting. Though an incredibly important man—the Crown Prince of Paradise Island, the commander-in-chief of the world's biggest army, and the most renowned running coach in the world—he had a way of making everybody feel special, no matter how inconsequential they might be.

Still, as she glanced around at the many consoles with computers, holographic maps, and various other technical paraphernalia, she could only manage one hesitant step into the room. If she was anxious about Chris walking into something called a war room, she was only slightly less uneasy about doing so herself.

"Here, I'll come to you," Josh said pleasantly, and expertly maneuvered around the consoles and gadgetry separating them. He smiled as he approached and greeted her with a kiss on the cheek.

By now, Susana had decided she was definitely dreaming; this whole thing was just too bizarre. Nevertheless, as Josh kissed her, she distinctly felt the brush of stubble against her cheek. She wasn't supposed to feel things in dreams, was she?

"Hello, dear one," Josh said. "Thank you for coming. We have a bit of a problem that you can help solve. You see, I could use Chris's help, but he can't enter this room without an access card, and that needs to be activated by your fingerprints."

"Why?" she asked in a small voice.

"Because you're his helpmate, of course." Josh pulled a keycard from the pocket of his red polo shirt and nodded toward the door where Chris was waiting. "Will you take this to him for me?"

Susana studied the card. She studied Josh's kind brown eyes. She studied the faces of all the military personnel, now riveted on her every move. And then, with a distinct wave of relief, she remembered: "I'm afraid I can't right now. It's important that I get these flowers to—um, where they're needed first. Maybe I can come back in a little bit?"

"The flowers are for my father," Josh said. "And you're right—they do need to be given to him first. You promised them to him some time ago. Don't you remember?"

She frowned. That did sound vaguely familiar.

"Well, it's all right," he said. "I can deliver them for you."

What? No!

At her hesitation, he studied her, a shadow of disappointment in his eyes. Then he refocused on the bouquet and lifted a delicate stem bearing a dainty, five-petaled flower. "Let's start with just one. This is scarlet pimpernel, also called poorman's barometer or shepherd's clock. It opens daily from about 8:00 a.m. to 3:00 p.m. It also closes in dull weather. And so its blossoms faithfully announce"—he pointedly met her eyes—"change. My father has a particular fondness for this tiny flower. He finds it very useful. May I give it to him from you?"

When she didn't answer, he asked, "Will you trust me with this one small flower, Susana? Will you trust me with the unforeseen changes in your life?"

She pondered the question carefully. She didn't want to disappoint him completely, and the flower was very tiny. Besides, there would be plenty of others to occupy her hands and give her an excuse not to deliver that access card to Chris.

When she bobbed a shaky nod, Josh carefully extracted the stems of scarlet pimpernel from her bouquet. Behind her, still standing at the door through which she'd entered, Paul exhaled a soft sigh and returned to the Observation Room. Before the door fully closed behind him, she heard him tell the waiting crowd, "This may take a while."

And then she noticed another clock above the door to the hallway. Faithfully it counted forward: 23:11:37—38, 39, 40 ...

CHAPTER 1
CONTENT

"I have learned in whatever state I am, to be content."
Philippians 4:11, NKJV.

"Your check's already been taken care of, sir," the waiter told Chris. "That gentleman paid for your meal."

Susana followed the waiter's glance to a polished gentleman who sat alone, staring out the window with a sad smile.

"There must be some mistake," Chris said. "We don't know him."

"Mistake or not, your dinner's paid for," the waiter said with a grin.

As he stepped away, Susana whispered, "Why would a stranger buy us an expensive dinner?"

Chris shrugged. "Let's find out."

Gathering their things, they stepped to their benefactor's table, where Chris introduced them and thanked the man for his kindness. Rising to shake their hands, the gentleman introduced himself: "Don Lang. And the pleasure's mine."

"But I don't think we've met before," Chris said. "Why would you pay for our meal?"

Mr. Lang glanced down to finger his wedding band. "My wife and I married twenty-two years ago today. We didn't have much money in those days, so we spent our honeymoon driving up the coast from San Gabriel, where we lived at the time. This hotel was our favorite stop. Every year on our anniversary, we've come back to spend a few days."

His gaze again fell to the ring, and Susana's heart stirred with sympathy at his obvious pain. When he looked up, unshed tears brightened his eyes. "Cancer took her since our last anniversary—only last month, in fact. I came back anyway, to be close—"

His voice cracked and he stopped to clear his throat. "I passed you when the maître d' seated me, and I heard you say you were on your honeymoon. Helping you celebrate just seemed like the right thing to do—something my wife would do."

"Thank you, Mr. Lang," Chris said. "And I'm sorry about your wife."

"Thank you. And you're welcome. But please call me Don." With a smile, he added, "Congratulations to you both. Enjoy your life together."

"What a nice fellow," Chris said as they left the dining room. "Reminds me of my dad. He once paid for a stranger's dinner—a soldier."

"Yes, he does seem nice. But I feel bad for him," Susana said. "He obviously loved his wife very much. It's sad that he lost her so young."

On their way to the hotel elevator, they passed a window with a stunning view of the lush vegetation, and they stopped to enjoy it. But Josh's insistent words interrupted her reverie: *Will you trust me with this one flower, Susana? Will you trust me with the unforeseen changes in your life?*

She sighed. Ever since she'd had that weird dream, that question popped up whenever she saw something especially beautiful. And she knew exactly what change Josh meant. He'd asked Chris to start up the Kids' Klub, an exciting project that his late father had envisioned. Meant to help children foster relationships with Doug while introducing them to running, it was certainly a worthwhile project, and she had no doubt about her talented husband's ability to see it through. But one question gnawed at her: Would it leave him any time for her? After all, they had only just married. They needed their alone time to build a marriage that would last. What's more, they'd both be entering busy doctoral programs in the fall. Certainly it would be wiser to settle in first and see if there was time left over for extra projects.

Yet her resolve was weakening. Balanced against all that Josh had done for them, her objections seemed more feeble each time she reviewed them. What's more, Doug had promised that he would never ask for more than they could give. Really, how could she continue to hold back?

Turning to Chris, she said simply, "Yes."

He glanced around, as if seeking context for the statement. "Yes, what?"

Since Doug had asked them not to speak about it in public yet, she searched for a roundabout way of expressing herself. "You know—the folders?"

"Oh! You're okay with it?" Excitement burst from his features like light through a sieve. "Suze, thank you—I promise, it's going to be great."

"I know it will be," she said, surprised at the joyful relief that filled her. "You'll do an amazing job."

Having finished her own workout in the pool, Susana sat at a table while Chris finished his. Despite the drizzling rain, she felt perfectly, sublimely happy. She'd been reflecting on a childhood drawing she kept in the bottom drawer of her dresser. Depicting her vision of her ideal family, it showed herself, a husband, one daughter named Bethany, and three sons running along a beach.

She had long since abandoned that dream as impossible; her face and hand had been so badly scarred that guys only noticed her to laugh at her. But Chris had changed everything, and her impossible fantasy was actually possible now.

She was releasing a soft, contented sigh when Don Lang's *"Buenos días, Susana"* startled her out of her reverie.

"Buenos días," she answered. *"¿Habla usted español?"* (Spanish: Good morning. Do you speak Spanish?)

He snatched a moist book off a nearby table. "I've been looking everywhere for this," he mumbled and then turned to her. "Yes, I do speak Spanish, but not as well as you do, I'm sure. My wife was *mexicana*—I learned the language from her." The book he was wiping with a towel slipped from his grasp, and he bent down to retrieve it from near her feet.

"Chris is learning Spanish, too," Susana said.

"He doesn't speak it? Isn't he Hispanic?"

"No. He's Native American. He does speak Tarahumara, the language of his grandmother's tribe."

"Oh. A friend of mine married a Native woman." Don gave his head a little shake as if remembering something unpleasant. "I'm afraid it didn't work out well, though."

"That's too bad."

"It certainly is. Native Americans have very strong family ties—which is fine, in its place. But they tend to put their relatives' concerns ahead of their spouse's."

Did they? She'd never heard that. Her gaze wandered to Chris. He certainly had strong loyalties. She had admired his family's bonding when they first met. But was there a flip side that could be a problem?

"Ah, I spy transmitters," Don said cheerfully, and Susana automatically felt for the smooth metal oval that hung from a delicate chain around her neck. Its presence marked its owner as one of Doug's runners. "I guess that explains why you're swimming in the rain," he continued. "Runners have to stay in shape."

Susana grinned. "Well, you get wet when you swim anyway."

"My wife used to say the same thing," he agreed with a laugh.

"Was she a runner?"

"Yes. We both were—that is, I still am." He pulled a transmitter out of his shirt.

"Oh, how wonderful," Susana said. "I love meeting fellow runners."

"All runners are brothers," Don said, quoting a common saying. "But if you'll excuse me, sister, I'm going back to my dry room. I just came out to look for this." He held up his book, which was written in some squiggly-lettered language—Arabic or something—and retreated to the comfort of the hotel.

Susana scratched at a mosquito bite on her foot while watching Chris's muscled shoulders ripple through the water in a perfect, seemingly effortless, butterfly stroke. She had always thought of his family the same way—effortlessly perfect. When his father died, he and his four siblings had all pulled together as a team to support one another.

Now that she considered it, though, there had been some tension between two of his brothers and their white wives. She'd assumed the stress of the funeral had caused it, but maybe she should have paid more attention. Could those conflicts have been culturally related? How much did she really know about Native values and customs?

What are you doing, Susana? said a voice in her head. *You talked about your cultural differences with your coaches before the wedding, remember? And Chris was raised white, not Native. Quit looking for trouble.*

I'm not looking for trouble. I'm being—well, proactive.

Yeah, right.

Susana wasn't a mistrustful sort by nature, and she found these doubts bothersome. Suddenly restless, she got up to do a few stretches. When that didn't help, she plopped down at the end of Chris's lane and dangled her legs in the water.

He stood up in front of her after completing that lap. "Tired of waiting?" he asked, panting hard. "Go on inside, if you want. I'm almost through anyway, just …"

He trailed off, searching her face. Then he hoisted himself out of the pool and sat beside her in one fluid motion. Drawing her close, he kissed the top of her head. "What's wrong, *tesoro*?"

"*Mi tesoro*," she corrected irritably, and then bit her lip. She had never meant to correct him. It was so sweet that he took the trouble to learn the word at all.

"What?"

"I'm sorry, it's just, well, *tesoro* means 'treasure,' it's true. But when you use it as an endearment, you put *mi* with it—my treasure."

"Oh. I like that even better, *mi tesoro*."

She peered into his ebony eyes—those tender, honest eyes that had melted her heart the first time she'd seen him—and smiled at his nonchalance. She should have known he wouldn't be offended. And how could she ever question his sincerity? She was just being silly.

"But you didn't answer my question," he pressed. "What's wrong?"

"Nothing. Everything's fine now."

And she really thought everything was fine—until later that morning. But after breakfast, they stopped at the hotel's computer room to check their e-mail, and Chris had a message from his oldest brother, who wanted Chris to call him. Immediately, something hot rose within her chest. Benny could be demanding, but did he really believe he had the right to interrupt their honeymoon? More importantly, did Chris think his brother had that right?

She soon learned the answer. Chris went right back to the room to call his brother. Susana listened in as she stared out the window at a view that now seemed less spectacular.

"Hi, Benny … It's okay. Is something wrong? Everyone all right?"

You didn't even think of that, did you? piped up that nagging voice in her head. *Someone could have died, for all you know.*

Susana winced. *That's right. What's wrong with me? I'm being so selfish.*

"Good," Chris said. "I'm glad everything's fine. What can I do for you, then?"

Aha—everything's fine. Then what's Benny's excuse for bothering us?

"Did you say that race starts February first?"

Oh, good—Benny and Marie must have decided to run the Parents' Race.

"Maybe," Chris said. "Susana and I don't start school again until the fall. So it would work out time-wise for us to take care of the boys while you run it. I could help out with the gardening service, too."

She sucked in an indignant breath. *Is he volunteering us to stay in Ventura without even talking to me? He knows I want to keep my job in LA.*

He hasn't said that, Susana. You're only hearing one side of the conversation.

How much do I have to hear? It's obvious, isn't it? It's exactly like Don said—he's putting his relatives first, and I'm supposed to trot along behind them like a little lost dog. What have I gotten myself into?

"I'll do that," Chris said. "Bye."

So that's it? He made his decision—no discussion, end of subject? He didn't even mention talking to me!

Hanging up the phone, Chris began, "Benny and Marie are—"

"Please don't tell me you led your brother to think we'll babysit while they run the race." She spoke as calmly as possible, but it honestly wasn't such a good imitation of "calm."

Chris had the audacity to act like the wounded victim. "What? Why are you upset?"

"Because you had no right to do such a thing, Christian. How could you? You're completely ignoring my plans."

"I'm not ignoring them, Suze, but I thought—"

"No, Chris, you didn't think at all. At least, not about me."

"That's not true. Just let me—"

"I'm going for a walk," she gritted out and grabbed her coat from the chair.

As she stormed out the door, that nagging little voice whispered, *This isn't like you, Susana. What's going on?* But she was too worked up to care about the answer.

CHAPTER 2

TWISTED TRUTHS

"You are being fooled by those who deliberately twist the truth."
Galatians 1:7, NLT.

"Suze, give me a chance to explain," Chris called as the door slammed. He started after her but decided against it. Her tone had definitely said she wanted to be left alone. And since she was about the kindest, most longsuffering person he'd ever met—definitely not one to blow up without cause—he must have done something wrong. But what?

Slumping into a chair, he dropped his head into his hands to review the phone conversation that had set her off. But, try as he might, he couldn't figure out where he'd messed up.

Finally he decided he'd just give her some space. She wasn't a hothead, and they'd always been able to discuss things. She'd go for a walk and cool off, and then they'd talk calmly and rationally and figure out what the misunderstanding was.

But why didn't she let him explain in the first place? All he'd done was listen to his brother's dilemma and promise to call back after talking to her. How could she possibly object to that?

The more he thought about it, the more his frustration tended toward anger. Finally he realized he was too mad to talk rationally if she did return. Deciding *he* needed cooling off, he changed into workout clothes and headed down to the gym. In truth, he half hoped he'd meet Susana on the way so he could storm away from her the way she'd stormed away from him.

Luckily, he didn't meet her en route.

He'd been pumping iron for about fifteen minutes when Don Lang walked into the fitness room. "Well, hello again, Chris. I keep running into you and Susana. But there aren't many people here this time of year—I always make new friends when I come."

Chris returned a polite smile. Although he wasn't in the mood for making small talk with strangers, he wouldn't be rude either. "Yeah, Susana mentioned over breakfast that she'd seen you at the pool. You're a runner too, I hear."

"That's right." Don pulled out his transmitter as proof. Stepping onto a treadmill, he began jogging as he continued. "Ran the race twenty-five years ago. Best thing I ever did—that and marry my wife."

Chris was suddenly interested. Maybe this interruption wasn't such a bad thing. Maybe an older, wiser runner like Don could offer him some advice. Would it hurt to pick his brain?

He adjusted the setting on the universal weight machine and lay back for a set of bench presses. "So you enjoyed marriage. Got any secrets you care to pass on to a couple of rookies?"

A thoughtful look came over Don's face, and he slowed to a walk. "Yeah. I'll tell you the same thing my father told me: resist the tendency to blow things out of proportion. The occasional disagreement is as normal as catching a cold, and both are best treated with the same remedy—tincture of time."

Wonderful. Now they were doing riddles.

Chris tried to keep the irritation out of his voice as he asked, "What's 'tincture of time'?"

"It means that most things will run their natural course and clear up on their own, like a cold does. You just need to be patient."

"I thought you were supposed to talk out problems."

"Sure, eventually. But if you talk it out too soon, you may make things worse. Say, for instance, Susana's tired, feeling grumpy. You say something she misinterprets and she gets mad."

Wow. It's like he was there.

"If you try to make her talk then, when she's still tired, it would be like pouring gasoline on fire. You have to give her some time to calm down. When she does, she'll probably realize her mistake on her own. The *Manual* says the same thing, you know: 'Let the sun go down on your anger.' In other words, be patient—wait for the right time."

at?"
ays known that you need some
ven weeks—before you can dis-

rves, especially since the whole
Susana cut her workout short
ict, before he started overthink-
l off. So that's what he'd do. In
e time he returned to the room.
hind him, Chris looked around
s copy of *The Runner's Manual*
afed through it, looking for the

raighter when another passage
hat represented his new mission
whatever you command me, and

x Chapter 2
- Somtimes people will claim to be Chirstian, or people that can offer good advice, sometimes it sounds good, But if you don't question advice and compare it with the bible it can be damaging in your life.

amour had earned Chris's trust and loyalty by paying a very steep price—his own son's life—to save Chris from death. As he remembered it now, his gaze shifted to the blood-red ruby in his wedding band that commemorated the event. He could never repay such a gift. He could only try to be the committed supporter Doug deserved. And certainly the surest way to accomplish that would be to do whatever Doug said. Simple.

After committing that passage to memory, Chris worked on some ideas for getting the Kids' Klub going. His father had envisioned the scout-like group for the RABs, or Runners' Assemblies Buildings. It had been his last project before he died, and Chris desperately wanted it to succeed. But Stan Moden was dead set against the club. Decades earlier, his lackeys had even stolen the original plans for it. That's why Chris had entrusted a duplicate set of these plans to his brother Mike, and why he kept this set in the room safe. One could never be too cautious where Moden was concerned. The guy was not only smart and determined, but he had the largest fortune in the country to finance his whims.

Chris brainstormed for some time, postponing lunch so he could eat with Susana. Finally he gave in to his growling stomach and went downstairs to grab a bite. Before he did, he carefully locked the Kids' Klub plans in the room safe again where they'd be secure.

🏃 🏃 🏃 🏃 🏃

When Susana finally showed up late that afternoon, she didn't mention where she'd been. In fact, she didn't say anything. She just sat down to watch some courtroom show on TV. She had never given Chris the cold shoulder before, and he quickly decided he didn't like it. He wanted to sit her down and say, "Look, this is nuts, let's talk it out!" But Don's words still rang in his ears, and he decided to accept the older man's advice. After all, Don had been married twenty-something years, and his philosophy was based on principles from the *Manual*. It must work.

Dinnertime finally rolled around, but Susana claimed she wasn't hungry. Although Chris didn't have much of an appetite either, he was desperate to escape the hostile atmosphere in the room, so he went down to eat by himself. When he returned, he found Susana in bed with the blankets pulled over her head—a definite leave-me-alone sign if he'd ever seen one. But this was crazy! How long did it take to cool off?

Tincture of time, remember? Be patient. She's obviously not herself. Let her get some rest. She'll probably be fine in the morning.

Chris shook his head in frustration, but decided to persevere. Retrieving the Kids' Klub plans from the safe, he again settled at the table to occupy himself with them. He had trouble concentrating until he opened one folder and noticed a blue pen mark inside.

Instantly alert, he scrutinized the room, checked the bathroom, and assured that the windows and balcony door were locked. He confirmed that Susana's expensive camera still sat in plain sight on the dresser and that their envelope of cash was still in the safe.

Once he'd convinced himself that they hadn't been burgled, he returned to the table. With his skin crawling, he methodically reviewed the full set of manila folders. Each one was complete and in exactly the right order. The only thing out of place in the entire room was one stray blue mark, the kind you might make accidentally when reaching for something with a pen in your hand.

Could it have been there before, and he just never noticed it? They were the original folders, old and dog-eared. They'd had plenty of use.

But he knew better. Dad had been very organized in his work, and he'd only used black ink. Chris, to keep his own notes distinguishable from his father's, always used red. There wasn't one blue word in the entire set. Not one. And since he was accustomed to noticing little things, he was sure he'd never seen that stray mark before—not even that very afternoon.

Maybe it was crazy to think someone would break into the room, even into the safe, and take nothing more than a gander at Dad's plans. But that's exactly what made Chris's skin crawl, for it told him that their visitor was no mere thief. The invader was a spy—Stan's spy.

Chris slept poorly that night, jerking awake at every sound. In the morning, Susana was curled up as far away from him as she could get. He rolled out of bed softly to avoid disturbing her and sat down at the table to read the *Manual*.

When she awoke, she seemed more subdued at first, and he thought maybe things had solved themselves, as Don had predicted. But when he invited her to join him in reading, she turned a look on him that might have been directed at some lowly—probably slimy—creature. Turning on her heel, she wordlessly stalked into the bathroom.

With that, Chris's anger rekindled. It burned a little hotter when she, after dressing, informed him that she was going down to breakfast—alone. As the door closed behind her, he banged the table with his fist. So much for her feeling better after a good night's sleep. This "tincture of time" thing sure didn't seem to be helping her—and it wasn't doing much for him, either.

You know, you still haven't talked to Doug about this.

Feeling stupid for not thinking of it sooner, he activated his transmitter. Doug responded right away, his native Paradisian being translated into English with a gentle Texan accent. "Howdy, pardner. How's your day?"

"Awful," Chris grumped.

"H'mm. Trouble in paradise?"

"Yeah, plenty of trouble. Susana's mad at me and I don't even know why."

"When did that start?"

"Yesterday morning. Benny asked about us watching his boys while he and Marie run the race. Susana only heard my side of the conversation, but she got really mad and ran out. She hasn't talked to me since."

"That's not like her. But, son, I've gotta tell you, you did wrong too."

"I don't know how, Doug. I don't even know what's bugging her."

"That's just what I mean. You let the sun go down on her anger."

"Yeah, like I'm supposed to. Tincture of time and all that, but it's not working. How long am I supposed to wait?"

"Wait for what, son—for things to get more blown out of proportion? There's a reason the *Manual* says 'Do *not* let the sun go down on your anger.' "

"Is that what it says? I've been looking for that passage ever since I talked to Don yesterday."

"The passage is in Paul's letter to his friends at Ephesus, fourth section, near the end."

Chris flipped to the place Doug specified and found the passage right away. "No wonder I couldn't find it. Don said it was in Solomon's writings."

"Who's this Don feller?"

"A runner we met here—Don Lang."

"Chris," Doug said slowly and in a tone that immediately seized Chris's attention, "I don't have a runner by that name."

A bolt of electricity shot through Chris, and he sprang to his feet. He'd heard of people claiming to be runners as part of a scam; had he and Susana been the objects of a con artist? But that didn't make sense. There had been no mention of money, except for the dinner Don bought them. And if he wasn't after money, why the con? Besides, as Chris objected aloud, "He's got a transmitter."

"Does it work?"

"I guess so—I mean, why would he have a nonfunctional transmitter? But I didn't actually see him activate it, if that's what you mean."

"Anything else you're not tellin' me? Any trespassers?"

"Well, I did find a stray pen mark inside one of the Kids' Klub folders. I know it sounds silly, but I'm sure it wasn't there before."

"It doesn't sound silly to me, son. Describe Don to me."

"About five-foot-eleven, brown eyes, and very light-brown hair—almost golden, really. He said he'd been married twenty-two years, but he looks younger than that. He dresses well, seems like he has money. And he apparently speaks a few languages—Spanish and something like Arabic, anyway."

"Do you know where Susana went?" Doug asked urgently.

"To breakfast."

"Go find her, son—now. She's in serious danger. Debora will meet you in the lobby and help you look for her."

Chris didn't have to be told twice. The last time Doug had sent him to look for Susana, he had found her in the clutches of a serial killer. He bolted for the door, no longer angry. Now he was just plain scared.

MASQUERADE

*"Satan himself masquerades as an angel of light, so it is easy
enough for his agents to masquerade as agents of good."*
2 Corinthians 11:14, 15, REB.

Susana charged through the lobby toward the hotel restaurant, her steps ringing sharply on the stone floor. She wanted nothing more than to be away
from Chris. Obviously, he didn't even care how she felt. Did he even try to talk
last night while she cried under the covers? No, he just watched the stupid TV.
And then he wanted to study the *Manual* together this morning like everything
was normal. Don was right. Chris didn't care about her feelings; he was just concerned about his family. Maybe marrying him was a mistake.

She stopped short. Where had that thought come from? Wasn't it kind
of dangerous to be thinking like that? It surely couldn't be a good sign after only
a week of marriage.

"Good morning, Susana!"

She pivoted to see Don coming toward her, a warm smile on his face.
Putting on a cheery expression, she said, "Hi, Don. How are you?"

His brow furrowed. "Uh-oh. You look a little down. Tell you what. I'm
on my way to a cute little café just down the coast. My wife loved the place. Why
don't you join me? I'm sure it will help and, from the looks of things, it can't hurt."

Not awaiting an answer, Don took her by the elbow, chatting easily as he
led her out the front door to his rented Bentley. She went with him without giving
it a second thought. After all, he was a runner, and runners were trustworthy—
right? Besides, she wasn't feeling quite herself. Her brain felt sort of slow and
numb. She vaguely recalled feeling this way before, but she couldn't remember
when. Or what it meant.

Don drove a short ways down the foggy coast as he talked and joked,
making Susana feel comfortable and safe. He stopped at a little café where they
had breakfast and more easy conversation. By the time they finished, the fog
had cleared, and Don offered to show her the view from a nearby bluff: "One so
magnificent, you'll see it in your dreams forever after."

"But I didn't bring shoes for hiking." She pointed to the slick soles of her
sandals.

"Don't worry. It's more like a leisurely walk."

She wasn't sure she wanted to go on this outing, but she knew she wasn't
ready to face Chris. So, although she didn't exactly consent, she also didn't refuse.
The result was that she soon found herself ambling along a picturesque trail that
led up a hill and into some trees. In that peaceful setting, with the calming rhythm
of the surf in the background, Don gently explored her discontent. His voice was

so mellow, his manner so soothing, that Susana found herself spilling the whole story. He listened patiently as they continued through the trees. As they crossed a clearing, he expressed appropriate sympathy—unlike Chris.

That's not fair, chided her conscience. *Did you give Chris a chance to listen?*

"I'm sorry to hear this," Don said, crossing a bridge of wooden slats and rope that spanned a tiny ocean inlet. "You deserve better."

Susana took one tentative step onto the bridge and looked over the side of the rickety contraption. Waves sloshed over large boulders some fifty feet below. Her head swam with the height. She glanced at her sandals, already slipping on the dew-covered grass, and considered turning back.

"Here, let me help you." Don returned and, slipping one arm around her waist, helped her across the bridge while continuing the conversation. "I have to say, though, none of it surprises me. I've heard it all before from the friend I told you about. It's really too bad Chris won't even talk about it. That doesn't bode well for your future together."

They had crossed the bridge now, and Don took Susana's hand to help her up the steep incline on the other side. She wasn't comfortable with the way he was touching her, as though it was the most natural thing in the world to do and he had every right to do it. Yet the very fact that he was so confident and nonchalant about it made her feel silly—prudish, even. After all, he was just being kind and helping her over the rough ground.

"Unfortunately," Don continued, "my friend ended up divorcing over the problems he had with his wife. I know this may not be what you want to hear, but you should consider that option sooner rather than later. Don't waste precious time on the wrong guy."

"Oh, I could never divorce Chris."

"And why not? Do you think the Damours want you to spend the rest of your life with someone who doesn't consider your needs? The *Manual* says they want you to have 'life in all its fullness.' They certainly don't want you to stay with someone who makes you unhappy."

Just then, they reached the top of the cliff, and Susana gasped in wonder. What beauty! This spot was everything Don had promised. The gently curving coastline with waves splashing against a rocky shore, the birds gliding through an idyllic azure sky—it all deserved to be in a painting.

Seeking the best view, she moved to the edge of the cliff and filled her lungs with the cool salt air. As the peaceful stillness washed over her, she murmured, "It's breathtaking."

"Indeed."

Although Don echoed her reverential tone, her peripheral vision informed her that he wasn't admiring the vista. He was looking straight at her.

This was a new experience—she'd never been pretty before. Still, an innate alarm sounded, and she turned toward him in confusion. "I think, um, I should be getting back. Chris will be worried about me."

"Don't go yet," Don said, easing closer. "Listen, Chris is obviously a blind fool who doesn't appreciate you. You should be with a man who knows how a woman of such beauty should be treated."

He reached out to stroke her face, and Susana almost stepped back—until she remembered she was already on the edge of the cliff.

"You should be with a man like me. There's no reason to fight it. I know you're attracted to me, too."

"No, I'm not," she cried.

He chuckled. "Of course you are. Think about it. This is your honeymoon, and where are you—with your new husband? No, you're alone with me. He doesn't even know where you are."

"I-I think I'd better go now." She lifted her eyes to look past Don—and saw Chris in the clearing on the other side of the gorge, a shocked look on his face. As she watched, he turned to go back through the trees.

"Chris, no!" She pushed past Don to descend the cliff the way they'd come. Rushing down the steep, rocky path, she stumbled and yelped as she slid partway down. She managed to regain her footing and scrambled, half-sliding, down the rest of the incline. When she reached the bridge, she plunged across.

Suddenly her feet slid out from under her. Her back slammed against the wooden slats, and the impact cut short her scream. Yet she was still sliding, her feet in midair above the rocky gorge. She twisted, clawing at the slats and ropes—at anything to stop her uncontrolled slide.

The sharp burn of a rope skimmed down her arm, and she grabbed at it convulsively. Then she was hanging there, fifty feet above sharp boulders, her only lifeline the wet rope in her hands.

"Help!" she screamed. "Help!"

🏃 🏃 🏃 🏃 🏃

Colonel Jané Lanáj of the Paradisian Royal Guard tore through the woods toward Susana. As she ran, she tapped the bony prominence behind her right ear, activating her implanted military radio. Without waiting for King Doúg's reply, s̲_____ion to rescue Susana, sir!"

"Perm____

Jané ____ forest—seconds from her dan____n, she could not intervene.

The____ch depended on these decisi____universe. Despite Susana's ob____cusing her king of unjustly cu____ust be allowed the opportunit____ to see the results. Otherwise

S____erhaps Doúg didn't understa____s imminent, sir."

"____danger, Colonel. If we interve____fairly won victory. We cannot justify____

Jané wilted. Of course ____ears of guarding Doúg's runners, she knew it very well. A person's tree w... always be respected. At times, His Majesty could intervene if petitioned, but even then he must weigh the

[handwritten note overlaid:] There are people who will deceive you, set you at your low points and disguise themselves of people that are good. It is important for you to lean and trust God the most before any people. If I was Susanna I would [?] my low point [?] reconsre the and [?] I [?] flgs

individual's welfare against the welfare of the universe. Furthermore, her blunder was making this harder for him—she could hear the grief in his voice.

"Copy that, sir. I'm sorry for my lapse. I can't imagine what I was thinking."

"You were thinking of your charge, Colonel," came His Majesty's sympathetic reply. "Your compassion is admirable. Please keep me updated."

After signing off, Jané double-tapped her radio to change frequencies. "Major Meshon, we have a no-go. Return to rendezvous. I repeat: Stand down."

"Copy that, Colonel," came Serji's reply.

Her partner's voice conveyed disappointment equaling her own. Although they'd never actually met Susana, both guards had become quite attached to her. This would be no easier for Serji than it was for her. Still, they trusted Doúg. Only he had the ability to balance the many factors involved in these decisions, using an eternal perspective that no mortal could comprehend. Even Queen Debora and Prince Joshua did not hazard to pit the well-being of the universe against the welfare of one individual. That job was Doúg's alone.

And he could have it, as far as Jané was concerned. For millennia, Stan had doggedly—ruthlessly—sought His Majesty's throne, but she had never understood the obsession. She trembled at the ponderous responsibilities that came with it. Each time she saw her king's head bowed low in sorrow, each time she saw his great heart of love breaking over the horrifying results of mortals' choices, it merely renewed her longing to help in whatever small way she could.

And so, she followed Doúg's guidelines for protecting his runners—even when it meant watching them take heart-wrenching paths—because she knew her king. He had proven his love, compassion, and faithfulness a million times over. She could, and would, trust his decisions. Absolutely.

But that didn't make it easy. She logged off, turned around, and covered her ears. She couldn't bear to watch. Reporting the aftermath would be bad enough.

"Help! Please help!" Susana screeched. Her right hand was slipping as she swung over the gorge, offering her no chance to pull herself up. She had seen Chris turn away and return through the woods, so he was no doubt out of earshot. But where was Don? He must hear her—why wasn't he helping?

"Help! *Please* help!"

Strong hands clasped her arms, and she looked up to see Chris. He struggled mightily, grunting with the effort of lifting her full weight from an awkward position, but she finally reached solid ground.

Her whole body trembled as she threw her arms around his neck. "I'm glad you didn't leave."

He held her tightly, his face buried in her hair. "I love you, Susana. *I* could never leave *you*."

Her heart stopped. What had he seen? What had he heard?

"How long were you standing there?" she whispered.

"Long enough to see him—" He looked away, his jaw clenching. "—touch you. I couldn't hear much, but I did hear you talking about—about divorce."

"No, Chris, no. I wasn't talking about it. He was."

"Correction—she was," came Debora's British-accented voice.

Susana turned to see her coach crossing the rope bridge toward them. Stepping into a long hug with her, she murmured, "How good to see you. But what are you doing here?"

"Helping Chris rescue his kidnapped wife." Her look seemed to reflect equal parts relief and reprimand.

"Kidnapped?"

"Yes, dear, kidnapped."

"What happened to Don?" Chris asked. "He just disappeared."

"Well, not precisely disappeared." Motioning to the other side of the bluff, Debora explained, "She fled over a steep trail when she saw me."

"She?" Chris and Susana both asked.

"Yes. That was Camille Desmon disguised as a man."

"Stan's partner?" Chris exclaimed. "No, it can't be. I'd recognize her eyes—they're a really distinctive blue."

"Indeed they are," Debora said. "However, she knew you would remember that, so she used contact lenses as part of her disguise."

"So how did you recognize her?" Chris asked.

"Doug recognized her from your description. She's vacationing here this month."

"But she had a transmitter," Susana objected.

"No. She had a transmitter prop. They manufacture them to deceive runners. Although they appear genuine, the props are nonfunctional."

"But if he was a she, she—" Susana's nose wrinkled. "Yuk. That's even worse."

"She was hitting on Susana," Chris explained.

"Yes. Camille knows Susana very well, well enough to recognize that she would rebuff advances from any other man. But since Doug placed a hands-off order on Susana after the attempt on her life a few months ago, Camille cannot harm her directly. Therefore, she intended to excite her into endangering herself by running pell-mell over this rough terrain."

"You mean like I did?" Susana said sheepishly.

"Wait a minute," Chris said. "You're saying she pretended interest in Susana *because* she would reject her advances?"

Debora nodded. "Precisely. And it almost worked, even though Doug had warned you she was in danger. Why is that?"

"Well, she—he—" Chris sputtered before finally exclaiming, "It didn't exactly look like she wanted my help!"

"So you felt it safer to rely on what you inferred from your senses than to trust Doug? Will you, then, carry out his commands only insofar as your limited understanding justifies them?"

Chris groaned. "Oh, man. You're right. I'm sorry. I can't believe I blew it already."

Debora took Chris's face in her hands and kissed him on the forehead. "You're forgiven, my son. The resolve you made yesterday will not be as simple to carry out as you believed. Nevertheless, your willingness to make that commitment reveals a noble heart."

She put an arm around Susana's shoulder as the three walked back toward the road. "As for you, my dear—do you realize how extreme the danger in which you placed yourself? How could you be enticed into such a situation? What lies did Camille tell you?"

"When we first talked, she said she had a friend who married a Native woman and that it didn't work out too well—that she put her family's concerns ahead of her husband's because of her traditions."

"What's that have to do with you?" Chris asked.

Susana stopped and blinked at him. Was he serious? Wasn't it obvious how that related to them?

Becoming increasingly annoyed as she spoke, she said, "Well—obviously—because you're Native, and you committed us to babysitting Benny's kids *sin hablar conmigo*, and just expected me to go along with it, *y tú ni pensaste en mi, y, y*—" She squared her shoulders. "Well, it all just confirmed what Don said." (Spanish: without talking to me … and you didn't even think about me, and, and—)

Now Chris was the one staring at her like he had no idea what she was talking about. "Suze, there were so many—um, let's call them misunderstandings in what you just said, at least the part I understood, I hardly know where to begin."

Debora raised a hand. "Perhaps I might take care of one small detail first, since I believe I know what has happened. Susana, do you have a mosquito bite?"

Although it sounded like a bizarre, where-did-that-come-from-and-who-cares-anyway question, Susana had enough experience with Debora to know that such questions always had a reason behind them.

"Yes. Right here." She sat down on a rock and pointed out the bite on her right big toe. "Come to think of it, January's an odd time for mosquitoes to be biting, isn't it?"

"Indeed it is." Squatting down, Debora examined the bump. "Just as I suspected." She pulled some tweezers from the pack she carried and extracted a very fine dart, almost invisible. It reminded Susana of a sticker from a cactus pear.

"A dart?" she asked. "That's why my brain's been feeling kind of slow."

"What kind of dart is it?" Chris asked.

"Self-pity," Debora said as she applied an ointment to the wound. " 'Tis rather a peculiar toxin. It gives one a certain satisfaction in thinking oneself ill-used. It can actually make calamity and misery attractive. It's not unusual for victims to exaggerate the severity of their misfortune, or even invent it altogether."

"Have I been inventing misfortune?" Susana asked quietly.

"Yes, dear, I'm afraid you have. Camille helped, of course, by planting lies in your mind."

"They seemed so reasonable at the time."

"Yes, which is precisely why you must measure everyone's advice by the *Manual*. As it says, 'If they do not speak according to this word, they have no light.' " Rising, Debora added, "But I suspect you two have things to discuss. I'll return to the car and give you some privacy, shall I?"

As Debora disappeared into the trees, Chris sat down next to Susana. "Suze, first of all, I'm sorry for letting things get out of hand. I should have insisted we talk about this yesterday. Don misquoted the *Manual* to make me think I needed to give you time to yourself—days to weeks, he suggested—and I didn't know the passage well enough to catch the distortion."

"And he was telling me how terrible you were for refusing to talk about it."

"I wish I'd called Doug sooner. He figured out what was happening right away."

"But what about the rest?" Susana said, her annoyance resurfacing. "Why did you tell Benny we'd babysit for him without talking to me?"

"I didn't."

"Yes you did—I heard you. You never even mentioned me."

"I didn't have to. Benny did. He said to talk to you and try to make a decision within the next week so they could make other arrangements if we couldn't do it. I told him I'd do that."

Oops. He did say that, didn't he? "I'm sorry. I guess I kind of jumped to conclusions."

"And as to the other stuff, it's true I'm a quarter Native, but I wasn't raised in the culture and haven't internalized the same values as someone who was. My family's close, but that's as much Dad's influence as Grandma's—and he was as white as they come. Besides, that business about loyalty to birth family overriding a spouse's needs isn't true anyway, as far as I know."

She covered her face with her hands. What a sucker she'd been. "I'm sorry. I should have talked to you instead of getting all mad and—and stupid."

"You could never be stupid," he said, pushing a strand of hair out of her face. "Anyway, culture or no culture, you are my family, Susana Strider. You are the most important person in the world to me. I will never put anyone, not even any children we have, above you. And—" He lifted his face into the breeze as he paused.

"Go ahead," she said, sensing a rebuke. "What else?"

He took off his baseball cap to rake a hand through his hair and then replaced it. "About a week before each of my brothers married, my dad took them out to breakfast and gave them a little talk. Since he couldn't do that for me, Mike did it and passed on Dad's message. One of his pieces of advice was this: 'From the moment you marry, you should think and act as though the word "divorce" doesn't exist. Don't even consider the possibility that marrying Susana was a mistake. Because if you do, I guarantee there will be times when divorce seems easier than working things out. It isn't, but it will seem like it.' "

Taking her hand in his, he said, "Suze, for me, marriage is forever. I'm in this till death do us part."

The shame she felt earlier returned. "I am, too, Chris, really. I'm sorry if what you heard sounded, well, otherwise. And I'm sorry I let Camille trick me, that I doubted your love for no reason. I really wasn't very fair to you."

"That's true. But it's also true that she tricked me, too." With a wink, he added playfully, "But she's going to have to do a lot better than that to break *us* up, right?"

She grinned. "Right."

"Very well, I accept the challenge," came a cold voice behind them.

They spun around to see Camille standing only a few yards away. Susana froze in fear, while Chris sprang up and assumed a protective stance between her and Camille.

Fists on hips, Camille continued, "Understand this, Christian Strider, son of Juan Misi. I am putting you on my List—"

"Be gone!" boomed Doug's voice from Chris's transmitter, and Camille shrieked in pain. Susana peeked around her husband's back in time to see their enemy retreating over the bluff, scrambling faster than seemed possible for that rough terrain.

Striding toward them from the trees, Debora said calmly, "Come, it's time we leave this place."

"What did she mean?" Susana asked, her voice trembling. She had no idea what this list of Camille's might be, but she found it scarier than dangling over the gorge. In a world where marriages fell apart every day, could theirs withstand Camille's focused attacks?

Debora gave Susana an appraising once-over and then turned to Chris. "Would you allow me a few moments with your wife? We'll meet you at the car, shall we?"

"Sure." Chris dropped a kiss on Susana's head and jogged into the trees.

The coach tucked Susana's arm into hers and patted her hand as they followed at an unhurried pace. "Camille is what you might call a sore loser. And these are troublous times. She knows that the end is very near. Still, you have nothing to fear from her as long as you place your faith firmly in Doug. I assure you, he is still on his throne."

When Susana didn't respond, Debora said, "Tell me your concerns."

Susana chewed on her lip. "Well, what is this list she mentioned? They've already made Chris a Target. Does this mean they'll be trying even harder to get to him, or to break up our marriage? I just don't know what I'd do if I lost him."

"My dear, dear daughter. You worry about so many things. Don't you find it tiring?"

"Sometimes," Susana admitted.

"Learn to give Doug your burdens. Surrender Chris to his wisdom. He knows what Camille's List is. Let him worry as to its implications. Look above and away from these cares."

"Surrender Chris?" Had she heard right?

"You have chosen to surrender all in the past."

"Yeah, but ..."

When Susana trailed off, finding it difficult to put her thoughts into words, Debora obliged. "But perhaps you didn't feel that you had as much to lose then? Perhaps 'all' was not as valuable to you then as it is now?"

"I—" Susana hesitated before deciding, "I can't, *Ami*. Not that—not Chris. You can't ask that of me." (Paradisian: Mommy)

"I ask only what is for your good, dear one. And I can enable you to accomplish it, if you will allow me."

Susana turned away from Debora's pleading eyes. "Later. I will—later."

"The choice is always yours, dearest," Debora said softly. "But you will save yourself much heartache if you do it sooner rather than later."

CHAPTER 4

WHATEVER

"Whatever is born of God overcomes the world.
And this is the victory that has overcome the world–our faith."
1 John 5:4, NKJV.

As Queen Debora spoke with Susana, Jané watched the surroundings closely for any sign of Camille. There was something akin to desperation in the rebel's eyes these days. If she had returned once, she might well do so again.

When Her Majesty bade the couple farewell and strode toward Jané, the guard snapped her right fist to her heart and bowed.

"At ease, Jané," Her Majesty said. "Your assessment was correct—self-pity. Thank you for your excellent work, my dear."

"Thank you, *Ami*. I have to admit, Susana finds a special place in my heart."

"And mine," Debora said with a sweet smile.

A giggle escaped the guard. "All your children hold a special place in your heart."

"True enough," Her Majesty admitted.

"Are there any further orders?"

"Yes. Doúg has just issued a seventy-two-hour lockout order for the couple as a result of receiving a petition from Susana's father."

"I'm glad to hear it. They'll need some time to repair the breach that's developed between them."

"Just so." Debora kissed Jané on the cheek and walked toward the car.

Chris and Susana also returned to the car. Thankfully, they were discussing plans to check out of their hotel and travel farther up the coast. Jané would be happy to see them out of Camille's shadow.

Still, the guard did not yet prepare to leave. All indications were that the time of the Final Battle was growing very near, probably within this very generation. And Lustanli and Kamíl—or Stan and Camille, as they now preferred—had recognized the signs as well. Besides the constant urgency in their expressions, the increased activity at Moden Industries clearly indicated their understanding of how little time they had remaining. So, if she knew Camille at all, she would be coming back to—

A moving shadow in her peripheral vision caused Jané to scrutinize the area. Just as she expected, Camille was creeping through the trees toward the couple.

The guard strode toward her enemy, who faced her as soon as she caught sight of her. Being so near to the woman who had been both friend and business partner for the first 2,000 years of her life always brought back a wave of nostalgic sentimentalism. But the Kamíl she remembered was forever gone, having gradually transformed into someone Jané no longer recognized—a treacherous stranger in her best friend's body.

"So you're assigned to the troublemakers, are you?" Camille asked.

"I have the honor of being one of Susana's guards, yes."

"And the other?"

"That honor is mine." Serji Meshon approached, having just returned from his post at the bottom of the cliff. "Perhaps you would care to know that Chris's two guards are here as well." He waved at the Lok brothers, who came out from behind trees on Camille's other side.

The rebel surveyed the four Royal Guards in turn. "A colonel, two majors, and a captain. That's a great deal of brass for two inconsequential humans. I surmise that your king has exalted intentions for them."

"All of His Majesty's runners are important to him," Jané replied.

Camille sneered. "I see. Well, no matter. I don't need you to confirm the obvious. But by what right do you detain me from my purpose?"

"We have a seventy-two-hour lockout order on the couple."

Camille's face assumed that flat, stonelike expression she now used to disguise her emotions—anger, in this case, no doubt.

"Justified by whose petition?" she snapped.

Jané had hoped she wouldn't ask; nevertheless, the rules of warfare assured her the right to question such orders. "Pedro López—Susana's father."

"Very well."

Camille studied each of the guards a second time. Jané's muscles tensed in preparation as her enemy, an adept warrior, weighed their individual skills in hand-to-hand combat—deciding whether an attempt to fight past them would be worth her while.

"Very well," the rebel repeated and abruptly stalked away.

Jané signaled Major Viktor Lok, who waved his brother, Captain Vanti Lok, after her. Vanti would notify them if Camille tried to double back.

While making their way to their motorcycles, Jané radioed in to advise Doúg that Pedro López's guards should expect a retaliatory enemy strike. When she logged off, Viktor said, "I'm glad you were here to handle her. I was certain we were to have another fight on our hands."

"She considered it," Jané said. "But her decision had nothing to do with me. She's not yet sufficiently desperate to challenge the four of us at once. And she doesn't pick a fight solely for its entertainment value—as does your elder brother."

Viktor nodded, his dark eyes far away. "Yes, I sometimes wonder if Garike hasn't lost some of his marbles over the last few millennia."

"They all have," Serji said with a sigh. "And the tragic thing is, they don't even realize it. If Doúg doesn't call the Final Battle soon, we'll be fighting an army of lunatics."

"Oh, it will be soon," Jané said. "Perhaps much sooner than we imagine."

Chris and Susana headed farther up the coast, hoping to avoid further contact with Camille. As they drove, they discussed Benny's request. Susana listened quietly as Chris explained how Benny and Marie wanted their boys to stay with runners while they ran the race because Benny had badmouthed Josh to his sons all their lives. He felt the best way to counter that negative influence would be for them to stay with runners they loved and respected. But the other runners in the family all had children of their own. None could take all three boys for several months, and that would mean splitting the kids up.

"I know you really like your job at the PT clinic," Chris finished. "And I know you want to stay there, but this is something that may affect the boys for a long time—it may even determine whether they choose to become runners themselves someday. Besides that, I really do owe Benny a lot. He's been hard on me, it's true, but he's also supported me however he could, even pitching in financially when it meant straining his own family's resources. I'd like to help him if we can. I suppose I even feel like I owe it to him."

"I guess there's more to this than I knew," Susana admitted.

They dropped the conversation once they arrived at the Santa Cruz Beach Boardwalk in Santa Cruz, where they spent the rest of the day. Afterward, they checked into a hotel and then went for a run. Nothing surpassed a good run for putting things in perspective, and as they jogged along a trail overlooking the ocean, Susana reviewed the last couple of days, consciously releasing all of the anger and strife that had cluttered her brain.

When the shadows lengthened, they settled on a bench to watch the sunset. All the world seemed at peace now. Far below them, a couple of sea lions lolled on a large rock. A lone surfer bobbed among waves far too small to be ridden, yet showed no sign of disappointment.

just [...] delighting in the sensation of [...] the pool the previous day. Why [...] at had been so important? It al [...]

[...] e conscience said.

job [...] important than keeping the [...] sequences for Benny's kids cou [...]

grac [...] in the bank before we start [...] job in Ventura?

seer [...] ou trust me with the unfore- [...] rstood the issue underlying her reluctance. The job, the money, the apartment they'd lined up—these were only excuses. The real problem was that she didn't want anyone messing with her carefully arranged plans, not even Doug.

Yet marriage, by its very character, would bring changes she couldn't foresee, and she and Chris would have to approach them as a team. Hadn't he been willing to adapt for her so she could work at her old job during the upcoming months?

> *[Handwritten note overlaying text:]* I am glad that Susanna was able to make the choice to leave her P.T job to take care of Benny kids. It seems like she is allowing Doug to take control to carry the situation. So she is putting in her faith having in every journey the fight is not over and committe is gong to still attack them.

So what will it be, Susana? You said you'd trust Josh with these unexpected changes. Are you going to renege on that commitment already?

She reached up to kiss Chris on the neck. "I think we should do it—take care of Benny's boys."

"Are you sure?"

"Yes, if that's what Doug wants us to do."

He kissed her on the head. "Thank you."

"Seems to me giving up my favorite job should be worth more than a kiss on the head," she teased.

"Mmm. Sounds like a challenge." He cradled her face and gave her a gentle, unhurried kiss. "Better?"

"It'll do."

"H'mm. Another challenge," he said, and kissed her again.

She giggled. "Let's go ahead and talk to Doug about it now."

"Aw, just when things were getting exciting," Chris said with a grin.

He activated his transmitter, and Doug responded, "Howdy, pardner. Looks like y'all ended up in Santa Cruz. That should keep you out of Camille's way."

"Good," Chris said. "We called to talk about Benny. I've filled Susana in on his situation."

"What do you think, little filly?" Doug asked.

"I understand why Chris thought it would be important for us to do it. I'll give up my job in LA if that's what you want us to do."

"I'm right proud of you, child. And yes, I would like y'all to accept that assignment. It's more important than you can appreciate right now. But I've also got a surprise for you. I have a friend who owns a PT clinic in Ventura. He specializes in pediatrics. One of his aides had to take an early maternity leave. She won't be back for six months, so he's lookin' for a temporary replacement."

Susana bounced up and down on the bench. "Doug, you are awesome! You know I love pediatrics."

"Yes, child, I sure do," Doug said with an audible smile. "But I'm gonna be straight with you. Y'all will be walking into a difficult situation at Benny's. Would you like some time to chew on it before you give me a final decision?"

"Is it what you want us to do?" Chris asked.

"Yes, son, it is. And I promise that I 'will be with you wherever you go.' "

Chris smiled, apparently understanding some private message. He looked to Susana, his raised eyebrows speaking his question, and she nodded her agreement. He answered Doug by quoting from the same story in the *Manual*: "Then 'we will do whatever you command us, and we will go wherever you send us.' "

CHAPTER 5

RETURN

"The LORD will return your wickedness on your own head."
1 Kings 2:44, NKJV.

7 February 8008 M.E.

Patric slipped quietly from the still-dark streets of Manhattan into the empty lobby of Desmon Tower, the world headquarters of Moden Industries. Keeping to the shadows, he moved silently to the reception desk and watched the blond crouching over a file box. When she seemed fully absorbed in her work, he exclaimed, "Boo!"

His sister jumped about a foot into the air, tripped over her high heels, and landed squarely on her rump. "Patric, I told you to stop doing that!"

"But it's so much fun," he returned with a laugh. He rounded the corner to help her up.

She scowled darkly as she rose, but she never stayed mad long. "Big day today, huh?"

"You know it," he said cheerfully, although the reminder awakened the butterflies camping out in his gut.

"Good luck. Will you be home for dinner?"

He shrugged and replied with a nonchalance he didn't feel, "If I'm not downstairs."

"Patric!" Glancing warily around the abandoned lobby, she nonetheless lowered her voice to scold him. "Don't even think such a thing. She can't take it out on you—it's not your fault."

Yeah—like that matters.

But even if he had something bad to say about his boss, he would never breathe a word against her, not even to his sister. Any little comment could be turned against you in Desmon Tower. Even siblings had been known to squeal on one another for the right price.

"Dr. Desmon's never been unfair to me, Elaine. If she corrects me, I probably deserve it."

"No, you don't, *zulu*, and she knows it. You wouldn't be wearing that ring if she didn't have good reason to trust you." (Paradisian endearment: brother) Taking his left hand in hers, she reverentially buffed the signet ring on his pinky finger. "My brother—first assistant to 'the most powerful woman in the hemisphere.'"

"So it is, m'lady." He bussed her hand with a playful kiss. "But I need to get moving. You have a good day."

"I hope it goes well," she said soberly.

"It will. It'll be A-okay, *zali*. Just you wait and see." (Paradisian endearment: sister)

But the butterflies were fully awake now, and as Patric ascended in the VIP elevator, he had to consciously suppress his rising anxiety. He loved his job—he truly did. And he adored his boss, Dr. Camille Desmon, the second of Moden Industries' two sibling-partners. But, since she was returning from vacation today, he would have to report on the happenings during her month-long absence, including one very difficult piece of news. And that old saying "Don't shoot the messenger"—well, it originated here at Moden Industries.

Remembering his sister's observation, Patric gazed at his ring, borrowing courage from the confidence it implied. Of the millions of employees at Moden Industries, only five wore a partners' signet ring. He had worn this one—a large, round lapis lazuli in an ornate setting of white gold—for over twenty-five centuries. To this day, he remembered the moment Dr. Desmon had presented it to him. He relived that pride every time the other employees ushered him to the head of a line, every time they carried out his directions without question, and every time he mounted the VIP elevator. While he wore the jewel that so precisely reflected the color of Dr. Desmon's eyes, he spoke with her authority, and people treated him with the respect they would afford the junior partner herself. He had not removed the ring, except to clean it, since he first put it on 2,540 years ago. And he would do anything necessary to keep it for the rest of his life.

He squirmed at that thought. Until recently, that phrase—"the rest of his life"—had no real meaning to him. For most of his 7,357 years, he had expected to live forever. But the tiny laugh lines that were sprouting around his eyes reminded him daily that death was lurking out there, drawing a little closer every year.

However, it wasn't in Patric's nature to dwell on downers. Instead, he assured his reflection, "No worries, Patric. The docs have got it covered."

Drs. Moden and Desmon were the two smartest people on earth—and linked besides. For over sixty centuries, they'd been working tirelessly to return the exiles to their homeland, Paradise Island. And they were close, very close, to finishing the job. Once they overthrew that tyrant, King Doúg Damoúr, and regained access to the Viv fruit, Patric's laugh lines would be banished forever. No getting old and dying for him—no siree. And he was part of the solution, Dr. Desmon's own first assistant.

The elevator doors opened, and Patric sauntered out onto the top floor—the inner sanctum of Moden Industries. Except for the armed guards that greeted him as he passed, the halls were deserted at this hour. But Patric had never resented the long hours his job required. Keeping Dr. Desmon's ring on his finger was worth arriving at 5:00 a.m. Besides, there was nothing he'd rather do with his life than help her get them back to the island. And he couldn't really complain when she worked even more than he did.

For the next two hours, Patric prepared his boss's desk for the day, making sure she had the best, most up-to-date information possible and clearing it from trivial matters he could handle himself. By the time she walked off the VIP elevator at precisely 7:00 a.m., Patric was standing beside it with a large mug of her favorite gourmet coffee, prepared exactly as she liked it. Although he had expected her to return in high spirits, a wave of relief nonetheless passed through him to see that her eyes matched his ring—rather than the charcoal gray color they assumed when she was unhappy.

"Good morning, doc," he greeted. "Welcome back."

"Thank you, Patric. It's good to be back." Her gaze traveled down his lanky frame, from his blond braid to his penny loafers, and took on a hint of puzzlement. "Why, Patric, I must say—you're very nicely attired today."

He grinned. "Thank you, ma'am." *And you, too, Dr. Moden.*

She'd never before complimented him on his clothing. The truth was that, although he loved color, he wasn't very good at matching the vivid shades he preferred with coordinating colors. His resulting fashion flub-ups could really irritate the doc's exacting sense of style. But while working with Dr. Moden during the doc's absence, the big boss had clued him in on a little secret he called "monochromatic dressing." So today, while Patric still wore his bright purple suit, he had paired it with a black shirt and abstract lavender tie. Apparently he'd gotten it right.

"Well, I'm sure we have a busy day ahead of us," she said. "We may as well begin directly—unless my brother's already called for me?"

"No, ma'am. He's been kind of tired—didn't get to his gym until 4:30 this morning. He'll probably be running late."

"Very well. Then come in and update me on what's transpired in my absence."

"You got it, doc." Patric followed the elegant figure into her office. Truth was, he would gladly follow his brilliant and driven boss just about anywhere … except downstairs.

The thought roused the butterflies in his stomach. As he settled into one of the Queen Anne chairs in front of her cherry wood desk, he decided to postpone mentioning the item that could result in such a trip. Instead, he would begin with other, less troublesome bits of news. He therefore reported on the progress of the races, where their agents were experiencing great success in discouraging Doúg's runners. Her gaze sharpened somewhat when he mentioned that Benjamin Strider Jr. had begun the Parents' Race with his wife, but it grew downright hard when he added that Christian Strider was babysitting.

"I beg your pardon?" she asked icily.

Patric hesitated. In retrospect, he should have foreseen this hiccup and saved that bit of news for later, too. Nevertheless, he obediently repeated himself. "Christian Strider and his new wife are babysitting Benny's three sons while Benny and Marie run the Parents' Race."

Her eyes narrowed momentarily and then wandered to her left, coming to rest on the nearest of the cherry wood cabinets that housed her collection of antique torture implements. He squirmed in the heavy silence that followed, even though she had never actually used any of those instruments on him.

"You assigned a master agent to Benjamin?" she asked.

"Yes, ma'am—Warner."

He unconsciously held his breath as she stared at him, and then released it when she nodded once. He quickly turned to the safer topic of the discoveries their scientists had made during her vacation. She seemed particularly interested to learn that they were attempting to duplicate the atmospheric conditions of Paradise Island. The physiologists theorized that periodic exposure to that environment might delay the progression of *lakviv*, the degenerative process they were all undergoing from the lack of Viv fruit.

Her interest also seemed piqued by the discovery of an enzyme the geneticists had dubbed *mij dinósh*, "restoring enzyme." When he finished summarizing that research, she held up a finger for silence while she pondered the information.

Presently she smiled. "Patric, keep me informed on every aspect of this research. It may well become the secret weapon for which we've been searching."

He had no idea what she meant—the enzyme simply undid mutations. And, after all the time their scientists had spent putting thorns on roses, the value of de-thorning them again sure evaded him. But she obviously saw something promising in the research, so he would be interested to see what came of it. More important, the discovery had restored her good mood—just in time for the big bomb.

"Is that all, then, Patric?"

"Almost, ma'am. Just one more thing, a report from the Division of Interpretation."

"Oh?" Her brow furrowed slightly. Things in that division, which was responsible for decoding the messages King Doúg sent his forecasters, didn't usually progress so rapidly that a mere month's absence would be significant.

Clearing his throat, Patric said carefully, "They have now pinned an estimated date to the Final Battle."

Dr. Desmon jerked upright in her chair. "That's impossible. Damour must first institute an organization capable of military recruitment."

"Yes, ma'am. He has—the Kids' Klub."

"Nonsense. Those plans have been buried for decades. Strider has only just received them."

"Yes, but he's moving fast." Patric's collar had grown tight, and he tucked a finger into it to give it a tug. "He launched the program this weekend—and not just in his local RAB. Six other locations around the U.S. are also forming clubs."

She stared at him with that hard look that meant trouble, and he shifted his weight forward in the chair, ready to spring up and run. Call him a coward—he didn't care. Dr. Desmon's fury was not to be taken lightly, and he wasn't above fleeing to escape it.

But as she glared at him, resignation replaced the anger in her expression, and he gradually relaxed. The doc was demanding, but she wasn't usually impulsive, and if she took the time to think about it, she knew this complication wasn't his fault. In fact, she was the one who had warned that something like this would happen if Strider and López got together. She had hoped for better, sure, but she'd predicted that combining their considerable talents would end in disaster. This unfortunate development only proved her right—although she'd probably rather be wrong in this case.

"So the estimated date for the Final Battle is in fifty years?" she asked tightly.

"Yes, ma'am." He unfurled a large laminated timeline onto her desk and pointed to the offending date. "8058 *Modén Eshí*," he said, using their organization's standard measure of time. (Paradisian: Moden Years)

She nodded curtly.

"The date *does* mesh with the projections you and Dr. Moden had worked out," he noted optimistically. "And the revised Global Strategic Plan *is* on track for that date."

"Only just."

"Yes, ma'am." Clearly, she had been hoping for a wider safety net. "But you may buy us more time with your plans for Strider. You already delayed the club's inception by a full generation when you attacked his father."

"Did I?" she snapped.

He gave his collar another tug. That was the big question, wasn't it? They hadn't exactly been copied on Doúg's timeline for the war. For all they knew, everything was happening exactly as he'd planned in the first place.

Shifting her gaze to the chart, she asked, "The next major event we're to expect, then, is the issuing of lifetime hands-off orders for Damour's key players?"

"Yes, ma'am. That should begin around 8038 M.E."

Her sharp gaze met his. "Let's see what we can do to delay that eventuality, shall we?"

"Yes, ma'am," he agreed with a soft sigh of relief. One of the things he loved about the doc was that she quickly channeled her anger into action. Once she did, the danger had passed.

The danger to him, that is. He chuckled inwardly at the thought. The danger to the outlander world? Well, that was another matter entirely.

✲ ✲ ✲ ✲ ✲

Patric's sanguine nature did much toward calming Camille's pique. It usually did. Still, her irritation had not completely subsided by the time he left her office. Furthermore, when she logged on to her computer to add Strider to her List of Guerdon, her indignation over recent events resurfaced. What humiliation—having to run from Doúg's ear-shattering voice as she had. And then to return only to find a lowly human challenging *her*. The nerve.

What's more, when she keyed in the command to place Strider on her List, the screen presumed to flash "Request Denied" at her. Some glitch, undoubtedly, for only one person's List of Guerdon trumped hers, and surely Stan hadn't—

"No!" she erupted as she pulled up his List. Why had her brother claimed Strider?

Well, she needed to check in with him anyway; she might as well do so now. As she proceeded down the hallway to his office, she wondered if she might talk him into relinquishing Strider, but promptly scoffed at her own question—as though Stan had ever renounced an object of vengeance.

When she approached the desk of Stan's executive secretary, relief washed over Madelyn's face. "Oh, Dr. Desmon—welcome back. We missed you." She added in a whisper, "Especially him. He's been speaking a lot of British, ma'am."

Camille groaned inwardly. Stan reverted to his British accent only when angry, and he wasn't likely to grant favors in such a state. She might have to put off her request.

"I think—" Madelyn reached up to twirl the white streak she bleached into her waist-length black hair. "Forgive my boldness, ma'am, but I think he needs your, well, help."

H'mm. Maybe he'd be willing to trade favors. "I'll see what I can do."

Madelyn released her hair. "Thank you, ma'am."

Camille placed her thumb on the security pad outside Stan's office, cracked the door, and automatically tuned in to his emotions through the innate link that connected them. But as she did, she learned that he wasn't actually angry; he was tired. No, beyond tired—he was thoroughly exhausted. In fact, when he sluggishly lifted his gaze to her, she saw that even the bright emerald of his eyes had dulled to a darker jade.

Madelyn was right—she should help him, even if he wouldn't give her Strider. Her fate, along with everyone else's in Desmon Tower, depended on them regaining Paradise Island, and Stan was by far the most qualified individual to lead that effort. If he was exhausted, his work would suffer.

On the other hand, a few minutes wouldn't make any difference if …

She explored his emotional state further, and a frisson of excitement shot through her. A tired Stan usually became as feisty as a bull facing a matador, but sometimes he became almost as pliable as putty. Today felt like one of those rare putty days.

Stan leaned back in his chair. "Good to have you back. This was, without doubt, the longest month in history. If I'd realized how much your work load had grown since your last vacation, I wouldn't have been quite so adamant about you taking a break."

Camille settled into a chair before the oversized mahogany desk that dominated the far corner of the room. "Well, you were right—I did need it. I'm reenergized and quite content to be back at work."

"Yes, you look much better." He scowled. "But you cut your hair. I like it longer."

"As do I, but it will grow again. I needed the shorter style to play the part of a man. I crossed paths with the Strider newlyweds."

"You did? How did that go?"

She hesitated. While she wouldn't ordinarily admit failure openly, the best way to get what she wanted from an exhausted Stan was the shortest, most direct route. "Truthfully, I had very little success with them, and that was short-lived." She leaned forward, capturing his eyes. "I want them, Stan. *I want him.*"

"Those sons of Juan Misi can get under your skin, can't they?" His keen gaze held her eyes. "Do you know why he's on my List?"

"No. Actually, I wasn't aware that he was until I tried to add him to mine."

"He disrespected me to my face at his trial."

Oh, no—foolish boy, she thought.

"I wanted you to know that"—he tapped at his computer keyboard— "so you'd appreciate what a big gift I just gave you. He's off my List. Merry Christmas."

"Truly? Why, thank you, Stan!"

He laughed at her unusual display of emotion. "You're welcome, Kami. Consider it a token of my friendship."

"Thank you." They had only recently agreed to put past misunderstandings behind them and repair their fractured relationship. Clearly, he meant this unprecedented concession as an indication of his sincere commitment to that goal.

"What do you have in mind for him?" he asked.

"Ultimately, I want him downstairs."

"Of course. And until we can arrange that?"

"I intend to assign Adlai to him."

He looked up sharply, and her posture sagged in the chair. Was he going to obstruct her plans? As senior partner, he could if he chose, and Adlai Menod was his favorite research assistant.

Yet he was also an exceptionally skilled agent. Talented, driven, and ingenious, Adlai was the only person in the history of the organization to hold the two highest titles of distinction—Company Best Agent and Entity Best Agent—simultaneously. In fact, he had held both titles for so long that everyone simply called him "Best Agent." None other approached him in skills or experience. She *must* have him for Christian Strider.

She was preparing to pour forth this compelling argument when Stan asked, "Are you telling me you don't know?"

"Know what?"

"Adlai's no longer doing management work—doctor's orders."

"What! How dare Pim 'order' us about!"

Stan waved his hand wearily. "Just a figure of speech. More accurately, he strongly adv⸻⸻⸻⸻⸻⸻⸻⸻⸻⸻⸻⸻⸻⸻⸻⸻en getting sick frequently. Not⸻⸻⸻⸻⸻⸻⸻⸻⸻⸻⸻⸻e. But Pim felt that the physic⸻⸻⸻⸻⸻⸻⸻⸻⸻⸻⸻ting his *lakviv*."

At this⸻⸻⸻⸻⸻⸻⸻⸻⸻⸻⸻with the other thumb. She ha⸻⸻⸻⸻⸻⸻⸻⸻⸻d, although she would miss his⸻⸻⸻⸻⸻⸻⸻⸻an unwelcome reminder of the⸻⸻⸻⸻⸻⸻⸻⸻nem, Adlai and his sisters had t⸻⸻⸻⸻⸻⸻⸻⸻o they were the first to experier⸻⸻⸻⸻⸻⸻⸻

She str⸻⸻⸻⸻⸻⸻⸻⸻⸻was a full-time assignment. Th⸻⸻⸻⸻⸻⸻⸻⸻—"

Madel⸻⸻⸻⸻⸻⸻⸻loden? Pardon the intrusion, si⸻⸻⸻⸻⸻⸻

Stan gl⸻⸻⸻⸻⸻⸻right out. Have the limo waitin⸻⸻⸻⸻⸻les under them, and swore agai⸻⸻⸻⸻⸻ later."

"Very w⸻⸻⸻⸻⸻ly searched her brain for any ot⸻⸻⸻⸻⸻⸻ty mood. When she could remember none, she silently cursed her bad luck. The opportunity of the millennium had arrived, and she could come up with only one request?

"Stan, before you go—" She held out her hand.

A flash of surprise lit his bloodshot eyes, followed by a wave of affection. "Thank you, Kami."

He took her hand in both of his, and she added her other hand to the pile. As they both focused, the subtle tingling of an energy transfer began—another ability granted them by their link. After a few moments, Stan nodded, his eyes brighter. He stood and took her face in his hands to kiss her gently on the forehead.

The simple act sent a surge of warmth through her, for they had not shared that most intimate of kisses for many centuries. Yet as they exited the

[Handwritten note: This chapter shows however more serious Camille is to put Chris Strider down. This chapter really foreshadow that a lot is going to go down especially in Chris life. I wonder how Chris will handle this]

office together, an unwelcome voice in her head hissed, *Beware lest in smelling the rose you are pricked by the thorn.*

Her brow furrowed momentarily. Where had that come from? Oh—that silly fortune cookie. How ludicrous that she should remember it. And why apply it to Stan? She had truly become too suspicious of him over the years. Siblings could display affection occasionally—it was within the realm of normal behavior. It didn't mean he was planning something disagreeable.

CHAPTER 6

HELLISH STEPS

"Her feet go down to death, her steps lay hold of hell."
Proverbs 5:5, NKJV.

7 February 8008 M.E.

Camille was surprised when Stan's bulk filled her office doorway shortly after the company's six o'clock quitting time. He generally preferred to summon her for discussions. It was one method he used to remind her that he was the *senior* partner.

"Hello," she said. "What can I do for you?"

"You can join me in the gym."

It wasn't an invitation as much as an order, but she responded as if she had a choice. "I'd enjoy that. May I ask why you're exercising at this hour?"

"Too tired this morning—couldn't finish my workout."

"A pity, indeed, but my gain. I shall change and be right over."

"Excellent," he said, and disappeared down the hallway.

The arrangement didn't arouse Camille's curiosity overmuch. Being diligent in his physical training, it annoyed Stan when he, for whatever reason, was unable to finish the routine he'd predetermined for the day. No doubt, he simply wished to continue their interrupted discussion while completing his workout.

Nevertheless the idea of being alone with him in the gym always made her a bit uneasy. This dated from the time he had goaded her into trying to bench press more than she was capable of lifting. Then he—her spotter—walked out with a laugh as she lay choking on the bar she couldn't lift from her throat. Thankfully, their director of security, Garrick Sondem, had happened in before she passed out. (Perhaps Stan had sent him, but Camille wasn't certain enough to credit her brother with the rescue.) In any case, she determined to confine her workout to the machines tonight—nothing involving free weights.

When she entered Stan's private gym, he was already on a rowing machine. She paused briefly to admire his physique—an exercise motivated not by sensuality, but by deep envy. Her brother carried 310 pounds of muscle on his six-foot-three-inch frame; Camille, quite simply, coveted those muscles. She had often bemoaned the female body that prevented her from developing such a body herself.

Although she could run well enough to wheedle her way into a runner's confidence, she truly despised that activity. She had certainly never respected runners as real athletes, since they strove primarily for enhanced endurance. Of what value was endurance except to outrun one's conqueror?

Strength, on the other hand, was what conquered. Strength won arguments, overthrew rivals, and discouraged rebellion. Strength kept one's position secure through intimidation.

Strength—that was the stuff of real athletes. Endurance was for losers.

When she mounted the stair-climber beside Stan's rowing machine, he glanced over his shoulder and acknowledged her with a nod. Then, losing no time on pleasantries, he said, "A huge problem developed in your absence—the Kids' Klub."

"Patric told me it launched in several locations this weekend."

"Yes, and its web presence has already garnered international interest."

"It's not military yet, is it?"

"No, it's a recreational group that encourages mentoring. However, as you've noted before, it has all the necessary components for evolving into a military organization." He spoke matter-of-factly, but she sensed a level of concern not reflected in his tone.

"What is it, Lusu?" she asked soberly.

He glanced up at her and then halted his machine. Rising, he positioned himself directly in front of her. "There's a spirit about this movement—an electricity—that has me worried. We've managed to keep the RABs in relative hibernation for centuries, but we've always known it would get ugly if the beast awoke."

"You believe this movement could awaken them."

He nodded, and she turned away to hide an involuntary flinch. Stan was not one to exaggerate problems. Moreover, he was the most astute sociologist on the planet. If this was his analysis of the problem, it was not overstated.

"What can we do?" she asked.

"Honestly?" He snatched up his water bottle and took a long draft from it. Finally he set it down, wiped his mouth with the back of his hand, and admitted, "I'm not sure."

This troubled her further. Her elder brother always had an answer, or at least a list of potential solutions.

"I have some agents infiltrating the organization to get us better information, but—"

"I have a copy of the plans," she remembered suddenly. "Along with Christian's notes on them. I let myself into his room in Big Sur and took pictures of the entire set."

Stan spun to her. "Great work. Do you realize how long Garrick's men have been searching for those plans?"

"I do. I'd even dared hope that their failure to find them meant the accursed things had been destroyed."

"Have you studied them? What's your best guess on how to thwart it?"

"Two points caught my attention. First, there was a clear emphasis on the *Manual* built into the father's original plans. But Christian is specifically zeroing in on the Laws."

"Legalistic obedience?" Stan asked hopefully.

"No, I'm afraid not. His focus is on restoring the relationship between humans and their creator." Scoffing, she added, "He sees the Ten Laws as Damour's 'gift' to mankind."

Stan muttered a curse. "I knew that kid was smart. A concentration on the Law undergirded the big reform under Ezra and Nehemiah. In fact, it's been the groundwork for every true reform throughout the history of the war."

He loaded several 100-pound plates onto a bar, positioned it across his shoulders, and began doing some squats. Camille resumed stair-climbing as she silently considered the implications. A revival of that sort disseminated by modern methods of communication—what could be more disastrous?

"Then we'll attack the Law," Stan said. "We've done it before. The pressure to conform to 'scientific' discoveries and 'rational' thought blunts humans' ability to process information clearly. In their confusion, they tend to accept public opinion."

"This is true. Furthermore, if they believe that they know the reason behind a particular Law, they're inclined to flout it. Either way, they're encouraged to exalt their own 'wisdom' over that of their creator."

"Mm-hmm."

"It still amazes me how easily we can devise idols for these creatures to worship," she mused aloud. "You'd think they'd catch on after a few iterations."

"You u[...] [...] said in a cautionary tone,

"That [...] added a makeshift bow.

grant [...] [...]y are stupid creatures, I

don't [...] [...]ese modern generations

forces [...] [...] at those who venerate

their [...] they—yet they suppose

lat pu [...] at of the Deón."

impo[...] [...]chine and began a set of [...]ther?"

takes [...] [...] unaware of it, will be an

mises [...] [...]lly," Stan said. "It really

fizzle[...] in a group. If he compro-

[...]is zeal and influence will

[Handwritten margin note: "This chapter really represents the great controv. It is really a reflection how Satan attacks people by destroy the 10 commandment, uplifting human wisdom, and misrepresting Christianity"]

"As we did with King David."

"Precisely. And that brings us back to Adlai. Who better to accomplish Strider's downfall than the agent who masterminded David's disgrace?"

"Yes," she agreed. "I'm increasingly inclined in that direction regardless of Dr. Pim's opinion. At this point in our history, Adlai's talent for creative manipulations is critical. I'd just as soon utilize those skills, even if it hastens his death."

"Agreed. But I saw Pim after our chat this morning, so I mentioned it to him. His biggest concerns were the workload and frequent traveling. If we make this a full-time assignment as you suggested—relieving him of his other duties and keeping him on location in the field—Pim says he should be all right. I haven't mentioned it to Adlai yet, but that's inconsequential, of course."

"Excellent. Then I'll speak to him in the morning."

"Camille, I do want to keep him useful for as long as possible."

"I agree. His skills are irreplaceable."

"Good. Then minimize the pressure on him. Remove the threat of punishment, but retain appropriate bonuses."

When she arched a disapproving brow, he growled, "Drop that brow. My decision's final."

"As you wish," she said tightly.

He came alongside her machine and softened his tone. "Adlai's a true believer. He doesn't need threats to do his job. And decreasing his stress level will maximize his utility in the long term."

She resented this restriction, but Stan wore that authoritative expression that forbade argument. Besides, she was flattered that he had bothered to explain himself at all. Better to leave the controversy behind and move the discussion forward.

"I've had an idea," she said. "It would help to undermine Strider's work— indeed, to undermine the authority of the RABs themselves since we could incorporate your attacks on the Law as well. However, it would fall more naturally under your purview as Company Master than mine as Entity Master."

"What's your idea?"

"The fellowship provided by the RABs helps to strengthen runners' ties to both the group and to Damour. We could set up a counterfeit institution, utilizing the same principle to foster a sense of community. Individuals could run—" She paused to catch her breath as she reconsidered. "No, not just run—they could exercise in the manner of their choice. That would attract a larger segment of the population."

"And it would be easy to rationalize by emphasizing the physical benefits of exercise in general. We'll alter the focus of the organization, probably in stages, so that it centers on exercise rather than on the relationship Damour forms with his athletes *while* exercising."

"And rationalizing in one area will make it easier for the participants to accept other changes."

"Then they'll meet together in groups that legitimize this new focus," Stan said. "We'll foster the belief that simply participating in certain activities earns them the reward Damour promises."

"Precisely. And we make the new plan less demanding than Damour's. They can exercise on treadmills that tally their mileage, allowing them to run the equivalent of his race without leaving their old lives behind."

"That will make the counterfeit more convenient since they don't have to give up anything important to run the race." He laughed as he added, "At least, nothing that they know about now."

"Precisely. As long as they're working, they'll believe themselves to be on the same path as Damour's runners."

The conversation lagged for a moment, during which Camille mused that it had been some time since she and Stan had brainstormed in such a productive and amiable manner. She'd missed it.

"Those interested in other sports would be easy marks," Stan said thoughtfully. "But I can also see it attracting pseudo-runners from the RABs and even some who would ordinarily run Damour's race—as long as they believe it to be a legitimate option."

"Yes, and the community spirit would be useful in strengthening the allegiance of our overt followers, the associates. We can use them as leaders in these groups."

"We'll be able to get government support, too. With our political contacts and the country's concern with obesity, I'll have no trouble there." He chuckled as he continued, "In fact, I'll even be able to finagle direct public funding for it."

"And our contacts in the media can publicize it for us."

"This is a great idea. I'll get to work on it." He finished a set of biceps curls and moved to a bench. She watched as he loaded a heavy bar with some 2,000 pounds of plates. Turning to her, he motioned gallantly to the setup. "Would you care to do some bench presses, *zali*? I'll spot you."

Camille considered herself above the articulation of the phrases that came to mind. She merely replied sweetly, "No, thank you, *zuule*." (Paradisian: elder brother)

Stan laughed energetically, as if he'd made some grand joke. Adding more plates to the bar, he lay back on the bench to lift the weights himself.

She changed the subject. "I found the information on that newly discovered enzyme, *mij dinósh*, particularly interesting. How was it discovered?"

Stan didn't answer at first. After completing a full set, he sat up and looked her square in the eye. "In researching my … condition," he said softly.

Camille was momentarily speechless. Although she had agreed to undergo surgery to give Stan one of her tonsils, a vital organ for Paradisians, he had thus far not deigned to explain anything of his illness to her. Even now, she dared not trespass by asking for clarification, for the look in his eye strictly prohibited further probing.

"We've learned the enzyme is present in all elder brothers," he added before laying back for another set. "It works during periods of rapid cellular growth to strip genetic mutations from the genome."

"Is this why Damour takes grafts only from elder brothers to create *yushún* siblings?"

"It appears so."

"Yet it's effective in other species?"

"At least in the ones we've investigated so far. The work is just getting started."

Stepping down from her stair-climber, Camille moved to Stan's bench. "It occurs to me that one species in particular deserves further study in these experiments—a species that could be of tremendous help to us. If returned to its original level of intelligence and trained under our watchful eye, it could even be used to fortify our own ranks."

Stan sat up, his eyes gleaming. "Humans?"

"Humans."

✲ ✲ ✲ ✲ ✲

When Adlai entered Camille's office the next morning, he appeared somewhat displeased. But then, Camille wasn't particularly cheerful herself. After considering the matter, she wasn't at all certain she wished to put Adlai on Strider's case—not with the restrictions Stan had imposed. She hadn't worked with him for a decade or so, and the threat of punishment was an important tool for keeping agents on track. How could she entrust an unleashed agent with their most important Target? She hadn't yet decided the matter, but expected that this interview would give her the information she needed to make the decision.

As she surveyed the man seating himself before her desk, she soon appreciated Stan's concern about his *lakviv*. Elegantly dressed, Adlai projected intelligence, sophistication, and diligence. Indeed, that was the man Camille knew him to be. But whereas most of the exiles looked thirty-ish by outlander standards, Adlai looked forty-something, with gray creeping into his coal-black curls and some wrinkles framing his eyes. Yet as he lifted his eyes to her, Camille noted that the mind reflected in them was as keen as ever. Further, when he folded his hands in his lap, a ring on his left hand caught her attention—a large oval emerald in a fine gold setting. She hadn't realized that Stan had given Adlai his signet ring. If her brother trusted him with such authority, the need for a leash suddenly seemed less imperative.

"Dr. Moden said you wished to see me about a new assignment, ma'am. Do I understand correctly that this is to be a dedicated, full-time assignment that will relieve me of all my normal duties?"

"That is correct."

"With no traveling back and forth to Desmon Tower, full salary, and bonuses for successful outcomes"—his tone was becoming increasingly incredulous—"but no discipline for failure?"

"Correct."

He glanced down. "Dr. Desmon, may I speak freely?"

"You may do so at your own risk."

He hesitated before proceeding in a tone that, while respectful, conceded no insecurity. "Ma'am, have I in some way engendered your ill regard—or Dr. Moden's?"

"You have done nothing to earn my poor opinion. As to Dr. Moden's, I should think your possession of that ring speaks for itself."

He glanced at the ring and straightened its position on his finger. "Then I hope you will not think me insubordinate, but I must confess that I find these terms extraordinary. I took the liberty of researching the matter. There's never been such a generous arrangement in the history of the company. Honestly, I feel like I'm being set up. I have no idea what I'm being set up for, but it just smells wrong."

Camille mentally tallied one point on the side of using Adlai. His astuteness was one of the qualities that made him such an excellent agent. And she certainly didn't resent his suspicion since it was warranted; she and Stan didn't always speak the truth, even to their fellow exiles.

Leaning forward, she rested her forearms on the desk and spoke gently but without patronizing. "I understand your concern, Adlai, but I can assure you that it is unfounded. You are our best agent—you're aware of this—and your health is becoming fragile. It is in our interests as well as your own to optimize your working conditions in order to preserve your health for as long as possible. To be blunt, we need your talent."

"So the unusual terms are meant to reduce my level of stress?"

"They are. There are very few individuals for whom we would consider such an arrangement. But your work has always been stellar, and you've consistently proven your unwavering commitment to the organization." Recognizing the truth of these statements, she mentally tallied two more points in Adlai's favor.

"Dr. Moden feels that your loyalty to our mission will be enough to keep you on track," she continued. "Frankly, I'm not certain of that, and I will have no qualms about replacing you at any time if I feel you're abusing your freedom." That's right, come to think of it—she always had that option. So why not try the arrangement?

His stern expression relented. "Fair enough. Dr. Moden said the subject was uniquely important?"

Camille tapped at her keyboard to pull up the file. Turning the screen toward him, she said, "Christian Strider, son of Juan Misi. Are you familiar with the ancestor?"

"By reputation only." Adlai looked behind him, apparently checking that the door to the soundproof office was closed. It was another indication of his caution—it would be imprudent to answer the question within Stan's hearing. "He was quite a problem in his day. Among other things, he's the one who gave Dr. Moden the scar on his cheek. Furthermore, we've never derailed any runner in his line."

"True, although derailment is not the object in this case. Our primary goal here is damage control."

"Ah." Adlai's blue eyes lit up like stained glass illuminated by the sun. "What damage has he caused so far?"

Camille chuckled. Still the same old Adlai—he'd always loved a good challenge. "He's the Leader-Activator behind the Kids' Klub. We expect he will also be the driving force behind raising an outlander division for Damour's army."

Adlai gaped at her. "Wow."

She nodded. "Now you understand our concern—and our willingness to make such unusual arrangements for his care. Dr. Moden and I will both rest easier with you on his case. You'll try to turn him from Damour, of course. But even if you do not succeed there, any limitation of his influence, particularly on children, will advance our purpose."

"I see," Adlai said with a nod. "Any delay we cause in the Kids' Klub will place Damour at a disadvantage."

"Precisely."

"Why don't we just kill the boy?"

"We've tried. Damour foiled it. In fact, he sacrificed Joshua to prevent it."

"That was this Subject?" Adlai exclaimed, and Camille understood his surprise. Doúg's willingness to risk his only son's life to save one lowly human was still the focus of much puzzlement and conjecture around Desmon Tower.

"It was. Joshua was Strider's coach during the race."

Adlai broke into a broad grin. "Then I heartily thank you for the opportunity, Dr. Desmon."

"Do you have a history with this Subject of which I'm unaware?"

"No, ma'am. My grudge is against Joshua. If this Subject's that important to him, then I'm really going to enjoy playing with him and bringing Joshua as much grief as possible." He chuckled. "Oh, yes. This will be great fun."

"Excellent. It appears we've found the perfect match. Speaking of which, one key to Christian's effectiveness is his wife, Susana López, on whom we have a hands-off order."

"Let me guess—a Connector-Catalyst."

Camille smiled. "I'd quite forgotten how much I enjoy working with you. She is indeed."

He shook his head. "Figures. Well, I'll have to give Damour this much— he certainly knows how to pair his people for maximum usefulness. But that also means that simply breaking up the team should help us."

"Indeed. On that front, I've made an interesting discovery. I recognized the wife's potential when she was quite young. We arranged a fire when she was eight that resulted in significant disfigurement."

"Ah, fascinating tack. If the fire didn't kill her, the scars would create a barrier between the Connector and the social network Connectors are so invested in. Inspired idea."

"Damour has since sent her some leaves from the *Viv Zabé*—"

"He healed her scars?" Adlai exclaimed.

"He did," she admitted grudgingly. "But prior to that, my manipulation worked so well that she despaired of being attractive to any male and renounced all hopes of husband and family. Instead, she committed herself single-mindedly to Damour's work and became one of the most dedicated runners I've encountered."

Enlightenment sparked in Adlai's eyes. "Let me guess: Then she met Strider, who wasn't put off by the scars. And now the runner who so freely surrendered all things material to Damour is having trouble trusting him with the one thing she thought she'd never have—a family of her own."

"Correct. I will admit that she had been so committed I did not foresee this result. However, as we've both seen before, humans sometimes fear most the loss of that which they once believed they could never possess. That is the case here."

"So if I can keep her satisfied with things as they are, she'll be my greatest ally in preventing what could be. Her own resistance will limit her husband's usefulness and delay the establishment of an Outlander Division."

"Precisely." All reservations Camille had entertained concerning Stan's interference on Adlai's behalf had vanished. He would do very well indeed.

PART II

MARR

> *Handwritten note:*
> Stephanotis – Bridal
> veil – known for
> marital happiness.
> We cannot solve our
> problems on our own
> simply because we
> don't know the best
> way, so we should
> give everything for Jesus
> to take of.

Susana heard the [l]... clock came grad[ually] ... igital wall
   Where was sh[e] ... ll fixed on her. What did they wa[nt] ...
   Standing dir[ectly] ... n his hand, Josh said, "What do y[ou] ...
   A flush warm[ed] ... distracted while the teacher was quizzing her. "I'm sorry—what was the question?"

A sigh seemed to go through the room. She had disappointed a room full of top-level military personnel, but she couldn't remember why. Neither could she place this setting, although it looked familiar. Hadn't she been here before?

No, it was in a dream—that's right. She must be dreaming again.

"I asked if you would give me the stephanotis." Josh indicated some fragrant white flowers in the bouquet she held. As she looked down at them, everything came flooding back: Chris at the other door, awaiting an access badge; Josh asking her to take it to him; the War Room. She shuddered.

"Does the stepha—um, this flower have a meaning, too?" Truthfully, she wasn't all that interested in the meaning of the flowers, but stalling seemed like a good idea. Anything that kept Chris and something called a War Room apart seemed like a good idea.

"Stephanotis," Josh repeated. "It has a lovely scent, don't you think?"

Susana sniffed the waxy, tubular flower. "Mmm. It's awesome." She was savoring a longer whiff when a question niggled at the back of her brain: Should she be able to smell things in a dream?

"Yes, it is awesome," Josh agreed. "Also called bridal veil, this flower represents marital happiness. It's a beautiful plant when cared for properly, but it can also be quite difficult. It's very sensitive to changes in temperature and susceptible to disease."

Susana gazed at the flower sorrowfully. She was rotten with plants. Cut flowers, live plants, even weeds—she was an equal-opportunity disaster when it came to anything green. And it seemed a terrible waste that such a perfectly fashioned, wonderfully perfumed piece of art should die prematurely under her clumsy supervision.

"Do you know how to care for it properly?" she asked softly.

"I sure do. Shall I look after it for you?"

Susana's eyes roamed over the many other blooms in her bouquet—plenty more to provide an excuse not to deliver that access card to Chris.

"Yes," she whispered. "Please take good care of it."
"Oh, I will, dear one. This is one of my very favorite flowers."

To: bestagent@management.com
From: MA-223@management.com
Date: 14 February 8008 M.E.
Subject: Humbly requesting aid

Please forgive my audacity in approaching you, sir, but I do so at Entity Master's instruction. I am assigned to your Subject's brother, who has started the Parents' course. I am working on an operation involving my Subject's oldest son—your Subject's oldest charge—but we are concerned that your Subject will interfere with its success.

I am fully aware that your Subject's priority level outranks my Subject's, and that your rank surpasses my own. However, my Subject has also been orange-flagged by Company Master. Therefore, I would be most grateful for your help in preventing your Subject's interference—if you are in a position to lend such aid without jeopardizing your own assignment, of course. I would also welcome any insights or suggestions that you, in your superior expertise, may condescend to offer.

To: MA-223@management.com
From: bestagent@management.com
Date: 14 February 8008 M.E.
Subject: Re: Humbly requesting aid

Your appropriate self-abasement is noted and accepted. I will happily lend any aid in my power to offer. In fact, I believe we may be able to dovetail our respective operations to benefit us both. By combining forces, we can devastate child, parents, and uncle.

I am working on a two-pronged attack utilizing overwork and distraction. However, I am at a particular disadvantage with this Subject as I have thus far been unable to identify any area of accessibility to him. He seems to guard his avenues well. I am, therefore, left only with indirect methods of influencing him, and the most promising of these is through the children under his care. For this reason, I have secured a position as a long-term substitute at the school attended by the oldest child—with whom you are doing an excellent job.

We should meet to coordinate the timing of our respective operations to maximum effect. I will expect you to travel to my location. Tomorrow at 4:00 p.m. would be convenient.

CHAPTER 7

COUNSEL

*" 'I counsel you to … anoint your eyes with eye salve,
that you may see.' "*
Revelation 3:18, NKJV.

Chris exchanged a worried glance with Susana as they watched their oldest charge, fourteen-year-old Kevin, hands stuffed into his pockets, trail into the house and plop into a chair.

"You'd better pick your brothers' brains really soon," Susana said.

"Yeah," Chris agreed. "Like today."

The Strider family was big—and busy. But, luckily, they got together frequently. Today they were gathering at Chris's old home, where his twin sister now lived with her husband, to celebrate Valentine's Day.

When dinner rolled around, Chris loaded his plate with the traditional family favorites like deviled eggs, carrot salad, and—his very favorite—Rosie's mouth-watering blueberry muffins. He'd gotten the last one of those; they were always the first thing on the table to disappear. Then he set off in search of his brothers, Mike and Steve. When he spotted all three of his siblings together, he promptly cornered them.

"I really need your help with something," he said. "It's Kevin. He's been so withdrawn, just not himself. And his grades are dropping. Do you guys know what's going on? It's got Susana and me worried, but he keeps brushing me off."

Chris's second-oldest brother, Mike, shook his head. "No, but I can tell you it's not new. His mom's been concerned about him too. I was hoping you'd get to the bottom of it—he's always been closest to you."

"Yeah, me too," Rosie agreed. "He's been this way since starting high school last fall."

"He's always been a quiet kid," observed Steve, Chris's third-oldest brother. "Maybe he's having trouble making friends at the new school."

"Well, he's got two new friends," Chris said. "But Susana doesn't have a good feeling about them."

Mike looked up sharply. "Then keep a close eye on them," he advised around a bite of Danish.

"How do you keep a close eye on three teenage boys?" Chris asked.

"Make your place the hangout for them. Equip the garage with stuff they'll want to do. And keep plenty of food around. Then tell Kevin he can see them all he wants as long as it's at your place."

"Hey, the old Ping-Pong table's still here in the garage, and Kevin loves to play," Steve said. "You're not using it, are you, Rosie?"

"No. Actually, Ivan would love to have it out of the way," she said of her husband. "Especially since we're getting a Mercedes and—"

"A *Mercedes*?" the others chorused.

"What?" she said defensively. "What's wrong with driving a nice car?"

Steve chortled. "Nothing if you can afford it."

"We got a really reasonable payment plan."

"That only means you're paying as much in interest as the car's worth," Mike said quietly.

"Oh, what do you guys know? You're happy driving old wrecks."

As she huffed away, Chris murmured, "You used to be, too."

After a few moments of uneasy silence, Steve said, "Come on, kid. I'll give you a ride home to get your truck so you can take that Ping-Pong table."

Chris looked at his still-full plate. "Thanks, but can I eat first?"

"Sure." Steve swiped the prized blueberry muffin. "I'll even help."

"Hey," Chris objected, but Steve had already stuffed half of it in his mouth.

"Speaking of helping," Mike said, "what on earth's happening with the Kids' Klub? The thing's exploded."

it." [...] ad were still around to see

proj [...] about their late father's pet

Chr [...] ne for football. Afterward,

In t [...] load the Ping-Pong table.

Chr [...] stuff in the garage. When

this [...] handed it to Kevin. "Here,

Kev [...] ris had seen in some time,

"Na [...] oxically, he tossed it aside.

[...] ," Chris puzzled aloud.

on [...] . I shouldn't waste my time

gar [...] around the corner of the

[...] ing on with that kid?

[Handwritten note:] It seems that the agents are up to something making the KK have many inconvenien and they are attacking Kevin, exactly what is going on with Kevin

As Susana opened the door leading from the house into the garage, she heard Chris's victorious "Ha!" and saw his well-placed volley bounce way out of his opponent's reach.

"Yeah," Kevin seconded and gave his uncle a high-five. "We won!"

Bringing the Ping-Pong table home had been a great idea. Kevin and his friends were happy to have a place to hang out, and they sometimes even invited Chris to round out the teams. The arrangement was already bearing fruit in a somewhat improved relationship with Kevin, and Susana felt better about having him home more often. She didn't trust his two buddies, since neither had much parental oversight.

"Chris," Susana called over the cheers, "phone's for you. A Kids' Klub leader from Idaho."

Chris tossed his paddle onto the table and headed for the door. "Sorry, guys. You'll have to get along without me."

"I just took some peanut butter cookies out of the oven if you want some," she told the boys. They were barreling past her before she finished the sentence, and she followed them into the kitchen. When the boys had finished their snack, she noticed Chris rubbing his temples. Still on the phone, he sat at the dining room table surrounded by his growing piles of notes and folders. She listened in long enough to get the gist of the conversation while she made the boys' school lunches for the next day.

When he finished the call, he came into the kitchen to help with the after-dinner cleanup. Pulling a bottle of acetaminophen from the cupboard, she wordlessly offered it to him. He gulped down two tablets and kissed the top of her head. "Thanks."

"You're welcome. With all the problems you've been bombarded with, it's no wonder you've got a headache."

"Yeah. I don't understand why these clubs get so bogged down with little bitty problems. Ours runs so smoothly."

"Because you've got Mike as an assistant."

His brow furrowed. "Huh. I guess you're right. He somehow manages all the piddling stuff so seamlessly that I don't even notice he's doing it."

"I'll bet he'd be willing to help with the other clubs' problems, too. Maybe he'd even work up a set of procedures to help new clubs deal with common pitfalls."

"I don't know. The leaders want to talk to me—I'm the one they know. With things just getting started, I really need to be on top of things."

"You want to make sure it succeeds because it's your dad's project."

He flashed a crooked smile. "Yeah."

"Don't you think Mike feels the same way?"

The phone rang—another Kids' Klub leader with another set of questions—and Chris returned to the dining room table. When he yawned as he listened, Susana shook her head. Doug had warned them that things would be difficult here, and she could see the makings of a disaster on the horizon. The Kids' Klub was only just getting started. The number of questions and problems would grow exponentially over the coming months, and Chris couldn't possibly keep up this pace much longer.

That issue alone was enough to worry her, but it wasn't the only problem. Something inside Kevin was still festering, something that he wasn't likely to reveal to anyone except his favorite uncle. Yet if things continued as they were, Chris would be too distracted and too exhausted to help.

She only hoped the result didn't devastate both nephew and uncle.

CHAPTER 8

HARD WORK

" 'I know all the things you do. I have seen your hard work and your patient endurance.' "
Revelation 2:2, NLT.

"Please, Uncle Chris, *puh-leeeease*?" eight-year-old Harry pleaded.

Chris glanced at Susana with a sigh. He loved his nephews. He did. But he was bone tired. The last thing he needed was an argument—especially not when the whole family would be arriving shortly for their monthly pizza night. What he did need was a break. Even a short one would help.

"Please, Uncle Chris?" Harry persisted.

"No." Chris turned away from his nephew's big brown eyes to carry the tray of watermelon to the backyard.

"It's only one hour a week," Harry said, following him outside.

"No. You can record it or watch it online on the weekends." He plopped the tray down on the picnic table.

"Aw, come on, Uncle Chris," whined twelve-year-old Adrian. "That's not the same. There's a whole *Fugitives* club at school now. Everybody meets in the history teacher's classroom at lunch on Tuesdays to talk about it. If we don't watch the new episodes Monday night, we miss the discussions too."

"It's the English teacher at my school," Kevin said as he deposited the paper plates on the table. "He's loves *Fugitives*."

"It doesn't matter," Chris insisted. "The answer's still 'no.' Remember, guys, we're only enforcing your parents' rule—no TV on school nights. The only exception is if it's directly related to a class."

"But if our teachers are organizing the discussion groups, isn't that school-related?" Adrian asked.

Chris rolled his eyes and headed into the kitchen with the boys trailing him. Catching Susana's eye, he complained, "You know, people always talk about kids being so innocent. But if there's one thing I've learned since becoming a surrogate parent, it's that kids are downright tricky and manipulative."

"Veritable scoundrels," she agreed with a giggle. In an obvious attempt to distract the boys, she said, "You guys really seemed to like the marching at the Kids' Klub last night. Should we make it a regular thing?"

"Yeah, it was awesome," Harry exclaimed.

But Adrian wasn't falling for Susana's tactic. "Hey, wait a minute. Mom and Dad always relax the TV rule during the last quarter of school if our grades are good."

"That's right, they do," the other boys agreed.

Chris heaved another sigh. He wished someone had mentioned that earlier. He could have avoided this whole battle. "Fine. We'll call your folks—"

The three boys cheered and made a beeline for the phone.

"—*after* everyone leaves tonight," Chris finished sternly.

The boys groaned and started bellyaching about the delay.

Completely losing his cool, Chris blew a shrill whistle between his teeth. "And if I don't get five lousy minutes of quiet right now, there'll be no phone call until tomorrow."

As the boys dragged themselves outside, Susana leaned up to kiss Chris's cheek. Offering him the bottle of acetaminophen, she asked "Headache?"

"Yeah. Thanks." He swallowed a couple of tablets just as the first of his siblings walked through the front door.

Despite the rocky start, Chris could feel himself unwinding as he socialized with his family—at least for a while. But after dinner and the requisite football game, a new source of unrest reared its head. The adults were sitting around the picnic table chatting when Steve's wife, Jeannie, approached her husband. "Do you have any cash? We need to pay Susana for our share of the pizza."

"Sure, hon." Steve handed her his wallet. "Just be sure to leave me enough so I can get my mistress some flowers."

The chatter at the table abruptly stopped, and all eyes turned to the pair.

"What?" Steve protested. "I'm joking."

Jeannie didn't seem to appreciate the wisecrack. She took some money, handed the wallet back to Steve, and walked off without so much as a polite smile.

Mike leaned across Chris to murmur, "Steve, some subjects aren't wise to kid about."

"Oh, it's just a joke," Steve said. "One she started, by the way."

A tussle between Chris's two youngest charges called him away from the table just then. When he returned, Rosie and Susana had joined the group, and their conversation gave him reason to cringe.

"Did you find someone to help out with those cooking classes for the Kids' Klub?" Rosie asked. "I could probably do it if you still need someone."

"Oh, that's really kind of you, but—" Susana glanced at Chris in an unspoken plea for help, and he reconsidered his cowardly notion that this might be a good time to check on the kids playing a Ping-Pong game in the garage.

"To be a volunteer, you must have completed the race," he explained.

He knew exactly what his sister would throw back at him, and she obliged. "But Dad wrote the guidelines—can't you just change them?"

"No. Dad wrote *down* the guidelines, but they came from Doug. He was very specific about the qualifications for the volunteers."

"That doesn't make sense," persisted Rosie, who could be as stubborn as her twin. "The kids are interested in cooking, and you haven't been able to offer it because you're short on people. Now you won't accept my help just because I haven't run the race? Which has nothing to do with cooking, by the way."

Chris's stress level was skyrocketing. He and Rosie had been best friends through high school. He liked doing things with her, and she would be a great cooking teacher for their Kids' Klub—if only she were a runner. But that one "little" thing had a big effect on her priorities, values, and lifestyle. A runner evaluated every decision, from how he fueled his body to how he spent his spare time, according to how it would affect his training. A non-runner simply couldn't relate to that.

Still, Chris understood his sister's desire to help. To her, as to him, the Kids' Klub was a way of remembering Dad. That made it really hard to turn down her offer, even though he understood the importance of doing so.

Thankfully, Mike came to his aid. "The primary objective of the Kids' Klub isn't to teach cooking—or astronomy or wilderness survival or scrapbooking or any other hobby—it's to expose kids to people who are living their lives according to Doug's principles, to help them understand how broad and interesting life is as a runner, to—"

"But I run sometimes," Rosie objected. "And I've always respected Doug's Laws, just like Dad taught us."

"It's not the same," Chris said. "The whole point of running is to spend time with Doug so you can trust him. You learn things running the race that you don't learn by running on your own. Really, Rosie, it's such an amazing experience. Have you thought anymore about doing it?"

"Yeah. I plan to, you know. I'm just not sure when. Someday when Ivan and I can do it together."

"Doug's great about helping you figure out how to work it into your life," Mike said. "Just talk to him about it."

"Okay," Rosie said. "I'll think about it."

But the way she said it made Chris's heart sink. Of all his siblings, Rosie was the one he especially wanted to share his new love of running with. So far, though, she'd resisted all of his attempts to enlist her.

When Rosie turned away to converse with Jeannie, Mike whispered, "There's only so much you can do, kid. She has to make her own decision."

Chris nodded, knowing his brother was right, but finding little consolation in his words.

"Speaking of which," Mike continued, "I just want you to know that I'm ready to help out with the Kids' Klub however I can. I don't have your talent for getting people enthused about a project, or your knack for getting the clubs going. But I could lend a hand with the problems that come up in the established clubs."

"Thanks, but Josh specifically asked me to do it."

"And he specifically asked me to help you," Mike countered. "Doug doesn't want anyone working themselves into the ground. It seems like that's what you're doing."

When Chris hesitated and entertained the thought of Mike's help, which *would* be nice, he was immediately hit with the sharp, familiar pangs of guilt. How could he even think of shirking his duty to his dad, who had worked himself sick to put him through college? Not to mention his duty to Josh, who had literally died for him. No, he owed them both more than he could ever repay. He had to do everything in his power to make this project a success. Giving anything less than his utmost would be unforgivable.

"I'm the one people know, the one they've talked to," he said firmly. "It's natural they should call me with problems."

"Sure, but that doesn't mean you have to handle all those problems yourself. You can delegate."

"Thanks, Mike. I'll think about it."

Mike snorted. "Funny, that's exactly what Rosie just said about running."

Chris looked away. Although he usually enjoyed getting together with his family, tonight's dinner—what with the boys' arguing, Steve's "humor," Rosie's complaints, and Mike's well-meaning pressure—wasn't doing much to ease the burdens he carried.

When everyone left, Chris called Benny and Marie, who confirmed that the precedent the boys cited did indeed exist. Kevin had to do a little negotiating since his grades had dropped earlier in the year, but eventually their parents agreed that they could each watch one hour of TV per school night as long as their grades didn't suffer. So, after a celebration rivaling that of New Years' Eve, the boys settled in to watch TV's newest craze, *Fugitives*.

Chris was instantly hooked. Not only was the show engaging, it felt *so* good to just lie back in the easy chair and zone out—no decisions to make, no problems to solve, no feathers to unruffle.

Finally, a place to relax.

He relaxed so well that he watched two more shows and the eleven o'clock news before turning in. The next morning his eyes were still heavy with sleep when the alarm blared. He blindly batted at it until he got the noise to stop and then opened one bleary eye to confirm the time: 5:00 a.m.

He groaned. How could it already be time to get up? It seemed like he'd just gone to bed.

But wait—did he really need to get up two whole hours before he was due at work? It only took ten minutes to drive there, and he could eat a granola bar in the car. Shower and dress—fifteen minutes, tops. Another fifteen to get the boys' breakfast—cereal would work fine. So, all he really needed was forty minutes. The rest was time he usually devoted to reading his *Runner's Manual* and talking to Doug with Susana. But he could do that later today; Doug wouldn't mind.

Yeah, that was a good plan. He'd talk to Doug later. Resetting the alarm, he rolled over and went back to sleep.

CHAPTER 9

SAFE

"They invoke a blessing on themselves, thinking,
'I will be safe, even though I persist in going my own way.' "
Deuteronomy 29:19, NIV.

To: entitymaster@management.com
From: bestagent@management.com
Date: 31 March 8008 M.E.
Subject: Monthly Report

    I am happy to report that MA-223 is doing an excellent job with his operation, and mine is also proceeding well. My temporary position has given me the opportunity to start a "discussion group" for a popular TV program, and to encourage teachers at other schools to do the same. I've thereby influenced the children under Subject's care and, with their help, distracted Subject with TV. He is already spending less time with his wife and with Dictator, and his runs are getting shorter. Yesterday he not only blew one off altogether, but he also decided to forego Dictator's ultramarathon this year.

    In conjunction with this, I've instructed our agents to persuade KK leaders to bring every concern directly to Subject himself, and our agents are having fun inventing problems that require consultation. I've also made excellent use of Company Master's new aerosolized form of guilt—which works very well, by the way. It has induced Subject to accept a load that even I would find challenging. In addition, his chronic haste often causes him to forgo the protective undergarments and sunscreen that Dictator provides, making him even more vulnerable to attack.

    In summary, Subject is both severely overworked and neglecting his communication with Dictator. As I am already seeing the obvious results of this combination, I will hold the course.

❋ ❋ ❋ ❋ ❋

    Camille chuckled to herself while composing a response to Adlai's report. As she finished, Patric bounced into her office. "Look what I found stuck in your calendar, doc." He held up two tickets for the Philharmonic that evening. "Bet you forgot all about them."

Her silence was all the confirmation he needed. With a victorious grin, he asked, "Shall I invite Fiona to go with you?"

A sudden commotion outside her open door drew their attention. All four of her secretaries were springing up at once, one so abruptly that she toppled her chair. Exclamations of "Dr. Moden, sir!" and "May I get you some coffee, sir?" filtered into her office.

"No, no, I'm fine. As you were," Stan answered as he strode through her doorway. "Camille, we need to talk. I just received an update on the human experimentation."

"Excellent," she said. "Then why don't you join me for a concert this evening, and we can discuss the research en route."

Her brother's eyebrows shot up, and Patric's mouth fell open. Frankly, she was just as astonished. She hadn't intended to say those words. She wasn't even certain that she meant them. Yet Stan's behavior over the last few months had grown increasingly amiable. Cherished memories, once consigned to oblivion, had begun to intrude upon her consciousness once again. Perhaps they had also lured her subconscious into hoping for a full reconciliation with her former best friend.

Shuffling some papers to cover her consternation, she added, "We used to so enjoy music together."

"Yes, we did," he agreed, a wistful smile floating briefly across his face. "I'd love to go, Kami. Thank you for asking."

Later that evening, in the limousine on the way to the Lincoln Center, Stan updated her on the research involving *mij dinósh*. When he finished, she summarized, "So by introducing this enzyme into an early embryo, we can reverse genetic mutations in any species, including humans."

"That's right."

"And humans bred in this manner will not have the weaknesses that the species has accumulated over the generations. They will have the strength, intelligence, and lifespan of the first humans."

"We have every reason to believe so."

Camille's excitement surged. She had hoped for such results. Here was an opportunity to create a large pool of workers—and ones they could genetically design to fill specific roles.

"Such individuals could be of immeasurable value to us, Lusu. We could use them in any number of capacities, from foot soldiers to executives for the business."

"I had the same thought," Stan said, his eyes dancing. "This may be the advantage we've been searching for—extra manpower to help us prepare for the Final Battle."

"Precisely. We can hire surrogate mothers to incubate the fetuses, but the offspring will be raised and trained entirely for our purposes."

"Our only constraint will be the number of germ cells we can obtain, but that shouldn't be a major limiting factor."

"I should say not," she scoffed. "Humans have been giving us their offspring for millennia, in every form from human sacrifices to uncensored consumers of video games. They don't even see embryos as fully human, and they feel still less responsibility toward their germ cells. I'm sure we'll have no difficulty buying ova and sperm, and then we can selectively breed embryos for intelligence, physical strength, leadership abilities, or whichever variable would be most useful to their future role."

"And then we'll deliver the infants in our facilities and put the names of the Paradisian 'parents' on the birth certificates. The kids won't know anything of donors or surrogates."

Camille's enthusiasm grew. "Such humans would be ours, Stan—wholly ours, to make of them whatever we choose. We could so completely control their environment as to virtually eliminate their freedom of choice. We'll immerse them in our values from the cradle and bedazzle them with the perks of wealth and power. They'll have no reason, let alone opportunity, to resort to Damour's dogma."

"I'd go even beyond that." Excitement began to radiate from him like sparks from a rocket. "Think of it: willingly sold to *us*; conceived in *our* labs, their very DNA altered by *our* enzymes; incubated in wombs *we* rent; raised in *our* homes—could there be any greater perversion from Damour's perspective?"

"Excellent point," she said. "How could such abominations possibly merit his love or forbearance? He wouldn't dream of offering them 'grace.' Instead, he'll abandon them entirely to our jurisdiction, making them more surely our slaves than any human that's ever lived."

"Exactly."

"However, I wouldn't relish the thought of raising such humans. It would be terribly inconvenient."

"True, but it would only be for a couple of decades. What's that to us after 8,000 years of life? For my part, the work I'll extract from the little brats will be well worth the effort."

"Perhaps." she said uncertainly. "Or perhaps we can raise them en masse, in large group homes."

"That would be the most efficient method for the common foot soldiers and laborers. But I want full control over any child I raise—I'll be training it to take over part of my work."

Camille shrugged. Stan could do as he wished, but she had no intention of complicating her life with something as noxious as a human child. However, if Stan wanted one …

"What is it?" Stan asked. "You're grinning."

She chuckled. "I was just thinking of a gift you might appreciate."

"A gift?" He leaned forward, delight glimmering in his eyes, and she chuckled again. It always amused her to see her brother with a present. Although he could send tough men fleeing with a glance, he acted much like a child when opening a gift.

She opened the cooler and, selecting some mineral water, poured it into a glass, purposely prolonging his suspense. "I happen to know," she said slowly, "of a certain daughter of Juan Misi—the twin sister of Christian Strider, in fact— who might be interested …" She took a leisurely sip of water. "… in selling her eggs."

He leaned forward, the picture of anticipation. "Go on."

"She and her husband have developed a taste for luxuries well beyond their means. Though married less than a year, they've already dug themselves into a deep financial hole."

A grin spread over Stan's face. "Raise a descendant of Juan Misi to help me fight Damour? Kami, I'd love that."

"Then I shall see to the matter myself," she said with satisfaction. "We'll establish a company to bank eggs and sperm, and I shall personally oversee the solicitation of Rose Strider Moore's ova. A little flattery, a little money, and I'm quite certain that you, my dear brother, will have a son or daughter of Juan Misi to—"

"A daughter. I want a daughter."

"You know I cannot promise that, Stan. But you shall have a child of Juan Misi. That I do promise."

He pressed a kiss to her forehead. "Thank you, *zali*. I like your gift. I like it very much."

Camille enjoyed the evening spent with her brother. The concert was excellent until intermission, after which it became exceptional. That was when Stan leaned over and laid his hand on her bare arm to whisper something to her. At his touch, the music instantly became richer and fuller, causing her to catch her breath in wonder. She had remembered enjoying music more with Stan than with anyone else, but it had been nearly five millennia since they had shared such an encounter. She had honestly forgotten the cause: skin contact completed a neural circuit that exponentially increased their enjoyment of art. For music, it was like comparing a tinny radio to a premium surround-sound system. Since they were already listening to outstanding live music, the effect was awe-inspiring.

Judging by the delighted surprise she sensed in Stan, he had also forgotten about this experience. He broke into a wide grin, abandoning whatever he had intended to say, and held out his hand. She gladly accepted it, and they enjoyed the rest of the performance in an auditory bliss unimaginable to anyone else in that audience.

As the lights came up at the end of the concert, Stan murmured, "Kami, on nights like this, when you're staying late in the city, you usually sleep in your suite at the office instead of commuting back to the North Shore, don't you?"

"That's right."

"I have an idea. You could stay in my guest suite instead, move your clothes and things in so it's convenient. It would be more comfortable, and my housekeeper can cook you a real breakfast in the morning."

She scanned his face and his emotions, and he shrugged under her scrutiny. With seeming indifference, he added carelessly, "If you want."

But the emotions she sensed through the link told another tale. Before being separated by misunderstanding several centuries before, they had shared a home, as was the norm for *yushún* siblings. Stan missed that companionship. He missed having someone with whom to unwind after a busy day, to share journeys or activities, and to experience new delights. He actually wanted to share his home with her.

She squeezed his hand. "Thank you, *zuulu*." She even employed the Paradisian endearment for "elder brother," which she'd avoided for millennia.

When they arrived at Stan's penthouse, they shared a cup of tea in front of the fireplace, reviving a cherished nightly tradition of their *yushún*. The simple custom gener[...] lise Island. Truly, she had great[...] er linkmate, and with good rea[...] sland in the first place.

Yet, e[...] hing deep within her stirred res[...] t of roses on the coffee table, t[...] re lest in smelling *the rose you ai[...]*

She v[...]

> This chapter was crazy seeing how far Stan and Camille would go to go against's Dog.
>
> I wonder ~~how~~ how their human experiment will go. And another thing /What does that fortune cake mean?

CHAPTER 10

LOST LOVE

" 'Nevertheless I have this against you,
that you have left your first love.' "
Revelation 2:4, NKJV.

Susana jogged to the reception desk at work to answer the ringing telephone. She was pleasantly surprised to hear Chris's voice. "Hi, *mi amor*. How's your day?" she asked.

"Busy. Listen, would you mind if we postpone or, well, cancel our date night tonight? It's going to be a long day and a busy week."

Cancel their date night? When he'd been so adamant that they both make it a priority?

"Suze?"

"Um ..." When her gaze fell on the desk calendar, she realized what was happening. "Oh, I get it. April Fool's, right?"

He sighed softly. "No, I'm afraid not. I'm sorry, but it'll only be this once. There's just so much going on right now, between work and the Kids' Klub."

She hesitated. He had been really busy, and he sounded genuinely apologetic. Besides, she didn't want their date nights to be a burden for him. "Okay. If that's what you want."

"Thanks, *mi tesoro*. I'm not planning to make a habit of it, but this will really help me out today. I can still pick the boys up, but then I'll have to go back to work, and I won't be home until late. See you then."

"Okay. I love you."

"Love you, too."

Susana hung up and stared at the phone, trying to shake off the feeling that something ominous had just happened. A little voice chimed in: *You should talk to Doug about this. Let him take care of the problem. "Surrender" Chris to Doug, like Debora says.*

No, she argued back. She didn't need to bother Doug with this. She was just being overly sensitive. After all, what was one date night in the grand scheme of their lifetime together?

But it wasn't just one date. It happened two weeks later. And then again the next week. Eventually she quit keeping track.

Several weeks later, she was in the bathroom applying the sunscreen that Doug provided them—one with a special protective agent, *fuj*, that repelled Stan's poisonous darts. Noticing that her tube was getting low, she made a mental note to get more from Debora. But when she replaced it in the drawer, she saw that Chris's tube was still full, even though they'd gotten them refilled at the same time.

Is he forgetting to use his sunscreen?

The idea chilled her. Those poisonous darts had made him critically ill during the race.

No, surely he wouldn't take that kind of chance again. She must just be remembering wrong. Or maybe he'd already gotten a refill from Debora that she didn't know about.

A yawning Chris poked his head into the bathroom. "Gonna be long?"

Submerging her fears in a pool of wishful thinking, she pasted on a bright smile, spritzed on some hairspray, and bounced out the door. "All yours. Good morning." She reached up to kiss him on the cheek.

"Mmm," he mumbled as he brushed by her to close the bathroom door.

Her worries threatened to resurface, but she determinedly shook her head against them and made her way to the kitchen to prepare breakfast. Stopping at a window, she admired the beauty of this Rest Day and reminded herself to think positive. Her heart was *not* heavy. Something was *not* wrong. She did *not* feel a vague sense of dread. Everything was fine—wonderful!

But it was getting harder and harder to convince herself of this. The truth was that she could feel something growing between them—something big and ugly. It was more than unused sunscreen and canceled date nights, which he wasn't even scheduling anymore. He used to greet her with a smile and a kiss; now she was lucky to get a grumbled "Morning." He used to wake her so they could talk to Doug as a couple before starting their day; now she wasn't sure he was even spending time with Doug on his own. And she couldn't remember when they'd last run together.

There were other changes, too. He was less trusting, less discerning, and less likely to help those in need—in fact, just generally pricklier. It wasn't at all typical for the kind, patient man she'd married. He'd even gotten apathetic about the Kids' Klub, and his attitude was affecting everyone involved. His insensitivity toward Kevin especially concerned her. Chris only saw that his nephew was talking to him more; he seemed blind to how superficial that interaction was or how restless the emptiness in Kevin's eyes had become.

What's more, whenever she tried to truly connect with him, he said he was tired. Weariness would be expected, with all the work he'd taken on. Yet he'd sit in front of the TV for hours. She told herself it was his way of unwinding, that he needed some time to catch his breath. But was that a healthy way to rest?

That voice niggled at her again—the one that liked to repeat Debora's counsel: *Talk to Doug about it.* But she had talked to Doug. Sort of. She'd mentioned, in a general kind of way, what was going on. Anything more would be complaining, wouldn't it?

You know what I mean. You haven't given Doug the problem. You haven't surrendered Chris.

The sound of shuffling feet drew her attention to Harry. Still half asleep, he had just staggered into the hallway. Thankful to have something to distract her from her nagging conscience, she called a cheery, "Good morning, Harry. Want to help make pancakes?"

As they sat down to dinner after the RAB services that day, Chris commented, "The meetings sure were boring today, weren't they?"

Susana's head jerked up. What was he thinking—saying something so disparaging about the RAB meetings in front of the boys?

"They're always boring to me," Adrian said.

"My class was good," said Harry around a mouthful of mashed potatoes. "But the Second Service was a little boring, I guess."

Motioning to Harry that he shouldn't talk with his mouth full, Susana said, "I thought it was very interesting. I'd never looked at the passage that way before."

"My class was okay," Kevin said. With a glance at Adrian and a teasing gleam in his eye, he added, "We talked about dating."

"Dating?" Chris exclaimed. "I'm not sure your teacher should be encouraging dating in a group of thirteen- and fourteen-year-olds."

That was all Susana could take. Rising abruptly, she said, "Christian, could you bring that empty bowl of mashed potatoes into the kitchen for me, please?"

Without awaiting a reply, she grabbed the almost-empty pitcher of juice and ducked through the swinging door into the kitchen. She heard Kevin intone, "Ooo, Uncle Chris, you're in trouble," as the door closed behind her.

Chris followed her into the kitchen with the empty bowl. "What's going on? Now the boys all know you're mad at me. What'd I do, anyway?"

"Ahorita te digo lo que hiciste, Cristian." (Spanish: I'll tell you what you did, Christian.) She grabbed the bowl from him and began mounding more mashed potatoes into it, her movements sharp and agitated.

"Wait—English, please."

"Sorry." She took a deep breath and, in a more controlled tone, said, "We've been working for months to introduce those boys to running and to give them positive impressions of the RAB. Now you're undermining everything by encouraging them to see the teachers' faults. If you've got a problem with something the teachers do or say, you should talk to them in private, not berate them in front of the boys."

"I'm just being honest."

Susana managed to keep from rolling her eyes. How often had she heard people use that excuse to justify making destructive comments?

Taking another calming breath, she said, "Perhaps, but those boys look up to you. They admire you. Even if they hadn't had a bad impression of what they heard today, your opinion will taint theirs. As a runner, as an adult, and especially as a beloved uncle, you're responsible for monitoring what you say in front of them. You need to ask yourself what effect it's likely to have on them, especially Kevin. And did you ever stop to think that—"

She broke off, afraid that, in her irritation, she would go too far. Turning back to the stove, she piled more potatoes in the bowl.

"Go ahead and finish," Chris grumbled. "Did I ever think what?"

She plopped the refilled bowl back into his hands and turned to the refrigerator for more juice. Then, feeling in better control of herself, she said, "The attitude we bring to something always affects what we get out of it, and that's especially true of the RAB meetings. If we come with a humble spirit, we can learn something from even the worst speaker. If we sit there with a critical eye, we'll find faults with even the best."

She paused, holding his gaze, and finished softly but firmly, "Your opinion of the meetings today may say more about you than it does about the teachers."

She could tell she'd hit the mark—he was too transparent to hide such things—so she knew he honestly hadn't considered the ramifications of his words. When his conversation during the rest of the meal became more circumspect, she hoped for a similar solution to the other problems. Maybe he just wasn't aware of them and needed her to spotlight them for him.

That night, Chris again stayed up late watching TV, but she waited for him to come to bed. As he entered the room, she put a marker in her book and set it aside. "Chris, do you think maybe we're watching too much TV? So many important things are slipping, like our training and time with Doug."

He scowled as he toed off his shoes. "It's only temporary. In a few weeks, we'll both be starting demanding doctoral programs. What's wrong with relaxing a little before then?"

"Is that the right question to ask?"

"What do you mean—what question?"

"Should we be asking what's wrong with it? Shouldn't we be asking what's right with it? That's what the *Manual* says, isn't it? 'Think about things that are pure and lovely and admirable.' "

He ducked into the bathroom without comment. When he came out, she tried for a lighter tone to broach the topic that hurt her most. "Do you want to go mini golfing tomorrow evening? We haven't gone out for a while."

"We'll see," he said as he undressed, but his tone of voice said, "No."

She frowned at his back. Why wouldn't he want to do something he liked on a night he was free? Oh, of course—money. They'd been trying to follow a strict budget in order to save up before starting school.

Well, she had an answer to that problem: "There's a free jazz concert Thursday. How about that?" He had a real soft spot for jazz. This idea should excite him.

"Uh, we'll see," he said in the same tone.

That's when it hit her: He wasn't rejecting the activity—he was rejecting her. That's why he didn't schedule date nights anymore. And it explained the other changes, too. He spent so much time watching TV because he was avoiding her. He was irritable because she annoyed him.

But what had she done—or not done? She was somehow driving away the man who meant more to her than anything, and she didn't even know how.

Her eyes flooded, and she quickly lay down and buried her face in the pillow so he wouldn't see her tears. He didn't—he lay down and went right to sleep. Or maybe he just didn't care.

In the darkness, Josh's voice echoed in her memory: *"Shall I take care of it for you?"*

"Yes," she'd replied. *"Please take good care of it."*

"Oh, I will, dear one. This is one of my very favorite flowers."

Her tears petered out as she remembered where the conversation came from—that bizarre dream. Josh had been talking about the flower that represented marital happiness, asking her to entrust it to Doug.

Maybe that really was the answer; maybe Doug could help.

Slipping out of bed, she donned her robe and went to the darkened living room, where she sank onto the sofa and activated her transmitter.

"Up kinda late, little filly," Doug said gently. "Everything all right?"

"I—" Sobs suddenly overcame her, and, for a time, she yielded to them. When she finally regained enough composure to speak, she told Doug about the problem and her concern that she had already lost Chris's love. "Can you help me, Doug? If I surrender our marriage to you, can you fix things?"

"The one shouldn't be dependent on the other, now should it? It's not real trust if it is."

Susana considered that. "A-all right. You can have our marriage. I surrender our marriage to you."

"That's a good beginnin', dear one. I'll see what I can do about the problem. But let me start by giving you a good night's sleep."

"Yeah, I guess I haven't been sleeping very well."

"Worry has a way of doin' that. Grasp the transmitter in both hands."

Susana did as Doug instructed, and a warm, tingly sensation spread through her hands and up her arms to suffuse her whole body with a pervasive, warm peace.

"Thank you, *Adu*. Now I feel—" A big yawn cut her off. (Paradisian: Daddy)

Doug chuckled. "Sleep sweet, little filly. Talk to you in the mornin'."

CHAPTER 11

FIRST WORKS

" 'Remember therefore from where you have fallen;
repent and do the first works.' "
Revelation 2:5, NIV.

> [handwritten note:] This chapter was an eye opener more than anything. When you neglect your family or purpose, you hurt people around you and you start to lack awareness. It's not the circumstances that affects their relation but you as a person and your attitude towards affect everyone around you.

Susana was makir... the TV.
She finally turne... ...ock news
aired, but he only had... ...e garage
with a basket of fresh... ..., "Harry
has to be at summer s... ...al, and I
can't get him there wit... ...e him?"

"We all try to b...

"But—" She ex... ...k a few
steps away, but then tu... ...e you're
sitting there?"

"Sure. Just leav...

She made som... ...to bed,
but, even then, Chris wa... ...t door
demanded his attention... ...imped
against the doorframe.

"Steve? What ar... ...here at this hour?"

"Can I sleep on your couch?"

"Of course." Noticing Steve's car parked out front, Chris asked, "You didn't drive here, did you? You smell like you've been drinking."

"Don't start with me, kid." Steve brusquely pushed past him.

This picture was all wrong for Chris's generally easygoing brother. With his puzzlement growing into concern, he asked, "What's wrong? Has something happened?"

Steve stopped, pulled a small piece of paper from his shirt pocket, and handed it to him. Then he trudged to the living room where he dropped onto the sofa and buried his face in his hands.

Following him into the living room, Chris silently read the note:

Steve —

I'm tired of trying to make things work by myself. The boys and I will be at my parents' house until I find a place for us. If you decide you want to talk seriously, call me tomorrow.

— Jeannie

"Steve, I—I'm so sorry." Chris fell into the easy chair, dumbfounded. "When did this happen?"

"Found the note when I got home today. House is too quiet—couldn't stay there."

"No warning? She just up and left?"

"I guess she's been trying to tell me she was unhappy." Steve rubbed his face. "I didn't catch on. You know how I am. I just kidded around about it."

He heaved a deep sigh, still holding his head in both hands. "All I've been able to think about since I found the note was the talk Dad gave each of us before our weddings. I guess you would have missed it. He tried to tell me, though. I should have listened."

"Actually, Mike gave me that talk."

"Good. I don't think either Benny or I appreciated it then." Steve flopped back to stare at the curtained window. " 'Stevie boy,' he said, 'make sure Jeannie's always the most important person in your life—don't let anything take her place. And make sure she knows she's the most important person in your life."

He rose and shuffled to the window where he stood before the closed drapes, arms crossed. "I blew it on both counts, kid. A complete failure. I can see it so clearly now. When did I stop appreciating what a great woman she is? When did I stop feeling like the luckiest guy in the world?"

He fell silent, and Chris shifted uneasily in the stillness.

"I used to be so good," his brother continued softly. "I opened her doors, brought her flowers, helped out with the housework—all the stuff I remember Dad doing for Mom. But then I just got, I don't know—distracted? Lazy, maybe?"

Chris couldn't help glancing at the basket beside his chair, the laundry still unfolded.

"I took her for granted. That's what it was. I guess she thought I didn't love her anymore. She even asked if I was having an affair—can you believe that? And you know what I did?"

Remembering his wisecrack about a mistress, Chris said, "You joked about it?"

Steve nodded. "I joked about it. What a thing for me to kid about, huh?" He shook his head. "Mike tried to tell me, didn't he? Honestly, I am so dense sometimes. I really didn't have a clue that she was serious."

When silence again settled over them, Chris reread the note. "Steve, it sounds like she's willing to work it out."

His brother looked around, his eyes lit with a spark of hope. "You think so?"

"Well, the note says to call her to talk. She wouldn't give you that option if she were absolutely set against getting back together, would she?"

"I don't know, kid. I honestly don't know. I mean, I've been so blind. I didn't catch on to what she thought of me—or our marriage—until I got that note. I'm not sure how to interpret anything anymore." His dark eyes probed Chris's. "Is that what they mean when they say people grow apart?"

"I—I'm not sure. I guess so." Truthfully, Chris was feeling a little out of his element.

"Dad warned me about that too. 'Make sure you spend time together,' he said. I haven't been too conscientious about that either."

Chris dropped his gaze. Neither had he.

Returning to the couch, Steve reached for the note to reread it. "She mentions finding a place of her own. That sounds pretty permanent."

"Only because she thinks you don't care."

"See, that's what I mean!" Steve exploded. "How did it come to that? How could I have been that blind? Why would my own wife decide that I don't care about her?"

"You do joke around a lot, Steve. If you were laughing about it, what else would she think?"

His brother nodded. "Maybe so. I'd like to believe we can work it out." He rubbed his face and stared at the floor. When he looked up, tears moistened his eyes. "I can't lose my family, kid." His voice cracked, and he continued in a whisper. "They're everything—my whole world."

Although Chris felt pretty much helpless, his brother wanted to talk, so he listened. By the time he turned in, it was nearly two o'clock, and the discussion had left him exhausted and uneasy. Needing a little reassurance, he slipped into bed, snuggled behind Susana, and kissed her gently on the cheek. "I love you."

"Oh, Chris, not now. It's late, and I'm tired."

Her words pierced him like a well-aimed arrow. He leaned up on one elbow and stroked her hair away from her face. "I'm sorry. I didn't mean to wake you. And I don't want anything except to tell you that you're the most important person in the world to me."

She turned over and gazed into his eyes. "Am I really?"

Another arrow. How could she not know that?

He stroked her cheek. "Absolutely, *mi tesoro*."

"H'mm." Her foggy, uncertain expression seemed to say, "But you don't treat me as if I'm important."

"Did you put the butterfly in the kennel?" she asked.

Butterfly? Oh—she was still asleep. Rosie used to do the same thing. She would seem to wake up, even stand up and talk to him, and then have no recollection of it in the morning.

He tucked the blanket under her chin. "Yeah, I put the butterfly in the kennel. Sleep well, *mi tesoro*."

She seemed to do exactly that. Nevertheless, Chris couldn't shake the feeling that her sleepy reaction to his profession reflected her true feeling—that she really wasn't certain of his love. When he eventually drifted off to sleep, baleful notes and giant baskets of laundry chased him around the house in his dreams. Stan's disembodied laughter echoed through the rooms while Chris frantically searched for an escape. He finally found the front door, only to throw it open and find Camille waiting for him. With a grin of malicious delight, she held up a note that looked just like Jeannie's, except it was addressed to him from Susana.

He awoke with a start, sitting bolt upright and breathing hard. By the light of the bright blue numbers on the clock, he inspected the room, but found no sign of either Stan or Camille, or even any malevolent laundry baskets. Susana was sleeping peacefully. All was well.

Except it wasn't. He had known it for some time now. He just hadn't wanted to admit it or figure out what to do about it.

He pulled on some sweats and wandered through the house, looking for a place to be alone. But, with Steve sleeping in the living room, no place offered the privacy he craved. Maybe that was the problem—being thrown into a family of three active boys right after getting married was just too much responsibility too fast.

He eventually ended up in the garage, pacing around the Ping-Pong table as he fingered his wedding band. One setting especially drew his attention. Comprised of two adjacent diamonds that, together, formed a heart, it represented the decision he and Susana had made to marry. It brought to mind a series of incidents, including the talk he'd had with Josh before proposing to Susana. His coach had given him such great advice. If only he could talk to Josh now.

The thought halted him midstride. Maybe he couldn't sidle up and chat with Josh anymore, but he still had an open line to Doug whenever he wanted to use it. How could he have forgotten that?

"What an idiot," he mumbled, and activated his transmitter.

"Howdy, pardner," came Doug's immediate response. "Whatcha doin' up at this hour?"

"Can't sleep, Doug."

"What's troublin' you, son?"

The tenderness of Doug's tone was all the encouragement Chris needed to spill his guts. "I don't know," he said as he finished the tale. "Maybe it's the whole situation, being suddenly responsible for three boys and taking over Benny's job and all."

"So you think I gave you too much to do when I asked y'all to watch Benny's boys for him?"

Chris hesitated. He might be slow tonight, but he could sense a trick question when he heard one. "When you put it like that—I remember Josh once told me you never give us more to do than we can handle."

"That's right, son. If the job's from me, I'll provide the resources you need to complete it."

"So the problem isn't my circumstances, is it? It's how I've responded to them."

"Right again. It's true that the assignment I gave y'all was a tough one, certainly not one I'd give to most newly married couples, but the two of you could have handled it without damaging your relationship." Doug allowed a short pause before prompting, "If …?"

"If …" Chris thought back to his coach's prenuptial advice. "If I'd taken the precautions Josh told me about: staying in touch with Susana and keeping us both in touch with you."

"There you go. Can you tell me what happened to make you slack off there?"

"Well, the Kids' Klub really took off."

"Yes, and you were too possessive to let Mike share the load."

A sheepish grin formed on Chris's face. "I guess I was doing more than the job you gave me to do, wasn't I?"

"Yessir, you sure were. You know, you said you wanted to 'do whatever I command.' Sometimes my command is that you step away from a job. Maybe someone else needs the blessing that'll come from doin' it. Or maybe they can do it better. Or maybe you just need a break. But there's still more to this story. What else has changed?"

Chris mentally reviewed his routine, and it suddenly clicked: "I turned on the TV."

"I do believe you hit that nail square on the head."

"Actually, it's like TV sucks the life out of everything else I do," Chris realized. "Things just don't seem as important as they used to."

"That's why Stan doesn't much care whether runners defect or just get apathetic. He wins either way. But there's still more, pardner, and I'm gonna be right blunt about it. You've been dancing' on very thin ice. When you relax your ties to me, you also limit the protection I can provide. Fact is, you place your whole family at risk."

Chris jerked to attention. "What?"

"Make no mistake, son, your enemies are a crafty bunch, and they prowl around just lookin' for a chance to harm you. I will save you *if* you take refuge in me. I can keep you as the apple of my eye *if* you hide in the shadow of my wings."

Chris's mind seemed to suddenly clear, allowing him a startlingly plain view of the situation. It set his heart pounding. Camille and her team had already tried to kill Susana three times, and that was before he was on this list of hers. How naïve—how dangerously careless—he'd been to relax the basic measures necessary to keep them under Doug's protection.

"What a fool I've been," he breathed. "And Susana tried to warn me. I just didn't catch on."

"Your wife's a remarkable woman. She'll be your strong and faithful partner for a lifetime. She'll provide wisdom and perspective that will ease your burdens and increase your effectiveness—if you let her. But she's got her limits, too, and you need to watch out for her. For instance, how much bellyaching have you heard from your beloved lately?"

"I don't remember her complaining at all."

"That's right. And, although it may not seem like it, that there's a problem. She can't do everything by herself anymore than you can, but you'll never hear her complain. Son, she's a woman who will literally work herself to death rather than bother anyone else with her troubles. Are you going to let that happen?"

Chris had justified his lethargy by telling himself he deserved a rest after a hard day of gardening. But Susana worked hard as a PT aide too, plus she'd become the one doing most of the cooking, cleaning, and laundering, to say nothing of helping the boys with schoolwork. Had he even cared what his idleness cost her?

"I'm such an idiot. Has she complained to you about me not helping?"

"No, that's not her way. She'll only blame herself, interpreting your indifference as meanin' she's failed you in some way. Still she tells me what all she's doing, and it sure sounds like she's doing most of the work alone—work that I gave both of y'all to do."

She was. To make matters worse, they were helping *his* family, and he had assured her they'd pull together to get the job done. Before they married, he'd even promised himself he would do everything he could to make her life rich and happy. He sure hadn't done much toward that goal lately.

"Doug, have I already blown it? Am I already on the same path Steve took? Is it too late to change things?"

"It's rarely too late as long as you're willing. It's just gonna take some work."

"What do I need to do?"

"You tell me."

"Well, first of all, I need to stay away from the TV. Once I start watching it, I just can't seem to stop. Then I need to get back to training consistently and spending regular time with you and the *Manual*. I remember Josh saying that was the only way to maintain *lashani*, and that's the root of my problem, isn't it? I've stopped seeing things from Susana's viewpoint because I'm too absorbed with my own." (Paradisian: selfless love)

"Right on the mark, pardner."

"Okay, then I also need to work on my relationship with Susana. How do I do that?"

"First, make sure you set aside time for that little filly. Sit down and talk to her alone every day—and really listen. Also, guard that date night that Mike told you about. And I know she misses running with you."

"Right—spend time together. What else?"

"Start thinking of the household chores and child-related activities as shared responsibilities. Pitch in to get it done together, so tasks bring you together instead of driving y'all apart."

"Good—work together. Is that it?"

"If you really want to bring her joy, start thinkin' of ways to show her you're her number one fan. Do the little things you used to do before y'all were married."

"You mean like bringing her flowers and stuff?"

"That's a start, but you can be more creative than that."

"I can? Like what, for example?"

Doug's chuckle rumbled through the transmitter. "Well, remember how she likes a cup of tea when y'all study the *Manual*? If you get up a coupla' minutes earlier, you could make it for her."

"Oh, I see what you mean—little things I can do every day."

"There you go. It may seem like work to start with, but soon you'll get the hang of it, and it'll come natural-like. You might even enjoy it."

"Thanks, Doug. I feel better with a plan, something concrete to do. And I'm really sorry I've been so apathetic, not spending time with you and letting myself drift away. Honestly, I miss our talks, especially those quiet early morning runs. They just seem to work all the anxiety out of me and give me a better perspective on things."

"I've missed those talks too, son."

After logging off, Chris returned to his room to read *The Runners' Manual*. But, after settling into the overstuffed chair with a book light, he discovered he'd picked up Susana's copy instead of his own. It fell open to the tenth section of a chapter entitled, "The History of the Judges," where Susana had inserted a pad of notes from the previous Rest Day's teaching. A passage she'd highlighted caught his eye: "But you have forsaken me and served idols, so I will no longer save you. Go and cry out to the idols you have chosen. Let them save you when you're in trouble." In her notes, she'd made a list of "Today's Idols" which included enter-tainment, ease, and inactivity. In the margin, she'd written, "TV?"

Chris shook his head. How ironic. The very message he'd called "boring" should have had special meaning to him.

He continued to read until it was time to fix that cup of tea as Doug had suggested. By then, Steve was getting ready to leave.

"Thanks for the couch," he said. "After sleeping on the problem, I feel more optimistic. I'm going over to my in-laws' place on the way to work. I'll set up a time to sit down and talk to Jeannie—seriously, like she said. I'm thinking it may even be a good idea for us to see a marriage counselor."

A rueful smile crossed his brother's face. "Never thought I'd say that. But it's scary how easy it is to slip into a rut that takes you in the wrong direction. Anyway, I may be late to work this morning."

"Yeah, I'll be late too," Chris said. "I've got some repair work of my own to do. I'm afraid I've been slipping in the same area. If it weren't for your wake-up call and Doug's advice, I may have been in the same spot myself before too long."

"Doug—you mean Damour? What's he got to do with anything?"

"He's a smart guy, Steve. He helps his runners in a lot of ways besides running, even in their marriages."

"Really?" Steve rubbed his chin. "Now that you mention it, Benny and Marie seemed a lot happier together the last time I talked to them. I may have to think about this race thing myself."

Chris fixed Susana's favorite mint tea as his brother left, and then he headed back to their room. He parked the tea on the bedside table and eased onto the bed, watching her as she slept. Her long black hair draped gently over the blue pillowcase and fell onto her right hand resting beside the pillow. He remembered the first time he'd seen that hand—scarred and limited in motion, yet reached out to help an injured runner. It was so characteristic of the compas-sionate, giving woman he'd married.

"You truly are the most beautiful woman I've ever known, *mi tesoro*," he murmured. He kissed her forehead, and her eyelids fluttered open to unveil her gorgeous, velvety brown eyes.

"Hi," she said sleepily. "How long have you been sitting there staring at me?"

"Not nearly long enough."

She smiled, but it quickly faded. "You don't look like you slept very well. Is everything okay?"

He hesitated. "I hope so." When her brow furrowed, he explained: "I had a long talk with Doug this morning. I realize I've slacked off and let things get in the way of what's really important. For starters, I'll be happy to take Kevin to school this morning."

"Oh, good," she said, sitting up. "I've already been late several times because of those tutoring sessions."

"You have? You never told me."

"Chris, you didn't seem interested in knowing."

He sighed. "I'm truly sorry, Suze. I really haven't been a very good hus-band, or even friend. Will you forgive me?"

Gazing intently into his eyes, she assured him, "Always, *mi amor*."

Then she seemed to catch a whiff of the tea and turned to see it sitting on the bedside table. "Did you make me tea?"

"Yeah. I remembered you like some while we study the *Manual*."

"Oh, how sweet."

"No," he said mischievously. "I thought you liked it unsweetened."

She giggled and took a sip. "It's perfect. And did you say we're going to study together this morning?"

"Yeah. I thought we should start again."

"Good. I've really missed it."

"Have you? Why didn't you say anything?"

"I did—twice. The first time you said we'd talk about it 'later.' And when I brought it up 'later,' you said—and I quote—'Don't bug me about it, okay?' So I didn't." She paused. "Chris, I don't mean to make your life more complicated. I just can't figure out what I've been doing wrong."

Doug's words rang in his ears—*She'll blame herself*—and he suddenly saw the results of his indifference in a whole new way. He had pursued Susana with all the passion in his soul, and Doug had given him the amazing privilege of sharing life with her, granting him the position that would allow him to bring the greatest joy into her life. Why hadn't he seen that the same position also equipped him to hurt her most deeply? The insight triggered a wave of self-disgust.

"Suze, you haven't done anything wrong. It was me—only me. I got, well, lazy, I guess. And I'm—" He sighed, feeling frustrated at his inability to express his feelings better. "I'm just really sorry. As for making my life more complicated, do you remember when we had that really big fight, when we broke up over …?"

"I remember."

"Thank you for not making me say it," he said with a small smile. "But it's funny the things you notice when your world's crumbling around you. And I really did think that's what was happening that night. I thought you were gone forever." He paused as the memory of that loneliness came back to him. "What I noticed then was how nice your motor home looked with the curtains and throw rugs and decorator pillows, and how stark ours looked with just the bare necessities. And I realized that's what you do to my life—you decorate it."

He cupped her precious face in his hands. "Maybe my life is more complicated with you in it, *mi tesoro*, but it's so much more beautiful. I wouldn't trade that for anything."

To: companymaster@management.com
From: bestagent@management.com
Date: 28 May 8008 M.E.
Subject: Idea for Compromising Outlander Division

      In the last report from our interpreters, they predicted that the children of the founding Director of KK—i.e., my Subject's future offspring—will lead Dictator's Outlander Division during the Final Battle. I hypothesize that if we were to prevent the birth of these children, Dictator would be obliged to scramble to find replacements with the rare combination of both natural talents and upbringing appropriate to his purpose. This should, therefore, seriously weaken (perhaps destroy) the future Outlander Division's effectiveness.

      I have several ideas for compounds, both contraceptives and abortifacients, and for imperceptible delivery systems. I'm certain that you could add to the list. If you consider this objective worth pursuing, perhaps we could discuss the matter further by video conference.

To: bestagent@management.com
Cc: companymastersecretary@management.com
From: companymaster@management.com
Date: 28 May 8008 M.E.
Subject: Re: Idea for Compromising Outlander Division

      Excellent idea. Arrange video conference through my secretary ASAP.

CHAPTER 12

LONELY

*"You will be left like a lonely flagpole on a hill
or a tattered banner on a distant mountaintop."*
Isaiah 30:17, NLT.

To: entitymaster@management.com
From: bestagent@management.com
Date: 2 June 8008 M.E.
Subject: May Report

    Company Master and I are working on another approach to limiting Subject's influence by preventing him from fathering the Outlander Division's future leaders. I am hopeful that this avenue will be of some help to us. It may take several years to perfect a useful chemical compound, but it seems unlikely that Subject will wish to reproduce immediately.

    Regarding my earlier optimism where Subject is concerned, I'm afraid it was premature. He has reversed his course and is returning to his old ways. You may well imagine my disappointment, since I am sure you share it.

    Nevertheless, I can report that MA-223's manipulation involving Subject's oldest charge is proceeding quite well. I believe this may yet produce excellent results on the child and MA-223's Subject, although I hold out little hope that it will have the desired effect on my Subject.

✽ ✽ ✽ ✽ ✽

Camille logged off her computer with harsh, angry strokes and stalked to the corner of the floor-to-ceiling windows to glare toward the setting sun. Excellent results on Benny? Who cared about Benny! It was Christian she wanted in her clutches.

Although she would like to blame Adlai for this outcome, she recognized that was merely her anger speaking. She knew from experience how obstinate Strider could be. She had been foolish to entertain such optimistic hopes in the first place.

She heaved a sigh and admitted to herself that Strider wasn't even the true cause of her irritation. He was merely the grounds at the bottom of a really bad cup of coffee. The bitterest part of her day had occurred much earlier and was far more personal, involving the end of a long and treasured friendship.

Camille's acquaintance with Fiona dated back to the island. They weren't as close as they had been then, of course. It wasn't safe to confide in people at Moden Industries. Whatever you said could, and probably would, be used against you. Still, their alliance had endured life's vicissitudes until today. But the problem with being a boss was that you had to discipline your subordinates. Fiona had always been a superb worker, so Camille had never had to discipline her before. Today, that clock ran out.

She expelled another deep sigh. Success and popularity didn't necessarily go together; she knew that. And she certainly was successful—the sixth richest person in the country, millions of employees at her disposal, on a first-name basis with many world leaders …

So why did losing one friend bother her so? She was a strong, self-sufficient woman. She didn't need Fiona. She didn't need anyone.

It's a good thing, her pesky inner critic taunted. *You don't have many girl-friends left, do you, Camille?*

Of course she did. She had plenty of girlfriends. There was—

Well, there was—

Oh, what did it matter? She didn't need friends of either gender.

Actually, she could produce the names of only two people who might qualify as friends: Garrick and Stan. And neither of them were any fun to shop with. Nevertheless, she was pleased that things had improved with Stan over the last year. Being able to once again call him a friend—a good friend—was no small gift. In fact, he was exactly the one she wished to see just now.

Striding purposefully out of her office, she proceeded down the hallway to his. But as she progressed, her designer heels echoed dolefully through the abandoned hallways. The sound grew louder and louder in her ears, grating on her and magnifying the empty feeling in her soul. Finally she removed her shoes and completed the trek in her stocking feet.

Stan sat at his desk with his shirtsleeves rolled up but his tie in place and hair perfect, as always. Glancing up as she entered, he said, "Good news—we've figured out how to approximate island atmosphere for our experiments."

"Mmm."

"Oh, and Pim estimates we can do the tonsillar transplant in two or three months."

"Mmm." Ordinarily, this reference to Stan's mysterious illness would have claimed her full attention, anxious as she was to glean any crumbs of information that he might drop regarding his secret. Today, however, the comment flew right over her head, unrecognized and unheeded.

Her indifference didn't escape Stan's notice. He looked up again, brow furrowed, and this time his gaze caught at the shoes in her hand. He slowly swiveled his chair to watch as she passed the desk and stopped at the window.

A recording of Debussy's piano works played on the sound system. As she gazed into the night, the tranquil melodies soaked into her troubled soul, providing a little measure of comfort. After several moments of her silence, Stan prompted, "Did you want to tell me about the problem? Or is the view from my window sufficient?"

She cast a repentant grin in his direction. "Apologies."

"Unnecessary," he said with a dismissive wave. "What's the trouble?"

"Well, to start with, I've just received an update from Adlai. You know what a superb agent he is, Stan. He's thorough and careful, and his plans are well considered and often quite creative. The agent's not the problem this time. Nevertheless …"

After another moment of silence, Stan urged, "Nevertheless …?"

She didn't answer.

"Camille?"

"H'mm?" She turned toward him. "I'm sorry. What did you say?"

He cocked his head. "You didn't finish your thought. Nevertheless …?"

"Oh. Nevertheless, he's having no success in driving a wedge between Strider and López."

"H'mm." Stan's chair creaked as he leaned back. "Come, Kami. What's really bothering you?"

She frowned. "Fiona breached security today. Badly. She tried to take a human into the agents' research room."

"She what?" Stan shot out of his chair. "With all those terminals accessing the Priority Computer? Did it see anything?"

"No, of course not. The guards barred them from entering the room. But the resulting confrontation was a noisy affair that succeeded in embarrassing the human, who happens to be the trusted assistant to a congressman with whom I'm negotiating. In any case, I had to discipline Fiona."

"Appropriately so."

"Yes, well, she disagrees."

Stan grunted. "I've noticed that about women. They're unwilling to separate business from personal affairs."

"Unwilling or unable," Camille agreed.

"So you're feeling lonely."

Stan's statement was link-related information. It didn't require a confirmation, and she didn't offer one. The same source allowed him to pinpoint Camille's needs, particularly what she needed to feel safe. As he rarely acted upon it, the ability was of little consequence. Tonight, however, without another word being spoken, he moved behind her and enfolded her in a protective, brotherly embrace. The gesture sent a tremor of gratitude through her. It also brought the skin of their arms into contact just as the pianist began Camille's favorite piece, *Rêverie.*

Instantly, the dreamy music burst into sumptuous harmonies that washed over her like a luxurious waterfall. Having gradually regained confidence in her brother, she surrendered fully to the haunting melody, basking in the sublime music that swirled around them as she rested in his shelter. Rich, magical warmth enveloped her and carried her along in its soothing current, bringing her to another world, an enchanted world of heightened awareness where her consciousness of Stan exploded into the vivid colors of full knowledge and mutual acceptance.

The beguiling strains enveloped them and drew them ever closer. For the first time in a very long time, she felt truly safe, truly loved, and truly whole. Her rapture was so complete, she could not have pinpointed whether the music came from within or without, from her or from Stan. Nor was it important. All that mattered was the music—the music and her and Stan, for they were all one inseparable unit.

She had long since forgotten this ecstasy. As it filled her now, soaking into every corner of her soul, her eyes flooded with joyful tears.

When the recording ended, they stood together in the charmed silence for some time, simply enjoying the pool of magic that swirled around them. When Camille at last became aware of her body, she perceived that even their breathing and heartbeats were synchronized. It had been nearly fifty centuries since they had swept away all the barriers between them and allowed themselves to connect so unreservedly.

Both understood the milestone they had just crossed. As Stan's arms relaxed, Camille turned to face him with a warm smile and unveiled gaze, for she no longer felt the need to limit his awareness of her emotions.

"Pad'amoúr, Kami," he breathed, and she sensed his sincerity. *"Pad'amoúr inje."* (Paradisian: I missed you, Kami. I missed you so much.)

Paltry English phrases could never express the depth of emotion encompassed by his words. They perfectly captured the deep longing, the ache, that she had also endured. Yes, this must be the place she had been seeking for so long.

Enjoying their rediscovered camaraderie, the siblings settled on the leather sofa in front of the fireplace, where they listened to all their favorite music and reminisced until late into the night. Thankfully, the office was soundproof, for the guards might have concluded that the two leaders had lost control of their senses. The boisterous pair who spent that evening laughing and exclaiming together certainly bore little resemblance to the high-powered, ruthless team that headed America's largest firm.

It was quite late when Stan, in the middle of an uproarious response to a shared recollection, abruptly went still, gazing intently into the fireplace. Camille immediately sensed the sorrow emanating from him. "What is it, *zuulu?*" she asked softly.

"It's been so long, *zali*. So long. I don't want to lose this connection now that we've rediscovered it."

"Must we lose it?"

He turned his intense emerald gaze on her. "Kami, I—" He scowled. "I asked Madelyn to marry me. She agreed."

"Marry you?"

The word had no meaning to a Paradisian. Partnering and procreation—these were things the lower species did. While the exiles found boundless entertainment in perverting such activities to manipulate humans, they considered themselves fortunate to be spared such messy undertakings.

"Obviously, I don't mean marry like humans do—sex and all that." He shook his head in distaste. "But we're ready to implant an enhanced embryo from Rosie Strider's ova into a surrogate, and I can't entrust this worldwide organization to a child who could be seen as illegitimate. She wouldn't be granted the same level of respect in certain human cultures, and that would just be an unnecessary obstacle in furthering our goals. The easiest solution is for me to marry and provide her with the respectability she'll need to represent Moden Industries most effectively."

"Ah, good point." Camille nodded thoughtfully. "Actually, the evidence indicates that humans are best raised with both mother and father figures, so the plan has merit from that standpoint as well."

Despite the arrangement's value to the business, Camille also immediately saw its personal disadvantage—which is what had elicited Stan's sudden change in mood. Paradisians were used to living with others, for, although the Damours created them individually, they lived in *yushuni*—family units comprised of several siblings. In their homeland, the norm was to live with one's siblings throughout one's lifetime. Even among the exiles, many still preserved this tradition.

However, each *yushún* had its own traditions and habits, which its members clung to with great tenacity. Living with a non-sibling would require meshing conflicting traditions—a most troublesome undertaking of which Camille wanted no part. On the other hand, she also didn't wish to end their comfortable living arrangements, for she had lately spent more time at Stan's penthouse than in her own home.

Capturing her eyes, he said earnestly, "I don't want to do this, *zali*. Frankly, I'm not sure I can, even for a couple of decades."

"I understand." She truly did.

"Still, I don't see any alternative. Unless …"

She understood his point at once. "Unless I marry you."

"Will you?"

She allowed herself a rather unfeminine snort. "You're asking me to raise a human."

"It would only take two or three decades. You and I have already done so much for the cause, suffered so many inconveniences. What's a couple of decades in comparison? And it's important that this child be raised right if she's to lead the organization. Who else could I trust so completely as her mother figure?"

"Madelyn will be most unhappy if you retract your offer. I'm certain she doesn't relish the idea of living with a non-sibling any more than you do, but she's probably already informed half the company that the great Stan Moden has chosen her to help raise his protégé. She won't take the setdown lightly."

He shrugged. "I can deal with Madelyn."

"Can you, indeed? She's in a position to cause you—to cause us—considerable harm."

"She'll forgive anything for a raise and some expensive jewelry." When his assertion didn't alter his sister's skeptical expression, the ruthless glint that she both admired and feared sharpened his gaze. "Look, she's not stupid. She knows better than most how I deal with those who cross me."

Though fully aware of how useful Stan's cruelty could be in altering an opponent's stance, Camille still wasn't convinced of its efficacy in this case—something about a woman scorned. Nevertheless, her concern over Madelyn's vengeance did not outweigh her own disappointment at having to give up the home she had only just rediscovered.

"We'd hire a nanny?" she asked.

"Of course. I'm certainly not going to change diapers, and I wouldn't expect you to, either."

When she didn't respond, Stan pressed, "Just imagine—a descendant of Juan Misi running Moden Industries for us. Isn't that worth some inconvenience?"

For Stan, maybe it was. But was it worth the bother to her? She wasn't the one with the vendetta against Juan Misi.

"This kid will also be the daughter of Christian Strider's twin sister," he pressed, leaning forward. "With the way Strider values family, such a child would be of incomparable value to him, wouldn't she?"

Now that was vengeance she could appreciate. Camille could not constrain the smile that overtook her. "Yes," she said emphatically. "Yes, it is. I will marry you, Stan."

This chapter really shows how determined to take down dona. They are willing to get married and raise an army. Where will this vengence lead to?

CHAPTER 13

DISTRACTED

*"Keep a tight grip on what you have so no one distracts you
and steals your crown."*
Revelation 3:11, The Message.

hris was washing up the dinner dishes when Susana came in from the garage. "Chris, could you come here?" Her someone's-in-trouble tone made him wonder if he'd left a mess out there, but as soon as she opened the door to the garage, he understood. The distinct odor of marijuana, along with a substantial layer of rose-scented air freshener, hung heavily in the air.

She leaned back against the washing machine, her eyebrows knitted together. "I came out to do some laundry after Kevin's friends left. It smells like pot to me."

"Yeah, it does." Chris began pacing around the Ping-Pong table, but something caught his eye, and he bent down to pick up a tiny twist of filter paper—all that was left of a joint. Holding it up so Susana could see, he added, "Definitely."

The weight of his own carelessness burdened him as he stared at the thing. He'd known some guys who got into drugs in high school, and they'd all started with pot. It sure wasn't a life he wished for his nephew. Yet what had he done to prevent it? Zoning out in front of the TV, ignoring Kevin's restlessness, discounting Susana's warnings that something was still out of whack with him. He'd been so negligent.

"This isn't your fault," she said softly. "Kevin was unhappy before we ever got here."

"I should have helped him. You tried to tell me. And Doug sent us here for a reason—I've always been the one he's closest to. I should have seen this happening. I let him down."

"We can still help him. Let's start by calling Benny and Marie."

But Chris wasn't so sure. He knew Benny. His brother could be gruff, but he loved his family fiercely. News of this sort would bring him home immediately, and once he left the race, he'd be too discouraged to take it up again. In fact, if Chris were the Moden Industries' agent assigned to Benny, this would be exactly how he'd attack him.

He frowned with the thought. Could this attack on his young, vulnerable nephew have been engineered by Benny's agent? Angered at the idea, Chris picked up an empty soda can and threw it into the recycling bin, where it clanged noisily against the other cans.

"I think you should be the one to call them," Susana said. When he didn't answer, she pressed, "What is it?"

He ran a hand through his hair. "Do you know why I didn't run the race sooner?"

"Because you were waiting for me to enter it?" she teased.

He chuckled. "Meeting you was the best part of running the race when I did, of course. But the reason I didn't run it sooner was because Benny was so set against it. Even after I started the race, Stan's people used his opposition against me, and I really wrestled with it."

"Pressure from loved ones can be very difficult to deal with."

"The thing is, if I struggled that much because of a brother, imagine how much Benny and Marie will struggle with the needs of a son. Don't you think Stan's agents will use this to discourage them from finishing the race?"

Stepping toward him, she urged, "Chris, we can't withhold something this important from them."

"Yeah, but suppose we could get it under some kind of control before we break the news—just postpone telling them for a day or two. They'd probably feel less of a need to drop out if the news came tempered with a solution or a plan."

"And how do you propose to get it under control? This is serious, and we don't have any experience with it." She cocked her head. "We don't, do we?"

"No," he assured her with a small smile. "I never did drugs either."

"Then the way I see it, the way this problem gets handled is really critical. If we treat it too lightly, Kevin will think it's not important. And if we punish him too severely, it may only push him farther away."

"Whoa—punish? Why would you punish him?"

She frowned. In a tone that suggested she wasn't sure he understood English, she said, "Because that's what you do to discourage children from repeating bad behavior."

"So if I made a bad choice, you'd punish me?"

"You're not a child."

Chris nodded slowly. "I see. So children should be treated with less respect than adults."

"Now you're twisting my words."

"Am I?"

She scowled at him and turned away to sort the laundry she'd left on the machine.

Reconsidering, Chris turned her toward him. "I'm sorry—that was unfair. I guess this is one of those cultural things Josh warned us about. The truth is, I don't really understand the whole rationale behind punishment. I wasn't raised that way. I still remember the shock I felt the first time I saw a kid being punished."

"You remember the first time you saw someone being punished? How old were you?"

"Maybe five or six. Rosie and I were grocery shopping with Grandma. A little boy about three years old grabbed something from a shelf and put it in his mother's cart. She hit his hand—hard, too. Grandma visibly flinched, and I could tell she was really upset. We all were. Rosie started crying. Anyway, I asked Grandma why the lady would do that, and she just shook her head. She said she'd never get used to how people here treat their children. Her people, she said, wouldn't even treat a dog so harshly."

"Are you telling me you were never disciplined as a child?"

"Disciplined, yes. But never punished—not like that, anyway. Grandma mostly talked to us, told us stories to help us make better decisions. I think that's the Native approach. If some kind of punishment was necessary, Dad let us suffer the consequences that might naturally result from our actions."

"So what are you suggesting—that we let Kevin suffer the consequences of drug addiction?"

"No, of course not."

"So we agree—something needs to be done. At the very least, we should forbid him from seeing those boys and ground him so we can keep a closer eye on him."

"And then what happens in three years when he's off to college, away from Benny and Marie's oversight? You may be able to train a kid with that approach, like you would an animal, but you haven't educated him. He hasn't actually learned anything to avoid making similar mistakes in the future. The whole point of discipline is to help kids become independent and self-sufficient. In this case, I can't see that grounding him does either. Simple rules help protect young children—I get that. But Kevin's not a little kid anymore. He's at the age where he's making decisions that will affect the rest of his life, and he needs to learn how to make better choices."

"And you think you're so wise that you're willing to risk your nephew's future by dealing with this yourself?"

"No. But I can take advantage of other people's experience. I want to talk to Uncle Ray—his son experimented with drugs. And I'll talk to Doug about it, too. And, of course, if Doug says the best course is to tell his parents right away, that's what we'll do. But I have a feeling he won't. I think the real object of this attack is Benny, not Kevin."

She flashed a wry smile. "I guess I can't argue with doing whatever Doug says to do, can I?"

They were up late that evening, talking to Doug and Uncle Ray. With their advice in hand, Chris determined to talk to Kevin the next day to see if he could understand the basis of his nephew's unrest. He picked him up from school early for a dental appointment. On the way, they passed a large yard where people were encouraging dogs to jump obstacles, climb ramps, and weave through colorful tunnels.

"I wonder what that's about." Chris was talking to himself, not really expecting a reply, but Kevin answered, "Agility training."

"What's that?"

"They train dogs to do obstacle courses. There are competitions in it."

They continued on to their appointment and, afterward, passed the same training center. This time there seemed to be a class going on, with more dogs and owners participating.

Intrigued, Chris asked, "Do you mind if we stop and watch for a while?"

Kevin shrugged. "If you want, but it's just a waste of time."

Despite his verbal disapproval, that now-rare spark of interest returned to Kevin's face as he watched the activities. He had always had a special aptitude with animals and, as a child, had wanted some animal-related job when he grew up. But lately he hadn't talked about his future at all.

"What do you want to do when you grow up?" Chris asked.

"Dad says I should be a doctor," Kevin answered in a monotone. "Like you."

The pieces of the puzzle suddenly fell into place. Benny was pushing Kevin—the same way he'd pushed Chris—toward a profession he saw as providing status and financial security. It had been fine in Chris's case since he was already interested in medicine. For Kevin, however, it meant a future he saw as boring. That's why he'd assessed the book and this agility training as unimportant; that's undoubtedly what Benny had called Kevin's fascination with animals. His loss of interest in school made sense too—it had become a road leading nowhere interesting. Maybe he even thought that if he didn't do well, his dad wouldn't expect him to go into medicine.

"Doctoring's an exciting field," Chris said aloud. "And so broad—lots of options. Men, women, adults, kids … animals."

"Animals?" Kevin's eyes popped. "You mean, like a vet? Are they doctors—real doctors?"

Chris laughed. "They get a DVM—*doctor* of veterinary medicine."

"Yeah, but would *Dad* think they're real doctors?"

Chris wished he could free his nephew of the need to choose his lifework based on Benny's expectations. But that would be difficult, maybe even unnecessary if veterinary medicine met both their requirements.

"You know, Kev, all your dad really wants is for you to be happy. For him, that translates into making sure you don't have to worry about money as much as he has. That's why he wants you to get an education, so you can have a career you can count on and make a decent living. It seems to me that vet med would be a great career for _____ only good at science and at figuring out how things work, but you _____ ould be a shame to see those talents go to w _____

With a trac _____ k I'm talented, Uncle Chris' _____

Laying a h _____ y. "I don't just think you're ta _____ ne as naturally good with an _____ ng of them that can't be taugh _____ d. They can tell your interest i _____

"Wow, it _____ iasm shining through. "Being _____ nimals, that's something I coul _____

"I'm sur _____ d to get good grades, when yo _____

Kevin _____ ce alight with excitement.

"Maybe _____ a better idea of what she does every day," Chris sugge_____ ave an appointment for Rex to get his rabies shot next week. Why don _____ ne with me, and we'll talk to the doctor about it."

"That would be so great. Thank you, Uncle Chris."

Just that quickly, the rapport Chris had once enjoyed with Kevin was back. And that made it easier to talk to him about the marijuana problem. He did that when they got home, before the other boys returned from school. Following Doug's suggestion, Chris broached the uncomfortable topic in the manner endorsed by family tradition: storytelling.

"There's a story I wanted to tell you, one I think you'll remember," Chris said as Kevin sat on the sofa. "It happened about a year and a half ago, when I was running the race. I had met Susana and was falling for her, but then I learned she was going to drop out of the race for a while. It really upset me, so I went into town and had a few beers. I met a girl there who slipped something into my drink and then shanghaied me. I ended up spending nearly three months picking crops in a slave camp in South America. Do you remember that?"

"Yeah. We were all really worried about you. Grandpa went to look for you, but he couldn't find you."

"I guess I worried a lot of people. And I ended up sick and miserable. All I did every day, sunup to sundown, was pick crops. I had iron shackles on my legs. They gave us two meals a day—always the same nasty porridge stuff. I got lice and several other infections. I slept with cockroaches—"

"Yuk. Sounds gross."

"It was. And it was all because I ignored my better judgment in order to feel good for a little while. Unfortunately, that pretty well sums up what happens whenever we try to use alcohol or drugs to improve our situation. Instead of improving it, we make the situation worse for ourselves *and* for those who love us."

He took a folded envelope out of his pocket and handed it to Kevin. Inside was the joint he'd found. Kevin unfolded the envelope, looked inside, and then closed it again, a deep flush crawling up his neck.

Sitting next to him, Chris placed a gentle hand on his shoulder. "I'm really sorry I made you all worry about me like that. I made some very poor choices that night. I haven't touched any drugs, including alcohol, since then. I don't want to ruin my life like that again, and I don't want to worry the people I love."

Kevin looked up at him, eyes glistening. "Zack said it would help me feel better."

"Did it?"

"No. Well, I guess it kind of did for a little while, but it didn't last very long. And then I felt worse, and nothing was different, and I kept feeling worse until—" He met Chris's eyes with a look of sudden insight. "Until we talked this afternoon."

"For me, solving the problem that's bugging me works a lot better than any drug. That's why I try to hang around with people who solve problems instead of those who try to forget them that way." Chris nodded at the envelope.

"I guess—I guess that makes sense."

"How often have you used it?"

Alarm widened Kevin's eyes. "Oh, no, Uncle Chris. I never smoked it before. I just tried it that one time. And ..."

Chris waited silently.

"Well, I did try some beer once too. But it was the same thing. I didn't like it." He shoved the envelope at his uncle. "I'll never do it again. I promise, Uncle Chris. I never will."

"I can tell you mean that, but sometimes we need help keeping those kinds of promises. I'd like to get you plugged in with a counselor at school, someone you can go to if you need some help."

Kevin's expression was something less than joyous acceptance. "Will you come?"

"Sure, if you want me to. And even when I'm not living here, you can call me anytime to talk about anything. In fact, if you get the urge to use any drug again, I want you to call me first. Will you do that?"

"Yeah, I'll do that. You make it easy to talk." His nephew relaxed back into the sofa. "Not like Dad."

"Your dad loves you, Kev. He really does. He just has trouble expressing it."

"H'mm," Kevin responded. After a moment, he asked, "Uncle Chris, are you glad you ran that race?"

"It was the best thing I've ever done. There's one for kids, too. Uncle Mike ran that one. You can do it in a summer."

"I was kind of thinking about it."

"I learned a lot from the race. In fact, I learned something really important. You might find helpful in weeding out the kind of decisions that lead to trouble, like smoking pot."

"What is it?"

"I used to think that Doug Damour's Laws were just there to cramp my style. You understand what I'm talking about, right?"

"Yeah, Grandpa talked about them sometimes. But everyone says those Laws are old-fashioned."

"That's what I thought, but *that's* the lie. They're not old-fashioned, and they're not just arbitrary rules, either. They're actual laws, like the law of gravity. Except these laws are about behavior, about how our minds work. They're meant to warn us that certain things affect us—harm us—even if we're not aware of it. Doug didn't give the Laws to us to make things harder for us. He did it to make things easier. The sooner we learn to follow them, the better our lives will be, and the happier we'll be."

"So, do you obey those Laws?"

"Mm-hmm. But I'm going to tell you a secret—I didn't always. When I went to college, I ignored some of them. I thought I was being smart, 'enlightened.' I was really being suckered into believing the lies. Now—" He sighed. "Well, I'm really sorry I did. I caused myself pain I didn't have to experience. And I almost lost the woman I love."

He paused, squeezing his nephew's shoulder. "I hope you'll be smarter than me, Kev. I hope you'll be able to see the wisdom of obeying Doug's Laws, even if you don't understand the reasons behind them right away. It all comes down to recognizing them for what they really are: Doug trying to teach us how to live in such a way that our lives are full of joy, not sadness."

Kevin's response was noncommittal, but Chris could tell he'd set the gears in his brain in motion. And when Chris went running the next morning, Kevin asked if he could join him.

CHAPTER 14

MISCHIEF

"Though I have bound and strengthened their arms,
yet do they imagine mischief against me."
Hosea 7:15, KJV.

```
To: entitymaster@management.com
From: bestagent@management.com
Date: 4 June 8008 M.E.
Subject: Request assistance

        As you may remember, Subject will begin a new academic
program at a new location in the fall. I would like to enter
a position there that would allow me better accessibility to
him, since this has been a serious problem for me here. Perhaps
Company Master could recommend me as a research assistant or
arrange a position as a visiting professor? My PhDs and experi-
ence should easily qualify me for some such position in Subject's
field of study, and either position would allow me to see him
regularly, thereby giving me the opportunity to infiltrate his
intimate circle.
        Thank you for whatever assistance you may be able to pro-
vide with this problem.
```

❋ ❋ ❋ ❋ ❋

Camille had just finished reading Adlai's e-mail when Benny's agent, Warner, called. Clearing his throat nervously, he said, "Ma'am, I'm afraid I have bad news."

"Go on."

"The manipulation—well, I succeeded in getting the child to experiment with both alcohol and marijuana, but Christian has the problem in hand. Actually, he managed the situation before even notifying my subject."

Jumping to her feet, Camille demanded, "Am I to understand that Benjamin is staying in the race?"

Warner gulped audibly. "Yes, ma'am."

Camille slammed her fist on the desk. This had been their best chance for derailing Benjamin—and it should have worked!

"Ma'am? Am I—to expect correction?"

Camille was furious, to be sure, and she certainly wanted to discipline someone for this. But Warner was an excellent master agent; she doubted the problem lay with his management. Certainly Adlai's reports would not indicate such. Furthermore, she had learned from experience that unjust discipline would alarm the agents generally, causing job performance to suffer.

"Be assured, I shall review the operation thoroughly. However, I doubt the blame lies with you, Warner. Christian Strider is the problem."

The agent released a breath. "Thank you, ma'am."

Hanging up, Camille stalked to the corner of her office where the windows met. Christian Strider—was there to be no end to that boy's interference?

But allowing emotion to rule was counterproductive; she would find a physical outlet for her anger later. For now, she must discipline her energy into meaningful action. And if Adlai's primary obstacle was inaccessibility to Strider, then her action must be focused on resolving that problem. After all, how could an agent influence a Subject if allowed no avenue of approach? And Adlai was correct: Stan did have several excellent contacts at Stanford. In fact, he could probably solve the problem with a phone call—if he was so inclined. Of course, his cooperation would come at a cost. Very little in her life came free of charge.

She frowned deeply as she considered other possibilities for accomplishing her purpose, but the exercise served only to reinforce her anger with frustration. She knew very well that her own contacts at Stanford were not in a position to help with this particular objective. She had no option but to seek Stan's assistance—and pay his price.

She exited her office, banging the door closed so forcefully that a book fell from the adjacent shelf. The janitor reached down to retrieve it with a sigh. "Sure are an awful lot of high-and-mighties stormin' around the premises today," he muttered, presumably believing his voice to be too soft for Camille to hear.

But she did hear. And now she had precisely the outlet she needed for her anger—a victim, and a reasonable excuse for correcting him. She felt better already.

Halting abruptly, she pivoted toward the hapless man. An expectant hush fell around them, and he snatched off his cap to make a full bow as she moved toward him.

Placing one long fingernail under his chin, she lifted his head. The guard at her door responded with an ominous chuckle. Company legend held that she had performed all manner of miraculous feats with that fingernail—such as slitting jugulars wide open. The truth behind the stories was that she kept a blade hidden up her sleeve, but she didn't correct the tales. She enjoyed the awe they inspired.

The janitor stood about six feet tall, slightly shorter than Camille in heels, so she gazed downward into his frightened eyes. In a cloying tone, she said, "Morton, I would be delighted to give you a personal tour downstairs."

"Th-that's all right, ma'am, if it's all the same to you."

"It wasn't actually a request, sweetheart." She glanced at the guard. "Ernie, would you see that my guest is made comfortable until my arrival?"

"My pleasure, ma'am." Ernie roughly grasped Morton's arm.

"Understand this, Morton," Camille said before releasing him. "This high-and-mighty does not tolerate disrespect. I trust you will remember that in the future."

"Y-y-yes, ma'am. I-I sure will."

"Excellent." She left Morton in Ernie's capable hands and marched toward Stan's office. When she entered, she slammed the door behind her at what happened to be precisely six beats before the cannon fire erupted in the *1812 Overture* playing over the sound system.

Stan peered up at the CD player with a puzzled expression. When he saw Camille, he seemed to understand exactly where the extra canon shot had come from. So did Garrick Sondem, their director of security and lifelong friend. Seated in front of the desk, he exchanged a quick glance with Stan.

"I have bad news," Camille bit off as she dropped stiffly into a chair.

"I think we've both deduced that much," Stan said wryly. "What's wrong?"

"Christian Strider has thwarted our best chance of preventing his brother from finishing the race."

Stan muttered a curse.

"Moreover," Camille continued, "Adlai is having difficulty in gaining access to him. He's asked if we might arrange a position for him at Stanford's medical school that would place him close to Strider—a research assistant or visiting professor, perhaps?"

"Yes, I could arrange that." Stan thoughtfully stroked his chin between thumb and forefinger, and Camille grudgingly prepared herself to accept whatever terms he might demand. Instead, he merely said, "I'll take care of it."

"Indeed?" Full cooperation, even beyond her expectation, and no mention of terms?

"Yes," Stan said. "It will be my pleasure to lend a hand."

With no conditions to negotiate, she struggled to find a response. Finally she decided on a simple, "Why, thank you, Stan."

That's when he revealed the price tag: "Not at all, *my dear*." He picked up a jewelry case and tossed it over the desk to her. "Courthouse. Two o'clock."

A sense of dread crawled over her as she snatched the case from the air. She opened it to find a trio of rings: two diamond-encrusted platinum wedding bands and a coordinating engagement ring. Inside the latter, a single word: *Together*. The jeweler who engraved that sentiment would have seen it as a mark of devotion. Camille saw it as it was intended: a reminder of her responsibilities to Stan under their business pact.

She fitted the engagement ring on her finger and held her hand up. Garrick leaned over and whistled appreciatively. "If you have to wear one, you might as well go first class."

"It is magnificent, Stan," she agreed.

Her assessment was not untrue. The central gem, a very large, emerald-cut blue diamond, probably weighed at least 15 karats. Moreover, it nestled amid several smaller, though still splendid, diamonds. Indeed, each of the lesser gems could have made a dazzling ring on its own, mementos that would elicit gasps of wonder from most brides-to-be. The total value of the exquisite piece easily rivaled the annual budget of a small country. Yet what Camille saw was neither the ring's beauty nor the exorbitant sum Stan had paid for it. What she saw was constraint. Encumbrance. Duty.

Nevertheless, she would accept the ring, along with the obligations it entailed. She would do this for the same reason she had accepted innumerable other inconveniences and disappointments over the last 6,000 years. Overthrowing the tyrant who had exiled her from her homeland was worth any sacrifice.

She placed the jewelry case carefully on the desk and lifted her gaze to Stan's. Forcing a smile, she answered. "Two o'clock will be fine."

PART III

FRIENDSHIP

When Susana's nose wrinkled against the icky smell of the yellow rose in her hands, the warm chuckle of a familiar baritone met her ears. She looked up in surprise. *"Josh!"*

"I tried to warn you. That's called rosa foetida. The English word 'fetid' comes from the same root. It may not smell good, but you'll have to admit, the color is beautiful. Did you know that Europe didn't have yellow roses at all until this was introduced from Persia in the sixteenth century?"

"Really? Oh—but I do know what yellow roses mean: friendship."

"Right you are. And now you know what I'm going to ask next, don't you?"

Glancing around, she quickly confirmed her impression that she was back in the War Room. *"You're going to ask if I'll give you these yellow roses so you can give them to Doug."*

"Right again. Will you entrust your friendships to my keeping?"

Her eyes rested on the vivid petals as she mused aloud, *"People never used to like being my friend. I was picked on so much because of the scars—they didn't want to be teased for hanging around with me."*

"I know," Josh said. A catch in his voice drew her eyes to his face, where tears brightened his eyes. *"And yet you still offered your friendship freely to those who would accept it. Your selfless, giving nature has made you very dear to us, Susana. It's why I call you 'dear one.' "*

Something warmed within her chest. *"Really?"*

"I never lie," he replied with a grin. *"But friendships will come much easier for you now. In fact, you'll find yourself on the other side of things. You'll now be the one others look to, the one with the power to reject those who need your friendship."*

"Oh, I never want to be like that."

"Then you'd better let Doug have those yellow roses. Human nature isn't always so faithful to principle. Let my father help you decide whom to befriend and how closely to let each one into your life."

Susana's gaze returned to the yellow blossoms in her hands as his words pricked at her conscience. How often had she seen it? Someone who was previously snubbed rises in social status and becomes the one who snubs others. Talk about a bad smell. She didn't want to become such a person. Nodding slowly, she tentatively held out the bouquet to Josh.

A shrill alarm suddenly pierced the quiet room, and Susana started at the unexpected noise. Gabriel jumped to a console to key in some commands while the other officers looked on anxiously. But Josh didn't seem surprised by the disturbance. He merely glanced over at the offending console with a slight frown. Then, with an *almost imperceptible shake of his head, he continued removing the yellow roses from her bouquet.*

Susana looked toward the door where she knew Chris was waiting. The large red digits on the wall clock still clicked steadily toward that midnight deadline: 23:22:32—33, 34, 35 …

To: entitymaster@management.com
From: bestagent@management.com
Date: 15 August 8008 M.E.
Subject: Reevaluation—New Location

I must thank you for the excellent position you and Company Master arranged here. It will certainly afford much better access to Subject.

My scouting has identified some initial avenues to explore:

1) A local RAB may be of help. The leader there is brother to one of your recent guests, and he is grieving. His response has bred apathy in many of the RAB's members, including the KK leader.

2) One of Subject's classmates has some interesting ideas regarding white supremacy. Although we have no information about Subject's response to this issue, I am encouraging the man's attitudes in the hope that he may become a useful operative.

3) I've discovered that the schedules of both Subject and Wife will be busy ones, making it difficult for Wife, a Connector, to form and maintain the social connections that are so important to her. Therefore, she will be particularly vulnerable in the area of friendships—giving me a fertile field to plow.

CHAPTER 15

HIS PURPOSE

" 'God has put it into their hearts to fulfill His purpose.' "
Revelation 17:17, NKJV.

Susana sighed as she watched another would-be friend disappear out the door of the local tea shop. In the few days that she and Chris had been at Stanford, she'd met a number of her classmates, but everyone was so busy that none had time to sit down and chat. How would she ever find a girlfriend to connect with at this rate?

"Busy, busy, busy," she muttered and took a sip of her iced lemongrass tea. "I guess I might as well get back to unpacking."

"Sit a spell, little filly," Doug said over the transmitter that she had left on during her run to this strip mall. "You can talk to me."

"Thanks, Doug. I do enjoy talking to you, but, well, it's not the same."

"I know, dear one. I'm well aware of your desire for a bosom buddy, and I will give you just such a girlfriend. But friendships of that caliber are forged over time, simmered in the slow cooker of life. Don't go lookin' for the sixty-second, nuked-in-the-microwave version, or you'll be disappointed, sure as I'm talking to you."

"Am I being impatient?"

"I'm afraid so."

She took another swig from her cup. Then, holding it against her face, she let it cool her overheated skin while the citrusy tartness cooled her mouth.

"I feel so displaced, Doug," she said at last. "Unsettled. I don't like feeling this way."

"Let yourself settle in with your husband first," Doug suggested. "Tonight's his class's dinner, isn't it?"

"Oh, that's right." Susana brightened at the prospect.

"Tell you what—I'll make you a promise. Give me a chance, and I'll make sure you meet someone there who, in time, will become a true friend."

"Really? Oh, thank you, Doug."

He chuckled. "You're welcome, little filly. You probably oughta be headin' back to get ready for that dinner, don't you think?"

"Yes, I'd forgotten all about it. Thanks again." Susana logged off and, draining the last of her tea from the ice, rose to leave.

Just then, a perky brunette bounced through the door. "Oh, hi. How great to run into you. I saw you moving into our apartment building this week. When I noticed that you were also a runner, I told my husband, 'Now there's a friend waiting to happen.' "

So Susana stayed to become acquainted with Vanessa Strong. Not only was she a runner, but she was married to one of Chris's classmates. When her new acquaintance mentioned that she would be attending the dinner that evening, Susana felt a gush of pleasure. Doug had kept his promise. And she could already tell that she and Vanessa would be the best of friends.

"I'm sure you'll have a great time once we get there and meet some people," Susana told Chris brightly.

"You're sure of that, are you?" In his irritation, Chris tapped his rearview mirror harder than necessary and then had to correct the over-adjustment. He'd never cared much for mixing with strangers, and he especially wasn't in the mood tonight—not after the rough week they'd had.

"Why are you so grumpy, anyway? This get-together is for your class."

"I'm not grumpy."

"I'm not Grumpy," she mimicked with a mischievous grin. "But you're certainly not Happy, either. So who are you? Oh, I know—you're Doc, just lovably grumpy."

Chris's face lifted with an unwilling half-smile.

"Ha, a smile," she said triumphantly. "See, that's not so hard."

He reached over to take her hand. "You're right. I am being cranky, and I'm sorry."

"It's been a hard week," she said sympathetically.

"It sure has. I feel rotten about leaving my family. Everyone was trying to be upbeat when we left, but Kevin was actually crying. We'd made such progress with him, and then we just deserted him. And Steve and Jeannie were doing so well with us there to help out with their boys. And Mike? We left right after dumping a bunch of Kids' Klub problems in his lap. I feel like I've, I don't know, abandoned ship."

Susana nodded sagely. "Because, of course, Doug didn't know what he was doing when he only sent us there for seven months. And he doesn't know how to help any of those people or solve any of those problems without ... you?"

He hadn't looked at it that way.

"Didn't you notice that Benny's interacting with his kids on a whole new level now? Or that Mike actually enjoys solving those problems? Doug's given each of you exactly the jobs you're good at."

"But the club's grown so big." Pulling into a parking spot, he turned to face her. "I don't know how much longer the two of us can handle the global management, especially with me starting med school."

"Then Doug will help us find more people to help. Who knows? Maybe you'll meet some runners tonight who turn out to be exactly the help you need."

"I probably wouldn't know it if they knocked on my head and introduced themselves that way. I'm too tired to think."

"The move was awfully tiring, and we're both exhausted. But this dinner could still be fun. Personally, I'm looking forward to getting better acquainted with Vanessa."

The spark of animation in her voice made him realize how inconsiderate he was being. He enjoyed solitude, so acclimatizing to a new place where they knew no one meant little to him. But she thrived around people, and her scars had made it difficult for her to make friends. Now she'd had to leave behind those few hard-won friendships. It must be a little daunting, and he should do his best to help her adjust.

Reaching for her hand, he suggested, "Before we go in, let's reconnect with Doug for a few minutes. I feel like I need to get my priorities straightened out."

As they chatted with Doug, Chris shared all his misgivings, and Doug assured him that he had things in hand. He even told them that Steve and Jeannie had decided to run the race—as had Kevin.

A tap at the window interrupted their conversation. They peered out to find Debora standing there. After they exchanged joyful greetings, she asked to speak to Chris alone. Susana waited in the car, conversing with Doug, while Chris and Debora took a walk. The coach came straight to the point: "You're not looking forward to this gathering, are you?"

"No," he said. "To be honest, I'm not. It's been a hard week, I'm tired, and we still have to unpack."

"Then why are you here?"

"Doug asked us to go, so I'm going."

"Rather reluctantly, I should say."

"I don't like mingling with strangers, especially when I'm tired. It's just a drain on my time and energy. It's not like anything important is going to happen tonight."

"Oh? Are you so certain of the future, then? Is it not possible that this evening will be the beginning of important friendships? Or that Doug knows of someone here who needs a nudge toward running? There are many possibilities, any one of which may justify the 'drain on your time and energy.' "

Debora's voice was a study in contradictions. Her refined, British-accented speech tended toward a more formal address, yet her manner radiated warmth and approachability. Her quiet gentility nonetheless conveyed authority. Even when scolding, her tone was kind and compassionate. So when a flush warmed Chris's neck, he knew it wasn't her manner but the truth of her words that caused his embarrassment. He could only admit, "I suppose you're right."

"A few short months ago, you told Doug you wished to do whatever he commanded and go wherever he sent you. Did you mean that you would do his bidding only when he asks you to do something you enjoy? Are you willing to obey only when in the mood?"

Chris had trouble meeting her eyes. Doug had done so much for him—freed him from constant guilt, given him an amazing woman to love, and even saved his life. Deep down, he wanted to live a life of grateful, faithful service to the one who had loved him so lavishly. He didn't want to do a halfhearted job with a stingy attitude. Yet, he kept stumbling and grumbling at the smallest things.

"I'm sorry, *Ama*. I want to be more reliable. I really do." (Paradisian: Mom)

She reached for his hands. "Then I can help you, my son. Simply breathe deeply."

As she blew on him, a gentle tingling spread upward from his hands and inward through his nostrils, growing into an electrifying current that drained away his fatigue. He closed his eyes and relished the bracing sensation. "Thank you," he murmured.

"You're welcome, my dear, dear son." Kissing him on the cheek, she added, "Now go, and have an enjoyable evening."

"But—well, Susana's really tired, too."

"It gladdens me that you wish to share your gift with her. However, the same social interaction that drains you will energize her. She will need nothing more."

As Debora had predicted, Susana visibly perked up as she roamed among the guests. Her musical laughter often greeted Chris's ears as he mingled in his own less effervescent way. He felt more at home when he found a group of men discussing cars. He particularly grew to like Efraím, a friendly So-Cal boy and runner about Chris's age.

Soon Susana returned, towing an attractive brunette. "Chris, this is Vanessa, the friend I told you about. You've already met her husband, George," she added as she indicated one of the men around Chris.

At that point, all Chris knew about George was that he was a classmate who drove a 1956 Thunderbird convertible that Chris wanted very much to see. With Susana's prompting, he soon learned that the couple lived in the same apartment building as they did and that they were runners who intended to visit the RAB Efraím attended. That point somehow triggered a discussion between Susana and Efraím in Spanish.

Not following their conversation, Chris's eyes casually roved the assembly until they settled on a man approaching their group. His nametag identified him as classmate Lester Stretch, but he drew Chris's special attention for two reasons. First, he was visibly tipsy. Second, he kept leering at Susana. Although she was oblivious to the newcomer's interest, Chris instinctively put his arm around her to draw her within his protection.

Turning to him, she said, "Efraím has invited us to his RAB. Can we go this week?" Chris readily agreed, and she responded with an enthusiastic, "Oh, good!" Then she paused, her forehead crinkling prettily in concentration, and said carefully, "Um, *natérarabá, keni kuná.*" (Rarámuri: Thank you, my husband.)

With a laugh, Chris rewarded her effort with a kiss to her forehead, and the female duo set off in renewed exploration. He smiled after them, pleased that Susana had found a girlfriend so quickly—and that the pie-eyed Lester was staying with the group of guys.

Drawing his attention back to the group, Efraím asked, "What language was she speaking, Chris? It wasn't Spanish."

"You're right. It's the language of my grandmother's tribe—Rarámuri, also called Tarahumara. Susana's trying to learn it."

Lester burst into a snorting laughter, but stopped when he realized no one else was amused. "Oh. You're serious? You're an Indian?"

Chris shifted uncomfortably at the guy's tone, which implied that his heritage was some kind of disease. "I'm a quarter Native American," he answered warily.

"You're not gonna scalp us, are you?" Lester again burst into his snorting laughter while the rest of the group lapsed into a charged silence.

Chris examined the soda in his hand. "No, not tonight. The sacred scalping day is tomorrow." Raising a sharp gaze to Lester, he added casually, "Shall I look you up?"

Lester's eyes grew wide. "Um ..." He glanced around and joined in uncertainly when the other men laughed.

Preston, a teacher's assistant in anatomy, spoke up. "Lester, I don't know much about the Tarahumara people. But if I'm not mistaken, they're known for their peaceful ways, as well as their endurance running. I don't think scalping was ever part of their culture."

"Injuns are injuns," Lester muttered with a wary glance at Chris. "You can't trust any of 'em."

Chris literally bit his tongue to avoid saying something he'd regret. Bigotry annoyed him—sometimes angered him. Still, experience had taught him that confronting those afflicted with it only fostered more hostility. So he focused on a safely unprejudiced spot on the rug and remained silent.

However, Preston and George, both white, spat some angry words at Lester who, looking genuinely surprised, quickly slunk away. After another awkward silence, Efraím cleared his throat. "So, does that mean you don't understand Spanish, Chris?"

"Not much, although I am trying to learn it."

"Then I apologize. I guess you didn't understand what Susana and I were talking about. I realized I'd heard your name in association with the Kids' Klub. Maybe you can help me with a problem."

"Sure. What is it?"

"The pacesetter at the RAB I'll be attending is a friend of my father's. He's asked me to help with their Kids' Klub, but it's kind of a mess. The volunteers are really apathetic, too busy fighting among themselves to do much with the club."

"I'd be happy to help if it's okay with the RAB's pacesetter. In the meantime, I may be able to give you some ideas. We've seen other clubs with that kind of infighting, and it usually comes down to their skipping one crucial step. Do you know if they ran the volunteers by Doug for approval?"

"I don't think so. Is that routine?"

"It should be. If it's not done, people can get assigned to jobs they're not gifted for, and individuals can slip in who shouldn't be involved at all. We've even had a couple of Stan's agents infiltrate groups. They use stolen trophies as 'proof' that they've completed the race. But clearing everyone with Doug solves that problem since he knows all his runners personally."

"That sounds like a great place to start, then," Efraím agreed. "Thanks."

About that time, Chris caught sight of Susana on the other side of the room. Noting that she was still with Vanessa, he chuckled. "Looks like we'd better get used to each other, George. With the way our wives are getting along, I think we'll be seeing a lot of one another."

"You will be anyway," Preston said. Pointing to their nametags, he said, "You're assigned to cadaver groups alphabetically. So Chris Strider and George Strong—oh, and probably Efraím Suárez, too—will likely be spending hours together in the lab."

"That's fine with me," Efraím said. "We seem to hit it off."

"Yeah," George said, "but I'm not crazy about that other guy that was here, and his name was Stretch."

All eyes drifted to Chris, who shrugged. "He may be a completely different guy when he's sober." He was trying to be charitable, but the truth was, he had a bad feeling about Lester. In fact, he was watching him as he spoke. The guy was near Susana again and still leering at her.

"There's a classic car show this weekend," Preston said. "Would you guys be interested in going?"

"Sure," Chris said as Efraím chimed, "I'm game."

George likewise accepted and added, "Do you want to ride with me, Chris?"

The opportunity to ride in a classic Thunderbird should have thrilled Chris, but he didn't even register the question. His full attention was riveted on Lester, who seemed to be moving in on Susana.

"Chris? Something wrong?" George asked.

The question came just as Lester moved behind Susana and brazenly grabbed her around the waist. Chris immediately charged toward his wife, but nearly ran directly into a tall woman who darted into his path. Since he brushed her hard enough to knock her glasses awry, he had to pause to offer a quick apology. By the time he reached Susana, Lester's fingers were digging into her arm, and he was saying, "Aw, come on, gorgeous. You can do better than a dumb Indian."

Chris struggled to react calmly, but Susana had gone stiff all over—as she did when terrified. Still, the guy was drunk. He probably meant no real harm.

Bending down to Lester's ear, Chris delivered his steely challenge from behind: "This is the dumb Indian asking you politely to let go of his wife."

"Why should I?" Lester slurred. "We're just—"

Chris wrenched Lester's arm from Susana's waist and shoved it up behind his back. A heavy silence fell, making Chris's quiet reply sound loud. "Because the dumb Indian gets less and less polite from here on. Say what you want about me, but you're not going to hurt my wife."

He gave the arm an upward shove to emphasize his point, and Lester released Susana's arm with a whimper. Susana dived into Chris's arms and, desperately clinging to him, hid her face in his chest. Fully understanding the reason for her distress, he tried to bury his ire—she shouldn't have to deal with his anger when she had such good reason for her current terror.

"Ow, that hurt," Lester complained, rubbing his arm. "Didn't mean anything, you know—just having a little fun."

"Does it look like she thought it was fun?" Chris shot back.

Lester's gaze shifted to Susana, weeping and trembling in Chris's arms, and a surprised expression came over him. Bursting into tears, he cried, "I'm sorry, I didn't mean to hurt her. I'm sorry …" He continued wailing as Preston and George hauled him toward the door.

The group chatter gradually resumed, and Vanessa asked gently, "Susana, are you hurt?"

Heroically trying to compose herself, Susana lifted her head and wiped her face. "No. It's just that—"

But she couldn't finish. Again bursting into tears, she buried her face against Chris. He softly explained on her behalf, "She was recently attacked by a serial killer who grabbed her the same way."

Vanessa gasped, and Susana clenched a fistful of Chris's shirt. He wrapped his arms more tightly around her. "I'm sorry I didn't stay closer, Suze. I should have. I had a bad feeling about that guy."

"It wasn't your fault, Chris," George said as he and Preston returned. "In fact, I thought you handled it especially well. You sure showed more restraint that I would have."

"Yeah, I would have decked the scumbag," Preston added.

Jané slipped quietly away from the group surrounding Susana. Like Chris, she had noticed the special attention her charge was receiving from the troubled young man. Lester was responsible for his actions, of course, but Jané could feel only pity for him. The real blame lay with Adlai, a true expert at tormenting and beguiling humans. For about a month now, he had been fanning the poor boy's insecurities to further his own sinister ends.

Still, Lester could do considerable harm in his current state of inebriation. Furthermore, such an attack so soon after the one last year would be very difficult for both Susana and Chris. So Jané had received permission to use force, if necessary, to protect her charge. Thankfully, Chris's attentiveness had obviated the need for her intervention.

Taking a seat well away from the action, Jané gingerly explored the bruise that Chris's elbow had left on her arm as she resumed her imitation of a wallflower—a useful skill for a Royal Guard. At 5′10″, she was a tall woman, but not so tall that she couldn't become inconspicuous with unbecoming glasses and drab clothing.

When Chris and Susana decided to leave the gathering, Jané prepared to follow them. Before she rose, however, Adlai claimed an adjacent chair. "You won't unmask me, will you?" he asked with no attempt at polite preamble.

"You know the rules as well as I," she replied. "We've no right to divulge such information to outlanders. If my charges discover your true identity, it will be of their own doing."

"Fair enough. I just wanted to make sure those *rules* you're so keen on hadn't changed during my little sabbatical."

The emphasis he placed on "rules" raised the hairs on Jané's neck. Stan's agents had a way of making Doúg's greatest gifts sound as attractive as last month's compost. Still, the time for arguing with them was long past. She merely assured him, " 'Until heaven and earth pass away, not the smallest letter or stroke shall pass from the Law.' "

"Right," he said with a derisive snort. Then he abruptly stood and strode away.

To: entitymaster@management.com
From: bestagent@management.com
Date: 25 August 8008 M.E.
Subject: Alert

As per Subject in public conversation, "a couple" of our people (no names or locations specified) have been identified at KKs, even though they used trophies. I would have been identified this weekend if not for overhearing this. Subject relates that KK protocol requires that Dictator himself approve all personnel. Subject is working to see this protocol implemented in all KKs.

Based on what I heard, I respectfully suggest that we: 1) consider the covers of any agents declined KK admittance to be compromised; and 2) that we desist all attempts to infiltrate KK, focusing our efforts on indirect approaches from the outside instead.

On a happier note, I can report an excellent first contact with Subject under my new cover. I have already been able to insert myself into his social group, and he has accepted an invitation to an off-campus social event, as well as to the troubled RAB.

Subject does not appear particularly susceptible to ethnic slurs, so I will abandon that approach. (I did manage to ignite an entertaining bit of anger in him through the operative mentioned before, but it was related to his protective instincts rather than his ethnicity.)

To: bestagent@management.com
From: entitymaster@management.com
Date: 25 August 8008 M.E.
Subject: Re: Alert

Thank you for this valuable information. I shall implement your recommendations immediately.

I am gratified to hear of your encouraging first contact. However, do not deselect that operative yet. Your design may not have unfurled as you intended, but experience has shown that Subject is predisposed to an especially useful form of anger. If this operative elicits that response, whether on the basis of ethnicity or family responsibilities, he is of value to you.

CHAPTER 16

ALIVE?

" 'I know your deeds; you have a reputation of being alive,
but you are dead. Wake up!' "
Revelation 3:1, 2, NIV.

As Susana drove to the RAB services on the next Rest Day, her stomach churned with a familiar mixture of anticipation and dread. She had always enjoyed visiting new RABs with their exciting variety of older runners with fascinating stories and younger runners who might become wonderful friends. Yet for most of her life, she had been shunned by new acquaintances. Even runners often had trouble seeing past her scars.

Her hand found its way to her face, to the smooth skin that had replaced the rough scars. It would be different this time. People would have no reason to instantly recoil at the sight of her ... would they? Oh, if only she could wipe the fear of rejection from her wounded heart as easily as Doug had wiped the marks from her face.

Chris caught her hand and, interlacing his fingers with hers, assured her, "Yes, the scars are still gone. People will only see you."

That was exactly what she'd wished for all these years—that people would see her instead of her disfigurement. But the old, deeply entrenched fears were not so easily ousted.

"Are you sure this dress is okay?" she asked. "It's not too showy?"

"It's perfect. So are you. Quit worrying."

She glanced at him with a weak smile. "Thank you."

"Besides," he said in a teasing tone, "if the people here don't love us and immediately beg us to stay, we'll just go somewhere else." Her smile grew into a giggle as he continued with mock conceit, "There are lots of RABs in this area. I'm sure at least one of them will have the good sense to see how indispensable we are."

Sobering, he added, "Which reminds me—since you've gone to a RAB all your life, maybe you can answer a question. Doug said he wanted us to decide which one to attend, but how are you supposed to pick? What sort of things should we be looking for today?"

"H'mm. That's a good question." And how like her rational-minded husband to think of it. "I guess I don't really know. I've never actually chosen one before. I just went to the one my parents attended. But you and Efraím seem to get along well, and he'll be coming here. Vanessa probably will too. Oh—and I have a cousin that attends this RAB."

"Don't you have a cousin in every RAB on the West coast?" he asked innocently.

"Very funny," she said with a grin.

"Besides, that doesn't seem like a good reason to select an assembly—the one where your friends go."

She shrugged. Seemed like a perfectly good reason to her.

"Well, I'm sure we'll figure it out eventually," he said offhandedly.

Eventually?

Although Chris's gentle teasing had relieved some of her initial anxiety, this casual attitude toward selecting a RAB stirred up a different concern. Throughout her life, she had always belonged to an assembly of runners. The idea of not settling into one right away made her feel all off-kilter. It would be like not knowing where her house was. And not having a specific pacesetter to call in the event of a problem? Well, that would be like not knowing which man to call her dad.

Eventually?

No, no—that certainly wouldn't do. While she didn't want to push Chris into joining an assembly he wasn't invested in, she did want a decision sooner than "eventually." Yes, she was partial to this RAB because her cousin and Vanessa would be attending it, but she could probably be happy in any group of runners—as long as she knew which one to give her heart to. So, her job today was obvious: She needed to help Chris make a decision. With the way his brain worked, that meant collecting information for him.

Susana began her list right away, even as the car turned into the RAB's parking lot.

Fact #1: We have personal ties to this RAB—Efraím, my cousin's family, and probably Vanessa.

They'd barely parked when Efraím knocked on Chris's window. "Come on, there's the pacesetter!"

Susana grinned at his exuberance. His obvious affection for the RAB's leader was contagious.

Fact #2: The pacesetter here is apparently able to stir up enthusiasm among the runners. (Note to self: Is the level of a pacesetter's charisma a valid reason for selecting a RAB?)

Efraím led them up the steps and clapped a broad-shouldered fellow on the back. The man turned around to reveal intense peacock blue eyes to go with his flaming red hair. Breaking into a broad, easy smile, he drew Efraím into a bear hug. "Efraím, my boy. How are you? All moved in?"

"Getting there. I want to introduce you to some people. Aedan McElroy, this is Susana and Chris Strider. Chris is a classmate—"

"And the new leader of our Kids' Klub—I'm so glad to meet you!" Aedan pumped Chris's hand eagerly, while Chris's eyes widened. When he glanced at Susana, she knew exactly what he was thinking: *Leader? I only agreed to a temporary consulting role.*

"Oh, now don't think I've made a snap decision on this," Aedan continued energetically. "I've done my research. I talked to the pacesetter in Ventura as well as some of the volunteers who worked with you there. And I've completed the requisite background check too."

The shock on Chris's face transformed into amusement. This man had already done all that in a few days—and without even meeting Chris?

"But now that you're here," Aedan continued, "there's no sense in wasting time. I'll announce a gathering of all the Kids' Klub volunteers for this afternoon so you can meet them. And I'll fill you in on the club's details when you come to lunch at my home after today's services. Efraím's joining us too."

Chris was now on the point of bursting into laughter, and Susana knew she would have to join him if he did. Aedan McElroy was quite a character, though not in a bad way. His entire presence spoke of openness and integrity—and of an enthusiasm that plowed ahead, impervious to silly obstacles like formalities. She liked him instantly.

Fact #3: Chris would find it easy to work with this practical, straightforward pacesetter.

Once she'd made this mental note, a tugging at Susana's heartstrings obliged her to set aside her fact-finding mission long enough to register a strong impression: Something big, something sinister, stalked Aedan McElroy. Not that he was dangerous—no, definitely not that. In fact, this was a man capable of great generosity and compassion. But he'd learned this empathy under circumstances that, based on the anguish still lurking in his eyes, could only be described as pure evil. A deep, dreadful sort of pain had recently shaken this man to his core. She didn't know what it might be, but his valiant struggle to move past it won her immediate admiration.

Some might question such impressions, but Susana was used to them. For as long as she could remember, she'd been able to sense things about people that others couldn't, and history had almost always proven her intuitions right.

A slim, middle-aged woman leaned over to the pacesetter and murmured, "Aedan, dear, you forgot a step or two."

"Did I?" he asked, clearly puzzled.

"Yes, dear. Susana, Chris—" She grasped their hands in turn. "I'm Julie McElroy. Please pardon my husband's eagerness. He sometimes runs ahead before the rest of us have our sneakers on. What he means is that we're excited you're *considering*"—she gave Aedan a meaningful look—"joining this RAB, and we're hoping you'll *accept*"—another look—"the leadership of our Kids' Klub. *If* you're free for lunch today, we'd love to have you join us after the services so we can discuss the club further."

"Oh," Aedan said with a self-effacing grin. "That."

"Well," Chris said, "I'll need some time to discuss accepting the leadership of the club with Doug. But I'd certainly be happy to help you evaluate it in the meantime. Maybe I can offer some ideas for moving things forward. As to lunch—" He looked to Susana. When she eagerly nodded her assent, he turned back to Aedan. "We'd love to. Thank you for the, uh"—he grinned—"summons."

When Vanessa and George arrived, Susana saw at once that George wasn't necessarily happy about being there. While Chris introduced him to Aedan, Vanessa confided to Susana that she'd heard good things about this assembly, but regretted that her husband would attend only rarely. He had grown bitter and stopped attending the RABs after his mother's death. In fact, he'd only agreed to come today because Chris would be there. Susana whispered back that Chris's father had reacted similarly after the death of his wife, and a spark of hope lit her friend's eyes. "Maybe Chris will know how to help restore George's faith in Doug."

Fact #4: Chris could be a positive influence on George—they think alike and relate well.

When her cousin and his wife arrived, Susana was appalled to learn that their fourteen-year-old daughter, after starting to attend the Kids' Klub, had dropped out because "they only do boring school stuff." Missy had immediately sprung to mind when Chris first told her about the club. The daughter of two busy working parents, just embarking on adolescence, and attending a school where Doug ranked somewhere between legend and myth—Missy was exactly the kind of kid Ben Strider had had in mind when he'd designed the Kids' Klub. And, though a sweet girl, she was easily led astray by her friends.

Fact #5: Missy needs our help.

As they drove to Aedan's home after the service, Susana used the opportunity to review the points she'd accumulated. Chris listened thoughtfully as she enumerated them. When she finished, he said, "I really liked Aedan's talk today about why we call our meetings First *Service* and Second *Service*."

She wasn't sure how this was related, but she nodded encouragingly. "I'd never thought of it before, but it's true. We should come to the RAB with an attitude of service to Doug and to the assembly rather than with a desire to be entertained."

"So that should also be a good way to decide which RAB to attend, don't you think?"

Susana groaned inwardly. This sounded like a question that would take a while to settle. Still, she had to admit the truth of his observation. "That makes sense—which assembly our particular gifts could benefit the most, where we're needed."

"Exactly. Several of the points you mentioned have to do with how we could be of use here."

"That's right," she realized. *Yes!*

"Maybe Doug led us here because it's where we're needed. I can help the Kids' Klub rediscover its mission. Aedan also thinks I should take the leadership on a permanent basis. And you seemed disappointed at how the teen class was limping along. Unless I'm reading you all wrong, you're just itching to get in there and help with their program."

"Oh, I would love that. Especially for Missy—I think I can help her. And, while we could form a relationship outside of the RAB, the Kids' Klub's small groups and camping trips would be perfect."

"Besides that, Preston, the TA from anatomy, comes here, but he's never run the race. Maybe, if I can connect with him and get him involved in some of the programs, I can nudge him in that direction. And George—he's run the race, but gave up running for some reason."

"Bitterness—after his mother's death. Vanessa told me."

"H'mm."

"So," Susana began carefully, "we have a number of opportunities to serve in this RAB. Does that mean we can come here?"

He grinned at her. "You really want to make this decision now, don't you?"

"Yes," she admitted. "I just don't feel settled without having a RAB to call home."

"Well, then, let's go here if you want—assuming Doug approves."

"Oh, thank you." Throwing her arms around his neck, she planted a big kiss on his cheek.

Being too excited to go anywhere until they'd settled the question, Susana wanted to talk to Doug right then, parked in front of Aedan's house. By the time they knocked on the pacesetter's door, they'd made two decisions: They would join this RAB, and Chris would accept the leadership of the Kids' Klub.

Thrilled with both decisions, Aedan ushered them into his living room to fill them in on the details pertaining to the club's decline. Susana's initial impressions about his forthrightness were quickly confirmed. When Chris politely commented that the kids he'd talked to that morning seemed to have little enthusiasm for the club, Aedan replied frankly, "That's my fault."

"How's that?" Chris asked, looking slightly shell-shocked.

"Yes, my fault." Aedan affirmed matter-of-factly. "When I saw announcements of the club in the RAB's magazine this spring, Doug asked me to start a club here. I did, but I did a lousy, half-baked job of it."

"There was a reason behind that rocky start," Efraím interjected.

The pain in Aedan's eyes deepened. "Reason, yes. Excuse, no." To Chris, he explained. "My kid brother had just died. I'm afraid I let it get to me."

"I'm sorry about your brother," Susana said sincerely—Aedan's pain was so palpable. "May I ask how it happened? He must have been quite young." Aedan himself didn't look over fifty.

"Yes, too young," Aedan said. "As to the manner of his death—well, that's a long story and perhaps better left for another day." He paused for a moment, as if trying to regain his footing. "Anyway, my melancholy and rationalizations affected the whole RAB. I managed to drag most everyone down into a mire of discouragement and apathy. I'm heartily ashamed of myself."

"But it's certainly understandable that you should feel saddened by your brother's death," Susana objected.

"Maybe so, but I shouldn't have let it affect my work. I'd always wondered about that story in the *Manual* where Doug forbade Aaron from mourning over his two sons when they died."

"Me, too," Efraím said. "Frankly, it sounds a little callous."

Aedan nodded. "Yes, I thought so, too. But no more. Now I understand it perfectly."

"Then please explain it to me," Efraím said with a laugh.

"All right. What happens if a pacesetter's running is chaotic during a race—what becomes of the runners he's leading?"

Efraím frowned, clearly not understanding the connection, but answered, "Runners trust him to set a pace they can maintain to the end of the race. So unless the runners are experienced and paying attention, following an unreliable pacesetter can cause exhaustion, even injury."

"Well said," Aedan agreed. "And that's why, when you have charge of the spiritual well-being of so many of Doug's children, you can't afford to give Stan any room to work, not even when you're mourning someone you love. Stan never takes a break from his work, and he never pulls any punches. In fact, he only hits harder when we're down."

"That's not your fault," Efraím said.

"No, but I'm called the 'pacesetter' of this RAB for a reason. I should have recognized that I was leading this entire assembly of runners into danger. In any RAB, there are some committed runners whose relationships with Doug are strong enough to keep them steady. Those are the runners who are 'paying attention,' as you put it. But, frankly, they're the minority."

"Really?" Chris exclaimed.

"Yes, I'm afraid so. It's not easy to keep the faith in a busy world. Many once-enthusiastic runners let their relationships slip because of trials, distraction, or mere indifference. And then there are those Stan's people call 'pseudo-runners.' They attend services, but they've never had a real relationship with Doug at all. There'll even be a couple of Stan's agents in disguise, just waiting for an opportunity to stir up trouble."

"But you shouldn't blame yourself for their problems under those circumstances," Susana objected.

"I can and I should," Aedan said firmly. "Doug entrusted me with the responsibility of providing a nurturing atmosphere for his children, and he always empowers us to carry out the jobs he gives us. It's we who fail to utilize the power he offers. What's more, I know that revival is on our horizon—"

"Is it?" Susana asked.

"Yes—and Stan will do anything to prevent it. Yet, knowing all this, I still allowed him to distract me. Doug's recently helped me understand all this, and I've repented. Still, it may take time to counteract the effects of my former negativity."

"You are honest, aren't you?" Chris said. "When I make a mistake, I have trouble admitting it to Doug, let alone to complete strangers."

"Strangers?" Aedan's gaze darted around his living room. "I don't see any strangers here, only brothers and sisters."

With a chuckle, Chris said, "I especially avoid telling my brothers about my mistakes."

Aedan laughed heartily before returning to his account. "So, after that lackluster beginning, I turned the club over to the volunteers almost immediately. Having no experience with such things, they didn't know how to handle the usual start-up problems. What's worse, they felt they shouldn't bother me with them." He shook his head. "I should never have put them in that position. Actually, the whole story is a great study in what not to do. We started with over fifty kids. Now there are less than fifteen."

And poor Missy's one of those dropouts.

Aedan sighed heavily. "I'm sorry to bring you into such a mess, but I'm guessing if anyone can figure out how to fix it, it'll be the guy who knows how things should be working."

"Well, I hope I can be of some service," Chris said humbly.

Aedan's stomach growled and he looked toward the kitchen. "Where's our lunch, anyway? Efraím, would you give Hannah some help in there?" He referred to his oldest daughter—a cute redhead that Susana had noticed Efraím watching.

As Efraím, quite willingly, set off to his appointed task, Aedan winked and whispered, "If he hasn't asked that girl out within the week, I'll eat my shoe."

He grinned as he stretched out his legs. "So, Chris, tell me what inspired you to start the club."

"Oh, it wasn't my idea. It was my dad's. He realized kids were starving for the attention of caring adults. With both parents working, sometimes the only time children spend with them is when they're traveling between soccer practice and music lessons. Even then, they don't talk to each other—they're on cell phones or listening to separate iPods. So he wanted to foster deeper ties between devoted adult runners and kids through shared hobbies."

"But he never saw the idea through?"

"No. My mom died when I was a baby, and it hit him pretty hard. He ended up blaming Doug. Actually, he stopped running entirely until just a few months before he died."

Aedan sat forward, his gaze sharpening in a way that made Susana uneasy. "Was her death an accident, by any chance?"

"Yeah," Chris said, his brow furrowing. "A kid threw a stone off an overpass and hit her windshield—killed her instantly. How'd you know?"

Aedan seemed elsewhere for a moment. He finally responded in a philosophical tone. "We rarely view ourselves or our accomplishments accurately in this lifetime. Our perspective is so restricted. We just don't live long enough to recognize the ripple effects our actions can have over succeeding generations."

Refocusing on Chris, he continued. "Your father probably envisioned the club as something that would help kids adjust to life, maybe influence them toward running. But that's not how Stan would view it. At the very least, he'd see a major threat to his program of distracting children. Through things like TV, video games, and the Internet, he's been able to functionally cut children off from the wisdom of their elders in large part—and that makes his work easier. But he may well identify some other potential in the club, too—something that we, with our limited vision, are incapable of seeing."

"Like what?" Chris asked.

Aedan shook his head. "I'm not sure. But, for whatever reason, it appears that Moden Industries has a special interest in the Kids' Klub. The circumstances surrounding your mother's death suggest that your father was what Moden Industries calls a 'Target.' "

"You're right. Josh told me so." Chris was obviously amazed by Aedan's conclusion, but Susana's response was closer to alarm. She had run into people like Aedan before—people who could see beyond appearances, who could analyze a situation and recognize Stan's involvement and motivations behind the scenes. These people were not common, in her experience, so she particularly valued their insight. However, the idea that someone with such acumen found Stan's awareness of Chris so remarkable—that she did not like. Not one little bit.

Clearing a sudden tightness from her throat, she said hoarsely, "Josh also said that Chris is a Target. And he's on Camille's List, too." With a nervous laugh, she added, "Whatever that means."

Jerking upright, Aedan demanded, "Camille's List of Guerdon?"

"She didn't specify what list," Chris said.

"She told you this *herself*?" Aedan's increasing incredulity only added to the flutters in Susana's chest.

"Yes," Chris answered, unfazed.

"How did you meet that witch?" The older man's voice suddenly throbbed with anger.

"Just chance, apparently," Chris said. "We've met her twice now."

"Chance, schmance! If you ran into her, it was no accident. And there's certainly nothing accidental about getting on her List."

"I don't know what any of this means," Chris said, "But, honestly, it—well, it scares me."

Her husband's candor didn't surprise Susana. Aedan was so open and artless; it was hard not to be equally forthcoming in his presence. But she was particularly grateful for Chris's honesty now, for she hoped his confession might lead to more information about this mysterious List.

Bowing his head, Chris continued softly, "My dad was an amazing man, Aedan. A good man—strong, wise. But even he buckled under Stan's assaults. It scares me to think that I could do the same. Especially after all Doug's done for us, I don't want to let him down. I want to be a man who keeps the faith, as you put it."

"That's a worthy goal," Aedan said, his anger receding.

"So can you tell me about this List?" Chris asked. "What is it? What kind of problems or challenges is it going to present? And how can I be sure to stick by Doug as faithfully as he's stuck by me?"

Susana wasn't sure how Aedan came by such in-depth knowledge of Stan's workings (truthfully, even considering the question left her feeling a bit uncomfortable), but she found herself inching forward on the sofa, anxious to catch every nuance of his response. She knew only two things about this elusive List: Chris was on it, and that wasn't good. But maybe it wasn't s bad as she thought. She itched to know more.

Aedan's anger revived as he began, "The List—"

"Be careful, son," Doug said through Aedan's transmitter. Having been left on in privacy mode, it allowed Doug to hear what was happening and to respond on a frequency that was only audible to runners.

"I'm sorry, Doug." Taking a break to compose himself, Aedan momentarily closed his eyes before continuing. "The particulars of the List aren't important right now."

Susana almost screamed in frustration.

He lifted a gaze to them that was so intense it pinned Susana to her seat. "Your focus should be on your last question, the one about staying faithful to Doug. The answer to that is simple, at least in theory: *You must stay in close communication with him.*" The way he emphasized the words sent a chill down Susana's back.

"If you keep that relationship strong, then when the time of testing comes"—he broke off and swallowed hard before continuing softly—"whatever form that takes, you'll be given what you need to meet it. I can tell you from personal experience that Doug *is* faithful. It's such an integral part of his nature; he simply can't be unfaithful. The deficiencies come on our side, when we allow ourselves to drift away from him."

Aedan reached into his pocket to hand them several of his business cards. "Put these in your wallet and purse, your apartment and backpack—just toss them around everywhere and keep them handy."

Julie popped her head around the corner and called, "Okay, my starvin' leprechaun, lunch is ready."

Aedan didn't move. His severe gaze didn't waver. "Call me, no matter the hour, if you need anything at all, even if it's just to talk—even if you're not sure what you need to talk about."

His passion set Susana's heart thumping in her throat, and she reached for Chris's hand, her own hand clammy.

"Chris," the pacesetter continued, pay attention to your wife in this. I can tell that you're a guy who likes facts and logic. But women's intuition isn't a myth, and it isn't something to laugh at. I can't say I understand it scientifically. Still, they often get a sense of things being out of whack before we fellows catch on. A wise man listens to that sense. He doesn't ignore it."

"Thank you," Chris said. "I will remember your advice, and we will keep your cards handy. But—" He turned to Susana and paused to kiss her hand before continuing gently, "But we will also remember that Doug 'is our refuge and strength, an ever-present help in trouble. Therefore we will not fear, though the earth give way and the mountains fall into the heart of the sea.' "

Susana's heart was beating hard. Still, she gave Chris a smile that she hoped conveyed some element of the confidence she didn't feel but thought she should.

At the meeting of the Kids' Klub volunteers that afternoon, Aedan introduced Chris as the club's new leader. Having chosen a spot where she could watch the proceedings, Susana noticed that almost everyone's face brightened at this news. The one exception was a heavyset man in his forties, whose face went as hard as iron—the current leader, she guessed.

A sense of dread crawled over her. Although Chris had a talent for diffusing antagonism, he could also be very unyielding when something hit one of his hot buttons. She hoped he was in a conciliatory mood today or this meeting would turn ugly.

Chris made a few introductory comments and then asked the volunteers to tell him about their program. As the discussion progressed, his face soon registered understanding. "So, if I'm hearing you right," he summarized, "you do some marching and then have large classes in a lecture format."

When heads nodded in affirmation, he asked, "Have you considered smaller classes? It might encourage more interaction between the kids and adults."

Efraím, watching from the back, nodded in a way that led Susana to wonder if his reasoning was taking the same course as Chris's. Meanwhile, the volunteers exchanged glances and then turned to the heavyset man, whom Susana now knew as Archie Turner, a teacher and ex-drill sergeant—and the leader Chris was unseating.

"That's not a very efficient use of time or manpower, now, is it?" Archie said gruffly, and Susana cringed. *Please, Chris, don't hit back.*

"No, you're right there. I have to admit, efficiency wasn't one of my dad's strengths," Chris said genially, and Susana almost grinned with pride. "But maybe you're getting enough interaction on the camping trips to develop a rapport that carries over?"

"We don't go camping," Archie said. "Too uncomfortable—sleeping on the ground and all."

Susana puzzled at that—an ex-drill sergeant complaining about a little discomfort? But then she noticed an older volunteer dipping her head self-consciously and realized that Archie wasn't voicing his own preferences.

Chris nodded. "It's true that camping isn't for everyone."

Efraím was also nodding with understanding, as though he was processing the interaction in the same way Chris was, with the same large-scale, mission-oriented vision. He'd also proven his ease and effectiveness at public speaking during the RAB's Second Service that morning. In fact, he'd exhibited many of the same talents that Chris had ... which meant he might be able to help Chris with his global responsibilities.

And as for the help Mike needed at the global level ...

She glanced around the room, consciously noting what had already caught her attention about Archie's work: supplies well stocked and carefully labeled, neatly charted schedules, lists of various kinds—all marks of a highly competent organizer, the kind of person that could help with Mike's work.

Chris handled Archie's unmistakable hostility well, and the meeting concluded without any arguments breaking out. Afterwards, he met with the volunteers individually, getting more detailed information about their talents, experience, and views of the club. It made for a long afternoon, but he gleaned most of the information he needed in that one mega-session. When the volunteers left, he gathered her, Aedan, and Efraím around to discuss their impressions.

"This club's focus is all wrong," he said. "It reminds me of the time I asked Josh why Stan was so interested in the Kids' Klub. He refused to answer me. He said that if I knew Stan's interest I'd focus on entirely the wrong thing and ruin the club's real purpose. That's something like what's happened here."

"Yeah," Efraím said. "They're concentrating on the forms—completing the designated activities, checking items off a list—and doing it in the most efficient manner. But the most efficient method isn't necessarily the one that best fosters relationships between adult runners and kids. And that's what the goal should be, right? Isn't it the friendship and sense of community that will encourage kids to develop their own relationship with Doug?"

When Chris nodded, Efraím continued, "Yet it seems to have gotten lost in—" He glanced around the room at the various charts and lists. "Well, in the routine."

"Exactly," Chris agreed. "But Archie's apparently ruled with an iron hand."

"That's true," Aedan said. "I'm afraid we've lost three volunteers already. They complained that he's too rigid."

"Because his focus is on the wrong goal," Efraím said. "He doesn't want input from the other volunteers—he just wants them to do their assigned tasks in order to convey a designated amount of material."

Chris nodded. "My diagnosis exactly. The problem is, he's a pillar in this RAB—an assistant leader and the grandson of its founders." He rubbed his chin. "Aedan, I want to observe this week's meeting and talk to Doug before making any recommendations, but what kind of position is it going to put you in if Doug says to drop him?"

"A hard one," Aedan said with a shrug. "But it won't be the first time I've been in a tough spot. If that's what Doug says to do, that's what we do. His ways are always best. Still, you should remember that Archie's a runner too. He can be stern, he can be intimidating, and I fear he's retained more of the form of godliness than the power of it, but he has finished the race. That means that, at least at some point in the past, he's committed himself to doing Doug's work."

He leaned forward, capturing Chris's eyes. "He's your brother, Chris. Do you understand what I'm saying?"

"Yes, I think I do," Chris responded soberly. Quoting the *Manual*, he added, "Doug is the only one who 'can rightly judge among us. So what right do I have to condemn my neighbor?' "

Aedan smiled and relaxed back into his chair. "We're going to get along just fine, you and me."

As they drove home, Susana grew quiet, mentally reviewing the happenings of that busy day. In general, it had been a good day; they'd accomplished a lot. She felt more settled now that they belonged somewhere. And they would be in a perfect position to help Missy, as well as some of the acquaintances they'd already made. However, her brain got stuck on the one thing that didn't happen.

She hadn't realized how morose she'd become until they arrived at their apartment building and Chris parked the car. Shifting in the seat to face her, he asked, "What's bothering you, Suze?"

She reached for his hand. "I love you. So much."

"I love you, too." He drew her head against his chest and waited for her to continue.

"Chris," she said at last, "do you know what it means to be on Camille's List?"

"No, but I don't think it means she's sending me a Christmas card."

She sat up to scold, "Don't joke about this. If something happened to you—" She swallowed a large lump in her throat. "Chris, I'm really scared. Maybe we should press Aedan to tell us more."

"I don't think he would, and I'm not sure we should ask. You heard how Doug cautioned him when he started to talk about it."

"You think Doug's hiding it from us?"

"No, not in the way you're suggesting. I think it's more likely that there's danger in us knowing too much."

"I don't understand."

"Well, when I was little, my grandmother gave me money for milk one day at a time—not a month at a time, or even a week at a time. She did that because she knew I'd be preoccupied with the money, and probably misuse it, if I had it before I needed it. I think this is something like that. Doug will give us the resources we need, including information, when we need it. If we had that information now, it not only wouldn't help us, but we'd also worry about it. That's probably why Camille told us about the List in the first place, and why Doug cut her off and refused to let her say more. She wants to spook us, to send us running for cover, so we waste time and energy worrying about *her* plans instead of focusing on the work *Doug* has for us to do. If we get sidetracked like that, she's already won on some level. That's why Doug wants us to cast all our anxieties on him and let him do the worrying."

He paused to search her eyes, and Susana wondered if he could read the disquiet that haunted her soul. He knew her better than anyone. Could he sense her deepest fear? Did he know that she sometimes couldn't sleep for wondering whether Camille would kill him?

"Suze, don't you see?" he pleaded. "Aedan told us the part we need to know now."

"He did? What was that?"

"The importance of staying in close communication with Doug." He stroked her cheek tenderly. "We need to trust Doug, *mi tesoro*. Absolutely. Can we do that?"

CHAPTER 17
THINGS WHICH REMAIN

*" 'Be watchful, and strengthen the things which remain,
that are ready to die.' "*
Revelation 3:2, NKJV.

Chris simply observed the Kids' Klub meeting that week in order to get a more complete picture of the problems plaguing it. The volunteers impressed him; they were good with children and represented a variety of talents and interests. The latter point was especially important because his dad's vision had been to offer a wide range of small group activities so every child would find something that interested him or her and an adult with whom to relate. However, the volunteers' diversity wasn't reflected in the meetings. Instead, only hobbies Archie pegged as "important" were explored. Astronomy and first aid, for instance, were "important," but quilting and model airplanes weren't.

Besides this limitation, Archie's rigid schedule completely eliminated spontaneity. So when the night afforded a particularly clear view of the sky and the kids asked lots of questions, he chided the teacher for getting off track. And, just as the teacher was about to show how studying the stars could teach them about Doug—the most important part of the whole night—Archie ended the lesson. The schedule said it was time for first aid.

The evening left Chris feeling frustrated. This club had wonderful potential, but most of it was wasted. Yet Archie resisted any changes Chris suggested, defending his own program instead. One conclusion seemed inescapable: they'd have to get rid of Archie. But how could he do that without making enemies in this RAB?

"Inflexible," Chris grumbled as he drove home. "Uncompromising."

"H'mm," Susana responded.

"Narrow-minded, too. And overbearing."

Susana didn't respond.

"He's totally misunderstood the whole idea. To him, it's just another school, where the only important thing is transmitting knowledge."

"Mmm."

"I don't even think he likes kids."

"Chris, that's harsh. And unreasonable."

"What?" He'd thought she was on his side—where did that come from?

"You saw how gentle he was with that little girl who was afraid of the dark," she said. "That's not a man who hates kids. And remember, he's a volunteer; he doesn't have to be there at all."

"Then why is he?" Chris exclaimed. "All he's doing is discouraging the other volunteers—that and messing up the program."

"Don't you think he knows that?"

That stopped Chris. He frowned at her in bewilderment.

"Do you honestly think that he doesn't know things are bad? That he can't see the tension and frustration all around him?"

"So what are you saying—he's doing it on purpose?"

"No, of course not. But maybe the only way he knows of dealing with the problem is by sticking more closely to his plan. Clearly, he's an organizer, and he's very good at it. Didn't you notice the beautifully arranged supply cabinet, all labeled and easy for any newcomer to use? Or the totes he prepared for the teachers, each one fully stocked with everything needed for their specific class? Or how about his up-to-date and easy-to-use filing system that quickly gives you any information you'd need in an emergency? The truth is, he's very talented and has a lot to offer this club."

"But there's no energy, no spirit, in totes and files."

"Exactly my point. See, he's like Mike—a great organizer, but not necessarily a leader. He simply doesn't have the larger perspective that you do." She laid a hand on his knee to continue softly, "And railing about what you see as his inadequacies won't change the way his mind works. He's already doing the best he can. Archie—just like this club—needs to be strengthened, to be built up, not to be torn down further."

"You're saying my attitude is making things worse."

"It's not helping, *mi amor*," she said gently. "And that's what we want to do, right?"

"Yeah, it is," he conceded. "So what am I missing in this picture?"

"The basic problem is that we're asking a manager to lead. When things get off-track, a true leader stands back, looks at the overall objectives, and designs a strategy to redirect things toward the right goal. It's a big-picture kind of approach. When an organizer runs into problems, he focuses on the details. He does what he knows best—tweaks the organizational system, thinking there must be a deficiency in it or in the way it's being implemented. When his 'perfected' plan still doesn't work, he's at least as frustrated as everyone else. My sense is, Archie's tired, he's frustrated, and he'd love to relinquish the leadership of this club—if someone would give him a way out that preserves his dignity."

Chris nodded. "Yeah, that makes sense. Aedan said he put Archie in charge because several people insisted that he'd be 'perfect' for it. Getting thrown out after that would be hard to live down."

"Especially because he's been in this RAB all his life."

Chris pondered her insights in silence for a few moments and suddenly realized—"When you say he's like Mike, do you think he could help Mike on the global level?"

She nodded emphatically. "Yes, that's exactly what I'm thinking—if he'll accept the job."

"Yeah, he's a science teacher at the middle school, so he's probably already busy."

"He's also part of the general apathy that's affecting this assembly of runners. Still, this is exactly the sort of project that a gifted organizer like him finds fun and inspiring. So he may well agree to help. I hope he does. Involvement would renew his energy and help him rediscover his true calling."

Susana's gift for understanding people was one of the things Chris had liked about her when they first met. Since they'd married, though, that appreciation had slipped. Sometimes he even scoffed at it. He now wondered why. Was it simply because she couldn't always verbalize the reasons for her impressions like she was doing now—in a way that made sense to him? Aedan had said he should value her intuition whether he could follow it or not, but that was hard to do. He tended to discount anything he couldn't reason out. Maybe this was one of those areas of faith that Debora was always challenging him on. He could almost hear her asking, *Will you obey Doug only when you understand the logic behind his command?*

Grasping her hand, he said, "That's a perspective I never would have seen on my own. Thank you for your insight."

"Chris ..."

"Go ahead," he said gently. "What is it?"

"You're a really talented guy and an amazing leader."

He appreciated her assessment, for he knew it to be honest. Still, he heard a "but" coming. "This is the part where you hit me with the truth. I'm ready."

"It's just—" She shifted in her seat. "Remember what happened in Ventura? You took on way more than any one person can do."

"I've learned my lesson. I'm going to let Doug tell me when I'm accepting too much."

"That's good. But wouldn't it be a lot easier if you had an assistant with complementary abilities? Someone who's good at managing the details that you get impatient with?"

"It sure would. Once Mike and I started working together, things went a million times smoother. I wish I could find someone with Mike's skills—"

Suddenly he understood her point. "Oh, no—not Archie! The guy hates me!"

⚡ ⚡ ⚡ ⚡ ⚡

Chris lifted his hand to ring Archie's doorbell, but redirected it to comb through his hair instead. He'd admit it: he was nervous. In fact, he'd spent quite a while talking to Doug about this meeting. He hadn't started off on the best foot with Archie, and now he was going to ask the guy for two big favors. And, while the planet wouldn't disintegrate if he turned him down, it certainly would make Chris's life a lot easier if he accepted.

When he heaved a sigh, Doug's voice came over his transmitter, which Chris had left on in privacy mode. "It'll be just fine, pardner."

"Thanks, Doug." He again lifted his hand, hesitated only briefly, and then resolutely pressed the doorbell.

Archie's wife answered and said her husband was working in the garage. That gave Chris a measure of comfort—he always felt at home in a workshop. And they apparently had something in common: they both enjoyed working with tools.

He joined Archie at his workbench, and they talked about the engine he was rebuilding for a few minutes. Then the shorter man glanced over his shoulder and said, "Look, Strider, I know you came here to kick me out of the Kids' Klub, so why don't you just get it over with?"

"Actually, that's not why I'm here."

"No?"

"The truth is, we need you. I'd really like you to stay in the club. So would Doug."

"Why? I thought you wanted me out of the way so you could take over."

"Take over?" Chris exclaimed. "I didn't even want the leadership. I only took it because Aedan and Doug asked me to."

"Then what do you need me for?"

Chris lifted a hammer down from the perfectly organized pegboard and turned it around in his hand. "My dad's favorite hobby was woodworking. When I was little, I'd work alongside him. He'd give me a scrap of wood and I'd hammer nails into it—at least, if I could keep my fingers out of the way."

Archie chuckled, and Chris continued. "One time a screw got mixed in with the nails and I hammered and hammered on the thing, getting more and more frustrated. My dad knew how stubborn I was—persistent, he called it—so he just let me keep trying to do the impossible. Finally I threw the poor tool down and yelled, 'Dumb hammer!'

"Without a word, my dad picked up a screwdriver and twisted the screw into the wood. When he finished, he placed both tools in my hands. 'Most of the time,' he said, 'tools work best when they're doing what they were designed to do. Just like people.' "

"Sounds like a smart man, your dad."

"Yeah, smarter than me. I think of that lesson whenever I find myself butting my head against a wall. Usually it's because I'm trying to hammer a screw in place again. It can be tricky, especially when other people mistake me for a screwdriver and think I should be able to do the job. Sometimes they even convince me. But at the end of the day, when someone puts me back in my spot"—he hung the hammer back in its labeled place—"I'm still a hammer."

Archie nodded.

"Look at this pegboard, for instance," Chris continued. "Everything's perfectly organized. Not only is there a labeled place for each tool, but the tools are in their proper places. Now, I can appreciate a workspace like this. I could even set it up if someone needed it done. But would I maintain it? Never." He chuckled at the idea. "As soon as I completed it, I'd be on to the next project, and, in my enthusiasm to get that next project completed, I'd let this one fall by the wayside. But you—you keep it organized, which is an amazing talent, one I've recently come to appreciate."

"Why's that?"

"When Josh gave me my dad's plans for this club and asked me to set it up, I was all excited. I love getting things going. Besides, it was my dad's baby, and he'd just gone to his rest, so it made me feel a little closer to him. But then it mushroomed, and I freaked out. I felt so overwhelmed—not at the number of clubs wanting my help to get started, but at all the complications that kept cropping up in established clubs. I felt like I couldn't possibly hold everything together, and I was going nuts trying. Worse, I was afraid I'd be failing my dad if the thing fell apart."

The rigid set of Archie's shoulders softened. "Yeah, I can relate to that."

"Long story short, I finally got smart and took my brother up on his offer to help. Once I did, everything fell into place." He smiled wryly. "See, I'd been trying to be a screwdriver again, when Doug only expected me to do what I'm good at and release the rest to those more gifted to do it."

Archie turned to face him for the first time. "I may have misjudged you, Strider."

"Well, that makes us even then," Chris admitted. "But here's the point. I'm still just a hammer. With Doug's direction and my wife's insights, I can help this club rediscover its purpose. But I don't have the patience or skills or whatever it is to keep things organized after that. I need a teammate who will help me keep the club in shape. The other volunteers are all great, but no one else has your ability to keep things running smoothly. So I'm really hoping you'll stay with us."

Archie studied Chris for a moment, and then his hard expression melted into a smile. "I think I'm going to like you after all. And yeah, I'll do it. Truth is, I'd much rather be an assistant than the leader. I really don't like making the kinds of decisions everyone's asking me to make, especially when they just get mad at the decisions I do make."

"Great. Then—well, I've got an even bigger favor to ask of you."

Archie laughed aloud. "What is it?"

"I know you teach, and that keeps you busy, so if this is too much, I understand. But the Kids' Klub has already way outgrown anything my dad envisioned. Not only is it in almost every state, it's in several other countries, which means we have to manage it on a global level too."

Nodding, Archie said, "Which would require a different type of structure."

"Right. So my brother and I sort of fell into this arrangement where I help with the initiating and recruiting for new clubs, and he deals with the problems once they're up and running. Still, it's expanded beyond what the two of us can handle—we both need help. Efraím's interested in helping me with the setting-up side of things, but we haven't found anyone to help my brother with his end."

"What does it entail?" Was it Chris's imagination, or did Archie actually sound excited?

"It's essentially helping clubs work the bugs out of their systems—organizing their supplies to maximize the use of time, collecting and keeping emergency information current—the kind of stuff you've figured out and solved in this club already."

"Yeah, I'd like that," Archie said. "Sounds like fun."

Chris laughed. "That's what Mike calls it."

With his mission a success, Chris could have left Archie's house then. But he didn't. He stayed to help him with the engine, and they got to talking. By the time he left, Chris had decided he liked the man.

As he drove away from Archie's home, Chris reviewed the amazing events of the last few days. A week ago, he'd been feeling overwhelmed with the Kids' Klub's rapid growth. He was so sure he'd never be able to find the help he needed to run the thing properly. Then he went to one little dinner (which he'd thought was a waste of time) and met Efraím, who was just itching to jump in and help him. And through Efraím, he also went to just the right RAB to find (thanks to Susana's insight, which he'd been questioning) Archie—the ideal runner to complete their team of global administrators.

Chuckling at himself, he activated his transmitter. "Thanks for all your help, Doug. I don't know why I bother worrying. You think of everything, don't you?"

To: entitymaster@management.com
From: bestagent@management.com
Date: 30 September 8008 M.E.
Subject: Monthly Report

As per my plan, Subject was successfully lured to the troubled RAB. However, the atmosphere there seems to be turning around; he appears to be affecting it positively rather than it affecting him negatively.

Do I understand correctly that plans are being made to set up a New-RAB in this area? Such a project could be quite useful in this Subject's management. Since he truly enjoys setting up new KKs, I believe he would be vulnerable to an appeal for his help with setting up a New-RAB. And, if he is kindly disposed toward the project at its outset, he will be less likely to note the subtle alterations in doctrine (or recognize their significance). In this manner, I propose to lead him gradually away from Dictator's standard.

You requested a report on agents of KK leaders. I have two observations of note:

1. Regarding Subject A.T. (new Assistant Global Manager for KK): A-1438's current work is adequate. Nevertheless, I believe she would also find this Subject quite susceptible to financial hardship—an area she has, thus far, left unexplored.

2. Regarding Subject E.S. (new Assistant Global Leader for KK): A-3945 needs to step up his efforts markedly. He has left some key areas of vulnerability untouched. I will advise him on these if you so desire. However, my observations suggest that he may lack the necessary skills to influence his Subject optimally. Because you have honored me by requesting my evaluation, I will be so bold as to offer my honest, though humble, opinion: I believe a master agent may be warranted for this Subject, especially considering said Subject's entrance into KK leadership. I await your further instruction on the matter.

Although I will not allow it to interfere with my primary duties, I must advise you that Company Master has engaged me to assist I.T. in hacking into the KK website. Our objective is to sabotage KK's Internet presence and overwhelm the leaders with website difficulties. Through my proximity to Subject, I can access vital information that I.T. can exploit to our advantage.

To: bestagent@management.com
From: entitymaster@management.com
Date: 30 September 8008 M.E.
Subject: Re: Monthly Report

I am encouraged at your success in luring Subject to the troubled RAB. Do not despair at his initial effect, which may well be temporary. Overcoming such general apathy over the long term will challenge his resolve.

Your plan to utilize Subject in our New-RAB is a solid one. And, yes, Company Master intends to set one up in your area next spring. As he is expecting your cooperation, I'm certain that he will be contacting you about it shortly.

Your honest and discerning evaluation is received with appreciation. I have had my own doubts of A-3945's abilities. I will replace him with MA-436 immediately. As to A-1438, please educate her regarding the deficiencies in her approach. I will arrange to have Subject A.T. laid off to aid this avenue of attack.

You are to cooperate fully with I.T.'s efforts to sabotage the KK website. KK is of greater importance to us than any individual Subject—even yours.

PAYBACK

1 October 8008 M.E.

Fixing Garrick with a stern gaze, Stan demanded, "Are you sure you didn't forget anything?"

"Stan," Garrick said with a touch of impatience, "I've been in charge of security for the entire organization for millennia. Surely I can handle the next few hours."

Sitting on the side of his gurney, Stan grunted and looked uncertainly toward the operating room. This prompted Camille to interject from her gurney, "I'm certain Garrick's right."

A heavy blanket of tension already hung over the preoperative area, and Stan's churlishness wasn't helping. As far as Camille was concerned, Dr. Pim was anxious enough—and understandably so; any complication would, quite literally, come out of his hide. However, while a certain level of stress would serve to keep Pim at his best, she didn't care to have her surgeon too nervous.

As Stan rose to pace the room, Camille admitted to herself that her brother's concern was warranted. Today's surgery presented a massive security threat. A rebel could ask no better opportunity for mounting a coup d'état than when the two leaders were unconscious—helpless—at the same time. Understandably, that risk had completely overshadowed the risks of the surgery itself in their conversations. In fact, they had scarcely discussed the procedure.

But then, what was there to discuss? Camille's half of the operation was simple: Dr. Pim was removing her right tonsil and transplanting it into Stan. Human children had their tonsils removed every day; how difficult could it be?

She watched her brother as he paced. "Stan, we've covered everything. We've missed nothing. Further delay is pointless."

He met her gaze and held it. Then he gave a single nod. With that, the room broke into lively activity. The nurses connected monitors and administered medications, and Dr. Pim scurried around double-checking everybody's work.

When Garrick's cell phone rang, the bustle came to an abrupt halt and the blanket of tension grew smothering. He had issued a firm mandate that he was not to be disturbed except for security threats.

With a wary glance at Stan, Garrick lifted his phone to his ear. After listening attentively for a few moments, he abruptly swore at the caller and demanded to be transferred to Cherisse, his sister and executive secretary. "Discipline and fire Rhoda," he ordered. "How dare she disturb me with trivia now."

After hanging up, he pivoted to Camille with an apologetic expression. "Sorry to bother you with this, but I might as well ask you now as later. It seems we're missing the paperwork on a body."

Stan muttered an oath while everyone else seemed to release a collectively held breath. Garrick swept the room with his dark gaze. "What? Would you rather it was a real threat?"

"Continue, Garrick," Camille said.

His voice dropped to a near-whisper, a quirk he'd acquired from centuries of eavesdropping on others' private conversations. "The man was a Sean McElroy from San Francisco. He was on your List of Guerdon—an associate who defected. He was apprehended months ago but is no longer among the guests downstairs. Apparently he hasn't been there for some time."

"Yes, I remember the man," Camille said. "I entertained him for several days. When he expired, I had Patric transport his remains to his apartment in California. His brother, Aedan McElroy, is a problematic pacesetter in that area, and I wanted him to find the body. I'm certain that Patric completed the appropriate forms and delivered them to your office. No doubt, they were misfiled by the same secretary who just needlessly disturbed you. However, knowing Patric, he undoubtedly has duplicates."

"I'll take care of it," Garrick said with a nod.

"All right." Dr. Pim clapped his hands together with false bravado obviously meant to disguise his nervousness. Sarcastically, he added, "Now that we've taken care of the important issues, can we proceed with this trifling little procedure to save Dr. Moden's life?" Pim cast a sneer in Garrick's direction—the two hadn't gotten on well since Garrick trounced Pim in their studies at medical school.

When Garrick opened his mouth with some retort, Stan cut him off. "Take it outside, you two. And take the others with you. Give us some privacy."

The room cleared, and Stan stepped to Camille's gurney. "Thank you for doing this," he said gruffly.

"Certainly, Lusu." Although she tried to portray confidence, she knew he rightly judged her fretfulness to arise from more than the security issues. A tonsillar transplant had never before been attempted. Yet without *anát*, a hormone produced only by the tonsils of Paradisians, Stan would soon die of an AIDS-like illness that could not be treated. In short, her brother's life—along with their goal of regaining the island—rested entirely on this one experimental operation.

Yes, a great deal was as stake today. Only a fool would be unaffected by apprehension.

Picking up her hand, Stan said, "Before they put us under, I just want to say—" He glanced toward the OR with uncharacteristic hesitation.

"I'm sure everything will be fine, *zuulu*," she said with more certainty than she felt.

He smiled, a wave of affection emanating from him. "Thank you, *zali*. I've really enjoyed having you as a friend again. Whatever happens today, I want you to know that." He paused. "I love you, you know. I always will."

He leaned down to kiss her gently on the forehead, and her heart swelled, spreading warmth through her body. She had given up everything to leave the island and support her brother. At times she'd wondered if she'd made a mistake. But now she knew she had not. Having someone to love, and someone to love her, made it all worthwhile.

That warm feeling lingered as they wheeled her into the OR and completed the preoperative preparations. It was what she remembered when the anesthesiologist put a mask over her face and injected something into her IV. As she sank into unconsciousness, her last thought was of how fortunate she was—how very happy she was—to no longer be alone.

✵ ✵ ✵ ✵ ✵

Camille awoke with a very sore throat. She had expected this, of course, but she had anticipated having pain on only the right side. To test her impression, she swallowed gingerly and discovered that not only did both sides of her throat hurt, but the left side actually hurt worse than the right. How could that be?

Seeing that she had awakened, Dr. Pim came to her bedside, chattering excitedly about what a wonderful success the surgery had been, about how proud he was to have performed the first tonsillar transplant, and about how well Dr. Moden's new tonsils were doing.

She squinted at the physician, struggling to think clearly despite the post-anesthetic fog that enveloped her. But did she really hear him say tonsils—plural? Surely that was inaccurate; it would benefit no one to kill her by removing both of her tonsils.

No one, that is, except …

She looked to her brother lying on the gurney on the other side of Pim. He appeared to be as woozy as she felt. Nevertheless, he returned her stare with an expression that conveyed a threat. He didn't want her to reveal her confusion.

And with that expression, she knew the truth: Her brother had betrayed her.

The realization hit her like an icy blade that plunged deeply into her chest, stealing away her very breath. Her linkmate had designed and carried out a calculated plot to steal her life-sustaining tonsils. He had chosen to sacrifice her in order to save himself.

Beware lest in smelling the rose you are pricked by the thorn.

She understood immediately the mistake she had made. With all the hubbub about security, she'd never actually talked to *Pim* about the specifics of the procedure at all. Rather, she had trusted Stan to transmit the important points of what was supposed to be, for her part, a minor procedure.

Two years ago, even six months ago, she never would have trusted Stan so implicitly. But he had carefully manipulated their relationship over those two years, first taking them to an unprecedented low to assure that she would be vested in warming their frosty relationship, and then carefully nudging her through successive levels of friendship until they were again living together as *yushún* siblings. And she, falsely secure in their rediscovered friendship, had so trusted him that she accepted his version of the surgical procedure without question.

She searched Stan's face for some hint that her conclusions were wrong, that this was all some kind of bizarre mistake. But she saw none. And he knew exactly what she'd surmised, too, for he was, even now, pressing a hand to his own heart as he sensed her pain at his betrayal.

Pim continued to jabber as Camille reached these conclusions, prattling on about what a courageous woman she was and how he admired her devotion to the cause. Meanwhile, she was growing more certain of her inferences and more angry at her brother. She couldn't care less about being a dead hero! Given a choice, she would have far preferred to attempt the completion of the war without Stan. But of course, that's precisely why he had withheld that choice from her.

In any case, as to allowing Pim to know of her confusion, she certainly would not. She wouldn't have him knowing how thoroughly she'd been duped.

Finally Pim asked, "Do you have any questions, ma'am?"

"No, an order," she said, her voice raspy. "I wish to speak to Dr. Moden alone."

Pim looked surprised. "Leaving fresh post-op patients alone is not recommended, ma'am."

"It was not a request."

He nervously reviewed both of their monitors and mumbled to himself, "Both conscious and stable. I-it should be okay." He moved toward the door, shooing the nurses out ahead of him, and cast one last worried look over his shoulder before exiting.

Camille turned a glare on her brother and spoke very deliberately. "Tell me, my dear, dear *zuule*—what did I ever do to you to deserve the slow, lingering, painful death to which you have consigned me?"

"Kami, listen—"

"Was it my giving up a thriving architectural firm, loving family, and beautiful home on Paradise Island to remain at your side through myriad difficulties?"

"Camille—"

"Was it my being your most faithful enthusiast throughout your entire life, supporting you through war and peace, fat and lean?"

"I—"

"Or perhaps it was my willingness to share with you one of the two most vital organs in my body."

"One tonsil wouldn't have been enough. We need—"

"I must admit, you did an excellent job of acting, Stan. I truly never considered the possibility that you would kill me for my tonsils. I even believed your last words to me before they anesthetized us. Do you remember what you said?"

This time Stan did not try to gainsay her. And was it her imagination, or was an embarrassed flush creeping up his neck?

" 'I love you,' " she whispered. "That's what you said, Stan. And I believed you. I believed that the man who once promised to protect and care for me—" Her voice caught in her throat, and she left the rest unsaid rather than allow the tears pricking at her eyes to overflow.

"I wasn't acting, Kami. I do love you. I've enjoyed renewing our old friendship. I'd like for it to continue."

She snorted in derision. "For the few days I have left?"

"Camille, I did what I had to do. Tonsils aren't like kidneys—we need them both. And we have every reason to believe that healthy tonsils can regrow. Pim purposely left a remnant of each of your tonsils. He conducted research on other species until he was fairly certain just how much he'd need to leave behind. It will be rough at first—I grant you that. You'll be in protective isolation to minimize the risk of infection, and he'll be monitoring you closely. But we have every hope that you'll be fine."

"You *hope* I'll be fine?"

"We *believe* you'll be fine," he backpedaled. "The possibility of both of us surviving is now quite good. The possibility of me surviving without the procedure was nil."

"Yes, much better to betray me and put my life at risk rather than your own."

"That's enough," he said sternly. Any shame she might have perceived earlier was gone and being quickly replaced by anger at her continued indignation. "I've explained the full circumstance to you. You're now bordering on insolence."

She stared at him. "*You* manipulated me, betrayed me, put me directly in harm's way—and you wonder at *my* attitude?"

His expression turned hard and wholly unrepentant. "It's what I do, *Kamíl*. It's what we both do. It's the reason we've stayed at the top of this organization. It's the reason the media's dubbed us 'America's Number One Power Couple.' We do *whatever* is required to accomplish a goal."

Her pain grew crushing as she realized that her linkmate's quest for power had gradually supplanted every other consideration. It had now extinguished even his capacity to genuinely love her, the one person to whom he was so intimately connected that he actually felt her pain. She had forfeited everything to preserve his love, and now she'd lost it forever. He was no longer even capable of providing the only thing she had ever truly wanted.

And then, although she thought she could bear no further pain, another shocking realization pierced her: she'd made a terrible mistake 6,000 years ago when she left Paradise Island with him. Yes, she was wealthier and more powerful now, but she had paid a dear price for these advantages. She had surrendered love in all its forms, her peace, her security, and now her very life. She'd been swindled. She'd paid a price far above the value of the merchandise she'd received.

The collective weight of these discoveries suddenly overwhelmed her, engulfing her in a despair darker, heavier, and lonelier than the deepest oceanic abyss. Feeling as though she was physically suffocating, she desperately gasped for air.

Stan clutched at his chest in response to the linked transmission of her pain. "Stop it! Just stop it!"

But, of course, she couldn't. She had traded everything she'd ever valued for nothing she truly wanted. And she could never undo the transaction. How does one "stop" the wretchedness of such a devastating insight?

For six millennia, Camille had trained herself to hide her emotions. She was so skilled at it that she had never before cried in front of another person. But now her utter hopelessness, combined with her drugged state, swept away all of her usual restraint, and she burst into great, heaving sobs. This only further unnerved Stan, whose astonishment quickly transformed into disgust. He impatiently hit at the controls on his bed until he found the call button.

Dr. Pim entered and leapt to her side. "What is it?" he demanded. "What's wrong?"

"She's in pain and having some kind of reaction to the anesthesia," Stan said. "Put her out."

"But if she's having a reaction—"

"Put! Her! Out!"

"Yes, sir."

It would have taken a bolder man than Pim to disobey Stan's direct order, even though he was obviously uncomfortable with it. He eased something into Camille's IV, his gaze darting nervously between her face and her monitors, while he bit his lip so hard that he drew blood.

As the medicine took effect, dragging Camille down toward unconsciousness, one clear thought moved to the forefront of her mind: She was all alone again.

That thought triggered a memory. She saw herself running along the beach back home with Debora. They stopped, shared a few long-forgotten words, and then the queen kissed her tenderly on the forehead.

Camille choked out one last sob before unconsciousness overcame her. *That* was the love she'd been seeking. All this time, she'd been looking for it in Stan, but his love was not—and could never be—the one for which she yearned. No, the love she sought was forever lost to her. She'd sold it. And received nothing in return.

CHAPTER 19
UNWILLING

"I have given her time to repent of her immorality,
but she is unwilling."
Revelation 2:21, NIV.

1 October 8008 M.E.

The Deón. Their voices, their presence.

Debora's beckoning smile.

Joshua's warm laughter.

Doúg's joyous voice echoing through the hills.

In her dreams, Camille could see and hear them so clearly. She longed to reconnect with them, to experience again that which she'd known only in their company: the warmth of absolute safety … acceptance … love.

She was in the Valley of the Rainbow now. Doúg sat on His throne, surrounded by the Dome of Lashani that radiated from Him and flowed into a magnificent, living rainbow. The glory of the sight defied words. Stan was positioned at Doúg's right hand and Gabriel at his left, both ready to do his bidding. And his bidding was always good, bringing happiness and delight—opening new fields to investigate, new art forms to experience, new worlds to explore.

Camille hadn't delved into these memories in centuries—millennia. As she revisited them now, they only intensified her yearning to go home, to return to that place of joy and peace. What had induced her to leave?

As the dream continued, it all came back to her. It had started with Stan asking simple, sensible questions and raising logical alternatives to their traditional way of living. For example, he suggested that, since they had no crime, they needed no laws. Silly Paradisians—they hadn't even realized there were laws until Stan pointed out how arbitrary they were.

Stan's questions had generated more questions, and, for a while, a good deal of discussion had followed. But the time came when debate was not enough. When he took a stand against Doúg's dictatorial rule, Camille and other forward-thinking patriots backed him. It had horrified her when their other siblings, out of stubborn, blind loyalty to Doúg, lined up on the dictator's side—opposing their own elder brother.

And then came war. As her dreams replayed it, the faces of the friends and siblings who were pierced by her sword passed before her. Perhaps her greatest battle that day had been with her own shameful feelings of pity and tenderness for those who deserved only disdain. But those foolish sentiments had fled forever when she saw Doúg's mighty frame bowed over a fallen warrior. Dirt and blood streaked his face, and his magnificent robes were shredded. Even as she watched, he tore another strip from his royal garments to bind the soldier's wounds. Then his face crumpled in heart-wrenching sorrow, tears flowing freely down his cheeks.

The image still sickened her—that such a great and powerful man should allow himself to be moved to the point of servility, to the point of tears. Such revolting weakness.

That's when she learned contempt. A new appetite burned within her—the desire to cause Doúg pain, to demonstrate his pathetic weakness for all to see. And so, she learned to enjoy wounding outlanders, especially Doúg's runners. Each time, she saw his sorrowing face in her mind and gloated in her ability to bring such agony to the great majesty of the universe.

The same ambition now reignited the fire in her soul. By the time she had fully awakened from the anesthesia, she was a new woman—or rather, a revitalized version of the old Camille, strong and independent. She had rediscovered her passion. She needed nothing more. Her consuming hatred for Doúg would energize and sustain her.

As to her current circumstance, it was her own fault. She was well acquainted with the drawbacks of love. Didn't she utilize the weakness and vulnerability it spawned in her work? Yet she had allowed herself to seek it. Foolish, childish sentimentalism.

But she would never make the same mistake. She was through chasing fairy tales.

CHAPTER 20

BRUISED REED

*"A bruised reed he will not break,
and a smoldering wick he will not snuff out."*
Isaiah 42:3, NIV.

Vanessa waved as Susana approached the café near the anatomy building, and Susana called a greeting. She truly appreciated Vanessa's companionship, particularly since making friends here had turned out to be more difficult than she'd expected. Not that people were unsociable; they were just busy.

Picking up a cup of tea at the counter, she settled at one of the outdoor tables with Vanessa and waited for Chris and George to finish anatomy lab. As they chatted, the conversation came around to her burn scars. Pulling out her cell phone, she flipped to a picture of her and Chris before the wedding.

"You're so beautiful now," Vanessa murmured as she contemplated the photo. "It's hard to believe that you could have had such extensive scars." She raised her head to examine Susana's face, but her expression went stormy. Addressing someone behind Susana, she spat, "Do you mind? This is a private conversation."

"Oh, I-I'm sorry," came a halting male voice. "I didn't mean anything."

Susana turned to see a guy blushing so fiercely that it was visible even through his full blond beard. Distressed at Vanessa's harsh treatment of the stranger, she said, "That's okay. You can look, too—I don't mind. I was just showing my friend a picture from a few months ago. Our sponsor, Doug Damour, sent us some special leaves that healed these burn scars."

"Th-thank you," the guy mumbled, drawing back. With the faintest hint of a smile, he added, "You're v-very nice." He hurriedly turned away, stumbling into someone in the process.

When Susana turned to see Vanessa's eyes flashing angrily, she understood the fellow's embarrassed confusion. "I really don't mind showing the pictures to strangers," she said quietly.

"You're too nice." Vanessa's voice remained hard. "No one expects you to put yourself in danger for pond scum like him."

"What do you mean, danger? Do you know him?"

Vanessa frowned. "You don't remember him? Oh, maybe you didn't actually see him—he was behind you that night. That's Lester Stretch, the guy who grabbed you at the dinner."

"That's him? He seemed so shy just now."

"Yeah, George says he's like that in lab, too—never talks. Personally, he gives me the creeps," she added with a shudder.

"H'mm." Susana watched him shamble down the sidewalk, not raising his head to greet anyone he passed—as if the fall leaves swirling around the pavement merited his undivided attention.

Vanessa leaned forward to squeeze Susana's hand. "Honestly, Suze, you're the kindest, most selfless person I know. But sometimes you're too polite. I saw the meanness in his eyes that night. It sent a chill down my spine. You need to watch out for your own needs better—especially your own safety. Remember, the *Manual* warns us to 'be wise like serpents.' "

Susana swirled the tea around in her cup while wondering if Vanessa was right. Did she put herself in jeopardy by interacting too freely with strangers? After all, she'd already been assaulted twice; how many people did that happen to?

Yet she was usually a pretty good judge of character, and, despite the scare Lester had given her at the party, his present behavior seemed more tragic than creepy. What's more, the memory of some yellow roses offered a different warning: *You'll now be the one with the power to reject those who need your friendship. Let Doug help you decide whom to befriend.*

Yes, that was the answer—she'd talk to Doug about it.

🏃 🏃 🏃 🏃 🏃

Chris's head was bowed as he exited the anatomy lab, his attention being entirely focused on the Kids' Klub's latest challenge, a virus that had erased the e-mail addresses for their newsletter's entire distribution list. The difficulties they were having with the website were getting exasperating, even dangerous. Last week several clubs had lost all of their emergency contact information—on the day of a big regional camping trip.

When he realized he was nearing the café, he lifted his head to scan for Susana. He wasn't sure what to make of the picture that met his eyes. Susana and Vanessa were sitting across from one another at a table, but Susana looked bewildered, even shamefaced.

He knew the instant that she saw him. Her eyes sparked with undisguised joy, and she broke into a beatific smile that made him feel like the most important guy on the planet. After taking their leave of Vanessa, they walked toward their apartment complex hand in hand.

"What were you girls talking about?" he asked. "You looked a little upset."

She hesitated. "Chris," she began uncertainly, "am I too trusting? Do I put myself in danger? Did I somehow cause the attack in Cleveland or encourage Lester's advances?"

The heat of indignation sparked in Chris's chest. Stopping, he turned to face her. "No," he said emphatically. "Neither of those incidents were your fault. Never."

"Are you sure?"

"Absolutely. I don't know what Vanessa told you, but the guy in Cleveland targeted you because you're petite and you were alone. You were an easy target— that's all. Lester's a bigot who saw you as a beautiful but non-white woman, which to him means less worthy of respect. He's just a jerk."

"He didn't seem like such a jerk at the café just now."

"What?" Chris exclaimed, alarmed. Could Vanessa have been responding to a real threat? "Did he approach you again? Did he hurt you?"

"No, not at all. He didn't do anything bad, just—well, inappropriate."

"*Inappropriate?*" His indignation roared into an angry fire.

"No," she said quickly. "That's the wrong word. Um, more like—"

"What happened, exactly?" he demanded.

"He only peered over my shoulder while I was showing Vanessa some pictures. But I didn't mind. I told her so."

Chris frowned. "And that's what Vanessa was criticizing you for—letting him look at your pictures?" Surely he was missing something.

"Yeah. I didn't realize he was the guy from the dinner. And I guess it was a peculiar thing for him to do. Still, I don't think he's dangerous, or even creepy— he just wants to be around people but doesn't know how to approach them. He's awkward is all. That's what I meant by inappropriate—socially clumsy."

Chris studied her. She honestly wasn't upset by the incident. And her assessment actually jibed really well with his own exchanges with Lester—when he wasn't drunk, that is. In fact, he should have already come to the same conclusion if he hadn't been so busy judging him for his inauspicious debut at the dinner. He had often noticed how Lester didn't meet people's eyes, blushed when someone so much as talked to him, and hung back around the lab until everyone else was gone.

"Do you see a lot of him?" she asked.

"He's in my cadaver group," he said. "Along with George and Efraím. But he's really quiet. It's easy to forget he's there."

"Poor guy. I get the impression he's lonely. I'll bet he doesn't have many friends. In fact, if he's a long way from home, he may not have any friends here. In spite of the way he behaved at the dinner, I think he's nothing more than a scared little boy."

Her dark eyes testified to a compassionate generosity of spirit that contrasted so sharply with his own condemning anger that it shamed him to witness it. Yes, the guy had behaved like a fool when they first met, but Chris had some experience in that role himself, and he knew how rotten it made you feel about yourself. He'd been lucky to have Josh there to help him through it, but whom did Lester have? What a sad situation to be in.

Cupping her sweet face in his hands, he said, "Susana Strider, you are the best, kindest, most wonderful human being I know. I am truly grateful—and proud—to be married to you."

ﾑ ﾑ ﾑ ﾑ ﾑ

As Chris walked to lab the next day, he pulled the collar of his jacket closed against the cool wind. Autumn in Northern California might not be cold to the natives, but to a kid from a beach town more than 300 miles to the south, fifty degrees was downright frigid.

But there was another reason for his chill: his newfound understanding of how unfeeling, even cruel, he'd been toward Lester. Even after his discussion with Susana gave him some level of sympathy for Lester's situation, he'd resisted Doug's suggestion that he should try to befriend him. Somebody should bite that bullet, sure—but why him? Lester had insulted his heritage and assaulted his wife. He didn't owe the guy anything. Quite the opposite—he had every right to be angry at him.

Ultimately, it took another visit from Debora and another of her pithy questions: *You said you would do whatever Doug commanded; did you mean to exclude your friendships from this commitment?*

And so, although the dying coals of anger were still smoldering in his gut, Chris had accepted the assignment as a point of obedience, trusting Debora to supply him with the goodwill he lacked to carry it out. Funny, but after she breathed on him, he had trouble remembering why he was supposed to be mad at his classmate. Instead, he felt genuinely sorry for him—and ashamed of the proud, exclusionary sentiment that had prevented him from offering his friendship to someone who so clearly needed it.

He also noticed something that he was beginning to see as a pattern: whenever he followed Doug's command, even when he did it reluctantly, a sense of peace and joy—of well-being—settled over him. In short, he was just plain happier when following Doug's directions.

Chris walked into the cadaver lab and proceeded to the bay where his assigned table stood. He hardly noticed the odor of formaldehyde anymore; it wasn't nearly as bad as some labs thanks to a venting system that sucked the formaldehyde-saturated air right out of the tables. He passed Efraím in the first bay where he was reviewing the day's assignment at the computerized virtual dissection table. George, likewise, was engaged in a discussion with Preston, the two comparing the textbooks' diagrams to their cadaver. Preston was a TA—not an official member of the group. But he had taken a liking to them, especially to George. In fact, the two got on like they'd known each other forever.

And then there was Lester, simply standing nearby—present, but not participating. He hardly looked like a member of the group at all.

It struck Chris that this picture was typical. They often excluded Lester—in attitude if not in action—even though he had as much right to learn from the cadaver as they did. And this same attitude extended to after-hours. Preston had even invited the others to his home for pizza or movies right in front of Lester without including him in the invitation.

Well, it stops now.

Making a point of looking the outcast full in the face, Chris approached the table and said, "Hi, Lester. How's it going?"

Lester immediately turned crimson. "F-fine, thank you."

It wasn't much, but it was a start. And it didn't go unnoticed. George and Preston exchanged a glance that said, *What's that about?*

As he worked that day, Chris occasionally asked Lester to pass an instrument he needed. The first time, his classmate again blushed, and even trembled as he handed it over, but the interaction forced him to draw closer to the group. After a few days, when Lester had started standing nearer the table, Chris also began thinking aloud as he worked. This invited whomever might be standing around to join in with their thoughts. Lester remained quiet at first, but eventually started contributing short observations and, as Chris received his comments with respect, gradually became somewhat bolder.

One day Chris was musing aloud, "Let's see, if this is the musculocutaneous nerve, it will run ... lateral to the axillary artery? or medial?"

"Below the pec minor? Lateral," Lester answered immediately. "It will give off one or two branches to the coracobrachialis near its origin, pierce the muscle about halfway down, continue downward between the biceps and brachialis, giving off branches to those muscles, and then pierce the brachial fascia lateral to the biceps tendon. It continues through the forearm as the lateral antebrachial cutaneous nerve."

Nothing less than stunned, Chris straightened up and stared at him. Two scarlet patches developed on Lester's fair cheeks, and he stammered, "I-I think."

Chris turned to George, who was directing the dissection. He had proven himself to be a really smart fellow, but even he seemed a bit astonished at Lester's recitation. He hunched over the books for a few moments, tracing his finger along the diagrams, and then straightened up. "He's exactly right on all counts."

"Wow," Chris exclaimed. "What are you doing back there watching, Les? Why don't you come around and help me?" Efraím had taken off early for a dental appointment, so the dissection was progressing slower than usual.

"But I—I—" Lester sputtered.

"I'll tell you what you are," Chris said. "You're good. You know where we're heading better than I do, which means you're less likely to mess things up than I am. Come on, doctor, I need your assistance."

Lester hesitated, appearing both excited and scared.

"Come on," Chris pressed. "What's the worst you can do—kill her?"

Lester nervously laughed his snorting laugh, but went to get his dissection kit. While he was gone, George murmured, "Chris, I really don't like that guy. It's bad enough just having him stand around. Do you have to encourage him to participate?"

"We're short at the moment and falling behind. He obviously knows the stuff. He just lacks self-confidence." Chris stopped himself before adding, *And you don't like getting your hands dirty, so …*

He immediately regretted his irritated tone. He was supposed to be encouraging the ex-runner to return to running. Getting impatient with him wouldn't further that goal.

George didn't miss the annoyance in Chris's voice. In fact, such a hateful scowl crossed his face that Chris glanced reflexively toward his dissection kit to make sure the scalpel was out of George's reach. But it was just Chris's guilty conscience manufacturing the expression because when his gaze returned to George, he saw mere irritation. And, with a little smile, his lab partner took the high road. "You're the one who should have a problem with him, my friend. If you're okay, why should I complain?"

From then on, Lester became a regular participant. At first he was uncertain and a little clumsy with dissecting, but Chris continued to encourage him, and he quickly improved. Over time, Chris learned that he was from Virginia, that his only family was his mother, and that his father had abandoned them when Les was five. As the member of a large, tight-knit family, Chris actually felt a pang in his chest when he learned this. And Susana had been right about his friends, or lack of them. He had so far made no friends in California, and had only a few back home.

As Thanksgiving approached, an idea began gnawing at Chris, and he finally determined to bring it up with Susana. Before he could, though, she mentioned it.

"I saw Lester at the café again today," she said over dinner one evening. "When I said, 'hi,' he turned all red, but said 'hi' back this time. Does he have any friends at all?"

"A couple in Virginia, but none in this area."

"He's all alone here?"

"Yup." Chris hid a grin. He could already see his wife's sympathetic nature revving into overdrive.

"Wow. How lonely."

"Mm-hmm. In fact, I was wondering—"

"What's he doing for Thanksgiving? We could invite him to come to my folks' house with us."

Laughing, Chris said, "That's just what I was going to say. Do you think your parents would mind?"

"We can call them, but I'm sure they won't. *Papi* always says holidays are meant for sharing with others—whether it's food or fellowship."

"I like his attitude. I don't know if Les will accept …" He hesitated. "Well, anyway, it won't hurt to invite him."

"What is it?"

"It's just that he's pretty prejudiced against Natives. I wouldn't be surprised if he's got some funny ideas about Hispanics—or anyone who's not white."

"Has he said something to you?"

"Not since that dinner party. But then he probably wouldn't verbalize it around me unless he was drunk, would he?"

"Well, if he's very prejudiced, he won't accept the invitation. So, like you said, it won't hurt to ask."

As Susana had predicted, her parents were happy to extend the invitation. So, after lab the next day, Chris invited him to join them for Thanksgiving dinner. "It's about a seven-hour drive to LA, but you can go down with us if you'd like. Actually, you'd be doing me a big favor," he added with a conspiratorial grin. "I could use a non-Spanish speaker around."

Silence fell, broken only by the sound of running water and the clanking of the instruments they were cleaning. Interpreting this as a prejudiced Lester working up the courage to refuse, Chris's irritation rose.

Finally Lester said quietly, "I don't know what to say. I'm—I really owe you an apology, to start with."

"Do you?" Chris looked up from the sink, surprised.

Lester kept his head lowered, but Chris could see that his ears were crimson. "For—for the stupid stuff I said and how I acted and—" His voice dropped to a whisper. "—and what I did to your wife when we first met."

"Ah," Chris said quietly. "I sort of thought you were too—well, that you didn't remember. In any case, apology accepted."

"I wish I'd been too drunk to remember. As it is, I remember every embarrassing word, and how controlled you were, and how she cried, and everything."

Chris turned off the water and began drying his instruments. "I won't lie to you. You scared her pretty bad. You grabbed her the same way a serial killer did last year."

Lester's hazel eyes grew wide. "Wow. H-how did she get away?"

"Our friend, Doug Damour, warned me of the attack. I got there before the guy could get her in his car, although he did break two of her fingers and stab her in the side."

"N-no wonder she was so upset." Lester said, hiding his face. "You mentioned Doug Damour. Before I met you guys, I thought he was a myth."

"Yeah," Chris said with a sigh. "A lot of people do. But we know his whole family. His son, Joshua Damour, is my running coach. I lived with him for a year and a half, so I can assure you—he's real."

Les chewed on his lip. "Chris, I-I appreciate your invitation. I really do. But I'm sure your wife wouldn't want me around."

"Actually, it was her idea. We'd both like to let bygones be bygones. You're not the first guy to do something stupid when you're plastered, you know. I've been there myself. Honestly, we'd like for you to join us. Especially me," he joked. "When my in-laws get together, they all seem to forget how to speak English."

Les snorted in laughter. "Thanks. I-I'd like to, actually. And maybe while we're there, you can answer some questions about Doug Damour?"

"Sure—talking about the Damours is one of my favorite things to do."

To: bestagent@management.com
From: companymaster@management.com
Date: 13 March 8009 M.E.
Subject: Meet me

        I've had a breakthrough on contraceptive BC-8 but require
your collaboration on the viability of a delivery system. I'll be
in SF next week. Arrange your schedule accordingly.

CHAPTER 21
BLASPHEMY

"[The beast] opened his mouth in blasphemy against God,
to blaspheme His name, His tabernacle,
and those who dwell in heaven."
Revelation 13:6, NKJV.

Susana wasn't an antsy person by nature. In fact, people often commented that she seemed to have an endless supply of patience. But not tonight. As she drove to the shopping center where she would meet Missy and her mom, Molly, Susana had to repeatedly ease up on the accelerator. It wasn't just her expectation of fun that had her so eager to arrive, although a girls' night out was always enjoyable. Nor was it simply her pleasure at being invited to share this special occasion—they would be shopping for a gown for Missy's first banquet. But her young cousin had also hinted, with a sly giggle, that she had some special news to share.

Susana thought she knew what the news would be—and she was dying to hear it. For months she had been working hard with the RAB's teen class in general, and Missy in particular. Some of her students were now on the verge of deciding to run Doug's race.

Missy, her face lit up like a billboard, waved as Susana pulled into the parking lot of the bistro where they were dining. When they met on the sidewalk Susana prompted, "Well, what's the big news?"

"News?" Missy teased. "What news?"

Playfully shaking her cousin's shoulders, Susana demanded, "Come on, don't keep me in suspense any longer."

"Go on," Molly urged her daughter with a laugh. "I think you've milked this long enough."

"Okay. I am"—Missy paused dramatically while grinning broadly— "running the race!"

"Yes!" Susana exclaimed, and bounced her way into a hug with her cousin. "I'm so excited. You're going to love it. You'll be running the Kids' Race this summer?"

"No, I've already started it," Missy said.

"In April?" Susana's brow furrowed. There were three recurring races: the regular race that began in July; the Parents' Race that started in February; and the Kids' Race, which ran through the summer. It was true that Doug sometimes designed an individualized racecourse for those who simply couldn't manage any of these three—he called it the Special Course—but a healthy teenager with a regular school schedule like Missy's wouldn't qualify for that.

"This is a new race," Molly explained. "Doug's just launched this option through the RAB that opened near campus. The start date is individualized."

"Really? How's that work?"

"Oh, it's so cool," Missy gushed. "You don't have to leave home or take off school. Instead, you run on a treadmill, and the computer tracks your mileage on a virtual racecourse. You can do however much you want for as long as you want and go whenever you want. I love it."

"I don't understand." In fact, Susana felt really puzzled. She knew about the new RAB since Vanessa was helping with the start-up. And her first impression was positive since it had even succeeded in winning George over. Still, Missy's explanation didn't mesh with what Susana knew of the race's broader goals.

"The whole point of running the race is to learn real commitment," she explained. "Whatever you don't relinquish, even your work or family, becomes a hook that will gradually pull you away from running altogether. So the race is designed to help you disconnect from everything else and learn to rely on Doug alone."

Molly shook her head and scolded, "That was a nice idea for us. But it's not very practical now. This is a new generation. They do things differently."

"The pacesetter said that the Damours have modified their expectations to reach the postmodern world," Missy added.

"And it sure seems to be working," Molly said. "These new RABs are exploding in size. New runners are enrolling in droves. Who are we to argue with success?"

"Wow," Susana breathed, wholly bewildered. It seemed so contrary to what she thought she knew. Yet it had broken through Missy's final objections to running the race, so it couldn't be bad ... could it?

🏃 🏃 🏃 🏃 🏃

Chris parked in the lot under his apartment building and grabbed his backpack. Before his car door was fully open, he heard Preston calling, "Chris—just the guy I was looking for."

He spied his friend jogging toward him as he climbed out of his pickup. "What's up, Preston?"

"Have you got a minute?"

Um, no, Chris thought. He'd had a long day. He just wanted to get home, eat dinner, and relax. He wasn't in the mood for interruptions. Nevertheless, he ditched his uncharitable reaction for a somewhat reluctant, "What can I do for you?"

"I'm on my way to a meeting about the new RAB. The pacesetter's looking for ideas about promoting it among the students, and I thought of you—you've done such a great job with the Kids' Klub."

Chris had heard that a new RAB had opened near campus—a worthwhile project that he really should support. True, he didn't have a lot of extra time, but certainly one meeting wasn't asking too much. Glancing at his watch, he said, "I haven't eaten yet."

"I'll buy you a burger on the way. Please? I know you're busy, but the committee promised me they wouldn't pressure you into more of a commitment.

It's just that your experience with starting up clubs would be really helpful at this stage."

Chris slung his backpack onto one shoulder as he mulled over Preston's request. If his friend had finally decided to become a committed runner, he should do whatever he could to support him. Besides, how long could one meeting take?

"Let me check with Susana."

As it happened, Susana wasn't even home—he'd forgotten she was going shopping with her cousin. So he hopped into Preston's car and they set off to the meeting. Shortly after they arrived, George and Vanessa also showed up. Chris scratched his head when the pacesetter introduced George as his assistant. Wasn't that rushing things a bit? After all, George had just returned to running. Still, the pacesetter undoubtedly knew what he was doing. And, as Susana had pointed out with Archie, the right kind of project could help a runner rediscover his calling. Apparently that's what had happened with George and this new RAB.

The meeting began with a videotaped message from Gabriel that the pacesetter played off a website. Preston explained that Gabriel had also recorded a number of tutorials for individual runners on topics like the dietary considerations for athletes, optimizing training time, and various types of cross-training. In one way, this seemed like a good idea—an efficient way to disseminate needed information. But Chris couldn't help comparing this impersonal method with the way he'd been taught: directly from his coach's mouth.

Unlike Susana, who had attended RABs all her life, Chris was relatively new to its inner workings, and he found the video quite informative. However, about halfway through the film, he became vaguely aware of a something's-off feeling. As he continued to watch, he narrowed the "something" down to a subtle distance in Gabriel's manner. Although he smiled and communicated easily, he didn't convey the warm, friendly manner that Chris knew from firsthand experience.

Once he identified this oddity, Chris dismissed it as inconsequential. People often get nervous on camera; any stiffness he perceived was easily explained by that.

However, at the very end of the movie, Chris noted something he could not justify as stage fright when Gabriel handed his assistant a marker. A quick transaction, granted, but the attitude on either end of it caught Chris's attention. Gabriel thrust the marker at the woman with a curt nod; the assistant kept her gaze lowered and stepped back in a motion that seemed astonishingly like a bow. The interaction resembled a king releasing a servant. Or a god dismissing a worshipper.

True, Gabriel was an important man. As the general in charge of the entire Paradisian army, he was probably the most important man in Paradisian society after the Damours. Yet Chris had never seen him behave as though he were more important than any other person, no matter what their station. And he had certainly never seen him require behavior that smacked of veneration.

The film ended, and Chris became engrossed in the committee's proceedings. Still, the mental image of that exchange—the nod, the averted gaze, the bow—stuck with him. He didn't know how to explain that interaction, and he didn't know what it meant. But it bothered him.

🏃 🏃 🏃 🏃 🏃

Over dinner the next evening, Chris echoed skeptically, "Modified their expectations to reach the postmodern world?"

Susana thought crossly that anything seemed less likely when expressed in that tone of voice. "That's what their pacesetter said," she affirmed.

Chris thoughtfully slurped down a mouthful of *pozole* and then pointed his spoon at her. "The *Manual* says Doug doesn't change. That he 'is the same yesterday and today and forever.' "

"Well, this isn't really Doug changing, is it? What's changing is the way his supporters train—a more convenient arrangement, so more people can do it."

" 'Wide is the gate and broad is the road that leads to destruction, and many enter through it. But small is the gate and narrow the road that leads to life, and only a few find it.' "

"Why are you being so negative about this? Personally, I'm glad for anything that gets Missy interested in running."

"Anything? Even if it's a counterfeit?"

Susana scowled. "Counterfeit? Why would someone counterfeit the race? Besides, if it is bogus, it's fooled even my cousin and his wife, and they've been running a lot longer than you have."

"Doesn't the *Manual* warn us that there will be false teachings designed to deceive even the elect?" Chris tore up a tortilla and scattered the pieces in his soup.

Like a gringo, she thought irritably.

But then, he was a gringo; how else would he eat tortillas? The fact that it annoyed her only demonstrated how ill-tempered she was. Furthermore, it wasn't his fault that her own misgivings about Missy's announcement had made her cranky. Nor was it his fault that she'd been hoping he'd only point out positive aspects rather than discerning the new RAB's shortcomings so faithfully. And she couldn't honestly accuse him of being close-minded or jumping to conclusions; he had listened closely to her full account.

She took a sip of her juice and consciously relaxed her shoulders, determined to be less confrontational.

"Isn't it odd that Doug hasn't even mentioned this to us?" he said, apparently unaware of her simmering petulance. "A new race—that's big news. I'd expect everyone in the RAB to be talking about it."

"That's true—although we do miss the announcements during Second Service when we're detained in our First Service classes. Maybe we just didn't hear it."

"I suppose that's possible. But why would Doug go to all the trouble of working out a Special Course for Les if he could just rack up miles on a treadmill? It doesn't square."

Susana frowned, unable to conjure up a reasonable answer to that point.

"Anyway, how could running on a machine prepare people to live on Paradise Island? How would that teach the same lessons we learned on a country-wide racecourse? You're the one who taught me the importance of surrendering everything when you follow Doug. What are these runners surrendering?"

She swished her spoon around in her bowl, having suddenly lost her appetite. "Nothing, I suppose ..."

Chris was sounding more sure of himself as the conversation progressed—whereas her confidence was dwindling rapidly. She so wanted to believe that Missy was on the right path. Yet if she wasn't—if her cousin had been tricked into joining some kind of worthless, or even dangerous, cult—then she needed to warn her.

Chris was staring intently into his bowl as if reading hominy like tealeaves. Finally he shook his head. "There's something wrong about this. I think we'd better talk to Doug."

However, when they asked Doug about it, he merely said, "Maybe y'all should check it out for yourselves."

So ... the place wasn't *a* new RAB; it was *the* New-RAB. And, from her very first glimpse, Susana wasn't at all sure the two institutions were related—even though she desperately wanted to believe they were for Missy's sake. In the place of a simple, unpretentious sign announcing "Runners' Assemblies Building," a neon billboard shouted "New-RAB—Something for Everyone!" Inside, rather than a peaceful meeting hall where friends discussed ways of improving their relationships with Doug, they found a noisy gym where people ran on treadmills. Still, many of those in attendance were legitimate runners, individuals who had finished the race and had trophies to prove it. Some even came from the very RAB that Chris and Susana attended.

"How cool is this?" Missy gushed as she showed them into the main hall. "See—the computer even shows scenery from your virtual route on the regular racecourse."

"But the whole purpose of a RAB is to interact with other runners," Chris said. "That way you continue to learn about Doug and about living life his way, and you can find running partners who encourage you to keep training. How does running in this big, noisy room encourage communion with him or fellowship with other runners?"

"Oh, people can still do that if they want to," Molly said. "See?" She pointed to a treadmill where the runner, instead of watching the virtual scenery of his route, had chosen to view a DVD in which Gabriel discussed applying the principles of running to the real world.

Preston joined their group about this time, and Susana was shocked to see that he wore a nametag identifying him as an assistant pacesetter. He hadn't even run the race; how could he possibly be a leader of the assembly—a role model for her young cousin?

Missy set off to a class for new runners, and Preston took over the duties of tour guide. Things only became more confusing from there. He conducted them through several rooms where people worked out in an indoor pool, on stair climbers, stationary bikes, elliptical trainers, and other machines. "For those who don't like running," Preston explained, "the computer converts the energy expended in these other activities into the equivalent of miles run."

"So you can be a runner and never run?" Chris asked incredulously.

"You're being close-minded, Chris," Preston objected. "You can gain the same health benefits from other sports, you know."

"But there's more to running than its health benefits," Chris persisted. "How can you commune with Doug in this noisy environment?"

"I understand what you mean, Chris," Molly said. "For those of us who took the trouble to run the race the old-fashioned way, all this stuff seems like cheating. But I figure it's up to the Damours to decide how they want to run their show. The world has changed, and not everyone finds the more conservative programs at the traditional RABs useful. Besides, if this helps to qualify more people to live on the island, who am I to object?"

"But there's not even a meeting place," Chris said. "Isn't that the whole idea of a Runners' *Assemblies* Building?"

"Yeah, it's true they don't have a general meeting like our traditional Second Service," Molly said. "But they do have focus groups. It's like what we do for First Service—they split up by age and study different topics in small groups. And that makes good sense; the small group format is more effective for learning."

"Those groups are beginning now," Preston noted. "Why don't you sit in on one and see what you think?"

They found George and Vanessa heading to a group on marriage enrichment, so they joined them. On the way, Susana asked Vanessa about Preston being an assistant pacesetter. A troubled frown crossed her friend's face. Glancing toward her husband, deep in conversation with Chris, she whispered, "Suze, please don't voice such intolerant opinions around George. That exclusionary attitude is part of what kept him out of the RAB for so long."

"But I didn't mean—"

"I know you didn't, but you sound like Preston is a second-class citizen just because he hasn't run the race. He's still been a lifelong member of the RABs, you know, and he supports them financially. The pacesetter here feels that we need a wide range of people in leadership. That way we can develop a broad platform from which to appeal to non-runners too. And I agree with him. In this day and age, we need to be more accepting of people, not less so."

A flush warmed Susana's face and left her to speechlessly follow her indignant friend into the classroom. Yet, even with Vanessa's rebuke ringing in her ears, Susana still found herself balking at the atmosphere in the study group. To start with, the group's teacher never opened a *Manual*. In fact, the only *Manuals* in the room were those that she and Chris had brought. What's more, the teaching itself made her uncomfortable. Oh, there were some good ideas, she had to admit, but other ideas were just—well, wrong. She didn't mean to be critical, but there was no other word for it. For instance, the teacher claimed that the expectations of marriage, including sexual exclusivity, were "flexible." "As long as the couple agrees," he said, "anything goes. Doug wants life to be a liberating, joyful adventure, not a confining experience." He even quoted the *Manual* on that: "Everything is permissible."

When Chris interrupted with the rest of the sentence—"But not everything is beneficial"—the teacher snapped his fingers. "Exactly. Not everything is beneficial for every couple. That's why it's so important that you talk it over and do only what you're both comfortable with."

As they made their way down the hallway afterward, Susana observed, "No one has a *Runner's Manual*."

"They keep one in a central location so people don't have to carry their own," George said. "Here, I'll show you."

He led them to a *Manual* on a table in the lobby. Although it was freely accessible to anyone, it looked as though it was rarely used. What's more, as Susana flipped through it she realized a few sections were missing. "Where's the section on the origin of life? And most of the chapter, 'The Book of the Law,' is gone, too."

"Yes, the invalid parts have been edited out," Vanessa explained. "You know, so you don't get bogged down with the passages that are obsolete or don't apply to our culture."

"Truth never becomes obsolete," Chris said.

Susana added, "The *Manual* says, 'The sum of his word is truth, and every one of his righteous ordinances is everlasting.' "

Vanessa shrugged to George, "Some people are just afraid of change."

"On the other hand," Chris said, "the *Manual* warns us that false teachers and false prophets will try to trick us into believing error to draw us away from Doug. It also says we should test new ideas by the *Manual*, and, if they don't measure up to it, we'll know they're wrong."

Preston, who had just rejoined them, challenged, "So you're questioning this method of following Doug—the whole New-RAB movement—just because it's different from how you read the *Manual*? That sounds awfully narrow-minded, even conceited. Are you so sure of your interpretations? Maybe you should talk to the Damours if you disagree with how they're running things."

"Have you talked to them?" Chris countered, and Susana subconsciously moved away from them. She hated arguments.

"Well, not them, exactly," Preston admitted, "but their agent."

Chris's eyebrows shot up. "Doug's agent? Why don't you just talk to Doug?"

"You do have a transmitter, right?" Susana asked.

"Of course," Preston said. "It's at home."

"At home?" Chris asked. "What good is it there?"

"I use it when I want to," Preston said defensively. "But here's the pacesetter—he's got one of the new transmitters."

Chris shot Susana a sidelong glance in which she read his question: *A new transmitter too? When did all this happen?*

The pacesetter, a portly man named Owen, came over and, once filled in on the conversation, pulled a transmitter from his shirt.

"That doesn't look like our transmitters," Chris noted. The transmitters that he, Susana, George, and Vanessa wore were about the size of a quarter while Owen's was considerably larger. "It doesn't look like it's made of *tsuma*, either."

"It's not," Owen said. "Yours is the original model. The New-RABs are growing so fast that the factory on the island has been overwhelmed by the demand. So they opened another factory off the island to speed up production. And, since *tsuma* is only available on Paradise Island, they utilize different materials and technology. It's fully functional, though."

Remembering the transmitter prop Camille had worn to deceive them, Susana asked, "Can you activate it?"

"Sure." Owen activated his device, and a British-accented male voice answered. Owen carried on a brief conversation with the man and then logged off. "See—works just fine."

"Except you're not connecting to any of the Damours," Chris said.

"Of course not," Preston replied irritably. "Don't you understand? The whole system's been overwhelmed since the New-RABs have mushroomed. There's no way the Damours could keep up with it themselves."

"Now, now, son," Owen cajoled in a fatherly tone. "A little skepticism never hurt anyone." Turning to Chris, he explained, "The Damours have just recruited some of the other Paradisians to help out—that's all."

When Chris glanced at Susana, she saw amusement in his eye, but she didn't understand why. For her part, she was just confused. Could Doug really have so many runners that he needed help keeping up with them?

That evening, Chris and Susana called Doug back to tell him they'd checked out the new place. Chris summarized, "We're more confused than ever, Doug. There are so many differences between this New-RAB and what we thought we knew from the *Manual*."

"I'm glad y'all noticed those discrepancies," Doug said.

"Noticed them?" Chris said. "They'd be hard to miss. This New-RAB doesn't seem anything like your regular RABs."

"That's 'cause they aren't mine," Doug said flatly.

"What?" Susana exclaimed. "Aren't you the head of all the RABs?"

"Actually, that's Josh. But the upstarts they're calling the New-RABs are Stan's latest attempt to confuse folks. They've got nothin' to do with us."

"But my cousins think they do," Susana whined. "So do Vanessa and George, and—"

"Many others," Doug summarized gravely. "And that number'll grow like wildfire before the Final Battle."

"But we saw a bunch of runners from your RABs there," she pressed.

"I know, little filly. There's no reason they should be deceived—the truth's plain as day in the *Manual*. But, for various reasons, those runners have decided to sample the grass on the other side. Even runners aren't immune to the opinions of their friends. That's just one reason why you need to let me help you decide whom to befriend and how closely to let each one into your life."

Was it her imagination, or had Doug said that with a finger pointed in her direction?

"Doug," Chris said. "The new members have different transmitters. They don't look like ours, but they are functional. They say they're connecting to 'agents.' "

"They are."

Chris glanced at Susana with a wary look. "As in Stan's agents?"

"Yep. They'll tell some truths to convince the gullible that they're working with me. They'll even quote the *Manual* when it suits 'em. But they also mix in some lies. The combination is quite effective in leadin' folks astray."

"Just like the teacher did in the focus group today," Susana reflected.

"That's right. The transmitters let agents become more efficient. They can influence folks without having to be right at their side."

This reminded Susana of Preston's claim that Doug had been overwhelmed by the extra runners. "Doug, how do you do it? How do you manage to personally talk to all of your runners, plus run your country, plus run your business? I mean, it just seems impossible."

"And yet you know from experience that it's not, don't you?"

"Yes. I don't mean that I doubt you," she hurried to explain. "I just don't understand it."

"Well, I don't rightly expect you can understand it until we meet. Even then, many of my abilities will seem strange to you. Stan's people take advantage of that, causing those prone to doubt to disbelieve my word because they can't comprehend my abilities. You see, there's a difference both in the capacities of our brains and in how they work. Your brain is finite, child, and generally able to perform only one cognitive function at a time. My brain is infinite and can perform any number of functions simultaneously. For example, I'm currently talking to 34,964,073 people by transmitters, and I'm speaking to Gabriel in person."

"Wow. How many mouths do you have?"

Doug chuckled. "Just one, little filly—the one I'm using to talk to Gabriel. I don't need a mouth to speak via the transmitters."

"Oh." Susana sat blinking in wide-eyed astonishment.

"Doug, that reminds me," Chris said. "They've got a bunch of DVDs recorded by Gabriel, only he acts kind of strange on them."

"That's 'cause it's not him, son. It's Stan."

Chris nodded, as though he'd already suspected this, but Susana exclaimed, "What? Poor Missy!"

"What can we do to straighten out our friends and relatives who are getting into this New-RAB revival?" Chris asked.

"Keep on speaking truth to anyone who will listen, just like we've been doing for some 6,000 years now. For the sincere seeker, truth is all that's needed."

After they logged off, Susana said, "Poor Missy. This New-RAB idea is a particularly cruel trick."

"Stan's making people think they're running the race when they're not," Chris agreed with a nod.

"Yeah, but it's more than that. If ever a generation needed time reserved for recuperating and recharging from the busyness of life, it's this one. And as Doug planned it, the Rest Day does just that. It gives us a little refuge in time where we can refocus our priorities and realign our pursuits to Doug's master plan."

"I see what you mean. The New-RAB program has no provision for that. People come whenever they want, and they come to exercise, not restore. So neither body nor soul gets rejuvenated. The basic message and intent of the Rest Day is lost."

"I suppose that maintaining the hectic lifestyle contributes to keeping people deceived. How can they recognize the discrepancies if they're too busy to reflect?"

"To make matters worse, Stan's agents tell them they can't talk to Doug directly."

"That's right," she cried indignantly. "What kind of impression does that give of Doug?"

"Still, like Doug said, the truth is plain in the *Manual*. Over and over, he invites us to approach him and get to know him."

"But, Chris, so many people are being deceived. Even my own cousin and his wife."

"Yeah, that's scary. We should invite them over for dinner after next week's services and talk to them about what we've learned."

"Oh, yes—let's do. I'm sure they'll see the problems once they're spotlighted for them."

Chris shook his head pensively. "We should take this as a warning, Suze. If solid, lifelong runners like them can be tricked, so can we. As Aedan explained it to me, we're already at a disadvantage. Having been born into *kanuf*, Stan's counterfeits are naturally intriguing to us. Instead of running from his deceptions, our tendency is to flirt with them. And then it dulls our ability to perceive error, too. I guess that's how people come to the point of openly accepting *kanuf*, without even being ashamed of it."

" 'Designed to deceive, if possible, even the elect.' " Susana shuddered at the thought.

"We simply can't trust ourselves," he said thoughtfully. "Our only protection is our connection with Doug."

To: bestagent@management.com
From: IT-12@management.com
Date: 4 May 8009 M.E.
Subject: KK Website

   What the #$&! is going on out there? I've been seeing great results from my efforts on the KK website until this last week. Now my attacks are suddenly being countered almost immediately. I'm pulling my hair out here!

To: IT-12@management.com
Cc: companymaster@management.com
From: bestagent@management.com
Date: 4 May 8009 M.E.
Subject: Re: KK Website

   How dare you address me in this manner. To treat the bearer of Company Master's signet ring with such impertinence is to disrespect Company Master himself. Therefore, I am referring this infraction directly to him. You may expect a communication from him or his representative shortly.
   To answer your legitimate concern (however crudely expressed): KK has added new runner L.S. to its administrative staff. His undergraduate degree is in computer science, and he has extraordinary abilities in this area. Entity Master is aware of the problem and has assigned MA-913 to L.S.
   Your solution: Discontinue your policy of continuous attack in favor of intermittent strikes. L.S. will assume the storm is over and grow complacent, thereby becoming more vulnerable to your next assault. For maximum effect, coordinate with MA-913 to time your strikes when L.S. has the least time to block them. If you are too dim-witted to best L.S., refer the case to your supervisor.

To: IT-12@management.com
From: companymaster@management.com
Date: 4 May 8009 M.E.
Subject: Re: KK Website

   My office. Now.

CHAPTER 22

SATAN'S THRONE

*" 'I know your works, and where you dwell, where Satan's throne is.
And you hold fast to My name, and did not deny My faith.' "*
Revelation 2:13, NKJV.

Susana arrived after the Kids' Klub meeting had started, having stopped to pick up some needed supplies. As she pulled into the loading zone near the RAB's gymnasium, she noted the full parking lot with satisfaction. Not only had this Kids' Klub grown dramatically in size during the seven months since Chris took over the leadership, it had also altered radically in attitude. It was now a strong, unified, and vigorous organization.

When she entered the building, her satisfaction swelled into a sense of joyful accomplishment, the kind that comes from seeing one's hard work bear fruit. The large group had already completed its opening meeting and split into several small groups, most of which were now scattered around in the gymnasium. The room buzzed with animated conversations between the adults and kids.

As she scanned the energetic mix for someone to help her unload the car, her gaze lingered on individuals whose lives had been improved by this club. Several of the kids she saw had already signed up for the Kids' Race. Efraím had become a dependable right arm for Chris, as well as a close friend. The relationship they had forged in these few months might well last a lifetime.

Archie, who was building a remote control airplane with some kids, had proven invaluable at both the local and global levels. He'd recently been through a particularly rough patch after being suddenly laid off from his longtime teaching position. Yet his renewed faith in Doug had remained strong. As it turned out, the timing couldn't have been better, for his freedom was exactly what the club had needed. He ended up becoming the global organization's first paid employee, and his focused labor had helped the club expand as never before.

In the far corner, Susana caught sight of Lester teaching African-American history to a group of children. One aspect of the Special Course that Doug had designed for him consisted of teaching interested Kids' Klub members about the history of various ethnic groups—an assignment that had caused Chris to burst into laughter when he heard of it. The assignment not only helped Lester overcome his prejudices, but also, by putting him in the role of a respected teacher, helped to stabilize his shaky self-esteem. His knowledge of computers had also contributed to the club in a substantial way. He'd brought much relief to its leaders when he single-handedly corrected the aggravating and time-consuming problems they'd been having with the Kids' Klub website.

And there was Chris, teaching a group of new runners. To encourage his members in continued training, Doug sponsored an ultramarathon in different locations every year. Taking a cue from this plan, the Kids' Klub hosted a 5k run/walk for the kids every six months. If the group around Chris was any indication, that race would be well-attended and bursting with enthusiasm.

As she drew closer to the group, she heard Chris answer one boy, "Why weight training? Because improving muscle strength helps us run better—faster, longer, more safely. See, choosing to be one of Doug's runners affects every part of our lives. We eat healthfully so we can run better. We avoid harmful substances like drugs and tobacco so we can run better. Running faithfully, in turn, rewards us with better health and endurance. And when our bodies are healthy, our minds work better, so even our grades improve. The mind is also how we connect to Doug. Everything—every facet of our lives—is interrelated."

A gentle smile came to her face. He had a knack for talking to kids, and their appreciation for both his interest and his candor was apparent.

Passing Chris's group, she next saw Missy and several other young teens huddled over a chessboard. Once presented with the discrepancies in the New-RAB teachings, Missy and her parents had completely severed their relationship with it. Nevertheless, Missy had stuck by her decision to run the race and would do that this summer. It warmed Susana's heart to see the joy in her young cousin's eyes.

However, when Susana noticed the volunteer leading Missy's group, she did a double take. George Strong—what was he doing here? He'd never even expressed an interest in joining the Kids' Klub. When had his name been presented to Doug as a potential volunteer?

As she advanced within earshot, her confusion grew. "Sex before marriage?" George was saying. "Sure, that's fine, too—as long as each person is mature and committed to the relationship."

"Really?" asked Missy, obviously confused. "My parents say it's not."

"Some parents are pretty old-fashioned," George responded, and Susana had to stifle a shocked gasp. "See, the Laws were written a long time ago and need to be interpreted within the cultural context of their day. Why, even in the *Manual* itself, you'll find that the later teachings invalidate some of the earlier precepts."

Susana felt like screaming. Was there no end to the lies Missy would be bombarded with—even through other runners? The poor child hadn't even started the race yet.

She took a breath to bring her anger under control. "George?"

He spun to her, obviously startled. But when his blue gaze hardened into icy daggers, an irrational, yet desperately urgent, impression flooded through her: She—and these children—were in mortal danger.

"Um—" She swallowed, her throat suddenly dry, her heart racing. "W-would you mind unloading some boxes from my car? They're too heavy for me. I can fill in here."

For just an instant, he stared into her with a keenness that sent a physical chill through her. In that moment, she seemed to be looking death itself in the eye. Her joy of accomplishment, her gratitude at being part of such a grand organization—all of the positive emotions she'd been experiencing—came to a rude, juddering halt. Life itself seemed frozen in his glare.

Then, in an eye blink, his entire mien changed. With a broad smile, he bounced up. "Sure, Susana. Happy to help."

The abruptness of the change might have made her doubt that she'd seen that fierce expression at all. She wanted to doubt it. Yet, even now, gooseflesh covered her arms.

She returned a shaky smile as she handed him her car keys. Avoiding his eyes, she watched the keys clink against a ring on his left pinky finger. The large oval emerald in an ornate gold setting had drawn her attention before. Not only was it easily the most elaborate class ring she'd ever seen, but its striking beauty eclipsed the simple gold wedding band on the adjacent finger. She'd always thought the contrast made the wedding ring look like an unhappy, unloved stepchild.

George headed out to the parking lot, and she sat down in the chair he'd vacated. Taking a deep breath, she willed herself back to the real world. Of course she'd imagined that vicious look. He was startled, that's all. George was a full-fledged runner, a member of the RAB, Chris's classmate, and her good friend's husband; what possible reason would he have to harm them? And over a mere interruption? What a ridiculous idea.

She glanced around the circle of kids to see them all watching her quizzically, as if they'd perceived her momentary lapse into insanity and didn't know what to make of it. She flashed another smile (less shaky this time), took another calming breath, and then set about to undo George's damage.

"Sometimes," she said carefully, "people who don't fully understand the *Manual* can be led astray by popular ideas. In trying to mesh worldly thinking with Doug's principles, they can come up with some dangerous compromises."

"Like what Mr. Strong just said?" Missy asked.

"Yes," Susana answered firmly. "It's true that the latter parts of the *Manual* say some earlier sections are obsolete. But those parts all have to do with traditions and ceremonial laws, never Doug's Ten Laws. Those ten are actual laws—like the law of gravity. It's just like it says in the Songbook, 'Your laws remain true today. Your decrees never change. All your just laws will stand forever.' We can argue with those laws, we can even convince ourselves they're old-fashioned, but we'll still suffer the consequences when we violate them. It's like jumping off a building. It doesn't matter if you believe in gravity or not, you'll still fall."

Thankfully, the task she'd assigned George took a while. For, as she continued to explore what other tales he'd been telling these impressionable youngsters, it took her the rest of the session to rebut them.

Afterward, she found Chris and told him what had happened. "What's he doing here, anyway?" she asked. "Did Doug approve him as a volunteer?"

"I didn't even think of calling Doug," Chris admitted. "It all happened so quickly. Just as I was leaving the lab, I got a call from the MacDonalds saying that neither of them could make it tonight. George was there, offered to help out, and hopped into the car with me. Honestly, I was so relieved to have the help, I didn't even think twice about it."

"That's understandable, but I'm not sure we can call his contribution 'helping.'"

When they returned home, Chris had to dash right off to his study group. "I'll be home by eleven," he said on his way out. Feeling vaguely uncomfortable, Susana had trouble concentrating on her studies. It must have been fatigue because at one point she laid her head down on her arms and drifted off to sleep, right there on her desk.

The weird thing was that George intruded into her dreams, chasing her and the group of children down the hallway of her apartment building while literal daggers shot from his gleaming blue eyes. She herded the screaming children into her apartment and locked the door, but a green laser from George's opulent class ring began to cut around the doorknob. He was charging through the door when she jerked awake.

Panting heavily, she rushed to the door of her apartment. Of course, it was securely locked. No kids needed protecting, and nothing was out of place. Her heart rate was beginning to slow when she glanced at the clock and realized that it was 11:05 p.m. Hadn't Chris said he'd be home by 11:00? And wasn't George in his study group?

It was preposterous. She knew it was. Nevertheless, she couldn't shake the sense of dread that settled over her, and she took up a position on the balcony to watch for Chris's truck. He still wasn't home when the clock chimed the quarter-hour, so she called his cell phone. When he didn't pick up, a wave of panic swept through her. She returned to the balcony and, staring fixedly over the parking lot, whispered, "Please be Chris, please be Chris," to every pair of headlights.

When he walked in the door at 11:32 p.m., she cried, "Where have you been?"

Glancing around the apartment in alarm, he said, "What's wrong?"

"You're late!"

A frown creased his face, and he checked his watch. "Oh, I'm sorry. I didn't realize what time it was."

"Why didn't you answer your phone?"

"I didn't?" He pulled it from his pocket and groaned. "Sorry—I forgot to turn the ringer back on." Scanning her face with obvious concern, he asked, "Were you really worried? I'm only a few minutes late."

"Of course, I was worried!" What she'd intended as a statement came out more like the cry of a raving lunatic.

"Suze, what's going on?" He drew her close and she, in her relief, began crying. He held her, stroking her hair, until she grew calmer. Then he tried again: "What's wrong?" This time, the fatigue from his long day rasped clearly in his voice.

"I—I had a weird dream," she admitted sheepishly. "George was chasing me and the kids. I know it's silly, but I guess it scared me."

"You seemed afraid at the Kids' Klub, too. George didn't threaten you in some way, did he?"

"No, but—I don't know, something about his look, something about … him," she finished lamely. How totally crazy she must sound.

Chris continued to hold her, and, in the refuge of his arms, she began to feel better—which meant she also began to feel really silly. She could offer no coherent reason for her strange feelings. She had to admit, her reaction was overblown and illogical. And Chris was so logical. He must think he'd married an insane woman. Actually, she was beginning to wonder about it herself.

"You haven't been sleeping enough," Chris said at last. "Maybe you're just tired. Why don't you get ready for bed. I'll make you some tea to help you relax."

"Okay," she said, wiping her face. "You're probably right. I am tired."

She made her way to the bedroom and undressed. A few minutes later, Chris came in with the tea. "Aedan's coming over. I talked to Doug, and he told me to call him."

"Why?"

"Because something's wrong and neither one of us knows what it is or what to do about it."

"But it's late."

"He said we could call anytime, remember?"

Now she really felt bad, calling Aedan out in the middle of the night, and for no real reason. Even so, as she threw on a t-shirt and jeans, she couldn't deny that a big part of her felt relieved. There was just something comforting about their pacesetter—something safe.

When Aedan arrived, Chris summarized the evening's events and Susana's reaction to them. "You know Susana, Aedan—this just isn't normal for her. She's a strong woman with a strong faith. I thought maybe she was tired, but then I remembered what you said about women's intuition and called Doug. He thought you could help."

"I'm glad you called," Aedan said sincerely. "First, let me ask—did Doug approve George's stepping in?"

"No," Chris said. "I messed up there. I was in such a hurry, and George is a runner, so …" He shrugged.

"Yeah. Been there, done that," Aedan said and turned to Susana. "I'm going to ask you a question that may be hard for you to answer. You have the admirable quality of seeing the good in people, and you're reluctant to speak ill of them. That's another wonderful quality. In fact, I wish all runners were so loath to gossip. But I need you to tell me what you think of George Strong—the unedited version, your honest opinion."

"Okay." She licked her dry lips. "He's, um, really smart—"

"Unedited, Suze," Chris said with a grin.

She ducked her head as warmth flooded her cheeks, and Chris slipped a finger under her chin, lifting her gaze to his. "You have an amazing gift of seeing people for who they really are," he said tenderly. "But you want so badly to see people as good that you tend not to trust your instincts when they tell you someone isn't so good. Trust your intuition, Suze. Tell Aedan what that's telling you."

She nodded tentatively and tried to comply. However, she found it hard to put her feelings into words. "Cold," she finally murmured.

"Cold?" Aedan repeated.

"Hard," she tried again. "Like—like he could do anything to anybody. Like you wish he wouldn't walk behind you because you're never quite sure what he might do. Like if I were married to him, I'd be afraid he'd strangle me in my sleep."

She immediately felt bad. She hadn't meant to be so unkind; she was just trying to express feelings that were hard to put into words. So she quickly added, "I'm sorry. That's not fair. I've never seen him do anything bad at all. And yet—"

"Please go ahead," Aedan prompted when she cut herself off.

"Well, he doesn't do anything bad, but somehow he seems to promote, even thrive on, other people's doubt and discord. He says things in a way that encourages people toward a mean-spirited view of those around them. He questions Doug—not overtly, really, but subtly. When people are discouraged, his influence is toward unbelief instead of trust. And when people are at odds, he seems to a get a weird satisfaction out of magnifying their differences rather than helping them mend things."

"Wow," Chris breathed. "She's right. I never recognized it before, but that's him exactly. It's subtle—I mean, he's courteous, he acts friendly and cheerful—but he still has a persistently negative influence on the people around him."

"You're saying he prefers to see the dark side of things—to cherish it, even—rather than expressing hope and faith," Aedan summarized.

"Yes," Susana said.

"And yet ..." Aedan fell silent, thoughtfully stroking his newly grown mustache. "A medical student? Married? Here full time?"

"Yeah, he is," Chris said. "They live in this building."

"Very strange." Aedan continued stroking his mustache. "Tell me, have either of you ever seen that look or had that feeling around any other person?"

"No," Chris said slowly. "I don't think—"

"Yes," Susana said suddenly. "Stan and Camille—that same hard, cold feeling." Bewildered, she added, "At least when I first met her. Later, I didn't notice it."

"Did you discover a dart later?" Aedan asked.

"Yes."

"Then that makes sense. A side effect of their poisons is to blunt our ability to recognize *kanuf*. Still ..." Aedan gave his head a shake and mumbled, "Very strange," as he activated his transmitter.

"Howdy, Aedan," came Doug's voice. "I see you're in the Strider's apartment. How are things there?"

"Safe and secure, Doug," Aedan said. "But I think Susana's uncovered an agent—"

"Agent?" the couple exclaimed together.

"—although he's taken on a most unusual cover if so," Aedan continued. "He's here full-time. He's even married."

"What does he call himself?" Doug asked.

"George Strong. He's in Chris's class."

Doug drew a deep breath in and out. "Well," he said slowly, as though he regretted having to divulge the information, "it looks like y'all have found the snake in the grass."

Susana glanced at Chris, who looked as confused as she felt. "You mean you already knew?"

"Yes," Doug said. "I've known since Stan arranged George's death."

"His death?" Chris exclaimed. "I don't think you understand. He's not dead. He's in my class."

"Yes, the real George Strong was supposed to be in your class," Doug said. "He was a committed runner who was killed by a drunk driver last summer. The agent then took over George's life and got married in order to be close to y'all."

Susana gasped. "Poor Vanessa."

"Are you sure, Doug?" Chris still looked dubious. "This guy's about six-foot-two, white, average build, looks like he's in his early forties, curly black hair with some gray, and bright blue eyes. He's a smart guy, top of the class. He says he's from New York and used to work as a chemist in a pharmaceutical company."

"Yep—nice lookin' feller with a long scar on his left forearm and a distinctive emerald signet ring."

Aedan's eyes widened in obvious alarm. Meanwhile, Chris and Susana exchanged another surprised look and exclaimed together, "Yeah."

"George Strong was a single student from Maine, a green-eyed blond, short and slim." Doug paused before adding sadly, "One of nicest fellers you could ever meet."

"What's this agent's position in the organization?" Aedan asked, but his tone hinted that he already suspected the answer.

"He's one of Stan's research assistants. Sean never met him."

"Who's Sean?" Chris asked.

Aedan pursed his lips tentatively. "Doug?"

"Go ahead," Doug said.

"Sean was my brother," Aedan answered. "He worked for Camille for many years before Doug helped him escape."

"An operative?" Susana asked.

"No, an operative is someone who's been manipulated into helping Stan without knowing what he's really doing. My brother was an associate—he helped Stan for money, knowing exactly who he was working for. Stan and Camille recruit their associates up front for their particular talents, and they pay them very well."

"And your brother quit?"

"Yes, but that's not allowed. He only managed it with Doug's help. Then he devoted his life to educating our side about their tactics, how to identify agents, and so forth."

"Priceless work done by a brave man," Doug said.

"Thank you, Doug." Aedan's voice betrayed the same sorrow Susana had noticed when they first talked about Camille's List several months ago, and she suddenly understood: Aedan's brother had been on that list—the same one Chris was on—and the list had something to do with his death.

She reached for Chris's hand as if for a lifeline. When he looked at her quizzically, she tried to smile reassuringly. From his expression, she wasn't very convincing.

"So what's this agent's name?" Chris asked.

"I think it'll be better if y'all don't know that," Doug said. "You don't want to call him by his real name accidentally. It's gonna be hard enough now, just knowin' what he really is."

"You mean—" Chris frowned. "I'm not sure I understand. Are you saying you don't want him exposed?"

"That's right," Doug said. "If you let on that you know who he is, he's just gonna show up again in another role where you won't recognize him. This way, you'll at least know who your enemy is."

"So we're supposed to—what, stay friends with him?" Susana tightened her grip on Chris's hand. She understood staying friends with Vanessa. She especially needed encouragement if she was living with an agent, and Doug would want her to support her friend. But hang around with George?

"You've heard the saying, 'Keep your friends close and your enemies closer'?" Aedan said. "There's a place for that."

"Aedan's right on the mark," Doug said. "I don't usually recommend getting familiar with Stan's crew, and you sure don't have to hang on him like a flea on a dog, but you also don't want to let on that you know who he is. You might even consider this a blessing. Stan's agents are always around to threaten my runners, but, because they don't know who they are, runners sometimes forget and get lulled into complacence. Y'all will have George to remind you not to grow careless."

"Doug," Aedan said hesitantly, "Is this the research assistant they call 'Best Agent'?"

"Yes. Sean's mentioned him, then?"

"Yes. He never met him, but he knew of him."

Aedan fell silent while Doug chatted with Chris and Susana, reminding them of the need to stay in close touch with him, and of his promises for strength and wisdom. By the time they ended the conversation and Aedan was preparing to leave, Susana would have felt much better—except for Aedan's sudden reticence to talk. She needed to know more about Camille's List, about Aedan's brother, and about what it all meant for her husband. At the same time, she was afraid to know. And she sure wasn't going to ask those questions in front of Chris.

But Aedan himself provided the solution. As he was leaving, he asked Chris, "Would you mind if I have lunch with your wife? I'll bring Julie along."

Chris seemed surprised. "Sure, Aedan." With a laugh, he added, "I trust you."

"Thank you," Aedan said. "But it's always best to 'abstain from all appearance of evil.' "

The next day, Susana met Aedan and his wife at a quiet little café where they settled into a secluded corner booth. True to his direct, no-nonsense self, Aedan got right to the point.

"Susana, I suggested this meeting because I got the feeling you had some questions you didn't want to discuss in front of Chris. And I was afraid you might think you were bothering me if you asked to talk to me privately."

"Thank you. I—I do have some questions," she said hesitantly. "I'm just not sure I want to know the answers."

"These situations can be very difficult," Julie said sympathetically. "In fact, they can be more stressful for the spouses than for the Targets themselves."

"Yeah, I—" Susana paused, trying to formulate her feelings into words. "I guess I mostly feel kind of lost. To start with, I don't understand what Chris has done to get on this List. And I don't know what it means or how it's different than being a Target."

"A Target is someone Moden Industries identifies as a threat." Aedan said, "Someone who's liable to interfere with their plans in a measurable way. They're very perceptive judges of character and personality and are exceptionally good at predicting who's likely to cause problems for them. Figuring out why they've marked Chris as a threat could be tricky, but, since they also targeted his father, it's fair to assume that at least part of the reason has to do with the Kids' Klub. There may be more to it—they've gone to unusual lengths here."

"What do you mean? What lengths?"

"Well, first of all, the agent they've assigned to him is their very best man. In fact, he's legendary within their ranks, second only to Stan and Camille. He even wears Stan's signet ring. In retrospect, I should have recognized his so-called 'class ring' as the one Sean described."

"What does the signet ring mean?"

"It means that Stan holds this man in such high esteem that he's given him the authority to act on his behalf. There are only three people in the entire company with that kind of power."

"You mentioned a title—'Best Agent'?"

"Yes. He's held that designation for centuries—the only person to do so. He's famous for recruiting both Nero and Darwin and he coordinated the efforts against the seven RABs of the *Manual's* last chapter."

"Wow." Susana digested this for a moment. "You said, 'First of all.' What else?"

"As far as I know, they've never planted an agent on a Subject full time before. See, agents generally retain their regular duties in the organization and carry out their assignments on the side—almost like moonlighting. But George has been relieved of all his usual duties and planted in a permanent, full-time position. He's even married—"

"Poor Vanessa. I can't imagine being married to one of Stan's agents."

"Yes," Aedan said thoughtfully. "That's certainly troubling. But the agents can be very convincing. They're all top-notch actors."

" 'To deceive even the elect, if it were possible.' Oh, Aedan, I have to tell her who he is."

"No!" He exclaimed, wide-eyed. "No, Susana, promise me you won't. Doug was very adamant about this. If George's cover is blown, it could be dangerous. It could even be lethal for Vanessa. Remember what you said about feeling that he could strangle his wife in her sleep?"

"Oh!" Susana clapped a hand over her mouth. "Then I won't say anything—I would never do anything to endanger her."

"You'll have to step very carefully, letting Doug lead the way. Trust him to protect all of his runners." He hesitated before adding, "But also understand that every individual exercises free choice. I know that Doug would not have allowed his runner to marry an agent without trying to warn her away from him. She must have been 'blinded by love,' as they say and ignored Doug's warnings."

Susana nodded sadly. She knew it had been a whirlwind romance; Vanessa had married George within a week of meeting him. So Aedan's assessment was undoubtedly right. Yes, she would have to be very careful indeed not to divulge such a discovery to her friend, but she certainly couldn't back away from the friendship now. Doug would never want her to abandon her to such a situation.

"So what does all this mean for Chris?" she asked.

"Susana, they've taken measures here that are at least unusual, if not wholly unprecedented." He glanced at Julie as he drew in a breath. "I think it means that Chris has become the prime Target for their agency, like being number one on their most wanted list."

Susana stared at him in horror. "So that's what the List of whatever-you-called-it is?" she whispered. "A list of higher priority Targets?"

"List of Guerdon," he said, spelling the word. "It's an old term that reflects the idea of needing to recompense someone, of owing them a reward—but they often imbue words with atypical meanings to disguise their true intent. And no, a List of Guerdon isn't the same as a list of Targets."

"How is it different?"

"Targeting someone is a tactical move. It directs resources at him to prevent him from fulfilling his work for Doug. In one sense, all runners fall in this category—we each have a unique work to do, and Moden Industries would prefer that we didn't accomplish it. But some people stand out—Moses, Elijah, John the Baptist, and so on. Those are the ones specifically marked as Targets."

"And the List of Guerdon?" This was weird, having to pull information out of Aedan like this.

Aedan looked to his wife, who said, "You need to tell her, dear. Didn't Doug say to answer all her questions?"

"He did," he agreed with a nod. Drawing in a deep breath, he said carefully, "The List of Guerdon is a list of individuals singled out for punishment—for revenge. That generally includes death."

Susana's heart began pounding. Punishment *including* death? Did that mean ...?

"I have an active imagination," she said softly. "Sometimes I imagine things worse than they really are."

Aedan looked away, his expression sober, and muttered, "Not possible here."

Placing a hand on Susana's arm, Julie explained, "Susana, Moden Industries is made up of people who hate Doug and his runners with a passion you and I would find hard to understand. They enjoy causing runners pain because it brings Doug pain. One man in particular, named—?" She looked to her husband.

"Garrick Sondem, their so-called director of security." Aedan passed a hand over his face and sighed. "He's also the world's foremost expert on torture, having spent six thousand years inventing ways to cause pain. He has degrees in medicine, pharmacology, physics, and psychology—all studied with a view to increasing his expertise."

Pausing, he added gingerly, "Susana, the point is, I sincerely doubt that you could imagine something that Dr. Sondem hasn't already invented."

Susana felt the blood drain from her face. Torture—Camille intended to torture Chris to death. That's what Aedan was trying so hard not to say.

When tears threatened to break forth, she blinked rapidly and bit her lip. Julie grasped her hand. "Susana, we know how you feel. We really do."

Looking to Aedan, Susana realized, "Your brother. Sean."

Aedan nodded. "Yes. He was on Camille's List of Guerdon for defecting. You once asked how he died. He died—" He squeezed his eyes shut as if trying to avoid seeing something awful. "—at Camille's hand."

"I'm so sorry," Susana whispered hoarsely.

"It's been hard. Particularly since—"

When his voice broke, Julie finished his thought. "In an attempt to discourage Aedan, Camille transported Sean's—well, abused remains back to his apartment. She knew Aedan was the only other one with a key, and she wanted him to find the body."

Susana clapped a hand over her mouth and looked to Aedan. How horrible! She'd sensed that his loss was a difficult one, but to find his brother in such a state? No wonder he'd had such difficulty processing it!

Silence shrouded them for several moments until Aedan cleared his throat. "My brother did a great work for Doug, even in death. Just as the blood of the ancient martyrs fueled the early spread of the RABs, my brother's testimony encouraged many of Stan's associates to ask for Doug's help in getting out. It's not easy to escape Stan's grasp once you're in so deeply, you see. Sean couldn't have anticipated that his death would have such an effect. But one day, when he sees how many eternal lives were saved, he'll be happy about it." He looked away and whispered, "All of it."

"And he left us a note," Julie added with a hopeful tone.

"Yes." Aedan's eyes lit up and his voice grew stronger as he continued. "In a safe deposit box with his will and other important papers. In that note, he told me that he suspected he would die at Camille's hands. He wanted me to know that, even though he could guess what such a death would be like, he wouldn't change a thing. He said he'd spent years undergoing torture of a different type—guilt, shame, remorse, constantly condemning himself. He talked about the life-changing effects of knowing the Damours, about daily basking in the peace that had eluded him all his life, of the joy and happiness that he savored every single day as a runner."

He paused, a joyful smile lighting his face. "He actually said he would consider it a privilege if Doug thought he was worthy to shoulder such a witness."

"But," Susana objected in a tiny voice, "I'm not sure I could bear knowing that Chris suffered such—" Tears flooded her eyes and choked away her words.

"Just because Chris is on Camille's List doesn't mean Doug will allow her to get him," Julie said gently. "But if he does, you'll get through it the same way you get through every other trial—by leaning on Doug, by relying on him for strength. Doug *is* faithful. He 'will not let us be tempted beyond what we can bear.' "

"Doug won't allow anything to happen to Chris that either of you can't bear with his help," Aedan added. "Even though you're not aware of them, his Royal Guards are always around—watching, protecting. And Doug's promise will never fail: 'In *all* things he works for the good of those who love him.' "

"Is there anything I can"—Susana shrugged helplessly—"do?"

"Surrender," Julie said at once. "Surrender Chris and his life to Doug, just as you've surrendered yourself."

"But that's different," Susana said weakly, tears now spilling unchecked down her cheeks.

Julie nodded sympathetically. "Yes, it is different—it's harder. But just as crucial."

🏃 🏃 🏃 🏃 🏃

Jané dabbed her napkin to her mouth and then furtively wiped a tear from her eye as well. Lifting a hand to signal the waitress, she asked for her check. Ordinarily she would stay behind until well after Susana had left and allow Serji to pick up the surveillance outside the café, but she could tolerate no more. Her heart ached for Susana. If she didn't leave now, she would surely burst into tears—which was not conducive to remaining inconspicuous in a public place.

After paying her check, she quietly radioed Serji and advised him to take over the surveillance. Then she ducked into the café's empty restroom. Activating the personal transmitter around her neck, she poured her heart out to Doúg. "She's so fretful, *Adu*. So frightened. Last night she awoke several times, being unable to sleep soundly. She finally resorted to cleaning the kitchen—at three o'clock in the morning."

"I know, dear one. It's difficult to watch."

"Sometimes I want to take her by the shoulders and say, Don't you realize how easy your load would be if you surrendered this worry to Doug? He would carry the burden for you and replace your restlessness with peace."

"Her mind has been affected by *kanuf* in a way that yours has not, little dove. These truths are not as clear to her."

"I wish I could do more for her."

"Who barred Taylor from approaching her when she was so vulnerable this very morning? Your job is to protect her from temptations beyond her capacity to bear, to shield her from dangers not of her own choosing. Every single day you filter out surplus attacks, thereby limiting her load and assuring that she is able to respond to our advice if she chooses to."

"Sometimes that seems so inadequate."

"Yes, I understand your yearning very well. But you and I can only do so much. We cannot make her choices for her, even when we clearly see the pain they will cause her. That is what makes your job—both of our jobs—so difficult. But I appreciate your love for Susana. And, I assure you, it is not in vain."

Jané pondered this for a moment. "How much longer, *Adu*?"

"Soon, little dove. It's not much longer now."

CHAPTER 23

LABOR

"Unless the Lord builds the house,
They labor in vain who build it."
Psalm 127:1, NKJV.

29 May 8009 M.E.

Just as Stan walked into the living room, a violent sneeze overcame Camille. She winced when she put a tissue to her face to blow her already raw nose. In over 8,000 years of life, she had never experienced this most human of ailments, the common cold. Given her preference, she would have gladly gone another eighty centuries without gaining personal knowledge of the misery it entailed. It had driven her home from work early today, and she was already preparing for bed, being sorely in need of a restful night's sleep.

Handing her a cup of tea, Stan said, "It's too bad you're so ill, Kami."

"As difficult as this is, it doesn't compare to the stomach flu I caught last month. Nonstop vomiting and retching—disgusting."

"Pim has assured me that this should be the end of it. He says your levels of *anát* are almost back to normal."

"How kind of him to so freely discuss my medical condition with any interested party."

Stan cast her a sidelong glance, and she sensed that her barb had hit its mark. "I'm not just 'any interested party.' I'm your elder brother. I care about you. It's my duty to watch over you."

Watch over her? Had he really just said that? She bit back the retort begging to be unleashed and settled on a meaningful sidelong glance of her own. He pretended ignorance of the unspoken rebuke by focusing his attention on his tea.

The last seven months had been difficult ones. For four full months, Camille had been kept in protective isolation. A small suite of rooms in Desmon Tower, specially sealed and filtered, had served as her living quarters and office during that time, and she saw no one who wasn't wearing a sterile gown, mask, and gloves. She knew the precautions were necessary, but she came to think of those high-tech accommodations as a prison.

When Pim finally released her from isolation, she had initially resisted Stan's suggestion that she return to his penthouse. However, when she developed an ear infection, she quickly reversed that decision. Her brother deserved to wait on her during these illnesses. Besides, when he was nearby, the link assured that he felt at least some part of the physical pain he had foisted upon her.

He had not always been the picture of patience during this trying period. Still, he had been more helpful than she expected—which was, of course, simply part of his campaign to convince her that their relationship ought to return to the same, cozy friendship they'd enjoyed before his betrayal. It seemed he had truly enjoyed that state of affairs.

She allowed him to bestow his little favors upon her. She deserved such considerations and more. But she had no intention of complying with his wish. Only someone supremely arrogant and insensitive could even believe it possible. She would discharge the duties required of her, playing the role of the perfect wife and mother. She would even avoid deliberately antagonizing him in order to maintain peace in her home. But he had no claim on her friendship. Never again.

Rising to load some Debussy into the CD player, Stan turned to the safe topic of work. "The latest numbers on the New-RABs came in today. The things are growing like weeds."

"Of course," Camille scoffed. "Humans think anything 'new' is synonymous with 'improved.' Pathetic creatures—so predictable as to be boring."

He resettled into his favorite chair and sipped his tea. "Let's call him Stanley."

"Stanley Moden Junior?"

"Mm-hmm."

"Not that I care what you choose to call the child, but I am surprised you would wish to endow a human with your name."

"I want him to know he belongs to me, that he's completely mine."

"He will scarcely be able to avoid that conclusion." The boy would be trained for his position from birth, beginning with language tapes in his nursery. To maximize his exposure to the business, they were even setting up a second nursery at the office. He would come as near to eating and breathing Moden Industries as was humanly possible.

"How are the preparations at the office coming?" Stan asked.

"Quite well. We did run into a few problems related to having an outlander—the nanny, that is—on the top floor full time, but Patric has resolved those issues. The key concern, of course, was with the security of the Priority Computer terminals. He and Garrick have devised an excellent solution. If she ever comes within ten feet of one, she'll set off all manner of alarms."

"Good. Any progress on finding a suitable nanny?"

"Yes, I've decided on a woman named Anna Jenkins—widowed, no children, excellent references. And Garrick's background check uncovered no ties to Damour."

"Fine."

"I am glad the child will be more intelligent than other humans. I couldn't abide having an imbecile underfoot, even if it is for only two or three decades."

"Nor I. But we've done well with the *mij dinósh*. I only wish we'd discovered it sooner. Still, having a whole generation of humans that are as strong, smart, and long-lived as Adam will be a great boon to our cause. "

After suffering another bone-jarring sneeze, Camille leaned her head back and closed her eyes, enjoying the relaxing music. Stan stepped behind her to massage her shoulders—though not for her benefit. It was merely an excuse to establish skin contact and engage their link to enhance the music. However, she could control the depth of the experience, and she wasn't about to allow him uninhibited access to her sensory experience by dropping all barriers.

"How are the atmospheric experiments coming?" she asked to distract him.

"The same. Everything we put in island atmosphere explodes, and we can't figure out why." He paused before adding, "It's almost as frustrating as trying to get you to link."

She didn't respond.

"You don't allow us to link completely anymore," he said, as if she hadn't heard him the first time.

She sighed. "No, I don't."

"The music would be even better if you did."

"Yes, it would."

"You like it better that way, too."

When she didn't respond, Stan released a sigh, and Camille pursed her lips against a victorious grin. This wasn't the first time they'd had this discussion, and Camille found it supremely satisfying, although she didn't want Stan to discover that truth. She had something he wanted—the intimacy provided through the link. Moreover, he couldn't take it from her forcibly, as he could with most things he desired, for coercion shut down the neural pathways involved in the link.

"I did what I had to do, Kami. I wish you'd accept that." His anger became distinctly apparent in his touch, and she pulled away from the aggressive massage. "You'd never have gone along with the plan if I hadn't withheld information from you, and I'd be dead within a year. This way, we both live, thereby dramatically improving our chances of success against Damour."

"That would all be well and good—if you had known what my outcome would be."

"We were pretty sure you'd survive."

She snorted in derision.

"Look, neither of us enjoys this distance between us. More importantly, it's affected our work—creativity and productivity have dropped for us both."

"My decreased productivity might have something to do with these recurrent illnesses," she noted mildly, but he continued as if she hadn't spoken.

"We were doing so well, too. We'd spawned some really great ideas."

Piercing him with a glare, she hissed, "I am not the one responsible for the change. You knew there would be repercussions when you chose to risk my life. So, unless you wish to admit your error and apologize for it, you had better accept our new relationship."

She sensed his anger flare, but the only outward sign was that the pinkish scar on his left cheekbone flamed bright red. He took one step back, sketched a stiff, mocking bow, and stalked to his bedroom, slamming the door behind him.

Putting the great Stan Moden to flight was no meager accomplishment, and she allowed herself a soft chuckle in triumph. Yet she could not fully celebrate the victory. Although her desire for retribution overrode her other feelings, the whole truth was that she missed her brother, just as he missed her. No one else understood her so well or shared her interests as closely. Furthermore, the closeness they'd enjoyed during those few months had been wonderful—intoxicating—and she now yearned for it more than ever before.

But she had issued an ultimatum, and she would stand by it. She would not reconcile until Stan apologized. And Stanley L. Moden, DSc, JD, PhD, had never apologized—not once in his 8009 years of life.

❋ ❋ ❋ ❋ ❋

Sitting on a bench in Baltimore, Jané turned a page in her book and glanced up at the row house across the street. Warm light spilled joyfully from its windows, oblivious to the gloom of the dark night beyond. She couldn't help wondering if that home's occupant, Anna Jenkins, was equally oblivious to the gloom, and the danger, of the darkness she had agreed to brighten with her presence.

Along with Anna's two guards, Jané had been monitoring the house all day but had found no indication that Anna was being observed by personnel from Moden Industries. In fact, since completing their extremely thorough security check two weeks earlier, Stan's people had shown no interest in Anna at all.

But then, why would they? From their perspective, she was a meaningless old woman, useful only for the dirty diapers she could change.

But to Doúg Anna was a beloved daughter, unique and cherished. To him, each life was precious. He went to extraordinary lengths to rescue even one. That's why Jané suspected that tonight's activities were part of something very grand. Stan and Camille believed they were creating a closed system, one that would allow them absolute control of their children's lives—one in which the poor youngsters *could* not accept Doúg's rescue. But Jané had never seen Doúg allow such a circumstance. He had given each of his reasoning creatures the power of choice, and he meant that they should use it. She did not for one moment believe he would allow the unchallenged possession of any being without their consent.

Pushing back a strand of hair, Jané tapped the bone behind her ear. When Doúg responded, she said, "Still no activity, sir. Permission to proceed."

"Permission granted. Take good care of my little lamb."

"Yes, sir, I will." Changing frequencies, Jané checked with Anna's guards once more. "Bo Peep, any wolves?"

"Negative, Radio Doctor. All clear."

"Very well. Proceeding with operation."

"Roger that."

Jané logged off and then strolled down several blocks before returning to Anna's apartment via a circuitous route. The kindly, silver-haired woman immediately answered her knock and ushered her into the cozy home. They engaged in small talk for a few minutes while Jané checked for listening devices. Finding none, she came to the business at hand.

"Before we proceed," she said, "Doug would like to make certain that you still wish to participate in this mission. The assignment you've accepted is quite dangerous. If your new employer discovers your connection to Doug, they will kill you, and in a most unpleasant manner. But you may still change your mind if you choose. Doug will love you no less."

"Oh, you're not going to talk me into backing out," came Anna's spirited reply. "Doug's been preparing me for this adventure for forty years. Do you think I'm going to pull out just when things are getting exciting?"

Jané chuckled. She had expected exactly such a response from the kindly, but very stubborn, woman. "Then do you have any questions before I implant the device?"

"No, Doug has already explained everything. I'm ready."

"Very well." Jané pulled the sterilely packaged implantable radio from her briefcase and showed it to Anna. "This is the device. My brother, Rubén, developed it after the rebels were exiled, so they know nothing of the technology. We believe they're still entirely ignorant of its existence. And they don't have the technology to detect it, even if they were to suspect it. Therefore, the device is completely safe."

"Wonderful," Anna enthused.

"However," Jané added, "your use of it may not be as safe. It's probable that they will plant listening devices in your quarters. In fact, you may almost count on it, especially during the early days of your tenure with them. Therefore, anytime you speak directly to Doug, you must first scan the room with this instrument to assure that the area is free of listening devices." Jané handed her an object that looked like a gold pen.

Turning it over in her hand, Anna asked, "Does it function as a pen, too?"

"Yes, so it should raise no questions. It's linked to the radio I'll implant, allowing you to hear a ping through the radio if a bug is nearby. That ping, as with all transmissions, will be audible only to you. In other words, the radio acts similarly to the privacy mode of the transmitter. Doug will be able to hear what is happening and speak to you without the enemy's detection. You need only be concerned about bugs when you wish to speak to Doug. Is this clear?"

"Yes. Oh, this is so exciting. I feel like James Bond. Can my code name be 007?"

Jané laughed. "I'm afraid Doug has already assigned your code name— Little Lamb."

A gentle smile lit Anna's face. "He's called me that since I was five years old."

"I know." Jané wasn't allowed to tell Anna this—not yet, anyway—but she had been her guard back then. It had been a surprisingly difficult assignment. Anna had been fearless even as a child.

After explaining the radio's use in detail, Jané removed a minor surgical tray from her briefcase and set up a sterile field. Then, using local anesthesia, she began the process of implanting the tiny radio behind Anna's right ear.

As she worked, Anna said, "Can you tell me about the Moden family?"

"Yes. Doug asked me to convey several key points. To begin with, you should know that Paradisians are not, in fact, human."

"What?" Anna's head spun toward her. "You look like us."

Jerking the scalpel away from her patient's head, Jané admonished, "Please try not to move, my dear, or you will have more scars from this small procedure than necessary. Perhaps we should postpone this discussion until I finish."

"I'm sorry." Anna turned her head back to the correct position. "But go ahead—I'll behave."

"Very well," Jané said with a chuckle. "And you're correct. Paradisians and humans do look alike in all major respects. Furthermore, the exiled Paradisians prefer to be considered human as it facilitates their deceptions. As far as I am aware, you're the first human to receive this information. Doug wanted you to know as it may prevent you from making dangerous mistakes. For example, Paradisians possess keener senses than humans. We can hear a whisper from a block away, so be very careful what you say whenever Stan or Camille are at home. You may also inadvertently see them perform feats that seem impossible to you since Paradisians are considerably stronger than humans. If you do, turn away so that they believe you have not seen it."

"I understand. I'm not to let on if I see or hear something that seems strange to me or they may feel threatened."

"Precisely. They're not benevolent individuals, although they go to great lengths to maintain exemplary public images. I'm sorry to say it, but they have no qualms about killing anyone who might divulge unsavory information. They wish to be seen as a happy, law-abiding family. You must never give the slightest indication that you believe any differently. Your life will depend upon it."

"I understand."

"Also, Paradisian families are fundamentally different from human families. Ours consist of brothers and sisters. There are no spouses, let alone intimate physical relations between them. Again, this is not something you 'should' know, but Stan and Camille are actually siblings."

"But—but the baby?"

"Their children are conceived in the laboratory and carried by a surrogate mother."

"Oh," Anna said, sounding somewhat overawed.

"Never divulge your knowledge of this fact, especially not to the boy. Camille will pretend that she has borne the child herself, just as she has pretended to be pregnant for the last nine months. You must not challenge her story, of course, but it is important that you understand their true relationship. They will occupy separate bedrooms, will not kiss one another, and will not display other behaviors normally seen between human spouses. Do not behave as though any of this is strange."

"Okay."

"Although they are both expert at maintaining covers, they have lived together as brother and sister for millennia. In a permanent live-in situation, you may well see them err in word or action. If so, let them think you have not noticed."

"I understand. And the boy—will he have any physical differences?"

"No, his appearance will be normal to you. However, he will be stronger than any child for whom you have cared previously. He will also be capable of learning large volumes of information at an accelerated rate. Furthermore, they will wish to train him for his role in their organization as quickly as possible. They will undoubtedly begin teaching him foreign languages from birth. His formal education will also begin early, perhaps as early as age three."

"Oh, my. I'm glad you warned me of that or I would certainly have made a face at the news."

Removing the surgical towels, Jané announced, "There, all done." They moved to the kitchen, where Anna had left some chamomile tea brewing.

As they settled at the table, Anna asked, "Is there anything else I need to know?"

"Yes. Each Paradisian family has unique traditions that are quite meaningful to its members. Of course, as a nanny, you're accustomed to conforming to family customs. I only wish to emphasize that you should not question them, for that would be highly offensive."

"Certainly. But what type of customs do you mean?"

"When Stan and Camille eat breakfast together, they will probably not wish to have the child present. They will use that time to share their plans for the day. When they leave home in the morning, they will touch the doorframe and pause there, silently reviewing each family member's plans and considering how they may help to make their day pleasant and successful." She hesitated, staring into her tea, as a sad thought occurred to her: "But perhaps they now ponder something else."

Her voice grew wistful as she continued. "Before retiring in the evening, they will share some herbal tea by the fireplace while they discuss their day. This is a most intimate time, and one you ought to avoid interrupting, or even observing, at all cost."

Jané stopped, still staring into her cup. She had not meant to stir up the memories that now overwhelmed her, much less the deep sense of loss they evoked.

"You're very well acquainted with their habits," Anna observed quietly. "Yet you said these traditions vary from family to family. How is it that you're so familiar with theirs?"

Jané looked up, only then realizing that tears blurred her vision. "I shared these traditions with them for two thousand years. You see, they are my brother and sister."

✳ ✳ ✳ ✳ ✳

Shortly after Stan stormed to his room, the phone rang. Camille ignored it—anyone who needed to talk to her on a Friday night would have her cell number. Besides, she didn't feel like moving. Her body ached all over.

Stan apparently answered the call in his bedroom. Less than a minute later, he dashed out, shrugging on a jacket. "That was Pim. The surrogate's in labor, so we need to check you in at the hospital unit in Desmon Tower so it looks like you've delivered the child."

Camille sneezed twice in a row. "Oh, bother—what timing that woman has." She blew her nose and dabbed at her watering eyes while Stan disappeared down the hallway to retrieve her coat and pregnant belly prosthetic from her room. "Well, it can't be helped, I suppose," she said to no one in particular. Pulling out her cell phone, she added, "I'll call Patric."

"Hi, Doc," Patric answered. "What's up?"

"Finish your preparations at the office this weekend, and then retrieve the nanny. The surrogate's delivering the child tonight. I want Jenkins in place by Monday."

"Will do. By the way, I just had a thought—shouldn't we remove your collection? A bunch of torture implements in your office might freak out a human."

"Oh my, I'd not considered that, but you're quite right. I would rather she never see those instruments. Unless, of course, she turns out to be a disappointment."

"Not to worry, Doc. She'll be fine. Dr. Sondem's men did an especially thorough check. She's as clean as they come—certainly no runner. And if measures are necessary, no one will question a little old lady suddenly keeling over."

The New York Times   Saturday May 30

Moden Crown Prince Born

Manhattan—Stanley L. Moden Jr. was born early this morning to America's #1 Power Couple, Drs. Stanley L. Moden and Camille L. Desmon. Delivered at 11:58 p.m., baby Stanley weighed 7 pounds, 4 ounces. The couple's private physician, the world-renowned Dr. Maurice Pim, states that Dr. Desmon and baby are doing well.

The newborn is heir to the combined Moden-Desmon fortune, estimated to be well over $200 billion. He is also likely to succeed his father as the head of Moden Industries, the country's largest and most profitable business.

The Modens have not released photos of their son, citing concerns for the child's safety, but Dr. Moden says, "He has his mother's blue eyes and his father's thick skull…" **continued on A14**

To: entitymaster@management.com
From: bestagent@management.com
Date: 1 July 8009 M.E.
Subject: Request Hibernation

I've noticed a marked cooling between Subject and myself. My partner has noticed this as well, independently of my own observation. Since this change occurred after establishing the New-RAB, we can only conclude that this is what occasioned the present constraint, particularly since Subject seemed to have no difficulty recognizing the pertinent differences between Dictator's RAB and the New-RAB.

I must, therefore, respectfully make two requests. First, I would like permission to withdraw my support from the New-RAB. That project is progressing well, and I doubt that my influence will be severely missed.

Second, I would like to hibernate for a time. I intend to return to Dictator's RAB and allow Subject to lead me to "revival" in order to regain his trust. Since this is a long-term assignment, I feel it more prudent to strengthen this relationship before attempting further operations.

To: bestagent@management.com
From: entitymaster@management.com
Date: 2 July 8009 M.E.
Subject: Re: Request Hibernation

I salute the wisdom of your plan and hereby grant both requests. The KK continues to grow at an alarming rate worldwide, particularly since the addition of the three new assets at the global level. Your unique position allows you to influence Subject and these assistants as none other can. Therefore, your first priority—both now and for the foreseeable future—must be to thwart KK, even if this objective requires sacrificing your support of the New-RAB movement.

You may curtail your partner's activities there—or not—as you see fit.

PART IV

CHILDREN

"How about the cactus flowers?" Josh asked.

"Cactus flowers?" Susana glanced around, trying to get her bearings. When she clocked the equipment and Paradisian army uniforms, she realized she was back in the War Room—intent on keeping Chris out of it. "Do they have a meaning too?"

"Oh, yes, they certainly do," Josh said. "Cactuses are remarkable plants. Braving the most arid lands on the planet, they not only survive, but store water, bloom, and produce fruit."

A high-pitched siren went off, followed immediately by a lower pitched but no less insistent alarm. Gabriel leapt to a console, working with other officers to key commands into the offending instruments.

Josh's eyes squeezed shut momentarily, but then he looked back to her and unhurriedly finished his thought. "Is it any wonder that their flowers symbolize perhaps the most enduring type of human love?"

"What kind is that?" Susana asked, stealing a peek at the digital clock: 23:33:03—04, 05, 06 …

A warm smile lit Josh's face. "A mother's love."

Susana caught her breath. "You mean—me?"

"That's exactly what I mean."

She excitedly examined her bouquet. "Which ones are cactus flowers? This one, right?" She handed him a multi-petaled white flower. "And this red one. And …"

With Josh's help, she plucked out several cactus flowers and transferred them to him. "I definitely want Doug watching over all my children, Josh. No question." Besides, she had already made sure there were several more types of flowers left in the bouquet to help her keep up this delay tactic. It had worked for over a half hour so far; only another twenty-seven minutes to go.

When she had transferred all the cactus flowers to Josh, she mused aloud, "It's so funny how I learn things here. I mean, I know nothing about plants."

"I know quite a bit," Josh countered.

"Yeah, but ultimately the knowledge has to come from the information stored in my brain, right? After all, you're not really here. This is just a dream."

Another alarm blared, and Josh glanced toward it before locking her eyes in a penetrating stare. "Is it?"

To: entitymaster@management.com
From: bestagent@management.com
Date: 1 September 8011 M.E.
Subject: Return

    Although it has taken over two years, I believe I have regained Subject's confidence. Our interactions are less stilted, and there is generally less distance between us. I believe I may safely awake from hibernation.

To: bestagent@management.com
From: entitymaster@management.com
Date: 1 September 8011 M.E.
Subject: Re: Return

    Welcome back.

CHAPTER 24

FORGIVENESS

"To the Lord our God belong mercy and forgiveness,
though we have rebelled against Him."
Daniel 9:9, NKJV.

Chris rode up the elevator of his apartment building in a preoccupied haze, having felt restless all day. Disturbing thoughts of Camille had been invading his consciousness a lot lately. Especially that look in her eye when she announced he was going on her list—an expression of pure loathing. Was that the look she had turned on Aedan's brother before torturing him to death? The thought made him squirm like a worm on a hook.

And that made him mad. Why should Camille have so much power over him? Why should she be able to so thoroughly bedevil him with a few threats? What he really needed was to make peace with the possibility—no, probability—of meeting her someday.

But how could he? How could he ever be prepared for an ordeal like that?

It wasn't fair that this should be bothering him right now, because his life was really going great otherwise. Now in his last year of medical school, he was looking forward to a residency in pediatrics. He loved his work, his future looked bright, and he still cherished the treasure of the woman he'd married. Yet this obsession with Camille was sucking the joy out of all that goodness.

The elevator door opened, and he headed down the hallway, passing a familiar picture of a man sitting under a tree. But this time he stopped to examine it, suddenly struck by the subject's resemblance to Josh. He'd once stumbled upon his coach sitting in exactly that position—against a lone tree, legs crossed, eyes closed—with an expression of absolute peace. At first, Chris had thought he was sleeping. But then he noticed that his head was erect and his back ramrod straight, as if he were on the alert.

"What are you doing?" Chris had asked as he sat down beside him.

"Waiting," Josh said. "Watching."

"Watching—with your eyes closed?"

"Not that kind of watching," Josh said with a grin.

"Then what kind?"

"The kind I do while communing with my father. The kind that keeps a runner from growing careless and deviating from the right path."

"Oh. And what are you waiting for?"

His coach hesitated, as if searching for the right words. "My kingdom," he said at last.

Chris had pondered that. By then, he had a general understanding of the big picture that Josh referred to. He knew that Stan had declared war on Doug's kingdom and questioned his right to rule the earth. Through lies and deceit, he had inundated the outlander world with his own principles—not only robbing Josh of the kingdom that should have been his, but wrecking havoc on it as well. And causing Josh untold suffering in the process.

"Do you ever get impatient?" Chris had asked.

"No," his friend replied firmly. "Dad has it under control. In the fullness of time, he will set everything right. My job at this time is to watch—to be ready."

"To be ready," Chris whispered to himself now. That's exactly what he needed to put Camille's threat in proper perspective. He needed to be ready to meet her, just as Josh stayed ready to fulfill his destiny. He needed the same kind of peace about the future that Josh had. He needed to trust Doug the same way. In short, he just needed to be more, well, Josh-ly.

But how could he become more like his coach?

At the RAB the week before, Aedan had said something that stuck in Chris's mind: "We can't get cozy just because we have the truth. Correct doctrine alone doesn't transform our lives. For that, we must spend quality time with Doug in a spirit of humility and allow him to teach us the graces of love, self-sacrifice, and watchfulness. We must allow him to show us our deficiencies and clothe us with his robe of righteousness."

That's what he needed—quality time with Doug. And maybe he'd gotten a bit sloppy about it lately, rushing through his time with the *Manual*, talking to Doug about superficial stuff. How could Doug prepare him for meeting Camille if he didn't give him the chance?

Chris nodded at the figure in the painting as if to say "Message received," and proceeded down the hallway to his apartment with a renewed determination to get back to basics. When he inserted his key in the lock, it flew open, and a dressed-up Susana threw her arms around him. "Welcome home."

"Wow. You look beautiful." He held her in a warm embrace as the savory smell of enchiladas engulfed him. "September seventh? It's not your birthday or mine, not our anniversary. What's going on? What are we celebrating?"

Susana laughed. "Can't a girl dress up for her husband just because she loves him?"

"Anytime she wants," Chris conceded with a kiss.

They shared the news of their days over dinner, and Chris ended up telling her of a patient that had especially impressed him. "The man's only thirty-nine—Benny's age—but has a nasty case of pancreatitis. He may not survive. He's not even conscious."

"How sad. How did he get such a terrible disease so young?"

"Drinking. His only family is a sister. She says he started drinking when he was thirteen."

"Thirteen?" Susana exclaimed.

"It turns out their dad was an alcoholic too. Shortly after their mom left them, this guy started getting into his dad's booze. She says he's spent most of his life since then drunk."

"That's really sad."

"Yeah."

A somber silence fell over them as they finished their meal. Finally Chris sat back and patted his very full tummy. "That was an amazing meal. Thank you."

"I'm glad you enjoyed it. But there's more," Susana said with a playful smile.

"*Mi tesoro*, I honestly don't think I could eat another bite."

"Don't worry. No bites necessary." She handed him an envelope. "But there is some work involved." Chris grinned as he opened the envelope. Susana liked to play these little games. Actually, he did too.

The note read, *First clue: on your desk.* He crossed over to his desk in the living room, where he found his copy of *Love You Forever.* It had been one of his favorite books as a kid, and he often read it to his younger nephews when they visited.

Looking up at Susana, he asked hopefully, "One of my brothers is coming to visit?"

"Nope. Sorry."

"Too bad." He pulled an envelope out of the book and read the note: *Next clue: hanging on the bedroom door.*

Chris made his way to the bedroom and found a new dress hanging on the door. It was a different style than he'd ever seen Susana wear. To tell the truth, he didn't think it would be particularly flattering on her—too fluffy. Hopefully she wouldn't ask him if it made her look fat.

He turned to her and shrugged. "Um, you got a new dress to go to … a children's book reading at the library?"

When she laughed, he shrugged and took a note out of the envelope pinned to the dress. *Give-away clue: on bathroom sink.*

"Oh good, the give-away. I really have no idea what this is about." He ducked into the bathroom to find a bottle of prenatal vitamins sitting on the sink.

Snatching up the bottle, he spun to her. "You're— We're— Really?"

She nodded vigorously and he lifted her up to spin her around. "This is fantastic!" He set her down and gave her a long, passionate kiss. "I love you, Suze."

She snuggled into his chest. "I love you, *mi amor.*"

🏃 🏃 🏃 🏃 🏃

The man with pancreatitis had regained consciousness by the time Chris returned to the hospital the next morning. Chris gathered around with several other students and residents while the intern presented the case to Dr. Díaz, the attending physician, for morning rounds. Then they filed into the patient's room.

As Chris entered, the patient gasped and, pointing directly at him, began a long, babbling monologue: "The rose's eyes. The rose is here? But the rose is dead. Mr. Strider's rose. The rock crushed the rose. Bert's rock. The devil's rock. But the rose is here. But the rock crushed the rose. But the rose's eyes are here …"

A piercing pain sliced through Chris's heart, reopening an old, old wound.

The patient's sister patted her brother's arm. "It's okay, Bert. That was a long time ago." To Dr. Díaz she explained, "I'm sorry. He goes on about killing roses like this sometimes." A puzzled look came over her, and she glanced at Bert. "Although, this is the first time he's mentioned eyes. Anyway, his psychiatrist thinks he must blame himself for our mother's leaving when we were young.

She was a florist, and he helped in her shop. Apparently he damaged a customer's roses and thinks that's why she left."

"The psychiatrist is wrong," Chris said firmly, and then realized he had nothing but a suspicion to back up his statement.

Bert, who had babbled throughout his sister's explanation, stopped mid-sentence at Chris's words. "The rose talks?"

All eyes turned to Chris, although he, focused on Bert, was hardly aware of it.

"Dr. Strider, what do you know of this?" Dr. Díaz asked.

"Tell them," Bert pled. "They don't hear Bert. But the rose talks. Tell them, Rose."

Chris swallowed hard. His suspicion had grown into a huge, cumbersome weight in his gut, and he felt as if a million ants were crawling all over his skin. The room had taken on the distortion of something reflected in a funhouse mirror: Bert, supernaturally large, took up most of his field of vision while everyone else shrank to insignificance around the edges.

"Chris?" It was George's voice and George's hand on his left shoulder, his hard grip leading Chris to understand that he had actually swayed.

Dr. Díaz made his way to Chris's other side. "Chris, are you all right?"

"Christian, the baby rose," Bert said. "Then Rose, Edward, Steven, Michael, and Benjamin Junior. All the little roses."

"Those are all my brothers and my sister," Chris hissed, glaring at him. "How do you know our names?"

Bert withered at Chris's tone. "Newspaper said," he explained apologetically. "All the little roses."

Any doubt Chris had about Bert's identity was gone. Yet this was so unreal, so huge. Fitting it into his brain felt like trying to stuff a sleeping bag into a toothbrush case.

Dr. Díaz placed a steadying hand on his other shoulder. "Chris? What's this about? If you have any information about this patient, please tell us."

"Tell them, Rose," Bert pled again. "Please. They don't hear Bert."

Chris looked around the room, from Dr. Díaz on his right to George on his left, considering each puzzled face. When he got to George, he whispered, "Pinch me."

George held Chris's gaze, clearly mystified, before giving Chris's forearm a hard, toe-curling pinch.

"Ouch," Chris said.

"You're not dreaming," George assured him. "What's this about?"

Chris turned back to the patient, who had tears streaming down his face. Once more he pleaded, "Please tell them, Rose."

Chris drew in a long breath and began in a hoarse voice. "My mother's name was Rose Strider. They say I have her eyes."

"Yes," Bert said, clapping. "The rose's eyes. Tell them, Rose."

"She was killed when I was a baby," Chris continued. "She was returning home after grocery shopping. A teenager threw a large stone off an overpass onto the highway—the 126 in Ventura. The stone hit her windshield and killed her instantly."

Bert's sister gasped. "I remember that accident. It was near our house. I saw the husband on the news with their kids ..." She looked at Bert with a look of sudden understanding and breathed, "Oh, no."

"The rock crushed the rose," Bert said, sobbing. "Bert's rock. The devil's rock."

"They never found the teenager responsible," Chris finished.

"The rose's eyes found him," Bert said, patting his own chest.

Bert's final confirmation of Chris's suspicion had the effect of focusing the nebulous, surreal world he had entered into one clear truth. Capturing Bert's eyes, he seethed, "You murdered my mother."

"Chris," Dr. Díaz hissed.

"Bert's sorry." The patient burst into a fresh flood of tears. "Bert didn't mean to."

Chris took one threatening step closer. "Why'd you do it?"

"The rock crushed the rose."

"But you threw the rock. Why?"

"Ned's calling Bert chicken. Bert's no chicken."

"You killed my mother to prove you weren't chicken?" Chris exclaimed incredulously.

"That's enough, Chris," Dr. Díaz said firmly.

Chris turned on his heel and stormed out of the room. "Bert's so, so sorry," the patient called after him before dissolving into racking sobs.

Catching up with Chris, Dr. Díaz grabbed him firmly by the arm and led him to an empty room. George ducked in before the attending physician closed the door.

"Leave me alone," Chris exclaimed, shaking off the attending's grasp. "Didn't you see what happened?"

"Yeah," George seconded. "We need to call the police. We've got a murderer in there."

Dr. Díaz cast George a stern look. "We've got a *patient* in there who's far too sick to be prosecuted for any crime."

Turning an icy stare on the attending, George gritted out, "He deserves to be punished."

"He's been punishing himself since he was thirteen," Dr. Díaz replied firmly. "And if Doug treated us as we deserved, none of us would be wearing transmitters."

"I need to do something, or I'm gonna strangle that creep," exclaimed Chris, who had taken up an agitated stalking from one side of the room to the other.

"There will be no police, no prosecution, and definitely no strangling," Dr. Díaz insisted. "Not now. I'm dismissing you both for the rest of the day. I suggest you each go for a long run and work this out. But I don't want to see either of you on this unit again until you get hold of yourselves."

"You have no right to bar a criminal investigation," George challenged.

"I not only have the right, but the responsibility, to do what's medically best for my patient. You get out of here now, Dr. Strong." He pointed emphatically to the door. "Go have a long talk with Doug."

George stared at the attending physician with that blood-stopping, frigid stare, but Dr. Díaz held his ground. Finally George said, "I'll wait outside, Chris." Jerking the door open, he exited.

"As for you," Dr. Díaz said, turning to Chris, "I think we should talk to Doug together right now."

"I don't want to talk to anyone," Chris responded.

"Then you'll wait here while I talk to Doug." Dr. Díaz undid a button under his tie and reached inside his shirt to activate a transmitter.

Doug responded immediately. "Howdy, Nate. How you doing?"

"I'm fine, Doug. But I'm with a fellow runner, Chris Strider, who just found the man responsible for his mother's death. His runner friend's not helping the situation, but I sent him out for now. He's got a real attitude problem, by the way."

"Who's his friend?" Doug asked.

"George Strong."

"Ah," Doug said. "Well, he's not actually a friend. Or a runner. His transmitter's fake—a prop."

Dr. Díaz whistled. "Well, that explains a lot."

"I'll have a chat with Chris," Doug said. Then, through Chris's receiver, he said, "How're you doing, son?"

Chris didn't answer, preferring instead to continue pacing.

"Nate, what's he up to?" Doug said.

"Pacing the room like a caged panther," Dr. Díaz answered.

Doug spoke through the receiver again. *"Áchimi tamí bichíima, towí ke akemi?"*

Chris abruptly stopped and grabbed his head. He didn't want to be here. His mom's killer was just a few rooms away; he wanted to do something—anything—about it. But he couldn't ignore those two Rarámuri phrases, both of which were laden with meaning for him. The first—"Will you trust me?"—normally caused his mind to click through a slideshow of memories about how Doug and Josh had saved him from bad situations. Today, in his agitated confusion, it raised only a general feeling that he should pay attention. The second phrase—"Runs-Barefoot"—was Chris's traditional name. It carried an appreciation of Chris's strong, indomitable spirit, while warning him away from the recklessness that could sometimes overtake him. The combined effect was a vague sense that, even though his brain was churning wildly, he may not be processing things normally—so he really should listen to whatever Doug had to say.

Activating his transmitter, Chris said, *"Ayena abi, Onó."* (Rarámuri: Yes, Dad.) He honestly didn't feel like trusting Doug, but he knew he should anyway.

"I'd like you to listen to a story," Doug said.

The request brought back visions of him listening to Grandma's stories after he'd misbehaved. The implication—that he was a child in need of correction—further angered him. He crossed his arms and lifted his chin.

"Áchimi tamí bichíima, towí ke akemi?"

Chris raked a hand through his hair and sighed. "Fine. Whatever."

"Nate," Doug said through Dr. Díaz's transmitter, "would you be so good as to tell Chris 'bout your brother?"

"Of course." Dr. Díaz came alongside Chris and gazed out the window in silence for several moments before he began. There was something about his mood, his obvious sadness, that drew Chris's sympathy, despite his own anguish.

"I was the only one in my family to go to college," Dr. Díaz began.

"Really?" Chris said. "Me too."

Dr. Díaz nodded. "My kid brother, Miguel, chose a different path. He joined a gang in our neighborhood. There were frequent wars between the Hispanic gang he joined and a nearby African-American gang. One summer when I was home from college, I went to pick Miguel up from a friend's place. As I pulled up to the house, I saw three guys from the other gang running away. Inside I found Miguel and his friend—" He broke off to swallow hard. "I found them shot to death."

"I'm sorry," Chris said sincerely.

Dr. Díaz mutely stared out the window for a moment before turning to lock eyes with Chris. "I determined to get even. I started looking for those guys, asking around to see who they were, where they lived. I got a gun and learned to use it. I stopped talking to Doug and reading the *Manual* so he wouldn't dissuade me. Doug kept calling me over the receiver, but I didn't want to talk to him, so I took the transmitter off. I tried burying it in a drawer and putting it under the mattress, but I could still hear Doug's voice. So I threw it in the trash. Funny thing was, every time the trash collectors came by, everything was dumped except that transmitter. It always stayed at the bottom of the trashcan like it was magnetized or something. When I could still hear Doug calling me from the trashcan outside my window, I buried the pesky thing in my mother's flower garden."

Dr. Díaz paused, rubbing an eyebrow. "I went back to school, but getting even had become an obsession. I became a different person—angry, hard. My grades dropped. My girlfriend broke up with me. When I went home for Christmas break, I looked in the mirror and honestly didn't recognize the guy I saw there. I actually looked different. My mother, who's also a runner, knew what was going on. 'Bitterness is eating your soul,' she said. 'And it will steal your life, *mi hijo*. Please call Doug. He can help.' " With a chuckle, he continued, "Then she went to a drawer, pulled out my transmitter, and put it in my hand. 'The flowers don't need to talk to Doug,' she said.

"Long story short, Doug taught me to forgive and life became good again. A couple of years later, when I was a medical student at LA County Hospital, one of the guys involved in my brother's murder came in with some nasty stab wounds from a gang fight. I recognized him right away—his name was James. I told him who I was. I told him that I forgave him, and I explained why. James underwent a radical transformation. He became a runner and, eventually, began working with the LAPD's gang unit.

"A few years later, my wife—the girlfriend who had broken up with me— was grocery shopping with our baby, Isabel. She reached down to get a box of detergent, and when she straightened up, a guy was disappearing around the corner with Isabel. They locked down the store immediately. The place was crawling with cops. But it was my good friend James, with Doug's help, who rescued our daughter. The kidnapper had disguised her as a little boy and himself as a woman. He was standing in the cashier's line, casually blending in with the regular customers."

Dr. Díaz laid a hand on Chris's shoulder. "I've known the pain and the anger you're feeling right now. Bitterness nearly ruined my life. But I've also seen forgiveness turn a killer into a savior. I wonder what it could do for a mentally ill alcoholic?"

"I don't care what becomes of him," Chris spat.

"Do you care what becomes of you?"

Susana shot off the elevator as soon as the door opened. Charging down the hallway toward their apartment, she heard George say, "I have a friend who's a lawyer. I can ask him about the situation—statutes of limitation, prosecuting a juvenile offender so much later, that sort of thing."

"Sounds good," Chris said in response, and Susana's eyes widened. Didn't he realize that George's lawyer "friend" would be Stan?

Or wasn't he thinking?

The thought stopped her in her tracks. Two of the things she loved about her husband were his quick mind and even temper. But, when angry enough, he could transform into the exact opposite—someone wholly in the grip of emotion. It happened rarely, but, to tell the truth, it frightened her a bit when it did. After all, at 6′3″ and 195 pounds, he was a big man. He'd never hit her, and she didn't honestly believe he ever would, but it was just, well, scary.

"It's all right, little filly," came Doug's soothing voice. "I'll give you the right words."

"Thank you, *Ada*," she said sincerely. With that assurance, she proceeded forward to meet Chris and George as they came toward her. Chris was in workout clothes, but George was still in his tie and lab coat.

"Chris, are you okay?" she asked as she approached. "Doug told me what happened. I'm so sorry." Even before she hugged him, she saw the fire in his eyes soften. He didn't answer, but held onto her like a stranded climber clinging to a safety rope.

"Susana," George said, "I was just taking Chris to play handball. The exercise will do him good."

She drew back to look into Chris's eyes. He was going with George—alone—while in this vulnerable, angry state? Nuh-uh—not in her lifetime!

"I'll come watch," she said brightly.

George seemed flustered by this, but Chris kissed her forehead. "Thank you, *mi tesoro*."

They went down to George's apartment so he could change. While they waited, Susana heard George talking in the bedroom. With a glance at Chris, who had gone out on the balcony for some air, she edged to the closed door to listen. However, she discovered he was speaking in some strange language. With her transmitter still on in privacy mode, she whispered, "Doug, what's George saying?"

"He's speaking in Zulu, just in case you can hear him," Doug said. "He's telling Camille's assistant, Patric, to send him more vials of bitterness tonight by courier. Seems the housekeeper broke his vial of the stuff."

Susana gasped. Looking toward her husband, she asked a question to which she already knew the answer: "But isn't that what almost killed Chris in Texas?"

"Yes, little filly," Doug said solemnly. "I'm afraid it is."

Susana didn't sleep well that night. Chris also tossed and turned a lot. From the mumbles she could make out, he seemed to be dreaming a lot about his mom—or at least her absence. When Susana awoke in the morning, he was lying awake, staring at the ceiling.

She rolled over and kissed his neck. "Good morning, *mi amor*."

"H'mm."

"How are you feeling?"

"Okay."

She laid her head on his chest and reached for his left hand. Slipping off his wedding ring, she turned it to the obsidian. "Tell me this story."

He stared at it. "That was different. Benny didn't kill anyone. And he's my brother. He deserved to be forgiven."

"The principle's the same. Forgiveness is for your benefit—"

He abruptly snatched the ring from her grasp and vaulted out of bed. Dodging into the bathroom, he slammed the door behind him.

Apparently his thinking side still wasn't engaged.

"Chris, I need to tell you something," she called.

The bathroom door opened and he warily peered out. "What?"

"When we went down to George's apartment yesterday, I was eavesdropping at the door while he changed. He made a call to their office. They're sending him some bitterness by courier. He probably has it now."

He ran a hand through his hair.

"Please promise me you won't leave the apartment today?"

He nodded, which calmed her fears somewhat. However, the information hadn't even dimmed the angry fire in his eyes, so this fix was a very tenuous, very temporary solution. He couldn't hole up in the apartment forever.

CHAPTER 25
VENGEANCE

"But that day belongs to the Lord, the Lord Almighty—
a day of vengeance."
Jeremiah 46:10, NIV.

Jané and Serji had no trouble finding the battle. They ran into it as soon as they burst through the stairwell door in the Strider's apartment building—agents Adlai and Taylor Menod vs. Royal Guards Viktor and Vanti Lok. The newly arriving guards sprang into the scuffle and, shortly thereafter, the struggling agents stood with their arms secured behind their backs.

"You have no right to detain us," Adlai hissed at Jané, the ranking officer for the combined teams of guards.

"Actually, we do," she replied calmly. "His wife has not ceased petitioning for him. In any case—as you well know—Doúg has the right to protect his children by limiting your access to them. As we explained last night, at present you may approach Chris personally only if he grants you an interview. Your other options, including telephone and e-mail, have not been curtailed."

"He's not answering those," Adlai gritted out.

"That is his right. Our objective is merely to ensure that you respect that right."

Adlai glared at her for a moment, obviously trying to discover a loophole, and then exchanged a quick look with Taylor. Apparently neither of them could concoct further arguments for he said tightly, "Fine. Have it your way." Pulling away from Serji, who was releasing him anyway, he spat, "Let me go, you big gorilla." Together, he and Taylor stormed down the stairs.

"Big gorilla, is it?" Serji said. "And to think, he used to be one of my dearest friends."

The four guards exchanged rueful smiles.

"Serji and I must return to Susana," Jané said. "However, since this is their second attempt at breaking the barricade, I sincerely doubt that we have seen the last of him. I'll request reinforcements until this crisis has passed. They should be here directly."

"Thank you, Colonel," Viktor said. "Adlai does seem particularly determined. I'm afraid he knows his subject's history too well."

Jané nodded. "Yes, Chris's previous experience with bitterness was not pleasant. Thankfully, Joshua was present to remedy the situation on that occasion. This time—" She sighed, and the four guards looked toward the Striders' apartment door in shared concern.

"Do you think they know how closely they approach the precipice of danger at times like these?" Vanti asked.

Jané shook her head. "No. I believe the poor creatures have no idea."

🏃 🏃 🏃 🏃 🏃

Chris stayed in all weekend. Even though George was on call at the hospital, he couldn't chance running into him until he figured out what to do. Yet figuring out anything was a problem. He couldn't even seem to study effectively. And the longer he stayed cooped up, the more restless he became.

Late Sunday afternoon, Chris and Susana were both at their desks in the living room when Doug's voice came over the receiver. He had already called several times, but Chris just wasn't in the mood to talk. The interruptions had become annoying enough that he had tried throwing his transmitter into a bottom drawer. Still able to hear it, he buried it under all the sofa pillows. When that didn't work either, he finally stowed the silly thing underneath a potted plant out on the balcony.

This time, however, Susana was home and heard the soft rumble on the balcony. "What on earth is that?" She followed the sound until she found the transmitter, which she held up with an expression that said, "Oh no, you didn't!"

When Chris silently turned back to his books, she replaced the pot over the device and came to stand beside him. "How long is this going to continue?"

He didn't answer—he didn't really know what to say—and she went into the bedroom, her step crisp with determination.

As Chris watched her disappear around the corner, he wondered what she was planning to do. She seemed upset, so maybe she was just going to change and go for a run. But she might do something dumb, like phone Aedan.

His cell phone rang just as he rose to spy on her from the doorway. Seeing that it was George calling, he set the phone on the desk and let it go to voice mail. But even though he didn't want to actually talk to George, he was very interested to hear the latest update from the lawyer. So he played the message back as soon as his phone pinged, putting it on speaker without thinking about the possibility of Susana hearing it.

"Chris," came George's voice, "I just heard back from the lawyer. He's got some good news."

Susana poked her head around the corner, staring at the phone on Chris's desk with a wary expression.

"The patient's condition has improved some," George continued. "Enough so I think the case against him could proceed. My friend contacted an attorney here in Frisco who will help out at no charge, as a favor to him. He's really topnotch, Chris. I know you want to see that"—he interjected some colorful words—"hang, so phone me, and we'll get things rolling."

Chris reached for the phone. Grabbing his hand, Susana cried, "No, Chris, he's talking about Stan! The friend in Frisco is probably one of his associates."

"I don't care who it is, as long as he puts that"—here he repeated George's choice of colorful words—"away."

Susana gaped at him. "Do you hear yourself? When did you start cussing? This isn't you talking."

"Of course it's me. Who do you think—?"

A knock at the door interrupted him, and he turned a narrowed gaze on her. "What did you do?"

She seemed to shrink away from him. Quietly she said, "I love you, Chris. I can't just stand by while you descend into madness."

She reached for the door, and he shouted, "Don't you dare open that door!"

"Don't you *dare*?" She searched his face with an expression he had trouble placing. "Who *are* you?"

With that, she swung the door open, and Aedan walked in.

Jamming his fists onto his hips, Chris demanded, "What are you doing here?"

"Susana called me," Aedan said as he strolled into the living room. "She thought you might want to talk."

"I don't."

"Of course not. You already know I'll say you should talk to Doug. Worse, I might convince you to do it."

"Not unless you can tell me he'll make sure that creep gets what he deserves."

"Oh, sure that's what Doug'll tell you. Isn't that how he's always treated you?"

Chris's eyes narrowed. "What are you talking about?"

"Doesn't Doug always make sure you get exactly what you deserve?" When Chris responded only with a glare, Aedan added, "Oh, I forgot. You're so perfect, you've never needed Doug's mercy, let alone his forgiveness."

"That isn't the same at all." Chris took two menacing steps toward him, fists clenched at his sides. "That man killed my mother. I've never killed anyone."

"Haven't you? My *Manual* says that anyone who's so much as angry with a brother is guilty of murder. You seem pretty angry to me."

"I have every right to be."

"And Susana has every right to feel safe in her home."

"What?"

" 'Don't you dare open that door?' When did you start threatening your wife, Chris?"

"I don't have to listen to this in my own house. Get out of here."

Aedan crossed his arms. "No."

"What? You want me to make you?"

"You can try." Aedan leaned onto his toes and positioned his fists in front of his face.

This boxer's stance reminded Chris that Aedan had been a professional boxer before running the race. Yet he was so angry that the idea of a good knockdown, drag-out fight actually sounded good to him. If he even registered the fact that he'd be opposing an expertly trained boxer, it meant nothing to him. He started toward Aedan, swinging wildly.

Susana screamed and burst into tears. But that, too, rebounded off him like a basketball off a backboard.

Aedan bounced around, surprisingly agile for such a thickly built fellow, and nimbly dodged Chris's punches. They danced about like this for several minutes, Chris becoming increasingly frustrated and angry at his inability to hit the skillfully moving target.

Suddenly, Aedan sprang away from the wall and grabbed Chris by the ear. The maneuver was painful enough that Chris froze.

"Look at yourself," Aedan ordered. He pointed to a decorative mirror on the wall. "Do you even know that man?"

Chris's reflection frankly startled him. Hard eyes glared out of a red face twisted in anger. Dr. Díaz's words returned unbidden—*I became a different person, angry, hard*. A contrasting image—that of Josh sitting serenely against the tree—flashed into his mind. It occurred to him that the guy in the mirror certainly didn't look very Joshly.

His hands fell to his sides, and Aedan released his grip on Chris's ear. "What's the matter?" he asked quietly. "Don't like what you see?"

"No," Chris admitted. "No, I don't."

"Then you'd better do something about it. Otherwise that's the man who'll be raising your child."

A vivid picture of that angry man yelling at his infant son came to him, and Chris squeezed his eyes shut against the horrifying image.

"That's also the man who'll be living with your wife." Aedan nodded to Susana, sobbing and wiping tear-streaked cheeks. "There's a reason Doug says vengeance rightfully belongs only to him. Neither we—nor our families—are wise enough to handle it without messing up our lives."

As Chris surveyed Susana, her expression of a few minutes before returned to him, the one he hadn't been able to place. Suddenly he realized what he'd seen in her eyes: fear.

Had he actually scared his own wife—his precious *tesoro*?

This revelation struck Chris at his most vulnerable point: his family. It elicited a pain no physical blow could have approximated. He dropped to the sofa behind him and buried his face in his hands. "I'm sorry, Suze."

She approached hesitantly, as if she still wasn't quite sure if he was safe, and sat beside him to rub his shoulders.

"I'm sorry," he repeated. "I don't know what to do."

"Yes, you do," she said gently. "You just don't want to do it."

As he considered that, the promise he'd once made to Doug came back to him: *I will do whatever you command me*. And, after what Aedan had shown him, he actually wanted to obey, to change. He wasn't sure what that entailed, but he didn't want to be the man in that mirror. He didn't want that man raising his son. And he sure didn't want the woman he loved feeling scared of him.

"I—" He sighed deeply. "I don't know how."

"What did Josh do last time?" she asked. "When you couldn't forgive Benny?"

Aedan tapped him on the shoulder and handed him a grace inhaler. "I'll bet he used this."

Chris took the inhaler. "Yeah. That's exactly what he did. Thanks."

While Chris used the inhaler, Susana went out onto the balcony and came back with his transmitter. "I don't think the grace will work without Doug," she said softly.

"You're right." Chris fastened the transmitter around his neck. "You were right all along. I'm sorry I was so stubborn."

"You'll be fine now," Aedan said, slapping him on the back. "I'll get out of your way."

"Thanks, Aedan," Chris said. "I'm sorry for, well, everything."

"You weren't that bad," Aedan said with a shrug. "The last guy I used that approach on actually landed a punch."

While Susana saw Aedan out, Chris called Doug. "I'm sorry I've been so stubborn, *Ada*. I really do need your help."

"Then it's yours, son," Doug said immediately.

They talked for a long while, with Doug leading him through several passages in the *Manual* on the topics of anger and forgiveness, self-control and patience. He encouraged Chris to memorize some of the excerpts to help him stave off future attacks on the same battlefield. "This," Doug said, "is why one of the *Manual's* songwriters said, 'I have treasured your word in my heart so I don't sin against you.' "

As the conversation was winding down, Chris asked, "What should I do now?"

"Well, there's a sick, tortured man in the hospital who needs to know what forgiveness feels like."

"Doug, I—" Chris rubbed his face. "I want to be able to do that, but I honestly don't know if I can."

"Well, as it happens, I know who can help you."

Susana answered a knock at the door to find Debora standing there. She talked to Chris some more and breathed on him. Enlightened and empowered, he went to the hospital with Debora and Susana accompanying him.

Bert struggled into a sitting position when Chris entered his room. "The rose is here," he murmured, almost reverently.

For the first time, Chris really saw the man before him. He was a thin man, prematurely gray, with lines of pain etching his drawn features. The sheen of fever-induced sweat covered his pale skin. A tube entered his nose to empty his stomach and give him some relief from vomiting.

It was a pitiful sight, and one that roused Chris's compassion. He sat on the bed carefully, to avoid shaking it and causing Bert further pain. "Bert, my name is Chris—Christian. I'm Rose's youngest son. I was a baby when—when she died."

He proceeded to introduce Susana and Debora, but Bert remained focused on Chris. "Bert's sorry, Rose," he said through tears. Chris got the impression that the poor, confused soul actually thought he was talking to Chris's long-dead mother. "Bert's so, so, so sorry."

"I know," Chris said. "And I forgive you." He bowed his head briefly. "I never really knew my mother, but from everything I know of her, I'm sure she would have forgiven you too."

Bert stared at Chris, his amazement clear. "The rose forgives Bert?"

"Yes."

"Rose says it's okay?"

Chris hesitated, having some difficulty with agreeing that what Bert had done was "Okay," but nodded and repeated, "Yes."

Bert burst into tears and threw his arms around Chris's neck. "Bert's so happy. Rose says it's okay."

Bert never left the hospital. He continued to go in and out of a coma and died several days later. During that time, Chris, Susana, and Debora visited him every day, although sometimes he was unresponsive. When awake, he never called Chris anything other than Rose, and Chris had to repeatedly remind him that he'd forgiven him.

Still, Bert always listened intently when "the rose's eyes" talked, so Chris read to him from the *Manual*, choosing some of the simplest stories so Bert would understand. He also taught him a couple of short songs from the Songbook. Bert especially liked #23, the one about the shepherd. After singing it, he would say, "The shepherd loves Bert," and Chris would smile and assure him it was true.

Chris never knew just how much of the *Manual's* stories and songs Bert comprehended, his mind destroyed as it was by the poisons of alcohol and guilt. But when Bert died, it was with a smile on his face and a transmitter around his neck. The rest, Chris knew, Josh would one day fix with the leaves of the *Viv Zabé*.

To: companymaster@management.com
From: bestagent@management.com
Date: 12 September 8011 M.E.
Subject: Results of Clinical Trial for BC-14

    I am sorry to report that BC-14, despite its promising results in other primates, does not appear to be effective in humans. However, our new delivery system works nicely.

To: bestagent@management.com
From: companymaster@management.com
Date: 12 September 8011 M.E.
Subject: Re: Results of Clinical Trial for BC-14

    Most disappointing. However, BC-21 appears promising and can be modified for the same delivery system. I'll change my focus to that compound.

To: entitymaster@management.com
From: bestagent@management.com
Date: 30 September 8011 M.E.
Subject: September Report

   The unexpected lucky break I mentioned when I requested
that special shipment didn't work out as well as I had hoped.
Nevertheless, it did confirm my impression that Subject has
become quite comfortable with me once more. Although he was char-
acteristically reclusive during that crisis, he did allow me to
offer him consolation and advice.

   I have, therefore, decided to proceed with an operation
that, if successful, will likely result in the separation of
Subject and wife. I have already accomplished the first step,
which is to influence Subject to take an extra rotation in the
unit where a certain operative works. I have high hopes that I
will be able to supply him with sufficient excuses to make him
susceptible to operative's charms.

   This plan should reach its culmination precisely when
Subject's infant is due to arrive, so the two women are likely
to meet. Furthermore, from her conversation and behavior, it is
clear that the wife has still not completely surrendered on this
point—although she apparently thinks she has—so her vulnerability remains high. (Isn't it entertaining when, while believing
themselves strong, they cling so tenaciously to the darling
peccadilloes that can only weaken them?) The stress of her doubt
and suspicion alone will likely tax their relationship and cause
permanent damage, even if I cannot ensnare Subject.

CHAPTER 26

BURDENED

" 'We are burdened by our sins and offences;
we are pining away because of them.' "
Ezekiel 33:10, REB.

3 October 8011 M.E.

As Camille rode the elevator to their penthouse apartment, she reflected on Adlai's report, greatly encouraged by his success. Adlai had learned well the usefulness of patience and restraint. His decision to hibernate for a period had obviously produced the desired effect.

How often that which once seemed impossible could become not only possible, but probable, given a little time. Furthermore, they had the advantage of perspective. The two years that Adlai had hibernated were as a coffee break to a Paradisian; yet, for a human, that insignificant period of time was long enough to erase memories and establish new patterns of thought. Familiarity bred indifference, which resulted in unexercised wills and feeble defenses. Soon subjects were living comfortably with the very *kanuf* they once considered horrifying.

She chuckled softly. *Just as Strider will be.*

Of course, she had been hopeful before, only to be disappointed. But they had a powerful, though unsuspecting, ally in Strider's beloved wife. López obviously had no idea how significant her inability to surrender one "small" area of her life was. But Camille knew, as did Adlai. "Darling" peccadilloes, indeed. It took only one tiny holdout to weaken a subject's connection to Doúg and put the whole family at risk. Ironically, López's fear of entrusting the Damours with what she valued most was precisely the means Adlai needed to take it from her.

She chuckled again. *Yes, this time it will be different.*

Entering the apartment, she proceeded into the living room where a cozy fire hissed and popped in the fireplace. She settled on the sofa and pulled an update from the Division of Research from her briefcase.

Mrs. Jenkins appeared from the hallway. "Welcome home, Dr. Desmon. Would you like some refreshment or a few minutes before the viewing?"

"Lady Grey tea and fifteen minutes," Camille said without looking up.

Mrs. Jenkins fetched the beverage and disappeared down the hallway. Precisely fifteen minutes later she reappeared with two-and-a-half-year-old Stanley at her side, dressed in a suit and tie for his nightly viewing.

"Come," Camille said, and Stanley moved to stand in front of her.

"Chin up, young man," she instructed. "You are heir to the largest fortune in the country. Be proud."

He lifted his head.

"Turn."

He did so.

Camille ran her hand over his shoulders. "Mrs. Jenkins, call Dr. Moden's tailor and have the child measured for a new suit. This one is already snug."

"Yes, ma'am."

"What language is he listening to this month?"

"Spanish, ma'am."

"*¿Como te llamas, niño?*" (What's your name, boy?)

"*Stanley Moden.*"

"*Usa la gramática correcta.*" (Use proper grammar.)

"*Me llamo Stanley Moden.*" (My name is Stanley Moden.)

"*Muy bien. Mañana me dirás lo que hiciste—¿si?*" (Very good. Tomorrow you will tell me what you did—yes?)

"*Si,*" Stanley answered with an eager nod.

"*Está bien. Te veo mañana por la noche.*" (That's fine. I'll see you tomorrow night.) As she patted him on the shoulder in dismissal, she heard Stan come in, and she looked toward the entry, surprised. He was early tonight.

Stanley ran to Mrs. Jenkins' side as Stan entered the living room. Stopping short, her brother demanded, "Why aren't you ready?"

Camille frowned. "Ready for what?"

He planted his fists on his hips. "I sent you an e-mail about this business dinner a week ago. A large contract's riding on it."

"Then it went to that mystical cyber bucket in the sky. I received no such memo." E-mails had been their preferred method of communication since a certain cocktail party two weekends before, but it was an imperfect medium. "What time is the meeting?"

"Seven-thirty."

She looked at her watch: 7:10 p.m. "If it's important, you'd better go without me. Tonight is Mrs. Jenkins' night off, so we have no babysitter and no time to find one."

Stan narrowed his eyes, and Stanley, though not even in Stan's line of sight, dropped behind his nanny, clutching her leg.

"You're doing this to spite me, aren't you?" Stan took a threatening step toward Camille, but she resisted the instinct to jump to her feet. Towering over her, Stan would have the advantage in an altercation; however, Camille doubted that he would attack her in front of an outlander.

"I told you," he growled, "he specifically asked to meet you."

"And I told *you*—I never got the memo. Furthermore, while I'd be happy to spite you, you know very well that I'd never jeopardize a business contact, regardless of my personal feelings for you at the moment."

Addressing the nanny, she said, "Mrs. Jenkins, mightn't you take tomorrow night off rather than tonight?"

"I'm sorry, ma'am, but no. My niece is only in town tonight." Turning to Stan, Mrs. Jenkins explained, "She's the only family I have left, sir."

"Hmpf." Stan's glare was still trained on Camille.

"Um," Mrs. Jenkins began, "I *could* take Stanley with me."

Stan's narrowed gaze refocused on her, and Stanley scurried back into the shadows of the hallway.

"Stanley!" Stan roared. "Front and center."

Stanley approached hesitantly.

"Don't ever again let me see you show fear," Stan said sternly. "Fear is weakness. It also points out to your enemies exactly where to attack. Is that understood?"

"Yeth, thir," Stanley squeaked with the lisp typical of his age.

"Very well. Dismissed."

Stanley bolted down the hallway toward his room, and Stan returned his attention to the nanny. "Why would you volunteer to take the child on your night off?"

"It will be no trouble, sir. We're just going out for a casual dinner."

Stan's sharp eye scrutinized her, but her gaze never wavered. Indeed, if his anger ever affected her, she never showed it.

"Very well, Mrs. Jenkins," Stan said. "Thank you for your flexibility. I'll include a sizeable bonus in this week's paycheck."

"That won't be necessary, sir. By your leave, Stanley and I will be off as soon as I get him ready." Stan waved his hand in dismissal, and she stepped toward the hallway.

Camille rose with a sigh. Humans who thought the wealthy could do whatever they liked were sadly ignorant of the realities of such a life. She was in no mood to go out tonight, but she simply had no choice if it was a business dinner. "I'll get dressed, Stan."

"Make it fast," he snarled.

Camille chose a royal blue halter-top dress whose plunging neckline was trimmed in metallic gold stitching. The color set off her eyes, the fitted bodice accentuated her perfect figure, and the short, fluttery skirt highlighted her shapely legs. The combination turned men's heads and drew their wives' jealous gazes—always an entertaining combination. Maybe she'd do some flirting of her own tonight.

The limo ride to dinner was uncomfortably quiet. After several minutes of silence, Stan said, "The new formula they're using in the atmospheric experiments seems to be an improvement."

Camille didn't turn from the window to reply sarcastically, "Yes, a big improvement. Instead of exploding, things burst into flames. I saw the report."

Stan grunted.

"Perhaps you should brief me on the particulars of this meeting."

He obliged by relating the contact's importance and his particular quirk of working exclusively with devoted family men and women.

"Then you should remember," Camille said, "that devoted husbands don't flirt."

Erupting with a curse, he exclaimed, "This is ridiculous. I've always flirted with humans. It's a highly effective method of manipulation. Why does it suddenly bother you?"

"Because you're now married to me."

"How can you possibly be jealous? You're my sister."

"I'm not jealous, Lustanli, as you know very well. Or, at least, you could know it if you bothered to consult your link-sense from time to time."

He gazed into her eyes briefly and then burst into laughter. "You're offended."

"Of course I am. The humans observing your behavior don't know I'm your sister. To them, your flirtations indicate that I'm not good enough for you. They look at me with pity, Stan—pity! It's intolerable."

He sobered. "All right. Let's cut a deal. I'll quit flirting if you allow us to connect through the link like we used to."

"I've already told you my condition for reconciliation on that front—you must apologize."

"Well, that's that, then. We're at an impasse." He turned to the window.

But Camille had another card to play. "If you do not behave as a happily married man, I shall no longer attend social functions with you."

He struck out at her, but she was expecting it and easily blocked it. "You should be more careful with this weapon," she advised, tapping his hand. "Devoted husbands don't leave marks on their wives' faces either."

"You have to attend social events. You're my wife—it's expected."

"And *I* expect to be treated with the respect due a wife. If my presence is as important as you say, you will meet my stipulations."

He glared at her, the scar under his eye turning beet red, but she had him cornered, and they both knew it. She didn't enjoy socializing, and her work didn't require it. It was Stan's work that demanded networking to forge and maintain relationships with heads of companies. And, now that they were married, her absence from key social events would be both noted and discussed in important circles and gossip tabloids—exactly the sort of publicity Stan went to great lengths to avoid.

He peppered the air with epithets and then went silent. She knew he was busily analyzing the Catch-22 she'd designed, looking for its flaw. But there was none; she had thoroughly studied the matter to ensure it.

Finally, he said, "Fine. I won't flirt if you don't."

"Agreed. I haven't flirted in your company since our marriage as it is."

"I don't just mean when we're together. If we're going to act happily married, it needs to be a consistent cover."

She considered that. Flirting *was* useful in some situations, as he had indicated. Besides, she enjoyed having her ego stroked, which was doubtless the real reason he didn't want to give it up either. On the other hand, those strokes weren't worth the insult of being pitied—by humans, no less.

"Very well," she agreed. "No flirting. Happily married at all times."

"Done."

They were the perfect couple during dinner, complimenting each other and laughing at each other's jokes. Before the evening was through, the contract had been won and their recent disagreement tabled.

On the way home, Camille broached another topic she had been considering. "Stan, these two-and-half years of raising a human have not been so very odious."

"Yes, I agree. I think the arrangement is working out fine. Mrs. Jenkins can raise the child, and I'll train him."

"Yes. However, I've decided that I want one to groom for my position in the company as well. Pim advises me that he still has frozen embryos available from the same donors, so he can implant another into a surrogate without delay if you have no objections."

"Objections? No." He studied her.

"What is it?"

"A sort of half-formed idea's been nagging at me. I hadn't made a decision on it." He rubbed his chin. "We originally talked about using humans as soldiers, remember?"

"Yes."

"Who would be best suited to lead those soldiers?"

"I'm … not certain. What is your point?"

"We have three key positions in our organization—mine, yours, and—"

"Garrick's," Camille finished with a nod of understanding. "You're thinking it may be wise to recreate that same team among the humans—"

"—especially if you and I raise all three so they're trained the way we want them trained."

She nodded thoughtfully. "Furthermore, the family relationship should strengthen the bond between them, increasing their cohesiveness. And having an offspring at the head of the army would also increase the loyalty of the offspring being raised as soldiers. They will all be of the same childhood cohort."

"Precisely."

She silently weighed the pros and cons. She didn't relish the idea of having her home invaded by more children, but she couldn't deny the obvious advantages of the plan.

"Very well. Let's expand our household by two more offspring."

CHAPTER 27

PERSECUTED

*"When the dragon saw that he had been cast to the earth,
he persecuted the woman who gave birth."*
Revelation 12:13, NKJV.

When Chris's alarm went off at 5:30 a.m. on May 8, Susana wasn't in bed. He heard noises coming from the kitchen, so he padded down the short hallway in his bare feet to find her making breakfast—for one.

"What are you doing up so early?" he asked.

In lieu of an answer, Susana reached for her big belly and started breathing in the controlled pattern they'd learned in childbirth classes.

"Contractions?" he asked, as though there could be another explanation.

She nodded without interrupting her breathing.

"When did they start?"

"Around midnight," she answered when the contraction ended. "They've been getting stronger and more regular since four o'clock."

Contractions. Right. That meant, um …

Suddenly everything he had learned in childbirth classes and his obstetrics rotations abandoned him. He knew he was supposed to do something, but he didn't have a clue what it was. So he looked around the kitchen as if the microwave or toaster might hold the answer.

"Didn't you bring home some gloves and stuff?" Susana asked. "Maybe you could check my cervix?"

Oh, right. That's what they'd talked about.

Chris examined her and thought she was three centimeters dilated. "But I'm not sure I'm very good at this," he added when he called their obstetrician, Dr. Norton.

"You're better than you think you are, *Doctor* Strider," she said. The title was still honorary, since Chris wouldn't receive his MD for a few weeks yet, but he appreciated her confidence. "I'm already here on Labor and Delivery," she continued. "Why don't you and Susana come visit me?"

At Susana's insistence, Chris wolfed down the breakfast she'd made for him, and then somehow managed to get them to the hospital. Just as they came off the elevator on the labor floor, Susana's water broke and puddled on the floor. Dr. Norton plucked a pen from her short afro, her eyes bright with laughter, and started making notes. "Well, I guess you're right, Chris. Looks like real labor to me."

They got Susana settled into a room and Dr. Norton checked her again. She was four centimeters dilated by then and, at her request, received an epidural.

Seven hours of pacing later, Chris found himself coaching, "Push, Suze, push!" An hour after that, he was about to become a father.

"Dr. Strider," Dr. Norton said, "it's time to get dressed."

Chris surveyed the delivery table to find that it was already laid out with two sets of sterile gowns and gloves; one set was his size.

He looked at her blankly. "Me?"

With a grin, she said, "You didn't expect me to deliver this baby, did you?"

Chris hadn't expected this, hadn't even thought of it, but liked the idea at once. As he joined Dr. Norton in getting gowned and gloved, he confided, "I haven't done all that many deliveries."

"Don't worry," she said. "You do good work. And today, all you have to do is catch. I'll do the rest."

Dr. Norton massaged and maneuvered until the top of the baby's head was all but out, and then turned to Chris. "All right. Your turn."

Moving into position, he said, "Okay, Suze, push!" Then he watched in amazement as he delivered the top of the baby's head, followed by the eyes, a cute little smooshed nose, a mouth, and finally a chin.

He suctioned the baby's mouth and nose and, with the next push, delivered the shoulders. Then—through some miracle he had yet to grasp—he was gazing at his own child crying in his hands.

Dr. Norton took a quick peek between the baby's legs. "Congratulations, it's a girl!"

"No, it can't be." Even though Chris was staring right at the anatomy in question, he didn't believe what he saw. "Striders don't have girls," he explained. "They just don't."

Susana hadn't wanted to spoil the surprise by learning the baby's gender on the ultrasound, but in Chris's mind there was never any question; of course they would have a boy. After all, in five generations of Striders, only one other girl had been born, and that only as a twin.

Dr. Norton looked up at him, her merry eyes dancing. "Well, unless they've changed the diagnostic criteria, my twenty years of obstetrical practice says this child's probably a girl."

But Chris was still incredulous. "A *real* girl?"

Susana giggled. "Do you think maybe I could see?"

"Oh, I'm sorry." Chris placed the wriggling baby on Susana's belly and began drying her off with a towel.

"I have to agree with Dr. Norton," Susana said. "Looks like a girl to me."

Chris cut the cord and took another look. "Wow. A real girl." He laid his finger in the baby's hand, which immediately gripped his tightly. His brain knew this was a simple reflex. Yet his newborn daughter's grasp triggered the most profound sense of wonder, of love, that he'd ever known.

"What's her name?" Dr. Norton asked.

Susana caught Chris's eye, her own welling up in joyful tears. "Bethany Rose."

"Yes. Bethany Rose," Chris echoed. The name conjured memories of lying alone in a prison cell, awaiting execution, and wondering if Susana would someday have a daughter named Bethany with another man. And yet, because of

Josh's incredible *lashani*—his willingness even to die in Chris's place—Chris was now standing here, staring in amazement at *his* daughter.

"Kuira, keni mará," he whispered. (Rarámuri: Hello, my daughter.) Then, overcome with gratitude, he spoke the words again, savoring the way they felt in his mouth. *"Keni mará"*—my daughter.

🏃 🏃 🏃 🏃 🏃

The next morning, Chris awoke when Susana twitched the arm that was lying across his waist. Around two o'clock, while trying to soothe his fussy daughter, he had lain down on the hospital bed with Bethany on his chest so she could hear his heartbeat. The soothing worked so well they both fell asleep, along with Susana lying beside them. The three had slept soundly like that the rest of the night.

When Chris awoke, George was standing at the foot of the bed taking a picture. He grinned as he handed Chris his cell phone. "For your baby book. I just couldn't pass up such a great shot. I'll e-mail it to you."

Chris smiled at the picture George had taken of the three of them sleeping. It really was a great shot. George cooed over the baby and chatted with them for several minutes before leaving. Then Susana began making the bed, but stopped suddenly, her eyes going wide.

Settling Bethany in her bassinet, Chris asked, "What's wrong?"

"Does that look like a foiled dart to you?" She nodded at something on the bed.

Chris moved to her side to see a small pea-green sphere lying among the folds of the sheets. He gingerly picked up the hard object and, examining it minutely, noticed four small, blunted projections. When he set it down and whacked it with his shoe, a coffee-colored gel oozed out. "Um, I'm going to go with 'yes.'"

She flashed him a this-is-no-time-for-bad-jokes expression. "I'm wearing sunscreen. Are you?"

He guiltily met her eyes.

"Oh, Chris. How could you forget that?"

"It was a little crazy yesterday morning." And, well, maybe he'd been a bit lax about it lately, too. After all, George had been so nice—not at all troublesome.

"Wait a minute—this dart is foiled, so it bounced off sunscreen. He must of shot at me."

"Or he shot at us both, in which case he would have gotten me," Chris added reluctantly. He proceeded to check all areas of exposed skin, but found no darts or bumps. Apparently he'd been lucky—but it was really stupid to count on luck when it came to Stan's darts.

Susana, however, found three small red spots where darts had bounced off her sunscreen. "Do you know which dart that is?" she asked.

"No, but Doug will."

Chris activated his transmitter and explained what had happened. When he described the dart, Doug said, "That's jealousy. George apparently couldn't find one of the foiled darts to take all the evidence with him."

"But why would he be trying to poison me with jealousy?" Susana asked.

"That's a good question, little filly. Chris, are you aware of anyone Susana might have reason to be jealous of?"

"What?" Chris exclaimed indignantly. "Are you asking if I'm seeing someone else? Of course not!"

"Okay, pardner. Don't get your dander up. But if you think of any reason George might believe jealousy would be of use here, you let me know."

"All right," Chris said petulantly. He logged off and looked at Susana. "There's nothing. No reason."

She held out her hand and he sat down beside her. "I believe you, *mi amor*," she said, and laid her head on his chest.

"Thanks." He kissed her head. "You're my one love, *mi tesoro*. There could never be anyone else."

"I know. But George is obviously planning something. We'll just have to be on the lookout for it."

That's what Susana wanted to believe. Yet as she stepped into the restroom to bathe, she silently admitted her doubts. Just little things, mind you, but after pondering the implications of Doug's question to Chris, and his irritable response to it, those incidents were taking on new meaning.

She stepped into the shower and let the warm water wash over her, rinsing away the sweat and soreness—and uncertainty. Of course Chris wasn't having an affair. After all, he was a terrible liar, so if he ever were to cheat on her, he wouldn't be able to keep it a secret. Besides, he wasn't the cheating type.

Except for that one time when they were dating …

She shook her head. No, that wasn't really an affair. More like a temper tantrum. And he'd repented and changed altogether. He'd never repeat that mistake; she was sure of it.

Wasn't she?

Quite against her will, her mind began clicking through the list of "little things" she'd noticed, like the recently disappearing date nights, missed dinners, and his lengthening hours at the hospital. In fact, he'd been spending more and more time at the hospital ever since he started this extra rotation in obstetrics. Sure, it was always a busy rotation, but he hadn't spent as much time on the wards when he took it the first time around. Besides, George, who was taking the same rotation, wasn't working as much as Chris was. Come to think of it, George also became vague whenever she mentioned Chris's late arrivals. But he could be doing that just to stir up trouble. That was his job, after all.

But then, there was also the aftershave thing. During his first week of the rotation, Chris had stopped using aftershave, saying he'd learned that pregnant women could be hypersensitive to odors and that aftershave could make them feel more nauseated. But lately he had begun wearing it again, even though he was still doing OB.

Oh—and the pink note!

A wave of heat swept over her that had nothing to do with a change in the water temperature. Even now, she could see the whole incident so clearly. Chris had been emptying his pockets when he found a piece of folded pink paper. She noticed him flush and cast a guilty glance in her direction before he crumpled it up as if to throw it away. But then he didn't dispose of it. She knew that because she, being curious, had looked for it in all the trashcans but never found it. That meant he must have specifically waited to throw it into a trashcan outside the apartment so she wouldn't find it. Or tucked it away somewhere for safekeeping like a—

Oh, no. That was it, wasn't it? He had been hiding a love note.

He *was* seeing someone. How could she have missed it? She was going to lose Chris. Maybe she already had. A giant weight fell on her back, one far beyond her ability to bear. One that would alter her life forever.

She leaned against the shower wall and simply bawled.

CHAPTER 28
PLAGUE PREVENTION

" 'Come out of her, my people, lest you share in her sins,
and lest you receive of her plagues.' "
Revelation 18:4, NKJV.

Chris scrutinized his wife as he listened to her conversation. Why wasn't she objecting to Dr. Norton's suggestion that she stay another day? She had said she wanted to leave the hospital as soon as possible. True, Bethany was having some trouble with breastfeeding, but they'd probably get that straightened out by this evening.

"Yes, I'll stay if that's what you think is best," Susana answered Dr. Norton listlessly.

She did look tired—exhausted, even. In fact, she looked like she'd been crying. Was she already experiencing that postpartum hormonal drop?

When the doctor took her leave, Chris bent over the bed to kiss his wife. "I'm going to take Bethany for a long walk so you can get some sleep, Suze."

"Mmm."

He wasn't sure what that funny look in her eye was, but sleep would at least help, if not cure, whatever was ailing her. So he scribbled a "Do Not Disturb" sign, stuck it on the door, and rolled Bethany's crib out of the room. "Come on, sweet pea. Mommy needs some rest."

🏃🏃🏃🏃🏃

Susana laid her head, filled with hopeless, helpless thoughts, back on her pillow as she watched Chris wheel the baby out of the room. She was drifting off to sleep when she became vaguely aware of someone standing at her bedside.

She awoke with a start, but then broke into a smile and gave the intruder a big hug. "Debora, I'm so glad you came."

"I would have been here sooner if invited," her old coach said mildly. "As it is, I hope my visit is not unwelcome."

"Of course not. You're always welcome."

"Am I, indeed?"

Susana wasn't sure what Debora meant, but neither was she in the mood to ask. "I'm sorry you missed the baby. Chris just took her for a walk. But they should be nearby. I'm sure we can find them."

She started to get up, but Debora laid a hand on her arm. "Don't trouble yourself. You're the one I've come to see."

"Oh." Susana put the head of the bed up and relaxed back against it while Debora drew a chair near. "Is there a problem, *Ami*?"

"You tell me, dear one. I wasn't the one weeping in the shower this morning."

What? Had Chris heard her? "Chris told you that?"

"No. He's unaware of it. He believes you're overly tired."

"I guess I am."

"Is that all?"

Susana stared into Debora's eyes and realized that her coach already knew exactly what had happened. She was simply asking if Susana would share it voluntarily.

"Chris is having, having—an affair." The tears began before she finished the sentence, which ended in a choking sob.

Several moments of silence intervened, broken only by Susana's weeping. Finally Debora replied, "I see."

Susana looked up with a sniff. "You don't sound surprised."

"I'm not surprised that you believe this to be true, although you have no real evidence."

"Are you saying it's not true?"

"I said nothing of the kind."

Okay, this was not going right. It was turning into one of those I-can't-tell-you-what-I-know talks, and that wasn't fair. Those talks always ended in what Susana was doing wrong.

"This is not my fault," she insisted. "I'm not the one cheating on my husband."

"No, you're the one jumping to conclusions about your husband's behavior. I will not say that Chris is blameless in this situation—"

"Aha, so he *is* guilty!" Susana wasn't sure why that made her feel victorious, but it did.

Debora pursed her lips disapprovingly and continued as if Susana hadn't interrupted. "—but what I find most disturbing is the reason behind your choice of conclusions."

Susana studied the sheets. She wasn't going to ask what Debora meant. She wasn't. She didn't want to know.

Okay—yes, she did. "What—what do you mean?"

Debora leisurely rose and crossed over to a chair to fold some baby clothes lying there. "Suppose you're driving down the street to your parents' home and see cinders and ash in the air. Do you immediately conclude that their home is on fire?"

"No, it's probably old Don Felipe burning trash again. He's never accepted that it's against the law here."

"And you would probably be right. But suppose that you had just set fire to your parents' house? Now would you conclude that their home is on fire when you see the same cinders and ash in the air?"

"Why would I set their house on fire?"

Debora turned around to fix her with a knowing gaze. "Why, indeed?"

Susana frowned. She'd missed a step somewhere.

"The point is, your own behavior influences your interpretation of the evidence."

Susana cocked her head. "Are you suggesting that I'm guilty of infidelity?"

"Of infidelity? No. But guilty? Yes."

See? Just as she predicted, Debora was turning this into her fault. She knew she would.

Susana brushed harshly at some fuzz. "Then what am I supposed to be guilty of?"

"Of withdrawing that which you once gave to Doug."

Susana's hand abruptly stopped. Maybe her coach was right. "You mean my—my marriage?"

"Just so. The enemy needs only one, small, unprotected point of entry—that's all. With that, he is able to accomplish all manner of mischief."

As Susana studied the wrinkles in the covers, her tears began again, and Debora added softly, "Such as making you one very unhappy young woman."

"You're right, *Ami*. You're right. Can—can you help me?"

"I am both able," Debora said with a sweet smile, "and willing."

🏃 🏃 🏃 🏃 🏃

After strolling the halls for a while, Chris ended up in the doctor's lounge, where he and Bethany both conked out. When he returned to the room a couple of hours later, he found Ellen, the lactation specialist, exiting Susana's room.

"Oh, Dr. Strider, congratulations. And there's the little bundle of joy. What a cutie."

"Thank you," he said, unconsciously running a hand over his hair. He must be a mess. He should have showered and shaved before leaving the room.

"I have a meeting just now, but Susana will call me for the baby's next feeding." Ellen reached into her bosom and drew out a folded pink note. "And this is for you," she said intimately. She slipped the paper into his shirt pocket and patted it.

Chris shifted nervously. Didn't she realize how inappropriate this was? His wife had just given birth to his child. "I—" He cleared his throat. "I'll see you later."

He dove into the room but stopped just inside, before Susana could see him, and read the note. With the heat of a flush crawling up his neck, he crumpled the paper and stuffed it in his back pocket.

Sweeping aside the privacy curtain, he forced a smile as he handed Bethany over for her meal. Susana seemed to be feeling better after her nap. She cooed and chatted cheerily with the baby while she fed her. As he watched his wife and daughter interact, a wave of love surged through him. He was a truly lucky man.

When Susana finished with the baby, Chris settled Bethany in her bassinet. Then he took away the pillows behind Susana and sat down in their place. Drawing her back against him, he said, "Have I thanked you yet for giving me such a beautiful daughter?"

Susana giggled. "Only a dozen times or so. But I'm not tired of hearing it yet."

"Then thank you for the most amazing gift ever," he said with a kiss to her temple.

"Smooching again?" came a familiar voice.

Chris bounded up from the bed. "Josh!"

The three exchanged greetings, and then they introduced Josh to Bethany. For a time, he simply watched her as she slept. When he finally lifted her into his arms, she awoke without crying and the two regarded each other. At last, Josh placed his hand on Bethany's head.

"May Dad bless you and keep you; may he make his face shine upon you and be gracious to you; may he turn his face toward you and give you peace." He kissed her on the forehead and laid her gently in the crib, but continued to hold her eyes until she returned to sleep.

"Thank you," Chris whispered, strangely moved by the simple ceremony. Susana sniffled and wiped her eyes.

"You're welcome, *boní*," Josh said with a smile. (Rarámuri: little brother) "You've been blessed with a very special child. She and her husband will do a work unprecedented in both type and importance. But take care to guide her gently. Along with her mother's eyes, she has inherited her sensitive spirit."

Susana smiled as she watched the babe falling asleep at her breast. "I think she actually got her fill this time, Ellen."

"She seems happy," the lactation nurse agreed. "And are you feeling more comfortable with nursing?"

"Yes. It's not hard once we got her to latch on the right way. I think we'll be fine."

"I'm sure you will."

Chris walked into the room just then. As his gaze landed on Ellen, something like embarrassment came into his eyes. Susana didn't think she liked that reaction. And she definitely didn't like the look she now saw in Ellen's gray eyes. She didn't mind the sparks of interest she sometimes saw in women's faces when they met Chris. He was not only a handsome, athletic man, but had a kind spirit. A little interest was understandable. But the look in Ellen's eyes was something more than that, more like the self-assurance of a woman who knows her interest is reciprocated.

But as Susana's gaze returned to Chris, she realized that he didn't appear even vaguely charmed. In fact, his eyes had gone hard—like maybe he was mad at being put together in the same room with his two love interests? Wordlessly stepping to the window, he stood there with his back to them.

Susana's heart began pounding. Something was definitely going on here; she was not just jumping to conclusions. Chris wasn't always the most sociable guy in the world, but he certainly wasn't rude to people. There was something between these two, and she was going to find out what it was. Even if she wasn't sure she wanted to know.

Ellen turned back to Susana. "I'll check on you before you go home tomorrow, but you can also call me from home if you have any trouble."

If this nurse was involved with Chris, it must not be the first time she'd been in the position of the "other woman." Smooth and collected, she didn't seem thrown by the situation at all. She calmly headed for the door and then stopped. "May I speak with you for a second, Dr. Strider?"

He turned around and said brusquely, "I'm right here."

"I mean, in private."

"Why? Do you have something to say to me that my wife can't hear?"

Ellen seemed a little flustered at that. "Um, no. Of course not." With a forced smile, she said quickly, "Well, you know how to reach me if you need anything" and scurried out the door.

Chris frowned and turned back toward the window where he remained, silently clenching his jaw, even after Ellen left.

Susana debated with herself. Clearly, something was going on between these two, but what was it exactly? That last interchange sure didn't sound like a couple of lovers. Should she broach the topic? Did she really want to know the truth?

Yes. Yes, she did. There might yet be an innocent explanation. And if it wasn't so innocent, she wouldn't stick her head in the sand. Besides, the truth couldn't possibly be worse than what her imagination would conjure up.

"You were almost rude to that nurse," she said quietly. "She's only here to help, you know."

"Oh, yes, she's very helpful," he replied sarcastically.

Susana hesitated. "What's the problem, Chris?"

He gazed out the window, clenching his jaw.

"Chris? Please tell me. What's going on?"

He sighed. "It's nothing, Suze. Nothing you need to bother about."

"Consider me bothered."

He pivoted to study her. "Okay. If that's what you want." He shifted his position, scratched his head, raked a hand through his hair, and shifted his position again, all while turning red.

"Okay. It's—" He stopped. Ran a hand through his hair. Grew redder.

Meanwhile, Susana became more and more uncomfortable. This was not like Chris at all. She'd never seen him this nervous. This must be the preamble to confessing an affair. What else could make him so jittery?

At last he cleared his throat. "Well, here. Read this. You'll get the idea. This isn't the first one." He drew a crumpled piece of pink paper from his back pocket and handed it to her. It looked exactly like the one she'd seen him blush over a few weeks before.

She smoothed out the note and read:

Your wife won't be able to meet all your needs for the next six weeks. Call me when you get lonely.

  - Ellen

A small shriek escaped Susana, and she clapped a hand over her mouth. So it was true! Her husband was having an affair.

"Suze, what's wrong?" he had the audacity to ask. He sank to the bed and grasped her hands.

Jerking them from his grasp, she cried, "Don't touch me. How can you? How can you—?" She dissolved into sobs.

"How can I what? What are you talking about?"

What planet did this man come from?

As he stared at her, he suddenly caught his breath. "Suze, you don't think I'm cheating on you, do you?"

Her sobs came to an abrupt halt. What other explanation could there be?

"Suze, no—never!" He grasped her chin, impelling her to look directly into his sincere eyes. Slowly, emphatically, he said, "Listen to me. I have never cheated on you. I will never cheat on you. I never could." He was looking her straight in the eye without wavering. It wasn't the gaze of a guilty man.

His voice softened. "I promised myself only to you, Susana Strider. I've never broken that vow, and I never will. I don't even want to. Why would I risk losing my most precious *tesoro*?

"But the note—"

"That's all her, not me. She's been chasing me ever since I started back on this unit. Actually, even before that. But I have never, ever accepted her offers. You have to believe me."

"That doesn't make sense. If a guy's not responding to her advances, a girl stops flirting. Why is she still pursuing you?"

"I don't know. She just doesn't seem to take a hint. But when I saw her chatting with you so easily after just giving me this note a few hours ago, it really ticked me off. I think I saw for the first time what a phony she is. She even wanted to continue her little game right here in front of you." He said the last part through clenched teeth. With a snort, he added, "You called her helpful? Oh, yeah. Very helpful."

"Have you discussed it with Doug?"

"No," he said thoughtfully. "Actually, I hadn't even thought of it. But it's a great suggestion. I will." He started to get up, but turned back to her. "Suze, you do believe me, don't you?"

She looked intently into those deep black eyes she knew so well, eyes that couldn't even keep legitimate secrets like birthday and Christmas presents. Her gut said this man was truly incapable of lying to her. Only her fear argued the point. Would she give in to that fear?

"Yes," she said. "I believe you. But please talk to Doug about this."

He smiled, relief evident on every feature. "I will. I promise."

🏃 🏃 🏃 🏃 🏃

Later that evening, when Susana and Bethany were both asleep, Chris went to the floor's conference room, where he knew he could be alone, and called Doug.

"Howdy, pardner. How are my little filly and that new daughter?"

"They're both great, *Ada*. Really great. And Josh came by earlier today. It was good to see him."

"He felt the same way. He flew down from Cheyenne just to see y'all. I know it was a short visit, but he enjoyed it."

"So did we. Even more now that I know how far he came."

"So, what's on your mind tonight?"

"Something I should have thought to talk to you about long ago. Maybe the answer to what you asked me earlier today. I've been having trouble with a nurse here by the name of Ellen ...?"

"Milner."

"Yeah," Chris said, surprised. "How'd you know?"

"I make it my business to know when an agent sics an operative on one of my runners."

Doug's words set the skin between Chris's shoulders crawling. An operative focused on him? The last time that had happened, Josh ended up dying.

"I've been waitin' for you to talk to me about her," Doug continued. "To be honest, I've been a little worried 'bout you. I'm glad you've decided to do something about it."

"I've been trying to do something about it. She won't take no for an answer."

"Maybe that's 'cause she knows the difference between a maybe-no and a real no."

Chris felt as if Doug had socked him between the eyes. "Are—are you saying you think I want to cheat on Susana?"

"No, I don't think that's it, but Ellen Milner doesn't know that. All she knows is that your mouth says 'no' while your eyes say, 'but ask me again.' "

"But I don't—I wouldn't—"

"No, I don't think you would. Still—and I'm gonna lay it all out as naked as a baby's bottom, son—I think you like being asked all the same."

"Doug!"

"Look into your heart and tell me it's not so. Tell me there's not a part of you that likes knowin' other women find you attractive."

In response to Doug's challenge, several questions rolled through Chris's mind: Why did he always find an excuse to stay late when Ellen was on duty? Why was he using aftershave again, even though he knew it could nauseate his pregnant patients? Why was he suddenly so aware of his appearance when Ellen was around?

"Can you tell me that, son?"

Chris sighed. "No, I can't. But then, you already know that, don't you?"

Doug chuckled.

Getting up to pace the room, Chris said, "Doug, this is scary. I don't want to feel like I need someone else's attention. And I certainly don't want to get caught in some kind of affair that could blow my marriage. That's where something like this could lead, isn't it?"

"Yes, son, it could. Doesn't have to, though. Especially in your case, 'cause this isn't about lust for you—it's about affirmation and admiration, which are normal needs. If your focus weren't all out of whack, you'd be getting those needs met the right way—at home."

"So what do I do?"

"Well, Dr. Strider, here's your prescription. First off, you need to dust off that grace inhaler and take yourself two puffs. Then you need to focus on Susana and meetin' her needs. You've been slippin' in that department, haven't you? When was the last time you took that little filly out on a date? When was the last time you brought her some flowers or watched the stars with her?"

"You're right, I have been getting sloppy about that," he admitted. "I've just been so busy."

"Busy with what I've given you to do?"

"Well, I thought I could use the extra experience in obstetrics since it's so closely related to pediatrics."

"Is that the only reason you've been spending extra time there?"

Chris knew what Doug was getting at. Ellen's attention was flattering. He had enjoyed it on one level, while denying it on another. "You're right, *Ada*."

"You can always find excuses, son. When you run out, George will be happy to supply you with more, just like he's been doing the last couple of months. Still, excuses don't change the truth. It all comes down to stickin' to those priorities of yours. When you take care of meeting Susana's needs, your own will get met too. It's just about that simple. On the other side of the coin is this—if you're not meeting Susana's needs, who is?"

"What?" Chris exploded. "What are you saying?"

"Calm down, son. I'm not saying *that*. But have you even thought about it? Remember, for example, when Susana needed her windshield wipers changed? Do you know who helped her do it when you forgot? Or who's been helpin' her lug groceries up to the apartment? Or who—"

"Who?" Chris demanded.

"A certain agent masquerading as George Strong. He's set up a double-sided trap for y'all, and you've been too distracted to notice that you're sliding right into it. At one end, he's been feedin' you excuses to stay at work where his operative is puffing up your ego and setting you up for an affair. At the other, he's been exploiting Susana's need for companionship through the vacancy you're leavin' behind."

"Why haven't you told me?"

"Son, you've hardly been talkin' to me in private. When you do, you're in a hurry and not interested in complications."

Chris's head dropped into his hands. Doug was right in placing the blame squarely on him, and he felt a chill of terror as he realized how near the danger had come—again. How could he get so apathetic when he knew who George was and what his goal was?

"I'm sorry, Doug," he said. "Really sorry. I can't believe I've been so blind."

" 'They associated with the people of the land and learned their ways,' " Doug quoted from the *Manual's* Songbook. " 'Then they worshiped their idols and were ensnared by them.' "

"In other words, the more I hang around with non-runners—at least if I'm not hanging around with you enough—the more likely it is that I'm going to mess up."

"That's a tolerably good paraphrase."

"And it's true, too. Somehow George just doesn't seem all that dangerous to me lately."

"They accomplish that by layin' low for a while to gain your confidence. They can even be downright helpful. Then, once you let your guard down, they're in a better position to hit you hard."

Chris groaned. Of course—that's exactly what George had done. "I should have recognized what he was doing."

"I hate to break it to you, pardner, but on your own, you're pretty near helpless against Stan's crew. They're smart, well trained, and have centuries of practice. Your only defense is—always will be—in using your protective gear and stickin' tight to me. It's relatively easy to stay alert when you know the enemy's active. When things look quiet, though, it requires a lot of patient watchfulness."

"Joshliness."

Doug burst into laughter. "Well, I've never heard it put quite that way, but yes, 'Joshliness' pretty much describes it." He paused before adding softly, "That's the reason I instituted the yearly ultramarathons, you know—to help runners make the fundamentals an ongoing part of their lives."

Chris shook his head at himself. "You mean *Susana's* being eight months pregnant wasn't a good reason for *me* not to run it this year?" How could he ever hope to fulfill his goal of being truly, unreservedly committed to Doug if he kept contriving such ridiculous excuses to shirk his duties?

They chatted a little longer, and then Chris went home to use the grace inhaler as Doug had directed. Afterward he went for a run—a short one, but his first in a while. He returned home feeling more settled and at peace than he had in weeks.

After showering, he took a critical look around the apartment. They'd left in a hurry and it was kind of messy, which he knew would bother Susana when she got home. So he took some time to straighten things up and make some spaghetti sauce for their dinner the next evening.

As he worked, he tried to picture what Susana's life would be like while she was on maternity leave. He saw lots of interrupted sleep, an endless cycle of breastfeeding and changing diapers, and not much of the socializing with friends that she enjoyed so much. While pondering this, a few ideas came to mind of ways he could improve things for her. He made a quick call to Susana's mother and then took one final look around the now-tidy apartment before returning to the hospital.

Ellen came in to check on them the next morning, and Chris asked to speak to her outside. When the door closed behind them, she flashed a knowing smile. "I knew you'd come around, Chris."

"Miss Milner, I'm really sorry if I've given you the impression that I was interested in any kind of liaison. The simple truth is, I love my wife. I'm the luckiest guy in the world to have married such an incredible woman." He paused as he wondered when the last time was that he'd told Susana that. "I am most definitely not interested in anything extra on the side, and I never will be. I hope that's clear because I really don't want to take it up with your supervisor."

Ellen's cheeks grew red. "Yes, that's quite clear, Dr. Strider. I'm sorry to have bothered you. Apparently my information was, well, wrong." She scurried off down the hall, seemingly anxious to be out of his sight. Chris stared after her, scarcely believing how easy it had been.

When he reentered Susana's room, she was hanging up the phone. "That was my mother. They were just leaving, so they'll be here tonight."

She looked up at him expectantly, but he wasn't sure what she was expecting, so he just said, "Good," as he sat on the bed facing her.

"Is that all you have to say?" Her eyes danced with amusement.

"Um, I hope they have a safe trip?"

She laughed. "My mother spilled the beans. So come on, tell me about the secret phone call."

"Oh, that," he said with a chuckle. "I asked her if she'd babysit Bethany one night a week after we move to LA this summer."

"She told me that much. That's what she was excited about. So excited, in fact, she'd forgotten why."

"For our date night."

A sweet smile spread over her face. "I was hoping that's what it was. I've missed them."

"Me too," he said soberly. "It's just that with my call schedule changing and everything, it's been hard—"

He stopped himself. That wasn't really the truth, was it?

"Actually," he said softly, "I think I just got lazy again."

She grasped his hand. "But you haven't forgotten. Thank you for that."

He smiled. She was far too generous with him. "We won't be able to stick to the same night every week since my schedule won't be regular during residency. So I thought I could give you my schedule every month and let you pick one night a week that works for both you and your mom."

"That's a great idea."

"Good. I also want you to schedule yourself an afternoon off every week to coincide with my afternoons off after call."

"An afternoon off? Off what?"

"Off, well, motherhood. An afternoon to do whatever you want—have lunch with a friend, read, whatever you want to do other than be a mom. I'll take care of Bethany. Just freeze some milk for her."

Her eyes widened. "Are you serious?"

"I know it's not much of a break from a 24/7 job, but I figure it should help."

She studied him, tears brightening her eyes. "Chris, you don't know how much—"

She paused to wipe at her eyes. "When you left earlier to pick that stuff up from home, Bethany got fussy again. I think she's going to be a daddy's girl. She always fusses when you leave. Anyway, I fed her, burped her, changed her, walked her, and everything else I could think of, but she just kept crying every time I put her down. And I was so tired and had to go to the bathroom really bad, but I couldn't just leave her crying. Anyway, I started wondering, if this is how I feel after two days, how will I ever make it through three months nonstop? But this, an afternoon a week all to myself, it's just—it's wonderful."

"I hope it helps."

"Thank you. It already does." She cupped his face in her hand and kissed him. "You know what else would help is if you would tell me your secret with her."

"It's not really my secret—I learned it from an OB nurse. 'Put yourself in the baby's skin,' she said. See, for her entire life, Bethany's been in a warm, tight place where she always hears lub-dub, lub-dub, so that's how she feels secure. Everything else feels strange to her, like something's wrong. So you just try to recreate that. You swaddle her firmly, make sure she's warm, and put her next to your heart. Or use this." He got up, took a red heart out of the crib and handed it to Susana with a grin. It was still making the sound of a heartbeat. "I picked one up this morning."

Bethany stirred and began whimpering, and Chris snatched the heart from Susana and set it back in the crib. When Bethany quieted down again, he turned to her with a grin. "See? That's my secret."

"I have a secret, too." Susana rose and slipped her arms around his waist. "You are the most amazing man I've ever known, and I love you more than I know how to say. I love being married to you."

The statement was simple, almost matter-of-fact. Yet she said it with such sincerity that Chris found he couldn't speak for how deeply it moved him. He kissed her on the forehead and held her close, relishing her warmth and softness, the fresh citrus smell of her newly washed hair, the way she snuggled against him. He didn't appreciate these things often enough. He took them for granted. In fact, he had started taking her for granted. He needed to break that habit—starting right now.

"I love you, Susana Strider," he murmured, his voice hoarse with emotion. "I am truly the luckiest man in the world."

CHAPTER 29
CURSED

> " 'I will bring a terrible curse against you.
> I will curse even the blessings you receive.
> Indeed, I have already cursed them,
> because you have not taken my warning to heart.' "
> Malachi 2:2, NLT.

June 8012 – November 8014 M.E.

On the evening of 18 June 8012 M.E., Camille was physically located in Stan's office, though officially registered in Desmon Tower's hospital. They were sharing Chinese takeout when they received the phone call informing them that a surrogate had delivered their second child. Upon answering the call, Stan listened with an increasingly narrowed gaze, and then erupted with a curse and slammed the phone down.

Camille pursed her lips against a snicker and asked mildly, "A male, then?" They already knew this from the ultrasounds, but Stan had insisted that ultrasounds were not completely accurate in assessing gender.

Frowning at her darkly, he complained, "Simple luck would allow a 50-50 chance of a female."

"Yes, well, I would say that the Striders have little such 'luck.' "

Why her brother cared about the child's gender was a mystery to Camille, though not enough of one to merit her investigation. She simply found his preoccupation amusing.

He crunched on stir-fried vegetables for a moment and then stated grumpily, "Stanley L. Moden III."

Camille rolled her eyes. "For the hundredth time, I will not sign a birth certificate with such a name. We already have one Stan and one Stanley in the house. What would you have us call this child—L?"

"Hmpf."

"Saxon L. Moden will suffice. He will still bear your indelible mark by way of your initials."

Stan grunted his displeasure, but did not argue further. Nevertheless, Camille determined to complete the birth certificate immediately after dinner. Since she had to pass the nursery on her way, she decided she might as well meet the child too. She found him surprisingly cute for a human. He was not given to fits of crying, was alert and apparently intelligent, and his blue eyes actually looked much like her own. This, of course, was a ridiculous notion. Not only was there no biological relationship between them, they weren't even of the same species. Furthermore, the baby's eyes would likely change color as he aged. Stanley's eyes had also been blue at birth, but had later become a plain, uninspired brown.

Still, Camille was inclined to like this Saxon creature. If first impressions were an accurate indicator, his personality would be compatible with her own. That was fortunate, since she would have to spend considerable time with him. Although his training, like Stanley's, would begin immediately, it would still require a couple of decades to fully prepare him to assume her business-related duties.

Twenty months later, Dr. Pim implanted another embryo in a surrogate, and Stan was again disappointed that the result was a male. Camille was working late in her office when she received the phone call announcing the birth of Sheridan L. Moden on 24 November 8014 M.E. About an hour later, Stan stalked into her office, trailed by a nurse carrying the newborn.

"I don't care to see the child at the moment," Camille objected. "I'm quite busy. I'll see it tomorrow."

"You'll see it now," Stan growled. He motioned the nurse to the desk.

Camille dutifully, if reluctantly, surveyed the infant. He was an unremarkable specimen—not as cute as Saxon, but not as squirmy as Stanley. In fact, he seemed rather good-natured, content to take in his surroundings without complaint.

"Fine," she said. "I've seen it."

"No. You need to see all of it." Stan nodded to the nurse, who began to unwrap the blanket.

"Why?" Camille said, suddenly concerned. "Surely it isn't defective, is it? The *mij dinósh* should have prevented any—"

She halted as the nurse bared the child's chest. A large red birthmark lay just below the left collarbone. The irregular border of the oval's upper margin gave it the appearance of a diadem. Specifically, Doúg's diadem.

Lifting her gaze to the nurse, she ordered. "Leave us."

As the nurse exited with the infant, Camille met Stan's eye, knowing exactly what he was thinking. He might have branded their children by means of his initials, but only Doúg had the power to mark a child's skin. "It's impossible, Stan," she said quietly.

"And yet, there it is." He strode to the window and gazed down on the city. "And on the wrong side."

"There are no other defects?"

"None. But the *mij dinósh* should have prevented any defect, including birthmarks. No other infant born through this means has had one."

Camille hesitated, reluctant to verbalize what they were both thinking. Yet they needed to examine the possibility. Clearing her throat, she ventured, "In Paradisians, birthmarks do not arise as defects."

Stan swiveled to her, his eyes narrowed. "He's not Paradisian."

"Then any concerns we may have are ... unfounded?"

He frowned. "I'm not sure that's a logical conclusion."

Neither was she—although it's what she preferred to believe. The truth was that they were in wholly uncharted waters here. There simply was no precedent from which to extract reliable information. Doúg had marked special Paradisians, including Stan, with that symbol, but he had never celebrated a human's birth in the same manner. Yet, if he could mark a Paradisian's skin, could he not do the same to a human?

Stan turned back to the window, and silence settled between them for several moments. "We should just kill him," he said at last.

"That would solve the problem," she agreed. "We will likely be able to obtain more ova from Rose Strider Moore. If you wish to take that route, I have no objection. However ..." She frowned in concentration as another idea came to her.

Stan looked around sharply. "What?"

"If this is merely a fluke—which would be the logical conclusion in a human—it means nothing, and we will be neither better nor worse off if we replace him. However, if that is indeed a *poli*, then the child has special innate *abilities*—not *loyalties*. We know this to be true because we have several *polini* among us already. So if that is the case, we should ask ourselves: Would we not wish to recruit any other human possessing such remarkable abilities? Indeed, are they not precisely the talents we would prefer in the commander of our army?"

Stan's brow furrowed briefly, and then he roared with laughter. Planting a resounding kiss on her forehead, he exclaimed, "Yes. Yes, they are. Thank you, *zali*."

To: companymaster@management.com
From: bestagent@management.com
Date: 12 May 8014 M.E.
Subject: Failed trial—BC-21

Despite promising results for several months, another pregnancy has just been confirmed. I believe the problem is that the delivery system requires regular reloading, which cannot be absolutely controlled or guaranteed in a Subject unaware of its use.

Sir, I fear I owe you an apology for wasting your time on this objective. Despite your brilliant solutions to myriad problems, this is the second offspring Subject has sired. Is there a reason to continue the project?

To: bestagent@management.com
From: companymaster@management.com
Date: 12 May 8014 M.E.
Subject: Re: Failed trial—BC-21

Disappointing results. However, Entity Master assures me that Subject's first offspring possesses neither the requisite personality nor talents to lead the Outlander Division. Although this second offspring may turn out to possess these traits, we do not know this yet. Until we do, our objective of preventing the birth of that leader remains critical.

However, contraceptive options do appear to be doomed to failure by the limits of the delivery systems we've tried. Therefore, I'll confine my efforts to the abortifacients. Unfortunately, it's unlikely that I'll have one perfected in time to abort this offspring.

CHAPTER 30
EVEN BETTER

> *"I know what you are doing, your love and faithfulness, your service
> and your endurance; indeed of late you have done even better than
> you did at first."*
> Revelation 2:19, REB.

C hris strolled down the beach carrying two-and-a-half-year-old Bethany on
his shoulders and enjoying the January crispness of the ocean breeze in his
face. Susana waddled along beside him, very pregnant. For some unknown reason, they'd had trouble getting pregnant this time. Yet, despite almost a year of
trying, the pregnancy itself had gone well, and she was now two days past her due
date. As he watched her smile at some sandpipers, her long black hair playing
around her face, a sense of pure contentment washed over him. He squeezed her
hand and asked, "Are you happy, Suze?"

She lifted her beautiful brown eyes to him. "I'm very happy."

Bethany bounced on his shoulders. "I happy. I sing."

"Yes, *chiquita*," Susana said. "Sing for us. Who's on his throne?"

Bethany happily obliged. "Doug *la-la* throne *la-la-la* no *la-la* worry."

The proud parents laughed as they applauded her performance.

Tugging on Chris's hair, Bethany said, "'Plash, *Onó*. 'Plash." She used the
Rarámuri word for father, as she always did.

Chris lifted her down. "Go on, then," he said in the same language, and
sent Bethany splashing into the water.

Wrapping their arms around each other, he and Susana watched her
alternately chase the waves and run from them. He mused that if he had spent
a fortune arranging things he could not have appointed a more perfect life for
himself. He loved his work, his family, and his friends. Susana was established
as a pediatric physical therapist here in Los Angeles and enjoyed her practice.
He was in his last year of a pediatric residency. In July, he and Efraím, who was
now married to Aedan's daughter, Hannah, would join a practice owned by two
brothers nearing retirement.

Yes, Camille's warning still hung over him. Sometimes he worried over
it. But now he saw these episodes for what they were—his own failure to grasp
hold of Doug's promises. George, of course, was ever present. He had chosen the
same residency program as Chris and Efraím, and had even tried to elbow into
the practice they were joining, although Doug spoiled that part of his plan. Still,
Chris had come to consider George's presence as a kind of blessing, as Doug had
once said. He now recognized the agent's constant labor, but his subtle suggestions of Doug's unfaithfulness, unremitting pall of doubt, and hints about the
futility of Chris's virtuous influence in a world of such evil all drove Chris to Doug.

With such continuing reminders of danger, he had learned to live very close to him.

"I had a dream like this once," Susana said. "I remember it clearly. I was walking on the beach, holding my husband's hand, our daughter running along beside us." She paused before adding softly, "It made me cry when I woke up."

"Cry? Why?"

"Because I knew it could never come true—that no man would ever have me, scarred and ugly as I was." She smiled up at him. "But then I met you, and you made all my impossible dreams come true."

"And you, mine, my most precious *tesoro*." He stroked her hair away from her upturned face and kissed her. It wasn't long and messy—just a nice, tender kiss that lasted a few seconds. But during those seconds, Chris shut his eyes.

When he opened them, Bethany was gone.

His mind immediately jumped to the image of his brother's hand slipping away from him as Eddie disappeared into the rapids of the river where he died. That was the moment when Chris learned the full meaning of the word "panic."

"No," he breathed. "No, no, no, no!" He frantically turned a full circle, scanning the ocean and beach for anything bright red, the color of Bethany's sundress.

Nothing.

He ran out into the waves up to his hips, using his full six-foot-three advantage to search the water all around him once ... twice.

Still nothing.

He couldn't have spent more than a few seconds in his search thus far, but it felt like an eternity. And it would feel even longer to Bethany since two-year-olds needed to breathe more often than adults.

He gulped in a lungful of air and dove, spiraling dread driving him beneath the waves. The chances of sighting her in the murky water were slim, but what else could he do?

Desperately he swam and searched until his lungs ached for oxygen. When he resurfaced for another gulp of air, he heard Susana screaming Bethany's name. Then, just as he started to dive again, he heard the sweetest sound he'd ever known: "What, *Mami*?"

Half believing he was hallucinating, he spun toward shore to see Bethany's head pop up from behind a large piece of driftwood. How she had gotten from the water to that driftwood in those few seconds, he would never know—but that didn't dampen his overwhelming relief.

Susana waded through the waves, tears streaming down her face. "Oh, *mi chiquita*. Come give *Mami* a hug."

"Okay," Bethany said agreeably and ran toward Susana, who fell to her knees in the sand and wrapped her in a long, hard hug. Dripping, Chris kneeled beside the pair and enfolded them both in trembling arms.

After a long group hug, he stood and reached down to help Susana up. But she had become preoccupied with a contraction, so he dropped back to his knees to rub her back. When the contraction was over, Susana said, "That was awfully strong for a Braxton-Hicks contraction."

"Hopefully it's something more," Chris said with a grin.

Meanwhile, Bethany ran back to the far side of the driftwood, where she dropped to her hands and knees beside a dead octopus—apparently the position she'd been in when they lost her a few minutes before. Looking up to Susana, Bethany asked, *"¿Qué es?"* (Spanish: What is it?)

"Pulpo," Susana answered. "Octopus."

"Pulpo," Bethany repeated, obviously preferring the Spanish version. After watching it for a moment, she looked up to Chris, concern etched in her gentle brown eyes. *"Pulpo* sick, *Onó.* Fix." If her daddy could fix sick children, surely he could fix sick *pulpos.*

Chris wasn't sure how she might react to the news of the animal's demise. Just as Josh had predicted, she had inherited Susana's sensitive spirit. He stepped around the driftwood and knelt beside her on the sand. "I'm sorry, baby girl, but I can't. He's—well, he's already dead."

"Dead?" she repeated, her eyes flooding. She had an idea what "dead" meant. She'd seen her friend's cat after being hit by a car.

"We can make a home for him," Chris suggested. "Like Missy did for Tabby-cat, remember?" He began digging a hole in the sand, and, together, they buried the dead octopus.

When they finished, Bethany put both hands on top of the grave and began singing, "Doug *la-la* throne *la-la-la* no *la-la* worry." She sat quietly observing the mound for several moments before looking up. *"Pulpo* happy, *Onó?"*

Chris thought she might be a little young for a full doctrinal study on the state of the dead, so he simply smiled and said, "Yes, sweet pea. Your *pulpo's* happy now."

"Pulpo happy now," she repeated and looked again at the grave. Then she hopped up. "'Plash, *Onó.*"

As he got to his feet, Chris saw Susana again breathing through a contraction, even though he'd been attending to Bethany less than five minutes. "No, baby girl. I think we'd better go home."

"No, *Onó,*" Bethany pled.

Chris came alongside Susana to rub her back, which drew Bethany's attention to Susana. Stepping in front of her, she gazed up quizzically, but her initial puzzlement quickly turned to alarm. *"Mami* sick, *Onó.* Fix!"

"No, sweet pea. *Mami's* not sick. It's baby Andy telling us he's almost ready."

By then, Susana's contraction had eased, and Bethany's expression turned to pure elation. Cupping her mouth at Susana's belly, she yelled, "Hurry, Andy, hurry!"

The contractions became stronger as they drove home and cleaned up. Six hours after arriving at the hospital, at 10:21 p.m. on January 12, the obstetrician, Dr. Mays, helped Chris deliver their healthy son, Andrew Benjamin Strider.

ᚴ ᚴ ᚴ ᚴ ᚴ

Josh seemed to have a knack for walking in when Chris and Susana were kissing. In fact, Chris had come to think he did it on purpose. In any case, when he showed up the day after Andy was born, Chris was leaning over Susana's bed, kissing her.

"Smooching again?" Josh said.

Interruption or not, Chris and Susana were always glad to see the coach, and they greeted him with exuberant hugs and cheek kisses. Even Bethany, although she hadn't met Josh since her own birth, could scarcely contain her excitement and fairly jumped into his arms.

Josh greeted each one warmly and then turned to the crib. "Now I need to meet Andy." He set Bethany down and stood over the sleeping babe. After watching him silently for several moments, he took him in his arms. Andy awoke without crying, and they gazed at each other for a time. Finally Josh turned to Bethany, who had waited, perfectly still, at his side. "Will you help me?"

She nodded solemnly.

Still holding the baby, Josh squatted down in front of her and placed his right hand on Andy's head. Bethany placed her hand over his.

"May Dad bless you and keep you," Josh said.

"Bless you, keep you," Bethany echoed.

"May he make his face shine upon you and be gracious to you."

"Face shine … grape juice."

Josh's mouth twitched. "May he turn his face toward you and give you peace."

"Turn face … um, peace."

When Josh kissed Andy on the forehead, Bethany did too, and then Josh laid him gently back in the crib. He continued to gaze into the baby's eyes until Andy returned to sleep.

Squatting again in front of Bethany, Josh said, "I'd like your help with a very important job. Will you help me?"

"I help," Bethany said soberly.

"I would like you to grow up to be a runner and help Andy grow up to be a runner. Because when you both get big, I need your help with something important. Will you do this for me?"

"I help. I love you, Josh-wa."

Chris thought he heard a catch in Josh's voice as he said, "I love you too, *huayé*. Very much." (Rarámuri: little sister)

As Bethany threw her arms around Josh's neck, Susana sniffled, and Chris put an arm around her shoulders to draw her close.

"I brought you the present you asked for," Josh said.

With a squeal, Bethany bounced up and down, clapping her hands. Josh pulled a transmitter from his shirt pocket, helped her put it on, and showed her how to activate it. She skipped off to a chair to tell Doug all about Josh's visit.

"I thought only runners got transmitters," Chris said. "Not that I object."

"We do give all runners transmitters," Josh said. "But we're happy to give them to anyone who wants one."

"I was about Bethany's age when I got a transmitter," Susana said.

"She can give it up anytime, of course," Josh said. "But if she learns to let Dad help her make decisions beginning at this young age, she'll find life that much more fulfilling.

"Now about Andy," Josh continued. "You've been entrusted with another special child, my friends. Together with Bethany and her husband, Andy will help us bring an end to this war. He has a strong and unyielding spirit"—he grinned at Chris—"even stronger than his father's. He'll need that spirit in his work, but it will be a challenge to his parents, although in different ways. Chris, you must take care not to weaken his will. Temper firmness with love. Susana, you must temper tenderness with consistent firmness, or you will lose control of him. And you should both remember that Dad's grace is able to provide the wisdom and the patience you'll need in training him."

Chris shook Josh's hand. "Thanks again. With Doug's help, I know we can do the job he's given us."

After chatting for a time, Josh stood and clasped Chris around the back of the neck, just as Dad used to do. "I'm afraid I won't see you again for some time, *boní*."

"And yet, somehow, you're always with us," Susana said.

Josh kissed her on the cheek. "That's right. And you with me." He gave them long, heartfelt hugs and turned to go.

"I don't suppose you could time your next visit so you don't interrupt a kiss?" Chris said with a grin.

Josh was chuckling as he turned back around, but his eyes betrayed sadness. "True love is a beautiful thing, *boní*. Treasure every moment."

CHAPTER 31
SLANDER

" 'I know how you are slandered by those who claim to be Jews but
are not; they are really a synagogue of Satan.' "
Revelation 2:9, REB.

"Suze, here's Andy."

The soft-spoken words barely penetrated Susana's sleepy mind, but when Chris touched her arm, she half-roused to put the three-month-old baby to her breast. Chris had initiated this routine in which he would get the crying baby, change his diaper, and bring him to Susana. She fed him lying down, rousing only slightly to turn over when the baby needed to switch sides. Chris then returned him to his crib, sometimes taking the sleeping babe without Susana even noticing. The system had made a huge difference for her, and she now slept longer and more soundly. But she never took Chris's help for granted. She'd heard enough stories from other mothers to know how unusual her husband's thoughtfulness was.

Tonight, however, something was different. Her awareness of the difference came in the form of a smell that wafted through the fog of her sleep. When she roused further to resettle Andy on the other side, she recognized the odor: dirty diaper. Now fully awake, she puzzled over this lapse. Chris had never forgotten the diaper part before.

When Andy finished nursing, Susana slipped out of bed and padded down the hallway to change his diaper and put him back to sleep. But, once fully awake, she had trouble returning to sleep herself—the reason Chris had designed the routine in the first place. While lying there, she noticed that Chris was sleeping fitfully. That was strange too. He'd always been a light sleeper, but his sleep was peaceful.

In the morning, per their usual routine, Chris left home first to drop the children off at her mom's house. However, when Susana prepared to leave, she saw that he'd forgotten all the kids' gear. The diaper bag, the ice chest with the frozen breast milk, and Bethany's "purse" were all left sitting neatly on the counter.

Frowning at the forgotten items, she said, "Huh. He's never done that before either. He must be really tired."

Deciding that her husband needed a good night's sleep worse than she did, Susana determined to beat him to Andy for his nighttime feeding. But the tired mother once again awoke only when Chris handed her the fussing baby. When Andy finished his meal, she shook herself awake and eased toward the edge of the bed to avoid waking Chris, only to realize that he wasn't in bed.

She stared at the empty place. The covers looked as if they'd been in a fight. And it was so unlike Chris to have trouble sleeping. It must be more than fatigue wearing on him; it must be a problem. Yet he hadn't shared it with her, and that was most unusual.

She put Andy back to bed and went in search of her missing husband. She found him sitting in his easy chair in the darkened living room. The picture tugged at her heartstrings. His anxiety was so palpable, like a living being that reached through the dimness and pulled her to him.

She drew in a steadying breath and moved toward him, easing onto the arm of the easy chair. Gently rubbing his shoulders, she asked, "Something wrong, *mi amor*?"

Chris turned to her with a start. "Did I miss getting Andy to bed? I'm sorry. I guess the time got away from me."

"That's not a problem. But what's bothering you?"

He kissed the palm of her hand and held it against his cheek, but said nothing. She waited, combing her fingers through his thick hair, while he organized his thoughts. Finally he said quietly, "It's nothing for you to worry about."

Her fingers abruptly stopped in their path. Chris wasn't one to share his problems with people in general, but he didn't keep them from her. How awful must the problem be to change that?

Sensing that his reticence to talk was itself an indication that he needed to, she moved around in front of him. Rather than meeting her eyes, he bowed his head. She sat on his lap and cradled his face with one hand, directing his gaze to her face. "But I am worried. Why can't you talk to me?"

He hesitated, squeezing his eyes closed. "Because," he whispered, "it's embarrassing."

"Too embarrassing to tell me?"

"Especially you."

Susana's stomach churned. This whole thing was so weird. Chris was a strong man, one from whom others drew strength. His unwavering trust in Doug had buoyed her own flagging spirits on many occasions. Yet tonight she perceived none of his usual vigor. Instead, he appeared totally exhausted, as though he had spent all his strength wrestling some hideous assailant, leaving him so drained that even breathing itself seemed almost more than he could manage.

If only she could help him. Instinctively, she gathered him into her arms and waited, unshed tears burning her eyes. Holding him close, she could feel his despair as if it were her own. Yet it also seemed that her presence was somehow bolstering his teetering strength. So she held him tighter, willing him her very life if it could help him win his mysterious battle.

At last he spoke, his voice scarcely more than a breath. "I've been accused of—" He swallowed. "Of molesting a little boy."

She gasped and drew away to look into his face. It never even occurred to her to ask if the accusation were true. He was no more capable of such a thing than she was.

"Oh, Chris. Who would ever—?"

She stopped, anger rising as the answer came to her: "George." And what a deviously brilliant stroke it was, too. There could be no more effective attack on her honest and caring husband than to bring both his integrity and his commitment to his profession into question with one underhanded strike.

Chris nodded without meeting her gaze, and that alone fanned her anger. What kind of monster would accuse such a kind man of something he finds so shameful that he can't even look his wife in the eye? She really wished George were here right now; she'd teach him to mess with her husband.

Chris's quiet voice interrupted her musings. "When I first rotated through pediatrics as a med student, there was an attending who warned us that, with all the reports of pedophilia in the news, it was something people are almost hyperaware of, and we would be in a position to be accused of it if we weren't careful. He told us to be aware of how things could look to other people, and he listed some precautions we should take. I've always tried to follow those, especially with George around all the time."

He paused and then continued in a low voice, never looking Susana in the eye. "When I was on call Monday night, a two-year-old Down Syndrome boy came in, dehydrated from a stomach flu. He was so scared. You could hear it in his cry. And his mother—well, I don't know what was going on with her. She kept leaving to have a cigarette. Later she left for several hours. Anyway, the little guy took to me."

She caressed his cheek. "Don't they always?"

Chris smiled weakly. "He seemed to feel better when he could hold my fingers." He held up the index and middle fingers of his left hand. "When he was transferred to the ward, they put him in a room by himself. I figured he'd settle down, and he did for a while. But then his mom left again and you could hear him crying all the way down the hall. It was heart wrenching, Suze. The poor kid was so scared and lonely."

"So you stayed with him." Of course he would. What compassionate person wouldn't?

"It wasn't a busy night. I figured I'd stay until his mom came back. Only she didn't come back for five hours. The little guy grabbed onto my fingers, and I told him stories until he fell asleep. Then I sat there reading a textbook. I tried to pry my fingers loose a couple of times, but he woke up each time. Eventually I fell asleep too, and then I guess one of the nurses shut the door."

Or George, Susana thought, but said nothing. Adding her anger to Chris's load wouldn't help him.

"When the mother reappeared, I was alone with the boy in a closed room. She thanked me at the time and tried to explain why she had to leave, which never did make any sense to me, but she clearly has issues of her own."

He stopped and sighed deeply before continuing. "During rounds that morning, I saw George talking to the mother. Shortly thereafter, she was raging through the building, talking to every administrator she could get her hands on."

While Chris sighed again, Susana had to fight a major temptation to give voice to her rage. But doing so would help no one. Her husband needed her support. He didn't need to be burdened further with the weight of her emotions. Those she would deal with herself—with Doug's help. Instead, she contented herself with combing her fingers soothingly through his hair.

He rubbed a hand over his face. "Anyway, it's all a big mess. The police are involved, the boy was examined for"—he clenched his jaw—"for sexual abuse.

Tomorrow I have to meet with the residency director and hospital administrators."

"But they didn't find any evidence against you." She stated it as fact, knowing what the answer would be.

"No, none. And the nurses, who were in and out of the room all night, have weighed in on my side. But these things turn into a big deal even if nothing happened. And, from the hospital's standpoint, you can understand why. They can't be seen as ignoring this kind of accusation." He shrugged feebly. "Meanwhile, everybody knows about it. I hear people whispering behind my back wherever I go."

She continued stroking his hair until he finally peered into her eyes, and she caught her breath at the anguish she saw there. "I was afraid—Suze, I couldn't bear to have you look at me with that kind of question in your eyes."

"Oh, Chris." Her voice broke and she paused to control it. "There is simply no way I would believe such a lie. No way at all. I know you could never do something like that, just as surely as I know the sun's coming up in a few hours."

Obvious relief flooded his eyes, and he reached up to stroke her cheek. "Thank you," he said, his voice catching. "You don't know how much that means to me."

Susana hugged him to herself. What could she say to make things better?

Softly, hesitating at first because of her emotion and her tears, she began singing #27 from the *Manual's* Songbook. When she finished, Chris smiled, a little of his usual energy returning to his face. "Thank you, *mi tesoro*. I guess I should have told you about this days ago."

It didn't take long for things to get straightened out—legally, at least. There was no evidence against Chris, and he had the supporting testimony of several nurses. And, if that hadn't been enough, many more nurses, residents, and attending physicians volunteered unconditional testimonials in his favor. Dr. Strider, they all said, was a caring physician who never behaved in a questionable manner toward his small patients. Both the police and hospital administration dropped the case within days.

But rumor mills operate independently of truth, and Susana prepared herself for the possibility of trouble resurfacing. She probably could never have prepared herself for it popping up in the place that it did, though, among people she trusted.

One Rest Day about a month later, while waiting for Bethany's class to dismiss, Susana stood in the hallway outside the classrooms of the RAB, Andy asleep on her shoulder. Hearing the rumble of Chris's voice in the preteen classroom where he taught, she moved to that doorway. The room was empty except for Chris and eleven-year-old Lorenzo Wells. Both sat in chairs facing away from the door as Chris recounted a story, his arm draped over the back of Lorenzo's chair in a posture of warm approachability.

A gentle smile came to Susana's face. What an extraordinary man she'd married. He often adopted kids like this. His method was simple: love the child, meet his needs, develop a relationship with him, and then help him develop a relationship with Doug. Chris didn't feel he did anything special for children, certainly nothing most adults wouldn't do for other adults. But whereas many people either ignored or minimized a child's fears and needs, Chris felt they were just as important as any adult's. Lorenzo was a good example. His mother had recently died of cancer, and his father, always inattentive, had only become more distant since his wife's death.

As Susana stood there, the mention of Chris's name in the classroom behind her caught her attention. "Dr. Strider?" one woman was saying. "But he does so much for children. And look at what he's done through the Kids' Klub. No, Judith, I'm sure you're wrong. Dr. Strider's a strong runner and a good man who loves children."

"He seems to be, Marty, I agree. But that's just the thing. How many men do you know who are that interested in children? It's just what pedophiles do. They act interested, get the child to trust them, then wham!"

The bile of hot indignation rose in Susana's throat. Fellow runners spreading George's lies? Were they so desperate for something to occupy their attention? They should spend their time spreading the news of Doug's rescue—not senselessly flapping their jaws about fellow runners. But such gossiping was far too widespread in the RABs. It only proved how worldly-minded they'd become, how badly they needed a revival of zeal and reformation of character.

Stepping to the doorway of the other classroom, Susana said, "Wham, what, Judith?" Her voice came out harsher than she'd intended, but she didn't particularly care.

The other two women started, and Judith turned bright red. "Oh, Susana. I-I—that is, we didn't know you were there. How nice to see you," she finished with a forced smile.

"Wham, what?" Susana wasn't about to let what she'd heard slide. "Wham, he helps a suicidal teenager find a reason to live?"

That too was harsh. The case she referred to was Judith's own nephew. But Susana could see that her meaning hit home as the gossipmonger blushed anew, and she continued, "Wham, he helps the grieving son of a negligent widower learn to find comfort in Doug? That's what he's doing now. Come, I'll show you."

Without waiting for Judith's consent, Susana took her by the arm and led her across the hall. Marty followed. They stood outside the room for a moment, listening in as Lorenzo spoke to Doug through Chris's transmitter.

"Notice," Susana whispered. "Open door. Have you ever known Chris to be really alone with a child?"

"No," Marty whispered firmly. "He's always in an open room, like this."

"In this case," Susana said, "I'll wager he'll not only help Lorenzo turn to Doug, but he'll try to get his father more involved too. Pedophiles, on the other hand, like inattentive parents."

About that time, Chris and Lorenzo rose and moved toward the door. "Our family's going miniature golfing tonight," Chris told him. "Would you and your dad like to join us?"

"Sounds fun," Lorenzo said. "But my dad won't come."

"I'll call him," Chris said. "He'll enjoy it."

Susana gave Judith a pointed look.

When Lorenzo headed down the hallway, Chris stopped at the group of women and reached for Andy. "Here, let me help you, Suze." Settling the sleeping babe in the crook of his arm, he said, "Hi Judith, Marty. Sorry for the interruption." Then he too headed down the hallway toward the Second Service, stopping to meet up with Bethany as she exited her classroom.

Susana activated her transmitter. "Doug, I'm talking to Judith and Marty."

"You sound angry, little filly," Doug said.

She took a deep breath. "I'm sorry, Doug. I guess I am. But I wonder if you can help here. It seems Judith heard rumors that Chris is a pedophile."

Doug's own voice took on an edge. "Then let me assure you ladies there ain't a lick of truth to it. That lie was started by Stan's people and has the potential of severely limiting the work I've given Dr. Strider to do. As the *Manual* says, the enemy 'sharpens his tongue like a sword and aims his words like deadly arrows.' "

"But—" began Judith.

"And he loves to trick runners into shooting those arrows," Doug continued. "One supposed friend can do more harm than a hundred enemies."

Judith bowed her head. "I'm sorry, Doug. I let my tongue get out of its harness again, didn't I?"

"We'll discuss that in private," Doug said, a little less sternly.

When Susana logged off, Judith looked up with eyes full of shame. "I'm so sorry, Susana. I should never have repeated such hurtful charges. I'll ask Chris to forgive me."

"No, please don't," Susana said quickly. "It would really hurt him to know you believed such things. But if you've repeated them to anyone else, I hope you'll tell them the truth."

```
To: bestagent@management.com
CC: entitymaster@management.com
From: companymaster@management.com
Date: 5 January 8018 M.E.
Subject: BC-33

        This has tested beautifully in all laboratory trials and
is ready for field-testing. (Special orders on your Subject's
wife have now expired.)
        #1 Offspring has assisted in development. I want him to
see the project through.
```

```
To: companymaster@management.com
CC: entitymaster@management.com
From: bestagent@management.com
Date: 5 January 8018 M.E.
Subject: Re: BC-33

        Your timing couldn't be better—Wife's third pregnancy in
progress. I'd be happy to show #1 Offspring the ropes as I conduct
the clinical trial.
```

CHAPTER 32
WAR

"The dragon was enraged with the woman,
and he went to make war with the rest of her offspring."
Revelation 12:17, NKJV.

Having just finished some research on a complicated patient, Chris sat back in his chair with a contented yawn. The pediatric practice he and Efraím had joined two years ago was thriving, and he loved his work. It gave him the chance to keep learning while helping kids; what more could a guy want? Yes, he'd been seriously blessed.

Glancing at the clock—1:00 a.m.—he turned off the light in the study and made his way upstairs to his bedroom. He slipped into bed and snuggled up behind Susana, who stirred in her sleep, whimpering slightly.

"Can you take the kids in the morning?" she said sleepily. "I've got a little headache."

"Sure," he said with a kiss to her cheek. "You sleep in."

He settled down to rest, but his mind churned. Something about Susana's headache bothered him—like he should be remembering something. But what? It hovered just beyond his reach, like a phantom taunting him from the edge of a circle of firelight.

As he considered the puzzle, he rested his hand on her pregnant belly. A wave of love surged through him for the tiny life inside. There was a time he wouldn't have understood that love—not really. To care so much for someone you've never met? Someone whose personality, temperament, and character are all giant question marks? He really knew only one thing about little Pete: he was his son. Yet that was all he needed to know to love this baby deeply and uncon-ditionally—the way Doug loved him. It was one way that fatherhood had helped him to understand Doug's love better—to trust him more.

Chris was starting to drift off when Susana's uterus became hard under his hand. He stiffened, suddenly alert. Why was she having a contraction? She wasn't even a full five months along.

She stirred in her sleep, but didn't awaken, and Chris tried to reassure himself. One contraction didn't mean anything. The odd contraction could hap-pen, after all. And Susana had no history of preterm labor—no risk factors at all. He was just being overprotective.

In truth, he had been edgy about this pregnancy from the beginning. It had been harder on Susana than the other two. She'd joked that "old women shouldn't try to have babies," even though she was only thirty-four. Maybe that's what had precipitated his own misgivings.

In any case, he'd started collecting things at home: IV catheters and fluids, urinary and umbilical catheters, cord clamps and suction bulbs. It made him feel better to have a few emergency supplies handy. Besides, wasn't there a corollary of Murphy's Law that said if you were prepared for disaster, it wouldn't happen?

But what did Murphy know?

The phantom was taunting Chris again. Something that Susana did this weekend? Or somewhere she went? That's it. She'd gone to a charity tea party that Vanessa hosted at her house today. Was that where the headache started?

Wait a minute. Wasn't Susana whimpering when he first lay down? He'd assumed she was reacting to his disturbing her. But might it have been from contractions?

He kept his hand over her uterus, scarcely breathing as his every nerve tuned in to the tactile messages his hand was receiving. He didn't have to wait long. This time, when her uterus tightened, Susana moaned in her sleep, and Chris sat up to wake her. He wasn't about to wait for a full-blown disaster. He knew too well the bleak prognosis for a baby born at twenty-one weeks gestation. His wife and child were going to the hospital now.

But before he could wake her, Susana awoke on her own with a cry of pain. At the same moment, a gush of something warm and sticky flowed against his leg, and a pang of outright fear shot through him. Ruptured membranes at twenty-one weeks? Not good!

He switched on the light, expecting to see clear amniotic fluid. What he saw was worse. He saw blood. Lots of blood.

Abruptio!

The word that leapt from the recesses of his mind sent an icy chill down his spine. He hadn't seen many placental abruptions, a condition in which the placenta tears away from the uterus, but he knew they could be bad. He grabbed the phone and dialed 9-1-1. With Susana moaning in the background, he said, "I need an ambulance to this address stat. My wife is twenty-one weeks pregnant and bleeding profusely. It looks like a placental abruption. I'm a physician. I'll do what I can until the ambulance arrives."

As he hung up, he felt grateful for the extra obstetrics he'd taken as a medical student. At least it had forever cemented the components of intrauterine first aid in his mind. They now clicked through his brain automatically.

Number one: Positioning.

Susana had rolled onto her back, so he tucked a pillow under her right hip to tilt her slightly to the left to improve the blood flow to the uterus.

Number two: Fluids.

"Suze, I'm gonna get some supplies. I'll be right back." He hoped his voice sounded calmer than he felt. But, honestly, she was paying little attention. She was in too much pain.

He raced downstairs to the study. As he sprinted, he activated his transmitter to begin a running conversation with Doug. He grabbed what he needed and dashed back, banging on Roman's door as he passed it. Mike's son was staying with them while he attended UCLA; he could take care of Bethany and Andy while Chris got Susana to the hospital.

Back in the bedroom, Chris started an IV in each of Susana's arms and slipped a catheter into her bladder. Mumbling to himself—or to Doug, he wasn't sure—he said, "That's positioning and fluids. Number three: Oxygen. Oh no, I don't have any oxygen. I should have—"

"It's all right, son," Doug said in a soothing tone. "It's all right. Don't forget to call Nancy Mays."

"I'll call her." Roman, who had stumbled sleepily to the doorway, was now wide-awake and nervously shifting his weight from one foot to the other. He called Susana's obstetrician and then stepped beside Chris to murmur in his ear, "She said she'll meet you at the hospital. She'll have an operating room ready to go."

Chris swiveled to stare into his nephew's eyes. An operating room? But that meant—

"You should probably call Les, too," Doug said.

The implication was almost too much for Chris. His old classmate, Lester Stretch, was now a respected neonatologist in their area. But having the OR ready and calling in a neonatologist meant they were gearing up to deliver Petey that night, although he wasn't even five months old. Wasn't there another option? Surely, once they were at the hospital, they could do something to stop the bleeding, to save the baby!

Chris surveyed his wife, still moaning in pain, with a practiced eye. Her uterus had stopped contracting in the normal on-and-off pattern. Instead, she was having one long, almost constant, and very intense contraction. And the bleeding hadn't let up at all. As her husband, it was scary for him to watch it. As a physician, he knew the treatment options were rapidly disappearing. But as a father, he couldn't accept the obvious conclusion.

"Call him," Doug repeated.

"No," Chris breathed wishfully. "We won't need him."

"It's a good precaution, son," Doug insisted gently. "You would do it for a patient."

"Right," Chris whispered. "Of course. I need to be objective." The danger in caring for family was in refusing to consider what *could* happen. And, if the worse happened, Les was the one he'd want caring for his son.

"Be objective," he repeated, and pulled up the number for Roman to call.

Susana was still losing frightening amounts of blood, so Chris checked her blood pressure—another reflex. But the result startled him: 190/105. She'd never had high blood pressure before. In fact, at her office visit just two days ago, it was a nice, normal 106/68. If anything, her blood pressure should be falling from blood loss. How could it possibly be so high?

Hoping he'd made a mistake, he rechecked it, only to be wholly shocked. *It can't be 194/108. This is crazy!*

He recorded this bizarre bit of data in his brain and continued working. The truth of the situation gradually dawned as he did—Pete's chance of surviving this crisis was slim. Still, Chris refused to dwell on it. Instead he kept himself occupied, performing the emergency functions that came more or less automatically.

When the ambulance arrived, Susana's blood pressure was normal, but her heart rate was elevated. The ominous pattern of dropping blood pressure and rising pulse continued in the ambulance, while neither the bleeding nor the pain showed any sign of abating.

Chris now knew that saving Petey was a pipedream. But, as his beloved wife grew visibly paler, he feared he would lose her too. He desperately watched her monitors, her accelerating heart rate sounding in his ears as he tracked the steadily dropping blood pressures. All the while, she became less and less responsive.

Despairing at his utter helplessness, he did the only thing he could do. Grasping her hand, he laid his cheek against hers and murmured in her ear, "I love you, *mi tesoro*. I love you so much." He hated admitting it, but it might be his last chance to tell her.

She groaned in response and he, unsure that she'd understood the message, repeated it. The second time she breathed a weak, barely audible "Love you," into her oxygen mask. Then she went silent.

Chris continued to murmur encouragements in his unresponsive wife's ear: "ETA three minutes, *mi tesoro*. Hang in there." Who knew if she even heard him, let alone understood. "ETA two minutes, *mi tesoro*. Don't give up. We're almost there …"

When they arrived at the hospital, Susana was no longer moaning; she was unconscious. The bleeding, now a diluted pink instead of bright red, might have looked better to an untrained eye, but not to Chris. He knew the color change indicated a critical shortage of the oxygen-carrying red cells that give blood both its vibrant color and its capacity to sustain life. Susana's blood was turning to water before his very eyes.

Dr. Mays, already in scrubs, met them as they came off the elevator on Labor and Delivery. Her evaluation was quick and accurate: "OR stat," she told the nurses. Turning to Chris, she asked, "Can I give her blood?"

"Yes," Chris consented. "Please."

"And start that type-specific blood stat," she called after the nurses as they wheeled Susana's stretcher toward the operating room. She turned again to Chris and hesitated, her hazel eyes sympathetic. "You wanted more children, didn't you?"

Chris understood her meaning. "Do what you have to. If saving Susana means a hysterectomy, don't think twice, just do it. Just—just please save her, Nancy." His voice broke. "Please."

Dr. Mays nodded once and disappeared into the OR.

As Chris ran down the hallway to change clothes, he reminded himself that they had an excellent doctor. He had handpicked her based on his considerable experience with all of the obstetricians as a resident. If anyone could save his wife and child, Nancy Mays could. But was it already too late?

Dr. Mays did everything possible to stop the bleeding. But tests quickly revealed that they were dealing with more than a "simple" abruptio. Susana had serious coagulation problems too. Whether this was a cause or a result of the hemorrhage—or both—was anyone's guess. None of the physicians, Chris included, had ever seen anything like it.

He lost count of all the blood products Susana received. Red cells, whole blood, platelets—every time he looked, another bag of something was running into her IVs. People constantly scurried in and out of the operating room carrying blood, lab results, needed supplies, and more blood. Always more blood. Chris silently thanked all those donors.

Still the bleeding continued. Dr. Mays worked tirelessly and efficiently. As sweat soaked her cap, she employed every procedure Chris had ever heard of and more to control the hemorrhage. Despite it all, saving Susana meant doing a hysterectomy.

Nevertheless, she did survive. That was a miracle Chris would never cease to appreciate.

Poor little Petey did not fare as well. Unfortunately, Chris had been right about him—he never had a chance. Within minutes of their arrival, Chris was standing at the warmer in the OR gazing at his tiny son. As small as he was—he fit in Chris's open hand—he was perfect: eyelids over his closed eyes; eyebrows arched like Chris's; a nose like Susana's, small and precious; even fingernails. Everything present and accounted for.

Except a heartbeat.

Chris put his index finger in Petey's palm, remembering the thrill it had given him when Bethany and Andy first grasped his finger. But Petey's hand, which didn't even reach halfway around his father's finger, lay limp.

Lester laid a hand on Chris's shoulder. "I'm so sorry, Chris." His voice wavered, and he cleared his throat. "There was just nothing I could do."

Chris nodded numbly, knowing it was true.

Les wrapped Petey up in a baby blanket that quadrupled his bulk. With a hand on Chris's shoulder, he led him to a chair and placed the bundle gently in his arms. Chris sat holding his son, knowing he was gone, yet not grasping the reality. The concept was too enormous to fit in his brain, the ache too painful to fit in his heart.

After surgery, Susana was taken to the ICU, where Chris sat beside her bed, still holding his lifeless son. Once the nurse got Susana settled, she asked, "Can I get you anything, Dr. Strider?"

He looked at her, not understanding the question. What could she possibly get him? A heartbeat for his son? A uterus to put him in for another four months?

"No. Thank you," he finally managed.

She hesitated. "Do you—shall I take the baby now?"

Chris looked into Pete's face and hugged him tighter. How could he give him up? "No. Please. A little longer."

She nodded and exited quietly, leaving them alone. Chris reached over and grasped Susana's hand, watching the reassuring rise and fall of her chest. She was still unconscious, but she was breathing on her own and her hand was warm, testifying to the life yet in her. When he withdrew his hand to grasp Petey's hand between his thumb and forefinger, it lay there, cold and limp. The contrast finally drove home the stark truth: Peter Jeremy Strider was dead.

As Chris stared into Pete's perfect but too-tiny face, his vision blurred. Tears began falling, one after another, turning into a constant rain that ran off Chris's hand and soaked into Pete's blanket.

He was hunched over, sobbing, when he felt warm hands from behind, one on his shoulder, one on his head. And then, in the midst of his grief, an inexplicable peace descended on him. It didn't take away the pain. It didn't lessen it. But somehow it strengthened him to bear it.

He knew immediately whose hands they were. Debora always brought peace with her. Still weeping, he reached up to grasp the hand on his shoulder. She rested her head against his, and he realized she was crying too. They wept together for some time.

At last his sobs subsided. "I'm really glad you came, *Ama*. I could never handle this alone."

"I know, son. You won't have to. I shall never leave you comfortless. I shall never desert you. I shall never forsake you." She rubbed his shoulders, humming a familiar old song—one that Chris had first learned from his grandmother, who had learned it from her father, Juan Misi. Then Debora began singing the song, her rich contralto voice the perfect instrument to convey the depth of meaning in the old song from *The Runner's Manual*—#55 in its Songbook. She sang it through a few times, and Chris gradually began to feel as though he might survive this terrible, terrible time.

She continued humming as she moved to his side. Squatting down, she stroked Pete's cheek and kissed him on the forehead. Then, drawing a transmitter from her pocket, she fastened it around Pete's neck and activated it. Though only the size of a quarter, the device took up most of the babe's little chest.

When Debora finished humming, Doug's voice came through the transmitter, low and tender: "Sleep sweet, little Petey. We'll see you soon."

Chris hadn't thought past the pain of the moment, but with Doug's words of hope, he glimpsed the light beyond the present darkness. Petey was only resting—and resting with a transmitter.

🏃 🏃 🏃 🏃 🏃

It was some time before Susana stirred. Chris's family had arrived by then, and his sister, Rosie, was in the room with him, although he barely noticed her presence. In truth, he was aware of little beyond his sleeping wife and the bundle in his arms. The nurses had tried to relieve him of that bundle on two other occasions, but he had declined their offer both times. "My wife will want to see him when she wakes up," he insisted.

As soon as Susana stirred, Chris handed Petey to Rosie, who unobtrusively moved to a corner where she would be out of Susana's sight. Sitting on the bed, he grasped his wife's hand and watched her face intently. When she opened her eyes, a wave of inexpressible relief went through him. Bending down to kiss her forehead, he choked out, "Welcome back, *mi tesoro precioso*."

"Hi."

She was still groggy from the anesthesia. Knowing she might not even remember this later, Chris simply waited to answer whatever questions she posed. When she moaned and reached for her abdomen, he rang for the nurse to bring some pain medicine. Then he answered her unspoken question. "Dr. Mays had to operate."

Susana looked around the room and he explained, "You're in the ICU. You had a placental abruption and coagulation problems. You were really sick, Suze. You—well, you nearly died."

Her eyes searched his tenderly. "Are you okay?"

He smiled. How like her to think of him despite her own critical condition. "I'm all right."

"And Petey?"

He bowed his head to steady his own emotions, and that was all she needed. "He didn't make it, did he?"

He shook his head, and Susana burst into tears. He bent over her, holding her as they cried together. When she was able to speak, she asked to see the baby. Rosie returned Petey to Chris, who held him for Susana as she caressed his little face, kissed him repeatedly, and cried still more. Finally the medicine and her emotional exhaustion enveloped her in sleep once again.

When she awoke a couple of hours later, she seemed to think that what had happened before was a dream, so a similar scene played out. The third time she awoke, she remembered about Pete, and Chris knew it was time to deliver the other piece of bad news. He didn't want her to hear it accidentally from someone else.

Gathering her hands into his, he said, "Suze, when you got to the hospital, you were literally at death's door. Your blood count was down to 5.1." Her eyebrows shot up. It had been 12.3 only days earlier.

"Yeah, things were bad," he continued. "Dr. Mays tried everything to stop the bleeding, but, in the end—" He paused. They had wanted several children. They'd talked about at least four. For his part, he was so relieved that she was alive that the hysterectomy no longer seemed like such a disaster. But the news would be difficult for her to hear.

"Suze," he said gently, "I'm afraid she had to do a hysterectomy."

Her eyes grew wide. "You're serious?"

"I'm sorry. There was just no other way to save you."

"Pero entonces no puedo …?" (Spanish: But then I can't …?)

He nodded. His Spanish was pretty good by now, so he could follow her occasional lapses. "We've got two beautiful children. And they're lucky to have their mother to raise them." Having never known his own mom, Chris meant what he said.

Susana burst into tears, and Chris again wept with her. When she drifted off, he almost fainted as he rose from the bed. At this point, he'd had nothing but juice for twenty-four hours and no sleep for thirty-six, but he still couldn't bear to leave Susana's bedside. Rosie convinced him to eat a sandwich and get some sleep in the easy chair the nurses had brought into the room. Even then, he slept no more than an hour or so at a time, waking whenever Susana did.

Later he would remember those days as one blurry mass of jumbled dreams and foggy wakefulness. Yet despite the muddle, one point became increasingly clear to him: This had all started after a visit to George's house.

CHAPTER 33

KNOWING

" 'I will make them come and bow down at your feet,
and make them know that I have loved you.' "
Revelation 3:9, NASB.

Chris lit the fire and sat back on his haunches to watch it grow into a crackling blaze. There was something about a good fire—whether a campfire in the mountains, a bonfire on the beach, or a cozy flame here on his own hearth—that imparted a sense of wellbeing to his soul. It reminded him of his youth, of camping with his family. If he closed his eyes, he could almost convince himself he was a boy again, watching Dad try to roast the perfect marshmallow before sending him off to bed. He could even smell the sweet aroma of roasting marshmallows—

"Uncle Chris?"

His eyes snapped open to see Roman bent over him, a steaming mug of hot cocoa, complete with marshmallows, in his hand. "What are you doing?" his nephew asked.

"Oh, just waiting for the fire to get started," Chris responded before a yawn overtook him.

His nephew surveyed the now-roaring fire. "I think it's good," he said with a touch of amusement. "I thought you'd fallen asleep, right here on the hearth."

"I'm not sure I didn't." Chris settled into his easy chair with the mug. "Thanks for the cocoa."

"No problem. I've gotten pretty good at zapping water and chocolate. Or water and oatmeal, or—well, water and dehydrated anything. I wish I could have taken care of the other stuff. But I couldn't find those light bulbs anywhere, and I was afraid to mess with the garbage disposal."

"You've been a big help. I really appreciate what you have done. Susana hides the light bulbs—Andy thinks they're fun to use as bowling pins. And it actually felt good to fix something." Chris paused before adding softly, "Anything."

"Yeah." Roman nodded and turned toward the stairs. "I'll be up studying for a while. Let me know if there's anything else I can do."

"Thanks." Chris settled back to watch the fire as he sipped the warming beverage and tried to unwind. This was his first evening at home since the crisis began. He hadn't felt comfortable leaving Susana while she was in critical condition, but Dr. Mays had transferred her out of the ICU today. Although Roman had taken the children to the hospital twice a day, Chris couldn't bring himself to tell them about Pete in that cold, sterile environment. Instead, he had faced that hurdle tonight.

Like their parents, Bethany and Andy already loved their little brother. The recording of Pete's ultrasound had become Andy's favorite "movie," which he watched over and over again, even though Chris doubted he really knew what he was seeing. Bethany, who had made a special frame out of macaroni for Pete's ultrasound picture, kept it on her dresser and gave it a kiss every night before bed. Breaking the news to them that their baby brother wasn't coming home had wiped Chris out.

But at least that job was done. Settling the children down afterwards had been a chore, one requiring the reading of several bedtime stories instead of the usual one apiece. Nevertheless, both kids were now sleeping soundly and would undoubtedly come through this okay.

He was less certain about his wife.

He gulped the chocolate and stared into the fire. Susana had ample reason to be blue. Not only had she undergone incredible emotional trauma, but her body was also recuperating from major abdominal surgery, never mind a brush with death. And, if that weren't enough, her hormones would be plummeting after the pregnancy. He should have expected some level of depression.

But he honestly hadn't. She was always so upbeat, so optimistic. Somehow he'd expected her to bounce right back after this too. Stupid, really.

In ten years of marriage, he'd honestly never seen her like this. Usually bubbly and friendly, she was now solemn and incommunicative. She barely spoke to anyone, including him. He had thought that seeing their good friends, Hannah and Efraím, might cheer her up. But she had almost ignored them when they visited today, preferring to stare out the window and let Chris carry the conversation. And when the nurses had tried to get her up to walk, she was uncooperative, even snapping at one poor nurse's aide.

"So unlike her," he mused aloud. He drained the last bit of chocolate from his mug and set it aside. "What did she mean, anyway?"

Her words still baffled him. When she'd drifted off to sleep, she began mumbling, "It's gone. My family's gone." She'd started crying as she continued, "Where is it? I can't find it anywhere. It's my fault."

He had awakened her and held her, reassuring her that he was there and that Bethany and Andy were both safe with Roman. Yet she continued weeping until she drifted back to sleep. And he was left with the feeling that he had missed something, that he hadn't addressed the underlying issue causing her nightmare.

"Well, it's not her fault, that's for sure," he mumbled. He still suspected that George was behind the whole mess. He didn't know how, but it made sense. Didn't the headache start at his house?

Dr. Mays had been at a loss to explain the abruptio. When Chris pressed her, she had shaken her head and rattled off the known causes of placental abruptions, starting with cocaine. But she also said they routinely ran drug screens with any abruption, and Susana's was negative.

Of course it was negative; Susana had never used drugs. Still, a drug provided the most logical explanation for all that had happened: the sudden onset, the headache, the transiently elevated blood pressures, the odd pattern of coagulation defects. What else could account for all those abnormalities?

Chris's head sagged back against the chair as a confusing mishmash of thoughts swirled around his tired brain: *cocaine ... clean drug screen ... headache ... hypertension ... abruptio ... cocaine ... George ...*

Chris crinkled his forehead, trying to make himself concentrate. Wasn't there something he was forgetting about George? He was Stan's agent, yes. He was a physician, yes. But wasn't there more? He must be thousands of years old—what had he done before going to med school? Worked at a pharmaceutical company? Yes, that was it. And what had he done there? Chris just couldn't remember.

Sleep must have overcome him then, for he was soon back at Stanford with his study group. George was running late, but Chris and Efraím were struggling with a problem in biochemistry that had them stumped. Suddenly Efraím looked up and grinned to see George walking through the door. "Great. Here comes our resident chemist now. He'll figure it out."

Awaking suddenly, Chris sat bolt upright and shook his head to clear sleep's cobwebs. A chemist? Were his dreamy recollections right? Think now—before medical school, George had worked at a pharmaceutical company; that much was true. But his actual job there was working in the lab to do what—develop new drugs? Yes, that's right. He *was* a chemist.

This opened up all kinds of possibilities. George not only had the intelligence and knowledge, but also the experience and resources to develop a brand-new drug—one the labs didn't test for, one they didn't even know existed. Is that what had happened?

Chris rose to pace the floor. If George had gone to the trouble of designing a new drug, he would still have to slip it to Susana somehow. Yet how could he have done that? She always followed Doug's precautions to the letter. She was careful about that anytime, and she was even more vigilant when she was pregnant. In all these long years, neither of them had ever had a problem before this.

He methodically reviewed the possibilities: A dart? No—Susana would never forget her sunscreen before going to George's house. In fact, Chris specifically remembered her asking him to slather it on her back to be sure she covered every square inch.

Could George have slipped it into her food or beverage? Doug's precautions specified eating or drinking only what George or Vanessa ate, and only from the same pot or package. Susana would not deviate from that routine. George would have to poison himself before he could poison her through food.

An inhaled poison? But she had donned the protective underclothing Doug provided, including the bra containing *jishana*. The J-waves it produced would have protected her against an inhaled poison.

So what was left? If George hadn't poisoned her through her food, drink, skin, or air, how could he have done it?

Chris shook his head. There were no other options. So even if George had developed a poison, he couldn't have gotten it into Susana.

He was being paranoid, that's all. End of discussion.

Gathering up his mug, he carried it to the kitchen sink and rinsed it. This reminded him that George made porcelain. And hadn't Susana brought a new teacup home from Vanessa's tea party?

He abruptly grabbed a hand towel and hurriedly dried his hands as another option occurred to him: Could George have made that teacup and mixed a heat-stable toxin into the glaze to poison Susana's tea?

He yanked open the cupboard and reached for the delicate piece of art. As he turned it over in his hands, he wondered if such an exquisitely beautiful vessel could really be created by someone so evil. He exhaled a sigh of relief when he looked at the bottom. The artfully inscribed initials staring back at him were not George's, but Vanessa's.

🏃 🏃 🏃 🏃 🏃

The work assigned to the Royal Guards would be difficult, if not impossible, for humans to carry out. For one thing, their senses wouldn't be keen enough to surveille their charges without special equipment. Jané, on the other hand, had no difficulty observing Susana's hospital room from the park down the street, even in the middle of the night. Although she couldn't see into the room, her keen hearing provided all the information she needed to assure her charge's safety.

However, the exiles were also Paradisians, and their senses, though affected by centuries of *kanuf*, were still much more sensitive than a human's. Taylor Menod, therefore, also had no trouble listening in on Susana's activities from the other side of the same park.

"Your charge will be receiving a visitor, Colonel," Doúg said through Jané's implanted radio.

"Now, sir?" she asked. It was after 10:00 p.m.—not a conventional time for visitors. More likely, His Majesty was informing her of something planned for the morning.

"Yes, now," Doúg said. "Aedan McElroy is on his way, and this visit is critical. I need you to bar any agents from interrupting it."

"Copy that, sir." Activating her personal transmitter on the military channel, Jané instructed, "Major Meshon, activate Code M." Each team of guards had their own set of codes for common procedures, and they changed these codes regularly to keep Stan's agents guessing. This week, Code M meant to set up a barricade around their charge.

"Roger, Colonel," replied Serji. He was currently working in hospital maintenance near Susana's room.

On the other side of the park, Taylor called Adlai to report the establishment of Code M. Jané heard Adlai's frustrated "Pfft!" in reply—because, of course, he had no idea what this week's "Code M" meant.

With a giggle, Jané said, "Be advised, enemy aware—after a fashion."

Serji chuckled. "Understood." Moments later he reported, "Code M activated. Operation underway."

Jané then heard the door to Susana's room open and Aedan McElroy's voice greet, "Hello, Susana."

"Oh," Susana responded lethargically. "Hi, Aedan."

"I hope you don't mind. I know it's late, but the nurses said you were awake and that I could come on in."

"Yes, it's fine. I'm always happy to see you."

Aedan scooted a chair near the bed as he replied candidly, "You don't sound happy to see me."

It was true. Susana hadn't seemed happy to see anyone of late.

"Just tired, I guess," Susana said.

"I know you've been through a rough patch," Aedan said kindly. "I'm very sorry to hear about the baby."

"Thank you." In an obvious attempt to change the subject, Susana continued, "I didn't realize you were in town. Visiting Hannah and Efraím, are you?"

"Oh, I'll get around to them eventually. Mostly I'm here to see you. Hannah was very worried about you after her visit this morning."

"Aww," Jané intoned. Aedan had traveled all day just to talk with Susana. He was such a sweetie, even if he did sometimes have an odd way of showing it.

"And that's why you're here?" The bed squeaked—Susana squirming, Jané guessed. "It's—it's awfully good of you to make the trip."

Always unwilling to be bogged down in niceties, Aedan plunged ahead. "So what's going on, Susana?"

"I-I don't know what you mean."

Silence ensued. Jané could imagine the look on Aedan's face—his is-that-really-the-story-you're-sticking-to expression that his daughters had always hated.

"I am pretty tired, I guess," Susana said weakly.

More silence.

"What do you want me to say, Aedan?"

"Only the truth. But the whole truth."

"The truth?" Susana sniffled. "The truth is that I just lost my baby, Aedan. Besides that, my belly hurts. My head hurts. I feel weak whenever I get up. I have no appetite, but everyone's forcing food down me anyway. And, and …"

"Yes?" Aedan prompted when she trailed off. "You're a strong woman, Susana, and a woman of faith besides. I know it's not easy. But you're not less capable of dealing with grief than any other runner who's lost a child. You're not less able to heal than anyone else who's had major surgery. So you haven't told me everything, have you? You're still holding back the one thing that's bugging you the most." He paused before prompting, "What is that one thing?"

"I can never have children again!" she exploded. "Never! And there's no possibility of that situation ever, *ever* changing! How am I supposed to deal with that?"

Susana had not mentioned this problem since Chris first broke the news to her, and the runner's obvious anger as she expressed it now honestly surprised Jané. Yet the vehement reaction told her that, although Susana had been hiding the problem from everyone else, this was the very thing that had been eating at her, separating her from those she loved, and driving her mood progressively lower.

Aedan didn't seem surprised by Susana's admission, and it again amazed Jané how Doúg always managed to bring the right person into a troubled situation—exactly the person who could best recognize the underlying problem and confront it.

His voice overflowing with compassion, Aedan quietly answered, "I don't know."

"Of course not," Susana continued bitterly. "How could you know? How can anyone know what I'm feeling?"

"Chris knows. He's lost the potential to have more children along with you. Why isn't he angry about it?"

"Maybe he didn't care as much as I did."

"Perhaps. Or perhaps he's just so grateful you're still alive that his gratitude dwarfs his disappointment."

When silence answered him, Aedan continued, "But let's consider your assertion. Why wouldn't Chris care as much as you do about losing the possibility of future children?"

"I—" She paused for several moments before admitting, "I don't know."

"*I* know."

"You do?"

"Mm-hmm. Shall I tell you?"

Susana squirmed again. "Am I going to want to hear it?"

"Probably not."

She groaned. "I bet I'm going to anyway."

"And I would hate to disappoint a beautiful woman," Aedan replied gallantly.

Susana scoffed. "All right, go ahead. Tell me."

A brief pause preceded his quiet question: "You still have that picture, don't you? The one of your ideal family that you drew as a child?"

"Um, yes." Susana was likely wondering why she'd ever told Aedan about that picture.

"That's the reason you're so angry."

"Because of a picture?"

"Because you still have the picture. Because that picture represents such an important dream for you."

"Is there something wrong with that?"

"Yes, there is. First, your anger at losing that imaginary family is robbing you of gratitude for your real family."

Aedan paused, as if to allow Susana to respond. When she didn't, he continued. "Second, your unwillingness to give up that dream demonstrates a basic lack of trust in Doug."

"What?" she exclaimed indignantly. "How do you figure that?"

"Think about it. The *Manual* assures us that 'Doug works out good for his children in *all* things.' Now, I know that losing the baby is hard. I know it hurts. I'm not minimizing your pain. And I'm certainly not saying Doug's responsible for it. Yet he has committed himself to work out something good, even in this painful situation—if you will trust him to do it. But you don't trust him with that just now, do you?"

When she didn't respond, he continued, "Susana, is that fictional family so important to you that you're willing to risk your real family? Are you willing to let resentment over what might have been ruin what is?"

"I never looked at it like that."

A long moment of silence ended with Susana whispering, "What do I need to do?"

"Tear up that picture," Aedan said immediately. "Burn it. You need to give up your 'right' to that ideal family of yours. Then tell Doug you will be happy—grateful—for the husband and two kids you have."

After a long pause, Susana said, "Okay." Her voice was weak, but Jané could hear the determination in it. "I will. As soon as I get home, I'll tear up the picture."

"And burn it?"

"And burn it."

"Yes!" Jané exclaimed, springing up to dance a joyful jig. She didn't care what passersby thought of her. She saw no shame in helping Doúg celebrate, for this was a huge step for Susana. She was surrendering a piece of her family—even if it was a piece that existed only in her imagination.

Frowning darkly, Taylor called, "I have more important things to do than sit here and watch you make a fool of yourself." Stepping to the car, the agent slammed the door and tore off down the road.

Taylor's scorn did nothing to blunt Jané's bright mood. In fact, she laughed in delight when she dutifully called to report to Doúg that Taylor had abandoned the scene.

"I'm glad to hear it," Doúg said somberly. "Because Aedan isn't through. He has something to tell Susana that I wouldn't want Taylor or Adlai to hear."

Somewhat bewildered, Jané returned to the bench and waited in silence as Doúg conveyed to Aedan his permission to proceed.

A moment later, she heard Aedan say cautiously, "Susana, there's something else you should know."

"Something else?" Susana echoed, as if the statement made no sense to her. In truth, it made little sense to Jané. After such a marvelous victory, what news could possibly merit his guarded attitude?

Aedan's chair squeaked, and Jané imagined him leaning forward to grasp Susana's hand in his fatherly clasp. The guard found herself holding her breath.

"Susana," the pacesetter said carefully, "George is not the only agent assigned to you guys. All these years, he's had a partner."

Jané caught her breath. "Doúg, he's not unmasking Taylor, is he?"

"Yes, Colonel," Doúg said gravely. "He made the discovery on his own."

Jané slumped back against the seat. "Oh, poor Susana."

Chris felt much better after a good night's sleep in his own bed. A big contributor to that, no doubt, was his decision to quit wasting his energy on searching out the whys and wherefores of this disaster. He would leave those questions to Doug and focus on helping Susana regain her strength and optimism.

When he arrived at the hospital, he was encouraged to see that she was out of bed and in the shower. Surely that was a step in the right direction. But her puffy eyes flooded anew as soon as she saw him. Wrapping his arms around her, he held her tightly as she dissolved into tears. She wept for several minutes before attempting speech at all. Then she rested against his chest in a silence broken only by her ragged breathing.

"We'll be okay," he murmured soothingly. "We'll get through this."

"I have something to tell you," she said. "You won't like it. I don't like it."

"It's George, isn't it? He somehow caused this. I know he did."

"Yes, he played a role in it. But he had help, a partner. Someone close to us. Someone I've trusted. A friend I've loved."

She fell silent for what seemed like an eternity, but Chris didn't push her, despite his burning desire to assign a name to these accusations.

Finally she breathed, "Vanessa."

"Vanessa?" he repeated incredulously. The years had proven her to be a loyal companion to Susana. Could she really have fooled them for so long?

"She's one of them," Susana affirmed.

He drew back to look into her face, still struggling to process this information. "Vanessa's an associate?" Was it possible that one of Doug's runners could knowingly work for Stan?

"Worse." She met his gaze, her eyes again flooding. "An agent."

A hot, prickly sensation worked its way across Chris's back and up to the nape of his neck. "An agent?" he echoed hoarsely.

She nodded wearily. "Aedan was here last night. He figured it out, and Doug confirmed it."

"But—an agent?"

"She made teacups for each of us seated at her table. We all drank from the same teapot and ate from the same buffet. Aedan thinks she slipped some kind of poison in my cup or in—"

"The glaze," Chris finished for her. "Some kind of heat-stable toxin that leached out into the beverage as it sat in the cup." Anger was replacing the disbelief in his tone. "A poison that George the chemist developed."

She nodded, tears flowing unchecked down her cheeks. "This is all my fault."

"Oh, no. This is not your fault." Taking her by the shoulders, he stared hard into her eyes. "Do you hear me, Suze? You are not to blame for their *kanuf*."

She returned his stare in silence before turning away to move toward the window. "I'd never lived away from home until we married. When we moved to Stanford, I was so nervous—so afraid I wouldn't make any friends there. Doug understood my fear. He assured me that, if I would give him a chance, he would bring someone into my life who could become a really good girlfriend. He even told me where we would meet—at that dinner your class had during orientation week."

Chris nodded. "I remember that. And then you met Vanessa there."

She turned from the window to face him. "No. I met Vanessa at a tea shop before the dinner. Because of my fear, I clung to her like a life preserver. And she took advantage of my insecurities, monopolizing my time and attention so that I never linked up with the girl Doug intended that I should befriend."

"Who was she—one of my classmates?"

She shook her head in an expression of desolation. "I may never know. Aedan said that Doug rarely answers what-if questions."

"And what about that hands-off order they have on you?"

"Aedan said they expire after a decade. I guess the decade's up."

Chris gathered her hands into his. "It's still not your fault, *mi tesoro*."

"My brain knows you're right. Aedan helped me see that they alone are responsible for their actions. Still, if I had listened to what Doug said instead of what I wanted to hear, if I hadn't allowed them such easy access to my life, ignoring the warnings Doug whispered along the way ..." She sighed wearily. "I just can't help wondering if—"

"They would have found another way," he said firmly.

"You think so?" She searched his face intently.

"I know so," he said, his anger returning. "This didn't happen overnight, and it probably didn't happen on the first try. It takes years to develop a drug, test it, and work the bugs out. Who knows how long they've been working on that potion? Who knows how many attempts they've made to deliver it? And they would have kept trying until they succeeded."

"Chris—" she began softly, her expression taking on a measure of wariness.

"They killed Pete," he bit off, his underlying rage bubbling to the surface like lava in a volcano. "And almost killed you. We're never going over there again." He clenched his jaw. "We're never having anything to do with either George or Vanessa ever again—none of us."

"But if we cut them off, they'll just assume different identities and pop up somewhere else. Then they'd be even more dangerous since we wouldn't know who they are. Doug said it would be best not to tip them off that we know."

"I don't care. I'm not putting my family in any further danger."

"Chris, you're not thinking straight," she said gently. "The threat won't go away. We'll never be completely safe from Stan's people this side of the Awakening. Besides, we're never in danger—not in the way that matters—if we're doing what Doug's asked us to do. Yes, we lost Petey, and I feel that pain as keenly as you do. But it is temporary. We'll be reunited and have eternity to spend with him. Besides, you're forgetting the people we meet through George and Vanessa—like his nephew. You don't see it, but you're affecting that little boy."

Part of Chris knew Susana was right. But in his anger and pain, he couldn't accept it just then. "H'mm," he intoned sarcastically. "My family or George's nephew—how will I ever decide?"

She came to stand in front of him. "Please go home where you can be alone, *mi amor*. Use the grace inhaler and talk to Doug."

"What!" he exclaimed, much louder than he intended.

Susana flinched, but grasped his hands and responded evenly. "I've lost a son. I've even lost the potential of having more children. I don't want to lose you too."

Chris pulled his hands away. "You're talking nonsense. I'm not going anywhere."

"Am I? Then look at me, Chris, and tell me this isn't the same anger that ended in bitterness toward Benny after your father died. Tell me this isn't the same anger you had toward Bert, the one that even made you willing to partner with Stan."

He stared at her, trying to muster the words to meet her challenge. But he couldn't. She was right.

Susana took his left hand, slipped the ring off his finger, and pointed to the obsidian, the stone that represented his fight with bitterness. She looked into his face, her gentle brown eyes pleading. "I love you so very much, Christian Jeremy Strider. You are the kindest, most caring man I've ever known. I wake up every day thankful that I get to share life with you. But giving in to bitterness and rage turns you into this man." She tapped the obsidian. "And I really don't want to lose you too."

He stared long at the black gem. He had to admit, he did become some-one else when he indulged this anger that energized him with a desire for revenge, that reduced everything else in his life to insignificance, that drove him to lay aside all caution and principle in order to make someone pay for their *kanuf*.

Not very Joshly. The thought came to him suddenly and clearly, almost as if someone had spoken it aloud. *He never wanted you to suffer for your* kanuf. *Instead, he suffered so you wouldn't have to.*

The thought acted like water on the flames of Chris's fury. He looked into Susana's eyes—so tender, so wise—and was suddenly overcome with shame. She was just getting back on her feet, and now she was dealing with guilt as well. Yet here he was, unloading his anger on her. He hadn't meant to—he was sup-posed to be helping her. But it had snuck up on him so suddenly.

Caressing her face, he said, "I'm sorry, Suze."

"Sorry for what?"

"I shouldn't be burdening you with this. But thank you for your insight. I'll go home for a while and talk to Doug."

On his way to the house, Chris's anger again resurfaced, and he recalled an occasion during the race when he'd been so angry that he had trouble thinking straight. Josh's solution? A good run.

Funny—I can't even remember when I ran last.

It had been several days at least, sometime before this disaster struck. And it always affected him when he let it slide. A little tumor of restlessness began growing, expanding until it finally exploded in anger. How many careless words and harsh interactions had resulted from his thoughtlessly skipping a run?

Josh's remarks from the finish line came back to him: *Don't stop running, for until the war with Stan is over, you must remain strong to withstand his attacks.* During a race, Chris had always found it relatively easy to keep going, no matter how lengthy the racecourse. As long as he had a distinct goal, a definite finish line in sight, he could push through the pain and fatigue to reach that goal.

But running through the distractions of real life was different. There was no clear-cut end, no point where he could say, "There—I'm done. Now I can relax." Instead, he had to run out of sheer faith—simply because Josh had told him to. And he had to keep running, even when he wasn't sure where he was headed. He had to keep pushing himself, even when he wasn't sure why. The strength he gained as a result—the kind of strength Josh had wanted him to maintain—wasn't the kind he could see or measure. Instead, he only recognized it when it was absent. Like today.

So when Chris arrived home, he changed and went running. As he loped along his favorite route, his anger began dissipating so that he could talk to Doug more coherently. At Doug's suggestion, he recited the passages he'd memorized about forgiveness and vengeance.

The treatment worked. His chat with Doug was shorter and his struggle easier than it had been when he'd wrestled with the same issue regarding Bert. Even though it now involved forgiving someone who had harmed him purposely, someone who didn't even want forgiveness, he was able to leave the matter in Doug's hands. By the time he hit the shower, absolute peace and serenity filled him, driving out every vestige of anger and agitation.

However, he soon learned how incapable he was of maintaining that peace on his own. When he returned to the hospital, Aedan, Efraím, and Hannah were visiting, and Susana was interacting with them like her old self. Chris paused just inside the door, before any of them saw him, and savored the sound of her beautiful laughter. He hadn't realized until that moment how much he'd missed it.

After he joined them, they fell to reminiscing, an activity that continued for a while. After all, they had a lot of shared history by this time. The two couples had gone to school together, and Chris and Efraím worked together. Their kids were similar ages, they went to the same RAB, and they'd run several ultramarathons together. In fact, they chatted for so long that Chris began yawning—he was still tired after several days of sleep deprivation. Efraím took that as a hint, and the couple left. Aedan hung back to offer a few encouraging words before starting his trip back up north.

Finally he said, "Well, I'm going to let you kids take a nap. I need to get on the road, and I think you're going to be just fine."

"Thanks so much for coming," Chris said as he clasped the older runner's hand firmly. "You've helped us more than you know."

"I thank Doug for the privilege of being of service," Aedan replied. He pulled Chris into a hug and kissed Susana on the forehead. Then he moved to the door, opened it, and stepped out … only to abruptly return and reclaim his seat. "I'm just going to stick around a little longer."

Chris frowned at this puzzling move—unusual behavior even for Aedan—and started to ask what the problem was when the door opened and the problem walked in.

George and Vanessa. And a ginormous bouquet.

Susana's gracious spirit had touched so many lives that flowers already covered every horizontal surface in her room. And they were all beautiful. But this bouquet was three times bigger than any of them. It was so big that it looked like it should be able to walk.

Boy, that must have cost a mint. Do they think flowers will ingratiate them to us? Or is it meant as payment for Petey's life? Is that how much they think my son was worth?

That's all it took—one bouquet and one thought—for a tired Chris to lose all the ground he'd won in his battle with anger.

Susana also went quiet, her still-pale face losing what color it had picked up. It was left to Aedan to offer the cordialities that society demands should be exercised upon visitors. However, his effort, much as Chris appreciated it, probably wouldn't have been missed. George and Vanessa seemed oblivious to the suffering and outrage their presence created. They made themselves right at home, with Vanessa moving plants around to make room for their monstrosity, and George inventing a conversation to keep himself occupied.

Susana glanced up at Chris and then did a double-take. Her eyes took on a pleading tone that required no words for Chris to decipher. Her thought message—*Please go talk to Doug before you do something you shouldn't*—came through loud and clear.

Stepping to Aedan, Chris whispered, "I need to step out for a minute. Can you stay with Susana?"

Aedan nodded. "Go." He slipped a miniature copy of the *Manual* from his breast pocket and pressed it into Chris's hand.

Chris stole away and found an empty room where he paced, pondered the *Manual*, and talked to Doug. Gradually he rediscovered that place of forgiveness and peace that Doug had granted him to replace his anger. And the process was even quicker this time. When he checked his watch before returning to Susana's room, he'd only been gone twenty minutes.

Upon reentering her room, Chris guiltily realized that he'd been so distracted by the flowers that he hadn't even noticed George's nephew, Jared. He had met the eight-year-old briefly on two occasions over the previous couple of weeks. Having expressed an interest in medicine, the boy was spending a school break with his uncle to see what pediatricians did.

But Chris somehow felt sorry for him. The boy was highly intelligent and suffered from the same haughty spirit that characterized George. Yet his gratitude for any measure of genuine interest that Chris invested in him was not only clear but exaggerated, as if such interest were a priceless gem he saw only rarely. The experienced pediatrician suspected there was a sad story behind Jared's stony exterior; in fact, if he was truly George's nephew, there had to be. But Chris hadn't been able to get close enough to learn more.

He greeted Jared and spoke with him only briefly before George's phone rang. George stepped into the hallway to take the call but quickly returned looking pasty.

"Something wrong?" Susana asked him.

"I-I—" He took a breath. "Just a call from the hospital—a patient. We need to go." The usually calm and confident George was so flustered that he set his cell phone down on the counter and forgot it.

Chris noticed the phone just after George left. As he picked it up, he couldn't help wondering who had placed that call. Who could possibly turn the arrogant, self-assured George Strong into a pale, skittering errand boy? Certainly not a routine call about a patient.

So Chris wasn't too upset when he just happened to hit the button that brought up the call history, and then just happened to notice that the last incoming call had been from someone with a New York City area code. George's phone identified the mystery caller as "SLM."

So that's who it took to upset George: Stanley L. Moden.

Chris stepped into the hallway, ready to chase after George with the phone, but he met Jared coming toward him to retrieve it. When he gave the boy the phone and a quick smile, Jared hesitated, gazing up at him with solemn eyes. Chris squatted down in front of him. He laid a hand on his shoulder, but quickly removed it when the youngster stiffened.

"What is it, Jared? Something you want to tell me?"

The boy glanced over his shoulder before meeting Chris's gaze. When their eyes met, a peculiar sense of recognition jolted through Chris. Jared's brown eyes looked exactly like Rosie's.

"Sir," Jared began with another glance over his shoulder. "I wish to express my sincere condolences about your baby."

Without waiting for a reply, the lad hurried after his uncle. He was returned to his parents before they had another opportunity to meet, but the encounter left Chris feeling very uneasy, as if he had failed to do something. He just wasn't sure what it was.

CHAPTER 34

COWERING

" 'Your foes cower before the greatness of your strength.' "
Psalm 66:3, REB.

15 March 8018 M.E.

Camille strode to the desk of Stan's executive secretary and leveled a glare at her. "Can you tell me now?" She didn't even try to control the irritation in her voice. After all, when a secretary summons a boss without divulging the problem, a certain amount of irritation should be expected. Especially when such an order comes on the tail of several difficult days in Washington, DC.

Madelyn's fingers fumbled for the white streak she bleached into her long black hair, but when she started twirling it, she winced and quite deliberately folded her hands in her lap instead. Upon closer inspection, Camille realized that Madelyn's white streak was nearly gone. Her suspicions mounting, Camille snatched the beret off the secretary's head to uncover a large wound where the missing patch of white hair had been pulled from her scalp.

Madelyn's golden skin flushed crimson. When Camille handed the hat back to her, the unfortunate woman wordlessly replaced it without meeting her eye.

Camille didn't have to ask what had transpired. Stan hated any show of weakness, and Madelyn's nervous tic particularly annoyed him since, as his secretary, she represented him to the public. No doubt he had yanked out that hunk of Madelyn's hair in a fit of rage. Such an incident would be unremarkable if the victim were anyone else. But Stan rarely attacked Madelyn; it was simply imprudent considering the wealth of sensitive information she possessed by virtue of her position.

He must be in a very foul mood indeed.

Her gaze still lowered, Madelyn said earnestly, "Believe me, I would tell you if I could, Dr. Desmon. But I honestly don't know, ma'am. He received a call from Mr. Damour three days ago and has been closeted in there ever since. He just placed a call to Adlai—"

"Adlai?" Camille exclaimed in surprise.

Madelyn looked up hopefully. "Yes, ma'am. Does that mean something? He's still in California, isn't he?"

"Correct. If this involves him—" *Did something go wrong with the BC-33 trial?* "What else?"

"I've never seen him like this, ma'am. I don't think he's been home since Mr. Damour's call. He has Patric training the two younger boys, he's hardly—"

"Stanley's still in California?"

"Yes, ma'am. As I was saying, he's hardly spoken to anyone except Garrick. He's canceled appointments he usually considers top priority, he's—he's—he seems—" She looked around her empty waiting area as though there might be a spy hiding in her ficus. Leaning forward, she whispered, "—desperate."

Straightening up again, she explained, "He hasn't actually asked for you, but he keeps asking when you'll be back."

"Very well. I'll see what I can do."

Madelyn expelled a relieved sigh. "Thank you, ma'am."

The armed guard stepped to the side as Camille advanced to the door. Putting her thumb on the security pad, she lowered her eyes to the retinal scanner. When the door unlatched, she heard Stan playing the cello portion of Rachmaninoff's Sonata in G Minor for Cello and Piano. She turned to Madelyn, her eyebrows raised in question.

"He's been playing a lot," Madelyn whispered.

Camille nodded. The reason Stan kept a cello and piano in his office was to play them when he needed to think, especially when he needed a creative answer to a problem. However, if he'd been playing them a lot, the solution was eluding him.

She entered the office and quietly shut the door behind her. Stan, facing the far window, didn't notice her entry. As she scanned the large room, an uneasy feeling rose within her. Stan himself was unshaven and wearing a jogging suit, both of which were unusual in the office. Unprecedented, actually. Furthermore, she had never seen the place in such a state. Papers were strewn around the sitting area like dirty clothes in a teenager's room. A new table sat near the far window where miniature soldiers battled on a world map. Apparently this strategy board was the source of the problem, for Stan sat before it as he played the cello.

While surveying the scene, she also reached out to sense her brother's emotions. She met a roiling mixture of frustration, anger, worry, apprehension, and fatigue. Madelyn's assessment of "desperate" wasn't far off the mark.

She moved to the piano, her footsteps muted by the tan carpeting, and joined in on the sonata. Stan jumped when she began playing, missing a few beats to glance over his shoulder at her. Then he nodded and resumed the cello portion, and they played the remainder of the piece together.

He stowed his cello on its stand and advanced on her, hand extended. "It's about time you got back. Give me your hand."

Camille hesitated. She still didn't know the cause of his angst, but she knew anger was involved, and he had once purposely broken her finger when angry with her.

"Stan, I had nothing to do with BC-33."

He glowered at her. "BC-33 worked like a dream. And I'm not angry at you *yet*, but I will be if you don't give me your hand."

Only somewhat reassured, Camille offered her left hand—just in case. She was, after all, a practical, right-handed woman. When he took her hand in both of his, Camille understood his need and joined him in focusing on their hands. The tingling of an energy transfer began immediately.

After a long minute, he gave a single nod. "Better. Now then, here's the problem: we have received a *lifetime* hands-off order."

Camille gasped, a cold terror shooting through her. They had worried over the possibility of their timeline being off by a year or two, but they hadn't expected this development until circa 8038 M.E.—a full twenty years in the future. This meant the Final Battle was much closer than they had believed, so close that Doug couldn't risk losing his key players. Rather than having four more decades to prepare, they now had only two—possibly less.

"A-a lifetime—?" she stammered. "On whom?"

"Susana López Strider." Stan moved to the new strategy table and stood over it, arms crossed.

"We're not nearly ready for this. That's why you've been—" She stopped herself before saying "holed up like a madman" and decided on a more diplomatic, "—so busy here."

Coming alongside him, she asked, "What have you done so far?"

"I just called Adlai, told him to lay off." He moved one soldier as he spoke. "Should have thought of that right away. Obviously, the Striders are important to Damour. It seems imprudent to rock the boat any more until we can get our footing."

"You've recalled Adlai, then?"

Camille hadn't intended for her voice to reveal her exasperation, but it had obviously done so. He turned to focus a cold glare on her that sent another wave of trepidation through her.

"You think me a fool?" he rasped, his voice too soft. "I know how hard we worked to place Adlai optimally. You think I'd jeopardize that on a whim? You think I'm running scared—is that what you think of me?"

Camille found herself frozen in place. Stan's anger had many faces, and she respected them all. But none of them chilled her so thoroughly as this quiet, intense fury. Doug's forecasters had spoken of her brother metaphorically as a dragon, and it was certainly an apt description. Naturally endowed with immense physical strength, he had honed that prowess into a precise and lethal weapon and then educated himself in all manner of torture and execution. Furthermore, he was now dispossessed of any tender feelings that might check his explosive temper. In short, the powerful and impulsive being that her brother had become was simply terrifying, even to her.

"Please forgive me, Stan," she managed. "My frustration is more with my own—" "Fear" was the word that came to mind, but she would never admit that. "I just—" She expelled a harsh sigh.

"Well, get over it. Now. I need my linkmate, my genius sister—not some blithering idiot."

His eyes still flashed with fury, but he turned away in a huff, and Camille desperately willed her pounding heart to quiet itself. Although her status as his linkmate had spared her thus far, his limited mercy would dissipate altogether if she did not produce the needed assistance. At this moment, she owed her continued wellbeing to one cause alone: his admitted need of her linked abilities, which shut down under duress.

He was once different. So very different.

The thought brought with it the bitter pang of regret, but she resolutely pushed it aside. She must calm herself to produce the required help.

She took several deep breaths and tried to think of the best friend he had once been—chasing her through the lush forest, laughing when he caught her, twirling her around and around until they both fell down, dizzy but delighted. Engaged thus in more pleasant memories, the thumping in her chest and prickling of her skin gradually subsided.

When she had regained sufficient control, she gingerly stepped closer to the table to hazard clarification of his actions. "So Adlai is still in position to take advantage of any unwise choices Strider may make, but has orders to desist any provocative action?" She hoped that's what her brother had meant.

He grunted a distracted confirmation.

She hid a relieved sigh. "And what else?"

He motioned over his shoulder at the papers scattered around the sitting area. "Garrick and I have been revising and updating our contingencies. And you and I will need to revise the entire Global Strategic Plan. But this is the biggest problem."

"Getting our military divisions into optimal strategic locations?"

"Mm-hmm."

"We'd planned on effecting a series of political changes that would allow us to set up bases in multiple countries with little resistance—"

"—but with two full decades cut from our timeline, we won't have time to carry them all out."

"And anything less than complete success will cripple us significantly at the time of the Final Battle," she concluded with a nod of comprehension.

"Precisely."

Camille fought for control of her frenetic thoughts. The problem of how to maneuver their troops into position had been one of their most significant challenges when they last revised the Global Strategic Plan. A complex tangle, the challenge required meshing their military needs with the geography of each intended stronghold, its political climate, and the host country's military and governmental structure. This necessitated monumental shifts in political structure around the globe. None of the changes was impossible in itself, but accomplishing all of these objectives within two short decades—that *was* impossible.

After a time of pensive silence, Stan retrieved his cello and sat down at the strategy table with a grunt that meant she was to accompany him. Welcoming the distraction, she obediently returned to the piano as he began playing Beethoven's Sonata No. 1 for Cello and Piano. She recognized it within a few beats and joined in, the notes filling the room with sweet harmonies that melded into one overriding feeling of completeness. Somewhere amidst the beauty of that interplay, the answer came. Just as their music was many different notes, harmonies, and patterns all tied together into one entity, the solution to their dilemma was in tying all the components together.

"Stan," she said as they finished the first movement. "We need our own country."

He spun to her, amazement on every feature. "Bingo! That's exactly what we need. If we were an independent country, we could raise our own army, develop our own stockpiles, and operate without justifying every move to outlander governments."

Abandoning their instruments, they returned to the strategy table. Seen within this new framework, the map wasn't nearly as daunting. The idea might seem preposterous to outlanders, but with the far-reaching political influence of Moden Industries at their disposal, they could easily manipulate legal and constitutional loopholes to their advantage. They had been doing it for centuries. Furthermore, their extensive files were rife with blackmail possibilities for virtually every leader on the world scene. And precedents already existed for having countries within countries. Lesotho sat smack in the middle of South Africa. Italy had the Vatican. Even the United States harbored a number of sovereign Native American nations.

Stan's mood progressively improved as they pored over the map and thoughtfully rearranged the toy soldiers. At last, he threw back his head and laughed. "I swear, Kami, you're brilliant. This will work. We'll call it the Allied States of Moden. Has a ring to it, don't you think?"

She thought the Allied States of Desmon sounded better, or at least Desmoden or Modesmon, but she didn't voice this opinion. Such a suggestion would require more finesse. Instead, she changed the subject entirely. "So tell me about BC-33. You said it worked? Tell me every delicious detail."

"You would have enjoyed Adlai's full account. The one disappointment was that it didn't cause a stroke. It probably would have in an older, less robust individual."

"Yes, yes, but the Striders! Don't keep me in suspense."

He chuckled. "It had both the acute hypertensive effect and the bleeding complications we hypothesized, causing a very nice placental abruption with severe hemorrhage."

"And ...?"

Stan grinned, his emerald eyes dancing. "Killed the fetus. Almost killed the wife. Oh, and they had to do a hysterectomy, so no more offspring for them."

"That's wonderful," she exclaimed. "This means that the Kids' Klub leader they would have produced will not be born."

"I hope you're right."

"Oh, I am, Lusu. I am. Neither of their two offspring possesses the right combination of personality and natural talent to fill that role. You, my dear sir, have thwarted our enemy's master plan." Catching his hands, she continued solemnly, "You too are brilliant, *zuule*. We're a pair of geniuses—a formidable team."

"Formidable? No, Kami. *Together* we're invincible."

PART V

SPOUSE

"This is no dream, dear one," Josh said emphatically. "It's closer to what you would call a vision. And it is very real, I assure you."

"It's real?" Susana scanned the room. The place seemed familiar, although the memory felt faint, like she hadn't been here for a long time. And she didn't remember it being this noisy, with so many alarms beeping and buzzing.

"Very real," Josh repeated.

"That clock?" she nodded toward the large red numbers on the opposite wall. They now read 23:39:49—50, 51, 52 ...

"It's counting down to the Final Battle at midnight. The time registered there doesn't correlate with any measure of time you know, but it is getting very late."

And that's when she remembered—Chris was standing outside the other door trying to get in. Josh wanted him to come in, but she had to give her consent. And she didn't want to give her consent because this big room—with all its fancy equipment, blaring alarms, and important military personnel—was a War Room. She didn't want Chris sent off to war.

When another alarm buzzed, Gabriel turned to a console and reported, "There's a marked increase in the activity of shamans, Modén."

"And heightened activity in the New-RABs, too," said an officer across the room.

"And wicca," added a third.

"What's that mean?" Susana asked.

"It means that Stan is rallying his forces," Josh answered. He paused before adding meaningfully, "And that I need to rally mine."

Susana had no problem with Josh rallying his troops. In fact, she whole-heartedly agreed with the plan—sounded like a great idea. As long as those troops didn't include Chris.

"Can I help?" she asked, although she already knew the answer. Still, as long as she could keep asking questions and holding onto flowers, she could keep Chris outside that door.

Josh released a small sigh. She had never seen him truly angry. In fact, she'd never even seen him become impatient. But he was clearly disappointed.

"As you wish," he murmured. "Then it's time we talk about the red rose."

Susana's stomach tightened. Red roses represented romantic love, right? A love that even transcends death. She couldn't remember the exact story behind the symbolism, but it had something to do with somebody's blood, didn't it?

As if reading her mind, Josh said, "Red roses signify love and romance. A true love that stands the test of time."

Susana's stomach began churning. Sometimes she hated being right. This was just a variation on the theme—Debora had been trying to get her to "surrender" Chris for years now.

"Do we have to talk about the red rose?" she said aloud. "How about—?"

"Within a marriage," Josh continued as if she hadn't spoken, "the red rose represents a domestic bliss that is both passionate and abiding." His eyebrows lifted. "Remind you of anyone you know?" There was an edge to his voice. In fact, the easy tone he had used on her previous visits was completely gone, having been replaced by a firmness that, while not unkind, was definitely uncompromising. He was obviously getting tired of her delay tactics.

She swallowed hard. She didn't want to be here anymore. At first, it had been kind of intriguing. Of course, she also thought it was a harmless dream then. But this was getting too close. Josh was just asking too much of her.

CHAPTER 35

DISCOURAGED

*"Fathers, do not provoke your children,
lest they become discouraged."*
Colossians 3:21, NKJV.

30 March 8020 M.E

Ten-year-old Stanley Moden sat in his plush office on the top floor of Desmon Tower staring at his computer screen. He had finished his work for the day, having completed his first hostile takeover—a small company, but a milestone nonetheless. He was not yet the acting President of Moden Industries, of course. He still had an MBA and a PhD to obtain before he would be endowed with the title that was his destiny and privilege by birth. Nevertheless, he was already taking over some of his father's duties pertaining to the business side of things. This allowed Father to devote himself more completely to the truly important work: the preparations for overthrowing Doug Damour.

Stanley needed to get home and finish a paper for school, but he wanted to do one more thing before leaving. Glancing around guiltily—although he knew he was alone—he pulled up his favorite file. Then he sat forward to gaze intently into the face on the screen: Dr. Christian Strider, son of Juan Misi. Stanley had heard of this man all his life. His parents watched him more closely than any other subject, he had more high-risk flags than almost anybody, and he was at the top of Mother's List of Guerdon. Father also cussed him out on a regular basis.

Yet Stanley's interest had nothing to do with any of that. He simply liked his eyes. He had even liked them before he met the man, but he hadn't realized how real, how sincere, the tender expression in those eyes was. How he wished he could see the same warmth in his father's eyes. He had tried to earn such a look. He had done everything Father ever asked of him. And, occasionally, he was rewarded with a look of approval or pride. But he had never, not once, seen the one thing he craved above all else. He had never seen love.

Despite his manly responsibilities, Stanley had not given up a child's imagination. So here, in the privacy of his office, he sometimes dared to dream. In this private world of make-believe, he had two favorite fantasies that had sprouted and grown since he met Dr. Strider two years before.

The first fantasy, the one he liked best, was that the eyes he was staring into were Father's eyes. Father would be saying, "Great job, Stanley. Oh, and by the way, I love you, son." Occasionally he would even dare to imagine that Father hugged him, for Stanley really liked hugs. But he usually had trouble pushing the boundaries of reality that far.

His other fantasy was that Dr. Strider was his father. Stanley had nursed this fantasy by learning everything he could about the Striders—which was quite a bit, actually. Moden Industries kept thorough records on all of Doug's runners. Stanley had even learned Tarahumara so he could carry on imaginary conversations with Dr. Strider in that language.

He was indulging this latter fantasy when Madelyn's voice came over the intercom, startling him. "Master Moden, your limo's ready."

Although Stanley jumped in his chair, his response into the intercom was even. "I'll be right there." He had learned long ago not to show weak emotions. It even annoyed him that he had jumped, although no one was there to see it.

As Stanley took one last look at the face on his computer screen, his right hand unconsciously found its way to his left shoulder, to the place where Dr. Strider had touched him. Stanley was not accustomed to being touched by anyone except his nanny. But he had liked it when Dr. Strider touched him. The doctor made him feel like someone important, not because of who his father was, but because of something else, something deeper—something Stanley didn't really understand, so couldn't put into words.

At last, Stanley closed the screen and logged off the computer, confirming his identity by both thumbprint and retinal scan. He'd only forgotten this step once. The entirety of Desmon Tower had gone into lockdown, and, when he exited his office, several guards were pointing rifles at him. And Father's look had certainly not been loving then.

Stanley collected his daily report and moved toward the door of his suite. Thumbprint recognition, retinal scans, and armed sentries secured this door, as they did every office in which the top secret Priority Computer could be accessed. The PC housed every detail of Moden Industries' operations against Doug Damour: all company and entity management files, battle plans and protocols, the formulae of all poisons, and more. It was, therefore, imperative that no outlander, and especially no runner, ever gain access to that computer.

There was just one small hole in the security system surrounding the PC—one small, but very wrong, assumption. As a result, unbeknownst to Moden's leaders, a runner had had unlimited access to the PC's database for nearly a year.

Stanley knew about this hole. He also knew of another problem, one that made the database incomplete. He hadn't told his parents about either vulnerability.

Exiting his office, Stanley bid the secretaries a good day and headed down the hallway to Mother's office. However, when a strange feeling pricked at his neck, he stopped. He had the sudden impression—but it was a strong impression—that he would never see his office again. How could that be?

A nearby secretary noticed Stanley's hesitation. "Is there a problem, sir?"

"I feel like I'm forgetting something," he said, improvising a reason to return.

"You don't have your backpack. Maybe you left it in your office?"

"Yes, that must be it." Stanley returned to the door and opened it, but the backpack wasn't inside. He already knew this, of course. He had purposely left it in Mother's suite.

He wandered around the office, touching a few things he liked—the sculpture Mother had let him choose, the seascape he'd painted last summer—but he decided there was nothing here that he really needed. As he again purposed to exit the suite, the same inexplicable feeling drew him to Father's office.

He crossed through the short hallway connecting the two suites and entered his father's office.

Glancing up, Father grumbled, "What is it?"

"I thought I may have left my backpack in here, sir," Stanley said as he meandered through the large office. When he brushed by one of the bookshelves, a book caught his eye, a copy of Charles Dickens's *A Christmas Carol*. It was his favorite book because Father had once read a few pages of this very copy to him.

Approaching the large mahogany desk, he asked, "May I borrow this book, sir?"

Father didn't look up. "Which book?"

"Dickens's *A Christmas Carol*."

"It's not the autographed first edition, is it?"

"No, sir. It's a paperback edition."

Father grunted, which Stanley interpreted as his consent. He tucked the slim book into his back pocket, but still something held him there. He focused on his father as he worked, taking in every detail: the red highlights the sun brought out in his chestnut hair; the muscles in his forearm that contracted as his fingers maneuvered the pen; the hard, inflexible set of his jaw.

Often when Stanley watched him like this, he was overwhelmed with a sense of what a great man his father was. Everywhere they went people kowtowed to him. Anything he ordered got done. People didn't argue with Father. They simply obeyed him. Such musings were always followed by an enormous sense of Stanley's own smallness. How could he ever be as great as Father? How could he ever take over the presidency of Father's company?

But this is not what Stanley thought of today as he watched him. Today he simply felt sad. He didn't know why.

Father finally looked up. "Now what?"

"I—" Stanley swallowed. The same impression that had drawn him into the office insisted that he say something poignant to his father. But what? I love you? No, never. Love was weakness. Father would smack him if he said that.

Then what—I like you? No, that wasn't it, and Father wouldn't care anyway.

I ... what?

The sentiment Stanley was groping for was an apology. He wanted to say he wished he could be a better son, for that must be why Father had never loved him.

"I'm a busy man, Stanley. If you have something to say, say it now before I get annoyed."

Yes, we wouldn't want that.

"I ... must have left my backpack in Mother's office, sir."

Father scowled. "Then get out. You're wasting my time."

"Yes, sir."

Well, that was less than satisfying.

Making his way to his mother's office, Stanley handed in his daily report. She nodded her approval as she reviewed it. "Good work. Quite well done."

She set it aside and returned her gaze to the computer screen as she spoke to him. This didn't bother Stanley. Not really. He was used to his parents' divided attention. But Dr. Strider had given him his full attention on the few occasions they had spoken. Stanley had liked that.

"And your schoolwork is on schedule for graduation Friday?" She spoke of his high school graduation. In the fall, he would enter Harvard.

"Yes, ma'am. I just have one paper left. I'll finish it this afternoon."

"Excellent. Then you may be dismissed."

"Yes, ma'am. Thank you."

As he gathered his things, she sat back in her chair and fixed her attention on him. "You did very well today, Stanley. You were creative, thorough, and efficient with that hostile takeover. Your father was very pleased with your work. You'll make a fine leader."

Stanley broke into a broad smile. "Thank you, ma'am!" Praise from either parent was a rare treat, one he reveled in whenever he could get it. But the unexpected commendation threw him so off balance that he really did forget his backpack, which he had never done before.

And he definitely knew better.

When Stanley arrived at the limo, his brothers, seven-year-old Saxon and five-year-old Sheridan, were already waiting. During the ride home, Sheridan entertained himself by shooting spit wads at his brothers. The older brothers retaliated by tackling him and pinning him to the floor of the limo.

The reason the Modens had a Paradisian driver, a job usually considered unworthy of a Paradisian's time, was precisely so he could act as a bodyguard. Nevertheless, Marcus apparently saw no need to protect the brothers from each other. He had long ago tired of their scuffles and routinely kept the tinted window between them closed.

When, after parking the car at their apartment building, Marcus opened the car door to find the youngest brother pinned to the floor, he simply shook his head. "Still the weakling, Sheridan?"

Sheridan never complained to Marcus about his brothers, since it had no more effect than complaining to Saxon's parrot, which only squawked and said, "Talk to the hand." But Sheridan did complain to their nanny, Mrs. Jenkins, as soon as the driver delivered them to the penthouse. Mrs. Jenkins' first response was to turn a reproachful eye on Marcus.

Holding up his hands, the driver said, "Not my job. Besides, it'll make him tough."

After Marcus left, Mrs. Jenkins sat on the sofa and gathered the three boys around her. While Sheridan expounded on his complaint, she unobtrusively fastened another button on his shirt. She didn't seem to like it when his birthmark showed. Or maybe she didn't like the look their parents gave him when it showed. Anyway, she was always adjusting his shirts.

After they all aired their grievances, Mrs. Jenkins sat back to gaze at each one in turn. Stanley hated it when she got that disappointed look in her pretty blue eyes.

Finally she spoke, her voice soft but firm. "Sheridan, you should not have been spitting things at your brothers. It's not nice. And it's nasty besides. Stanley, Saxon, you should not gang up on your brother. He's smaller than either of you. All of you were *most* unkind to one another." Her wavy silver hair bounced as she emphasized "most" with a vigorous nod.

Stanley bowed his head. "Yes, ma'am. I'm sorry, Sheridan."

Saxon scoffed. "I'm not." He marched toward the kitchen, where their housekeeper, Mrs. Morrison, would have a snack waiting. Sheridan ran after him and delivered a solid punch to his brother's back. Saxon spun toward his brother, fist raised.

"Boys!" Mrs. Jenkins cried.

Saxon stopped, fist frozen over Sheridan's head, and scowled at the nanny. "Father says fighting's good for us." Nevertheless he dropped his hand and turned back to the kitchen, his younger brother following on his heels.

Mrs. Jenkins sighed and bowed her head. "Give me strength."

A moment later, she looked up with a kindly smile and held out her arms. Stanley grinned and stepped into them. These were the moments he lived for, even though he knew hugs were weakness.

Mrs. Jenkins wrapped Stanley in a long hug and planted a kiss on the side of his head. He rested in her arms, savoring the moment. Then they proceeded to the kitchen, where she also embraced Saxon and Sheridan. Both boys smiled broadly, and all arguments ceased. Hugs were precious commodities in the Moden household since Mrs. Jenkins was the only one who gave them out. Maybe that's why their battles were short-lived around her.

Mrs. Morrison doled out apple slices and milk, and Stanley saved a piece of apple for Saxon's parrot, Max, the only pet in the large apartment. Although the other boys wanted pets, Mother only let Saxon have one. Stanley once asked her why, and she answered frankly: "Because I like him best."

But Max had become a pet to all the brothers. In fact, Stanley was the one who saved him from certain death almost every night. The day Saxon got Max, Father had told him he'd never eaten parrot but had no objection to trying it if that "stupid bird" didn't shut up. The boys quickly learned they could keep Max quiet by covering his cage. The problem was, Saxon didn't always remember to do it until he went to bed. So when Father came home before Saxon's bedtime, it was Stanley who raced into Saxon's room to cover the cage.

After playing with the bird for a while, Stanley went to his own room to study. He automatically checked under the bed and in the closet, as Sheridan had a habit of hiding and pouncing on him when he least expected it. Then he closed the door and settled at the computer to finish his last paper for high school. It shouldn't take long.

CHAPTER 36
PERVERSITIES

> "To the loyal you show yourself loyal ... but skilful in your dealings
> with the perverse.
> You bring humble folk to safety, but humiliate those who look so
> high and mighty."
> Psalm 18:25-27, REB.

30 March 8020 M.E.

A while after Stanley left, Camille passed into her attached living quarters for some iced tea. On her way back, she noticed the boy's backpack and snatched it up, impatient at his forgetfulness. However, she mistakenly grasped the bottom of the unzipped backpack, spilling its contents onto the floor.

"Careless child," she muttered as she bent down to replace the items.

But then she caught sight of a small oval object atop the pile. She jerked away from it, a cold wave washing over her.

It could be a prop, her optimistic side suggested. Except Stanley had not received an assignment requiring a fake transmitter.

Slowly, she circled the backpack, stopping at intervals to examine the device from different angles. Then she edged to her desk and phoned Stan, never removing her eyes from the oval object, as if it might attack her when she turned her back.

"Stan," she asked hopefully, "have you assigned Stanley anything that would require the use of a transmitter prop?"

"What are you talking about? You're reviewing his work this month. You should know if he needs one or not."

"Stan, please. Do you know of any reason why Stanley would have a transmitter prop in his possession?"

"No!"

The hair on Camille's neck tingled.

"Camille, I haven't got time for—"

"I think you should come to my office right away."

"Can't it wait? I'm—"

"Stan, if I'm right, I've just uncovered a very serious threat to the organization."

"I'll be right over."

While Camille waited for her brother, she called maintenance to bring up a sledgehammer. Moden Industries lacked the technology and materials to produce exact replicas of Doúg's transmitters, so they manufactured two other types of transmitters. The functional devices, made for the New-RAB supporters, were too large to be confused with the real thing. Therefore, they also manufactured props that looked like Doúg's transmitters; though inoperative, they were useful for giving agents the appearance of being genuine runners.

There were only two ways to determine whether the device from Stanley's backpack was authentic. They could activate it, or they could try to smash it, for no earthly force could harm *tsuma*, the metal used in the real transmitters. At Moden Industries, they preferred the smashing method since activating a genuine device brought Doúg's ear-shattering voice.

Stan strode impatiently into Camille's office. "What is it?"

She pointed an accusing finger at the pile. "Stanley forgot his backpack this afternoon. I picked it up the wrong way and that's what came out. I've handled nothing."

Stan did the same observational walk-around that Camille had done and then looked at her. "You haven't touched it?"

"I wouldn't take the chance of activating the accursed thing! You know that. I've not laid one finger on it."

Stan reached for the sledgehammer that had arrived during his walk-around. Picking up the transmitter by its chain, he held it out like a venomous snake and deposited it on the stone flooring around the door. Then he swung the hammer, cracking granite and jamming the transmitter into the floor.

The device remained intact.

He glanced at Camille, anger sparking in his eyes. Turning back, he moved the device to another portion of the floor and swung again, shattering the granite a second time.

The transmitter stood firm.

"I told you that children require a more consistent father figure!" Camille screeched. "You do nothing with them but work; you don't even eat dinner with us!"

"You're blaming me for this?" Stan shot back. "Miss I'll-just-run-off-to-the-North-Shore-when-I'm-vexed? Is that what you call consistent mothering?"

The resurfacing of Stan's British accent caused Camille to rethink her tirade. She took a step back and drew in a deep breath. "Perhaps you're right. We should both reconsider our training methods."

"Reconsider later! The point is, the child's a traitor—and one who's had unrestricted access to the PC!" He lunged for the phone as he added, "He must be destroyed straightaway!"

Camille caught his hand. "Let me."

His eyes narrowed, and Camille hastily released his hand. "Forgive me, Stan, but your accent has gone British. She'll suspect a problem."

He snarled an oath but backed away from the phone.

Camille dialed home. "Good afternoon, Mrs. Jenkins. I require Stanley's assistance for a special project. I'm sending the limousine back to retrieve him."

"Yes, ma'am. I'll have him ready."

※ ※ ※ ※ ※

Stanley was still settling in at his computer when Mrs. Jenkins entered his room. "Your mother just called and needs you back at the office. She's sending the limo."

"Okay," he said, pushing his chair back. "I'll just—"

Holding up a hand, Mrs. Jenkins listened for a moment and then pulled out her "favorite pen," as she called it, and scanned the room for listening devices. "Doug needs to speak to both of us urgently," she whispered. She turned away from Stanley to activate the transmitter hidden in her bosom.

"Anna, I need you to take Stanley and get out of there real quick like," Doug said.

Stanley rose from the chair, his muscles tense.

"Don't stop to pack anything," Doug continued. "Don't do anything but gallop off. There's a dark blue sedan at the front door. The driver's name is Lanse. He's a tall black man with a British accent. Go with him. He'll know what to do."

Ever since he'd become a runner, Stanley had known this call might come some day. He'd played a very dangerous game for the last year. Mrs. Jenkins had played it for nearly eleven. However, his parents had unknowingly trained him well for exactly this situation. He had been through simulation after simulation of kidnappings and threats on his life. His parents or Dr. Sondem reviewed the films of these exercises minutely, noting Stanley's every expression, reaction, and decision. They discussed with him ideas he might have tried or how he could have reacted better. And they punished any sign of weak emotions like fear.

So, rather than being scared by Doug's call, Stanley felt a surge of adrenaline that readied him for the game. He rushed through the living room with Mrs. Jenkins, who didn't even return to her room for her pocketbook. His senses already booted into high alert, he methodically registered every sight, sound, and smell. He noted the time and enabled the compass on his watch. He mentally catalogued everything on his person that could be used as a weapon—shoestrings and belt—and congratulated himself on recently sharpening the knife hidden in the sole of his custom-made shoes.

Calling to Mrs. Morrison to watch Sheridan and Saxon, Mrs. Jenkins urged Stanley ahead of her as they hurried out of the apartment. While they rode the elevator down to the lobby, he unscrewed the face of his watch and extracted the chip his parents would use to locate him. They exited the building to find a tall man waiting beside a dark blue sedan.

He opened the car door and, with a bow and a British accent, said, "Mrs. Jenkins, Stanley, I'm Lanse Meshon."

Though a large man—almost as muscular as Father—Lanse's manner was gentle. He wore the casual uniform of Doug's army: navy blue slacks and red polo shirt. The embroidered gold initials "LM" on his shirt pocket, combined with the three gold stars below them, told Stanley that this man was the lieutenant general in command of the *Lejani Mejad*, or Royal Guard, the most elite division of the Paradisian Army.

Stanley made a quick detour to pop his head into the open window of a nearby taxi. "Are you—? Oh, sorry. I thought you were someone else." He surreptitiously dropped his tracking chip into the cab before turning away.

Once in the car, they drove only a few blocks before entering an underground garage. There they exchanged the sedan for a white SUV. Lanse delayed just long enough to show Stanley a hidden space under the back seat. "If I tell you to hide, you're to enter this compartment and lock it straightaway. Do not come out again until you hear two knocks, a pause, and three more knocks. Understand?"

"Understood, sir."

Lanse gave Stanley a new transmitter and asked Mrs. Jenkins to show him how it worked before maneuvering the car back onto the street. Stanley activated his device and spoke to Doug for a few minutes, and then Doug asked to speak with Mrs. Jenkins.

When she activated her transmitter, he said, "Anna, my little lamb, you've done a great job. I want you to know how much I 'preciate all you've done over the last eleven years and before that too. I know this assignment's been 'bout as easy as running through molasses, but you've run like a thoroughbred."

"I'm happy to do it. You've given me so much more than I could ever repay."

"And I've been happy to do that, my precious, precious lamb. I look forward to the day I can hug you myself." There was a click as Doug turned off the translator. "*D'alasház, Anna.*"

"*D'alasház, Adu.*" (Paradisian: I love you, Daddy.)

When Mrs. Jenkins logged off, she had a thoughtful expression on her sweet face. She deliberately fastened her transmitter around her neck for the first time since Stanley had known her. Then she clasped his hand in both of hers.

"Stanley, I want you to know that I love you so very much. You are to me the son I never had." She paused, smiling what seemed a sad smile. "You're a good and brave young man with many talents. You'll do a great work, I know. Just keep running. No matter what happens now or in the future, keep running and talking to Doug. That way, if we're ever separated, we'll meet again at the Awakening."

Stanley peered up at her with wide eyes. If they were separated? What did she mean? He didn't want her to leave. She'd been the only constant in his life, the only one who had ever truly cared for him. Until now, this had been a game—another simulation, an exercise in outsmarting the bad guys. The facts that this time his parents were the bad guys and that his life was truly in danger were only beginning to register. But the idea of losing Mrs. Jenkins, the dearest person in the world to him, was too much.

"What is it, Mrs. Jenkins? What's going to happen?"

She drew him close and kissed the top of his head. "I honestly don't know, sweetheart. But I do know that we're going to be okay, because our ways are in Doug's hands. We can count on him. He always does what's best for us, and he never lies. Never. I've been through many trials in my long life. I didn't always understand them at the time, but I can see their purpose now, and I wouldn't change anything for the world. 'I will trust in his unfailing love,' " she quoted from the Manual. " 'My heart rejoices in his salvation. I will sing to him, for he has been good to me.' "

She rubbed Stanley's head. "Let's sing that song I like so much."

When she began singing #91 from the *Manual's* Songbook, Stanley joined in, gradually relaxing as they sang. He didn't understand everything Mrs. Jenkins said. He didn't know what the future, or even tonight, might bring. But if she could trust in Doug's unfailing love, he would too. As she often said, no matter what happened now, Doug would make all things right at the Awakening. And that was coming soon. Mrs. Jenkins said so.

While waiting for their driver to return with Stanley, Stan and Camille strategized until they had a solid plan for terminating him and deflecting all suspicion of foul play. This was no particular challenge, for they'd had millennia of experience in such matters. Accidents happen.

They were finishing the details when Marcus called, and Stan answered the phone. His eyes narrowed as he listened. When he spoke, his British accent had returned. "Follow his chip. And check the footage of the security cameras outside the building. Then ring back."

Camille's blood turned cold in her veins. Stanley was missing? Along with all he knew?

Stan hung up and roared, "You activated the thing! That's the only way they could have known!"

"Stan, I swear to you, I did not touch that transmitter. Unless it was somehow activated as it fell out or—" She hesitated, unwilling to verbalize the possibility that he activated it when he'd tried to smash it.

Stan apparently got the message. Looking at the device, he replied, "Yes. Quite."

"Perhaps he went to a friend's apartment?" Camille suggested.

"No. Morrison said Jenkins and the child left immediately you rang. The doorman saw them get into a dark blue sedan. They've fled, Camille."

"Then Garrick needs to get started. We must find that child."

"Garrick's in Arizona at the gym, but I'll recall him. Meanwhile, have Patric start the search with Garrick's men."

Stan stepped to the phone to recall their general, and Camille summoned Patric. When he appeared, he took in the unharmed transmitter in the middle of the shattered granite and said, "Ah-oh. Somebody's in trouble. Whose transmitter?"

"Stanley's," Camille said flatly.

All color drained from Patric's face. "Oh, that's not good."

"Indeed not!" Stan bellowed. "Find the child! Straightaway! Dr. Sondem said to work with Errol until he returns."

"Yes, sir."

"Cast a net," Camille said more calmly. "Tell Errol we want this to be the widest, tightest net we've ever cast. Utilize every employee in the city if need be, but find that child. I'm sure you understand how important this is."

"I sure do. With his photographic memory, Stanley's a walking backup disk for the PC."

Stan spit out an epithet, and Camille said sarcastically, "Thank you for that concise summary of the disaster, Patric. We were in need of just such a reminder."

"Sorry, sirs," Patric mumbled before slipping quietly out the door.

Soon Marcus called, relaying the news from the security footage. When Camille hung up, she must have been pale herself, for Stan stepped to her side and made her sit down. "What news?"

Camille took a steadying breath. "First, after tracking Stanley's chip all over the city, we have finally found it—on the floor of a cab."

Stan exploded with a curse. "*I* taught him that."

"There's more. He and Mrs. Jenkins were indeed caught on a security camera. They left in a dark blue sedan." She lifted her eyes to meet his gaze. "With Lanse."

"But if Lanse's driving, he's not in command of the operation. And only Gabriel outranks him. If Gabriel's involved, our chances of finding him are—"

He stopped, seeming to deflate. "—not good," he finished weakly and collapsed into a chair.

Camille leaned back against her desk and silence engulfed them. At length, she whispered, "This is as bad as I think it is, isn't it?"

"I don't know how it could be any worse. With everything that child knows …" Stan trailed off, shaking his head. "We would have gone about his training much differently if we'd known Damour would offer even these offspring his so-called grace. Who would ever guess he'd do that?"

"I still can't believe that's the case."

Stan nodded thoughtfully. "Maybe he's just using the boy for his knowledge."

Camille's gaze roved the office as randomly as her thoughts wandered about her mind. When it came to rest on the troublesome transmitter, she gasped. "Stan, if the thing was activated, then it still is. How could we be so obtuse?"

Stan snatched up the device and turned it over and over in his hand, his expression growing increasingly puzzled. "Camille, there's no way to activate this thing. Why would he have a transmitter that can't be activated?"

"Are you sure?"

"Look for yourse—" Stan suddenly went still and white, his mouth frozen in mid-sentence.

Camille knew Stan better than anyone. She had lived and worked with him for millennia. She had fought at his side in war. She had seen him in countless heart-stopping situations. Yet she had rarely seen him show fear. It was his expression, perhaps more than the words that followed, that filled her with terror.

"It just got worse," he rasped. "This thing doesn't have a means of activating it because it doesn't need one." He met her gaze. "It's live *all the time.*"

"So, not only does Damour have Stanley and everything he knows, but he's been listening—?" Her eyes shifted to the backpack, which routinely spent the afternoons in either her office or Stan's.

"—to our highest-level meetings and phone calls," Stan finished for her. "He's probably listening to us right now."

"That's right, Stan," Doúg said.

Stan thrust aside the transmitter and clapped his hands over his ears, as did Camille.

"It's a new model that Stanley was good enough to try out for me," Doúg continued. "It's worked pretty well, I must say. Not a nanosecond of dead air."

"For how long?" Stan demanded.

"Well now," Doúg drawled, "considerin' that you and I have sorta been on the outs lately, Stan, I may have to decline to answer that question."

"You turned our own son against us?" Camille cried.

"Oh, I can't take credit for that. Y'all did that yourselves. And while your parenting skills could use some work, I do want to thank you for the fine training you've provided him. You're right, Camille, he will be an excellent leader. He'll have a key role to play before this here feud draws to a close."

Camille couldn't have been more thunderstruck if Doúg had poured a bucket of ice water over her head. Stan had spent considerable time and energy to prevent the Striders from producing the child who would organize and lead Doúg's Outlander Division. After all that, had *they* produced, even trained, that child themselves? They had not only literally bred Stanley for excellent leadership potential, but had assiduously cultivated his superb natural talents. Had she and Stan not, just today, been congratulating themselves on their success with him?

Her astonishment transformed quickly into rage. Storming to the door, she crooked her finger at the first secretary she saw. Lana approached the door guardedly, and Camille pointed to the transmitter. "Remove that—that *thing* immediately and go bury it deeply."

"Yes, ma'am." Lana gingerly picked the transmitter up by the chain, holding it at arm's length, as Stan had.

"Howdy, Lana," said Doúg.

Lana screamed. Instantly blanching, she flung the transmitter up in the air and clapped her hands over her ears.

"Would you refrain from terrorizing our people further?" Camille screeched. "Haven't you done enough of that already?"

With Lana clearly too overcome to be of any use, Camille called to another secretary. "Dustin, get some earplugs and remove that accursed device. Take someone with you and bury it deeply. Be warned: it cannot be deactivated, so the villainous tyrant may torture you with his comments along the way."

"Yes, ma'am." Dustin was pale, but that seemed to be going around today. At least he was calm and rational. After stuffing some tissue in his ears, he picked up the device in the venomous-snake fashion everyone seemed to prefer and walked warily toward the elevator. The other employees tripped over themselves to give him a wide berth as he progressed.

Standing in her doorway, Camille addressed the group of secretaries and agents that had gathered. "That device belonged to Stanley." Ignoring the collective gasp, she continued. "Obviously we have had a traitor in our midst—we do not know for how long. Iona, send out an e-mail to all employees immediately. They should consider all instructions issued from Stanley's desk to be suspect. Should he return to the building, restrain him immediately. Also, call an emergency meeting of the Steering Committee to begin reworking all confidential procedures and protocols."

The immensity of the task she'd just described hit her, and she had to stop to take a calming breath. "Rest assured, the traitor will be found and will be dealt with according to his crimes. We rule the outlander world. Stanley cannot evade us for long. Now return to work."

Camille retreated into her office and closed the door. The full weight of the disaster then caught up to her, causing her to slump back against the door and slide to the floor. *All* of their plans and procedures as pertained to the war against Doúg were now exposed. Their *entire* battle plan was vulnerable as it had never been before. Such a situation would have been catastrophic at any point in their history. But for it to happen now, with their limited preparation time shrinking by the minute? The ramifications were staggering.

She had put on a strong front to buoy the employees' morale, but she knew that what she told them was false. Doúg already had Stanley. They would do their best to find him, but their chances of outwitting Gabriel were slim. Their brother knew them too well and was too much like them: cautious, thorough, and highly intelligent.

No, they had probably lost this skirmish already, and it was a crucial loss—perhaps the decisive battle in the entire war.

She watched Stan as he stared stiffly out the window. How she needed his consolation just now. If only she could return to the old days when she could fall into her elder brother's arms, find comfort in his strength, and hear him say that everything would be all right.

Having sensed her despair, Stan turned. The link informed him of her need, and she could sense his yearning for the same sort of camaraderie. But as he stepped toward her, she reconsidered. She couldn't accept his comfort without weakening the barricade she'd erected between them. And he had never met her condition; he had never apologized for his betrayal.

A tinge of sadness, followed immediately by anger, emanated from Stan as he sensed her change of heart. When he reached the door, he stood before her, arms crossed, and demanded, "Move."

Camille studied him for a moment, her decision vacillating as her emotional needs warred with her ego. In the end, ego won. She rose and stepped away from the door.

✳ ✳ ✳ ✳ ✳

Stanley began yawning as night fell, and still Lanse drove on. Stanley and Mrs. Jenkins passed the time by singing, reading from the *Manual*, and entertaining the general with stories from the Moden household.

Suddenly Lanse cut Mrs. Jenkins off in mid-sentence. "Stanley, now—hide!"

Stanley immediately ducked into the hidden compartment and locked the door, not pausing even to identify the problem.

The car stopped. Muffled voices drifted into Stanley's dark quarters.

He didn't move.

The back of the SUV opened and closed. Car doors opened and closed. Random knocking occurred on the compartment door, but not in the pattern Lanse had specified.

Stanley lay still.

A yell came next, followed by some scuffling. Then Lanse's "No!" and two gunshots in quick succession.

A chill shot down Stanley's spine, but he remained frozen and quiet.

The car lurched forward, proceeding at high speed over rough terrain. Stanley bounced around, but the compartment was well cushioned and he wasn't hurt. It seemed an eternity before the car stopped again. Then he heard on his door: knock-knock, pause, knock-knock-knock. He unlocked the door and cracked it open.

"It's all right now," Lanse said. "You're safe."

Stanley climbed out of the car to see that they were in a dimly lit barn.

"My apologies for the rough ride," Lanse said.

Glancing around, Stanley demanded, "Where's Mrs. Jenkins?"

Lanse sat down on a bale of hay behind him and looked at his shoes. When he raised his gaze, his brown eyes were moist. "Mrs. Jenkins was a strong woman. She was very brave."

Stanley's mouth went dry. "Was?"

Lanse wiped at one eye. Laying beefy hands on Stanley's shoulders, he drew him closer. "She gave her life to save you, Stanley. And she did it happily. She loved you very much." His voice quavered as he continued. "I'm so sorry. I know you were close. I tried—" He sighed and glanced down.

Stanley straightened his shoulders and relaxed his face. "I see." If ever in his life he wanted to cry, this was the time. He wanted to cry and scream and run away. Mrs. Jenkins was everything to him. She'd been better to him than his own mother. Until he had come to know Doug, Mrs. Jenkins was the only person to love him. And, yes, he loved her too, although he knew it was weakness.

But showing any sign of pain was also weakness, a message to your enemy of your vulnerabilities. And besides being dangerous, showing weakness was beneath a Moden. So Stanley did as his mother had taught him and concentrated on keeping every muscle in his face relaxed. It was especially hard with Lanse touching him the way he was—a strong grasp, but gentle and full of sympathy. It seemed to invite Stanley, even encourage him, to give in to his emotion.

But Stanley blocked all that out and concentrated on his chin muscles, which wanted to quiver and give him away. When those were under control, he repeated, "I see."

Lanse waited several moments. Finally he cleared his throat and stood. "Well, if you're ready, there are some others you need to meet."

"Certainly, sir."

Lanse led him out of the barn and toward a farmhouse. Still in alert mode, Stanley noted the location and weaponry of the two guards who saluted the general as they passed. He checked his compass reading. He noted the cloudy night, some woods and shrubbery toward the north, the sounds of a highway to the west, and the smell of cows. He had also noticed that Lanse left the car keys in the SUV. Several escape routes formed in his mind, just in case he should need them.

They mounted five steps and entered the farmhouse. Stanley heard people speaking Paradisian. Three men—no, four—and a woman.

When he rounded the corner into the kitchen, Stanley saw four burly men and a woman seated around a table, all dressed in navy pants and red polo shirts.

And, standing a little apart and looking directly at him, he saw his father.

CHAPTER 37

SAVED

" 'He has sent his angel to save his servants who, trusting in him,
disobeyed the royal command.' "
Daniel 3:28, REB.

Stanley instantly understood: Lanse had betrayed him, betrayed Doug. He was probably the one who killed Mrs. Jenkins too. In the next split second, he tallied his odds: one boy with a sharp knife, shoestrings, and a belt versus Father and six fully armed renegades from Doug's army. H'mm.

He spun around to run. Plan A: grab the SUV.

Before he could take a step, Lanse caught him by his shirt and lifted him off the ground. Stanley tapped his heels together, releasing the knife hidden in one sole. But Father understood his intent and pulled off the shoes before Stanley could reach the knife.

In a motion made familiar with practice, Stanley whipped off his belt and swung it around, the metal buckle whirring menacingly through the air. He managed to land several hard hits before the soldiers wrested it from him.

Determined to persevere, Stanley struck his attackers using the knee strikes and kicks he knew from Muay Thai. It was awkward going, with Lanse holding him tightly from behind, but several grunts testified that his attempts weren't worthless. He also repeatedly bit Lanse's hand and arm, even tasting blood.

Lanse held firm throughout. He just kept yelling, "He's not your father!" He obviously didn't have a very high opinion of Stanley's intelligence.

Despite his best efforts, Stanley soon realized that his attempts were achieving little and stopped struggling. They had him for now. Better to conserve his strength and watch for an opportunity to escape—if Father didn't kill him immediately, that is. Still, he wouldn't dwell on that thought. He needed to keep a clear head to plan his getaway.

Lanse set him down but clamped Stanley's shoulders firmly from behind. "Well, your father has certainly trained you well."

A vaguely familiar giggle came from the one woman. Stanley studied her, wondering how she could sound so much like Mother—although Mother didn't actually giggle very often. He was taken aback when their gaze met. Her eyes looked exactly like Mother's when she was in a good mood—a pretty, deep blue color. The woman didn't seem to mind Stanley's scrutiny. She smiled and winked at him, even as she dabbed at the bleeding gash on her forehead, a testimony to the effectiveness of Stanley's belt buckle.

Stanley returned a scowl before focusing his attention where it belonged: on Father. He, too, wore the informal uniform of Doug's army. His shirt pocket had four stars below the initials "EMP," which would be the uniform of the general in command of the *Ekanu Mejad Paladisi*, or Paradisian Royal Army. But why would Father try to masquerade as the commander of Doug's army? Surely he didn't expect to convince Stanley that he'd defected to Doug's side.

Bending down to his level, Father said, "Stanley, look at my face." His accent was British, so Stanley knew he was angry—no surprise there. But his manner was strange. And he'd certainly never put himself on Stanley's level before.

Father repeated, "Stanley, look at my face."

"Sir?" Stanley now stood at attention.

"Look at my left cheek."

Stanley did and then blinked in confusion. "What happened to your scar, sir?"

"As Lanse has been trying to tell you, I'm not your father. I'm Gabriel, his twin brother. I'm your uncle, Stanley."

"My father doesn't have a twin. And I don't have an uncle. All my relatives died in the war."

"Well, I beg to disagree. Besides Jané and I, you have two more uncles still living on Paradise Island. We brought some pictures. We thought you might care to see them. None of your relatives were killed in the war, whatever your parents might have told you."

"I will not fall for your manipulation, Father. I am now Doug's runner and have been for a year. I will not yield, sir. You yourself taught me that yielding is weakness. Interview me if you must, terminate me if you must, but I will not succumb."

To Lanse, Father said, "It seems my brother's raised quite the little soldier, hasn't he?"

"Yes, quite," Lanse agreed. "Anna was slain en route. He made no response whatsoever when I told him."

The woman gasped and burst into tears. Father took her in his arms and tenderly soothed her. Stanley had never seen him do anything like that. Usually he yelled at anyone who expressed weak emotions, especially through tears. But this play-acting was just part of Father's manipulation. Placing a subject in proximity to a weeping person increased the likelihood that the subject would surrender to his own weak emotions. And then Father would have Stanley just where he wanted him.

Well, he wasn't going to fall for it. He stood ramrod straight, concentrating on relaxing the muscles of his face and blocking out the woman's act. Finally the woman gave up, stopped crying, and drew away. Father then bent over again, hands on knees, to gaze intently at Stanley. His bright green eyes overflowed with a tenderness Stanley had never seen there before. But then, Mother had always said Father was the world's best actor.

"You must feel very alone, Stanley," Father murmured.

Stanley lifted his chin. If Father thought he'd trip him up with all this mushy stuff, he was sorely mistaken. He'd learned his lessons better than that. What's more, he was a Moden. If anything, it only made Stanley angry to know Father expected such a ploy to succeed.

"All right," Father said with a nod. "What other scars does your father have? Let's see, one on the left shoulder." He shucked his shirt, revealing a transmitter prop and—

Well, that was strange. He had a red birthmark under his left collarbone near the breastbone, just like Sheridan did. Father did have a birthmark like that, but it was on the right side.

Father ran a finger lightly over the birthmark. "Yes, you're right—your father's is on the other side. We're mirror twins, you see. It was the only way people could tell us apart." He chuckled. "Well, except for your mum. We never could fool her."

Stanley wasn't impressed. Father was playing games with him, that's all. Mirror twins—whoever heard of such a thing? Father had apparently painted on a birthmark to throw him off. Covering the real birthmark so well was harder to explain, but Moden Industries had some very skilled makeup artists. However, when he focused on the man's shoulder, he saw no scar there either. His gaze traveled to the right forearm, where another scar should be, but wasn't.

Father tapped his forearm. "Yes. That scar, unfortunately, was at my hand."

Though puzzled, Stanley carefully maintained an expressionless face and level tone as he said, "You have one on your side too."

"Ah, yes, of course." Father hesitated, a pained look in his eyes. "Also at my hand." He turned, but Stanley could see no scar there either.

The man bent down. "So, what do you think now?"

What Stanley thought was that someone had done an excellent job of disguising all of Father's scars. He didn't know how, but it was the only explanation that made sense.

"Permission to touch you, sir." He spoke firmly, allowing none of his uncertainty to show.

Father nodded, so Stanley rubbed vigorously at the shoulder where the scar should be, but found no make-up and no scar. He tried again where his real birthmark should be, again uncovering no disguise, and then rubbed at the fake birthmark. It didn't come off.

His hand dropped to his side. This was getting really confusing. He couldn't figure out how to explain this, but he did know of a simple, foolproof way to unmask his father. "With respect, sir, please pronounce His Majesty's first name."

"Doúg." The man said it, easily and clearly, with the Paradisian accent that triggered a cough in the exiles. "My lord and king is Doúg Deón Damoúr, and I am honored to be his servant."

Stanley was wholly baffled. Father and Mother had both said repeatedly that all of their relatives had died in the war. While it was true they were skilled liars, they only lied to accomplish a specific goal; otherwise it was easy to confuse which lies you'd told to whom. So why would they lie about this? What purpose could it possibly serve?

As he considered that question, his head began to swim. This was all so surreal, like he'd stumbled into an alternate universe. Mrs. Jenkins, the one constant in his life, was gone. His rescuers weren't who they seemed to be. His father even claimed to be on Doug's side. Nothing was as it should be, and he didn't know how to make it right again. Furthermore, he knew no one he could trust to help him make sense of the muddle.

No—there was one person. But Father would never allow him to call Doug. He couldn't even stand the sound of his voice.

When Father glanced up at one of the other soldiers, Stanley took advantage of his momentary inattention to quickly activate his transmitter. The man noticed his movement, but didn't try to stop him. Instead, he nodded. "Excellent idea. You should call Doúg."

"Howdy, buddy," came Doug's voice, and Father didn't clap his hands over his ears. "What can I do for you?"

Still expecting Father to try to stop him, Stanley quickly rattled off, "A man dressed like the commander of the EMP is claiming to be my father's twin brother. Who is he?"

"Ask the man to activate his transmitter, so I can get a fix on him."

The man complied.

"Stanley," Doug said, "the man standing directly in front of you is your Uncle Gabriel, who is indeed the commander of the EMP. Your father once shared that position with him, by the way. I couldn't tell you 'bout this ahead of time in case you mistook your father for him. But you can trust Gabriel, son. He's a good man."

So the world wasn't totally crazy. His parents had just lied to him. Even though he still couldn't understand why they'd bother to maintain such a lie, it was within the realm of possibility in the universe he knew. What a relief.

What's more, he had an uncle—a real uncle.

Stanley logged off and studied Gabriel, categorizing the physical differences between him and Father. Then, holding out his hand, he said, "Pleased to meet you, sir. Stanley L. Moden Jr."

Gabriel chuckled as he shook his hand. "Gabriel Lanáj, at your service. Lanáj is what the middle initial in your name stands for, by the by."

"Oh, I always wondered about that. Mother said it wasn't important, but it seems strange to only have an initial on my birth certificate."

"There's a reason for that."

"Yes, sir?"

"What does Lanáj mean?" the general asked.

"To help or serve," Stanley recited.

"Does that sound like a motto your parents would wish to perpetuate?"

"I see what you mean," Stanley said with a grin.

Gabriel chuckled again. "Well then, let's have a look at you." He straightened up to circle him. Accustomed to his father inspecting him this way when he assessed his workouts, Stanley immediately removed his shirt and started to undo his pants, although not without casting an embarrassed glance in the woman's direction.

Gabriel laid a hand on his shoulder. "Upper body is sufficient."

Stanley gratefully rebuttoned his pants. He assumed the stance Father preferred for inspections—feet apart, fists on his hips—and stood still as Gabriel circled him. But his gaze kept wandering to the woman, whose shirt pocket identified her as a colonel in the Royal Guard. Now that he knew she wasn't an enemy, he felt disposed to like her. She was nice to look at—pretty, with a warm, friendly expression. Actually, she looked a lot like Mother, especially her eyes. Could she be Mother's sister? It would be nice to have an aunt, too. And hadn't his uncle included her when he was mentioning relatives?

When he finished the inspection, Gabriel said, "You're remarkably well-developed for a ten-year-old. How much do you work out?"

"With respect, sir, I'll be eleven next month."

Gabriel smiled. "Of course you will. I do beg your pardon."

The apology perplexed Stanley. Was his uncle making fun of him?

Warily, he answered, "I work out with my trainer ninety minutes a day, usually six days per week. Each workout includes aerobic and strength training. Father reviews my workout journal with my trainer weekly to determine the appropriate changes."

"This is in addition to the martial arts?"

"Yes, sir."

"And you're completing high school this year, correct?"

"Correct, sir—on Friday," Stanley answered evenly, although the question reminded him of all the changes in his life. The fact was, he wouldn't graduate on Friday now. What's more, Mrs. Jenkins wouldn't be there when he did graduate. His world was still pretty messed up.

"Plus job training and music lessons—cello at present, I believe?"

"Yes, sir."

Gabriel bent down to look him in the eye. "When was the last time you played, Stanley?"

"Yesterday, sir. I had not yet practiced my cello when Doug called this afternoon."

"I'm sorry, I should be more specific. When was the last time you played like a child, just for fun? You know, baseball, or tag, or a board game, or—or rode a horse, for that matter?"

"To the best of my knowledge, sir, I have never engaged in such frivolous activities."

"I see." Gabriel's head dropped, and he muttered, "What have you become, dear brother? Your own son?"

When his uncle looked up again, his eyes were glistening, which disoriented Stanley further. Crying was one of the lowest forms of weakness. Yet this Uncle Gabriel, who certainly looked strong enough, was on the verge of tears. Why?

"Would you like to learn to play?" Gabriel asked. "Or ride a horse, perhaps?"

Stanley could scarcely believe his ears. "Really, sir? I'd love to! I saw horses sometimes around Central Park and I always liked watching them, but Mother said there was no reason to ride one because they were too slow, and Father said we have better methods of transportation now, but Mrs. Jenkins took us in a carriage once, and we even got to pet the horse a little and feed him a carrot, but I never thought I'd actually—"

Oops, he was rambling again. Father hated that.

Stanley snapped back to attention, but his uncle just seemed amused. "Then that will be our first assignment. We shall go riding tomorrow morning."

The woman cleared her throat, and Gabriel looked over his shoulder. "Oh, Jané, forgive me. I quite forgot you were here."

The woman came alongside Gabriel. She was tall for a woman, like Mother. But, like Gabriel, she bent over to Stanley's level. In a British accent, she said, "I fear I'm one of those relatives who shouldn't exist, Stanley." Shaking his hand, she added, "I am your Aunt Jané—Jané Lanáj."

"Lanáj? So are you Uncle Gabriel's wife?"

She giggled, and Stanley thought how odd it was that a grownup lady should sound so much like a girl and not care that she did.

"No," she said. "Gabriel is my brother."

"So, you're my father's sister, too?"

"Yes. Why does this confuse you?"

"I just thought you must be related to my mother. Your eyes look like hers, and you sound like her, too." He paused as he reevaluated the woman in light of this information. "But you do have the same hair color as Father. Oh—and you have the same cleft in your chin. Yes, I should have seen the resemblance."

Gabriel and Jané exchanged a glance, but neither said anything.

One of the other men moved toward the refrigerator. "Are you hungry, Stanley?"

As if reminded of a grievance, his stomach rumbled a reply. With all that had happened, he had scarcely noticed how famished he was. He settled at the table and devoured the omelet and hash browns set before him while he chatted with his aunt and uncle. He quickly decided that he liked them. He liked them very much. In fact, he felt safer right here with them than anywhere he'd ever been. Considering that he was running for his life, that wasn't reasonable. Yet it felt perfectly natural.

With dinner over, they moved to the living room for tea in front of a cozy fire. When Stanley said that he had sometimes seen his parents doing this, his aunt explained, "It's an ancient tradition of the Lanáj *yushún*, one that Gabriel and I, along with our other two brothers, Rubén and Felíp, still enjoy."

Stanley looked from her to his uncle, who was staring silently into the fire, his expression wistful. It touched him deeply that they would include him in their intimate circle. He had guessed that this time was special for his parents, but the children had always been excluded from it.

As they sipped their tea, Gabriel and Jané brought out pictures of their family—of Stanley's family—and shared stories about them all. When the stories wound down, Stanley asked, "May I ask what happens next?"

"Certainly," Uncle Gabriel said. "We'll leave from a private airstrip tomorrow afternoon." With a grin and a wink he added, "After riding horses in the morning. We'll fly to Chihuahua, Mexico, where we'll rendezvous with your new family. You will all remain at a hacienda there for about a month while you become accustomed to one another and to your new names."

Stanley nodded. "I understand. I'm in the NMH."

"Yes, you're now in the *Nij Mashil Halini*," his uncle said with a chuckle. (Paradisian: Program to Shelter Runners) "I forget that you know too much of such adult things. But I suppose you know the names of those in the program as well as I do."

"Yes, sir. Alphabetically, there's Lewis and Mary Aaron of Lincoln, Nebraska, disappeared from Springfield, Massachusetts on September—"

Aunt Jané giggled, and Uncle Gabriel burst into outright laughter. "Indeed, but I didn't intend that you should recite the entire list."

"Oh, I apologize, sir. When Father quizzes me, he often begins his questions with 'I suppose.' "

"Yes, of course," Uncle Gabriel said with a chuckle.

"You said I'll have a new family? Can you tell me about them? Who are they?"

"I'm afraid I can't tell you their names at this time."

"Understood, sir." Stanley was well acquainted with need-to-know situations.

Uncle Gabriel smiled. "You're a remarkable young man, Stanley. But then, Doug said you were strong and capable."

"Did he, sir?"

"Yes. And I can see it to be true."

When the mantel clock chimed, Aunt Jané said, "We should ready for bed, Stanley. Especially if we're to have riding lessons in the morning."

Stanley obediently followed them to an upstairs room in the old farmhouse. While Uncle Gabriel turned down the bed, Stanley changed into some pajamas that Aunt Jané had rounded up. She then folded his clothes and laid them on a chair. In the process, she discovered the paperback in Stanley's pants pocket. He had forgotten he had it.

Holding it up, she said, "*A Christmas Carol?*"

"Yes, ma'am," Stanley said. "Father once read to me out of that very book."

"Did he, now? Not typical bedtime reading for most children. Some find it quite terrifying."

"That book? It's a comedy, ma'am."

His aunt and uncle exchanged a puzzled look. "A comedy?" Uncle Gabriel said. "Why would you think so?"

Stanley shrugged. "I've never seen Father laugh so hard as when he reads that book. The whole idea of selfless humanitarianism and ..."

He trailed off as understanding came to him. Looking into his uncle's face, he said softly, "It's not supposed to be funny, is it, sir?"

Gabriel slowly shook his head. "No. It was written to draw attention to the plight of the needy and to draw forth man's sympathy for his fellow man."

Stanley's cheeks grew hot, even though it didn't seem like his uncle was ridiculing him.

"The fault lies not with you, my dear nephew," Aunt Jané said. "I fear our brother has confounded the world, making good appear bad and bad appear good. He has even succeeded in causing the tragic to appear humorous. We should have realized he would do no less with you."

She continued in a lighter tone. "But what else did he read to you? What are his favorite authors these days?"

"I don't know, ma'am. I was having trouble sleeping that time. I wandered into the living room where he was reading, and he read out loud until I fell asleep."

Aunt Jané lost her smile. With a glance at Gabriel, she said, "Do you mean to say your father read to you once—in your lifetime?"

Her reaction bewildered Stanley. "Yes, ma'am."

His aunt and uncle both appeared sad. They stared at the book for a moment, and then Uncle Gabriel took it from her and put it in his own pocket. Forcing a smile, he said, "Then this book will be special to you. I shall keep it on my person. In the event we need to leave suddenly, we wouldn't wish to leave it behind."

"Thank you, sir." Stanley still didn't understand their reaction, but he felt glad his uncle understood how special the book was and would keep it safe.

When Stanley crawled into bed, several men stood guard outside the house, Aunt Jané at his open door, and Uncle Gabriel beside his bed. He tried not to think about why he was so heavily guarded or about the day's events, for whenever he thought of Mrs. Jenkins, he wanted to cry again, and he would not be caught crying in front of soldiers. A Moden shouldn't be caught crying at all.

So he directed his thoughts to the usual evening routine at home, hoping that would bore him into unconsciousness. He pictured himself practicing his cello and sitting down to dinner. As they ate, Mother would conduct lessons on the culture and etiquette of various countries, and the brothers would report on their days and ask any questions they had about their schoolwork or job training. At home, they could speak with their parents only in the language they were practicing at the time, so tonight's table talk would be in Punjabi, and that was the language in which the scene played out in his mind. He was getting drowsy as his mental pictures came around to bath time. Father often came home as they were finishing their baths, so Stanley would—

He jerked up, suddenly wide-awake.

"Something the matter?" Uncle Gabriel asked.

"No, sir." Stanley lay back, ashamed of displaying behavior that might look like fear. He certainly never would have if he hadn't been almost asleep.

Gabriel gazed into Stanley's face, the soft moonlight enhancing his sympathetic expression. "I shan't laugh, Stanley."

"Well," Stanley said sheepishly, "it's just—" He stopped. No matter what his uncle said, he would certainly laugh.

"Yes?"

"I—" Stanley swallowed. "I hope Saxon remembered to cover Max's cage when Father came home."

"Max is a pet?"

"Yes, sir, Saxon's parrot. Father will eat him if he makes noise, and Saxon usually forgets to cover his cage on time."

His uncle showed no sign of amusement. Instead, anger flashed in his eyes. Yet his manner toward Stanley remained gentle. Sitting on the bed, he said, "I believe Max will be safe for the present. Your father will be too busy searching for you to return home tonight. Perhaps, if I apprise your mother of Max's danger tomorrow, she'll see to his safety in the future?"

Stanley smiled with relief. "Yes, sir. She's the one who let Saxon have Max. She likes Saxon best, so I think she might help him remember."

Another flash of anger lit his uncle's eyes, but he did no more than tuck the blankets around Stanley's neck with a sad smile. "Then I must conclude that your mother has gone quite batty, for I cannot imagine why she would prefer any child to you."

Stanley lay blinking up into his uncle's face, stunned. Did this man just compliment him?

"I shall address the issue tomorrow before nightfall," Uncle Gabriel continued. "If anything else concerns you, please inform me at once, and I'll attend to it directly."

"Thank you, sir." Even Stanley's strict training couldn't keep the astonishment from his voice.

"Not at all. If neither the birds of the air nor the lilies of the field are beneath Doug's care, certainly nothing that concerns your peace is either." He bent down to place a warm, lingering kiss on Stanley's forehead, which Stanley knew was a very special kiss to a Paradisian, although he had never before received one.

With no shame in his voice, his uncle said, "I love you, Stanley."

Stanley was too dumbfounded to think of a response, but his uncle didn't seem to need one. He pulled a chair beside the bed and, with one hand resting on Stanley's shoulder, began humming a song from the *Manual's* Songbook. In the doorway, Aunt Jané hummed along in harmony. Stanley found it soothing, but also mystifying. This Uncle Gabriel was strong and muscular, yet gentle and caring. He cried, he apologized, he delivered unnecessary compliments, cared about a bird, and even admitted love. What kind of man was this?

The kind of father you've always wanted, replied a voice in his head. And, as Stanley watched his uncle in the moonlight, it was easy to imagine that he really was Father—the very father of his daydreams. The fantasy was relaxing, and he dropped off to sleep.

During the night, Stanley relived his ride to the farmhouse. But he was most unmanly in his dreams, crying and screaming Mrs. Jenkins' name. The cushioning of the hidden compartment grew close around him, cradling him and making him feel safe even though she was in danger. He banged and clawed at the door, trying to get out to help her. But the compartment only closed tighter around him.

Then, somewhere far away, Father began singing—not the father of Stanley's reality but of his fantasies. Over and over, he sang Mrs. Jenkins' favorite song, his deep bass voice resonant and clear. Each time he came to the end of the song, he assured Stanley that he would see Mrs. Jenkins again.

In his dreams, Stanley knew Father was right. He gave up struggling and rested in the comforting warmth of the cushioned compartment—enjoying the music, absorbing the promise.

In the morning, Stanley awoke clutching a button that was attached to a fragment of red fabric. Uncle Gabriel's shirt was torn, and he had a scratch on his neck. Neither asked the other about these oddities.

CHAPTER 38

CALLED

" 'Fear not, for I have redeemed you;
I have called you by your name; You are Mine.' "
Isaiah 43:1, NKJV.

" **A** nd thank you for the gift of my most precious *tesoro, Ada*."
. . . Chris's murmured words to Doug came through the fog of Susana's dreams just before she felt his warm lips on her cheek. For the past two years, ever since the day Chris thought he was going to lose her, she had awakened this way. It had become their routine, and she loved it.

What wasn't routine was the request Doug had for them that morning. "I've got something special I need to talk to y'all about," he said when they settled down to their morning chat. "My Royal Guards just rescued a ten-year-old boy from a dangerous situation, and he needs a new home."

Chris turned raised eyebrows to Susana. She nodded her answer without hesitation. About a year after losing Pete, they had started discussing the possibility of adopting more children; just last week they had decided to proceed. So if Doug had someone he wanted them to adopt, it was an easy decision.

"Sure, Doug," Chris said. "We'd be happy to take him."

"I 'preciate y'all's ready willingness, but there's more you should know about this situation before you answer. First, you have met this boy. At the time, he was masquerading as George's nephew, Jared."

Chris nodded. "I knew there was more to that kid than met the eye. I wanted to help him—he just seemed to have this deep sadness. But I didn't have the chance to get close enough to find out what it was all about."

"Now's your chance."

"You said he was masquerading as George's nephew," Susana said. "Who is he really?"

"Well," Doug drawled, "hold onto your hats. He's really the son of Stan Moden and Camille Desmon."

"What?" Chris and Susana both exclaimed. "Aren't they brother and sister?" Susana added. "That's just—yuk."

"Well, the full explanation is kind of complicated. Suffice it to say that the exiles are makin' up their own rules. But the point is, little Stanley was raised to take over the management of Moden Industries."

"Wow," Chris exclaimed. "How much does he know about their operations?"

"That's the thing," Doug said. "Stan and Camille made the mistake of training this child in the most critical aspects of their organization first. They were working under the assumption that he wouldn't be able to change sides."

"A mistake I'm sure they won't repeat," Chris interjected.

"You're right there, pardner. Anyway, Stanley's a bright little whipper-snapper. He's got a photographic memory, was scheduled to graduate high school on Friday, and is fluent in thirty-two languages."

"What?" Susana exclaimed.

"You heard right, little filly. He also knows most everything of interest about their organization. Although they were training him to assume control of the business, it's so intricately connected with their battle plans that he's had access to the details of their war effort too. He even knows the specific plans for thwarting individual runners. He's been feeding me priceless information since he ran the race last summer. And besides all that, he has intimate knowledge of how Stan and Camille operate, allowing us to anticipate the changes they'll be makin' because of his defection."

"How'd he manage to run the race?" Chris asked.

"His parents sent him to a leadership camp last summer. We were able to cancel his stay at the camp without Stan and Camille's finding out, and he ran the Kids' Race instead. His parents haven't wasted any love on him. They never even tried to contact him during the summer."

"Oh, Doug," Susana cried. "That's awful."

"Yes," Doug said gravely. "It truly is."

"So, besides his value as an individual," Chris said, "this kid's strategic value is off the charts. But doesn't that also mean that Stan and Camille will be relentless in searching for him? What would they do if they find him? Would they kill their own son?"

"In a heartbeat," Doug said sadly. "So what I'm asking y'all to do involves pulling up stakes and disappearing. Y'all, including the little ones, will be in grave danger from Stan and Camille."

"Leave our home?" Susana asked. "Our families?"

"What about our patients?" Chris asked in a more matter-of-fact tone.

"I'll handle things at the office for you both. No one's gonna be left in the lurch. However—" Doug's voice grew solemn. "Yes, Susana, there is the possibility you may never see your families again this side of the Awakening."

Chris glanced at Susana, and she knew what he was thinking. He was ready to do as Doug asked; was she? But the possibilities terrified her. Adopting a child into their home was one thing, but this? Did he really understand what Doug was asking? Did he get the picture of never seeing their families again? Most important, did he realize it meant putting Bethany and Andy in danger?

No, this needed more thought. A lot more thought.

"How long do we have to decide?" she asked.

"You can take up to a week if you need it. Y'all are the best suited for this child. He's a mighty smart little fella, but he's been taught to look on outlanders in general with contempt. He needs parents he can look up to and respect, who won't be put off by his intelligence. He needs people who will expend the extra energy it'll take to understand the world from his perspective and to help him see it from mine. Y'all are exactly that set of parents."

Doug continued, "On the other hand, I hope y'all won't take as long as a week. During Stanley's rescue yesterday, his lifetime nanny was killed, and she's the only human who's ever loved him. What's more, the way he's been raised is only hinderin' his ability to deal with this trauma. My guards are doin' their best, but he really needs some TLC from someone who can relate to his pain. I'd prefer to get him hooked up with a new family as soon as possible."

Although Chris's ebony eyes had grown intense with concern, she couldn't acquiesce so easily. What Doug asked was life changing. They could never, ever turn back from this decision. She thoughtfully shook her head. She just needed more time.

"Okay," Chris said. "We'll try to get back to you soon."

"In the meantime," Doug said, "don't discuss this with anyone, including the kids. Don't give the slightest indication in anything y'all say or do that you may be leaving. Also, don't call or e-mail any relative or friend for any reason until we sort this out. Hear me well on this. It could be dangerous for them."

"All right," Chris said. "We understand."

"There's one more thing I'd like y'all to know," Doug said. "Chris, you 'member at your weddin', when I told you I had special plans for y'all?"

"Yes, I remember."

"This is what I was talkin' about."

That parting thought haunted Susana through the rest of the day. As she went about her work, every little boy reminded her of that one particular boy who needed her special attention. She often found herself pausing to look at her right hand—healthy, strong, and fully functional—healed miraculously by Doug so she could do the work he had for her. During lunch, she pondered her wedding ring, reviewing the stories of Doug's guidance and care that the jewels represented. Through it all, one particular passage from the *Manual* kept running through her mind—the maxim that Chris liked so well: *We will do whatever you command us and go wherever you send us.*

But balanced against her desire to help Doug were several deep concerns—legitimate concerns. The idea of never seeing her parents and siblings again, for example. "Never" was a hard word to get around. Still, that really meant "never until the Awakening." Compared to what Doug had done for her, was that such a sacrifice?

Giving up her present lifestyle was no problem. Sure, she enjoyed having the luxuries she'd never had as a child, but she wasn't bound to them. Trading a life and work she enjoyed for a complete unknown was more difficult, but she could give it up for Doug too.

Knowingly placing her children in danger to help their enemy's son? Well, that was a different story. It was to this terrifying possibility that her mind returned hour after hour. By the end of the day, she had still not reached a decision.

As she closed up the clinic, she took a careful look around, and a strong impression came to her: this work—as important as it was, as much as she loved it—was not the work Doug most needed *her* to do. Other people could do this work. Apparently there weren't others who would raise a lonely, frightened ten-year-old fugitive the way she and Chris would raise him.

This thought recalled something Chris's father, Ben Strider, had confessed to her when he returned to running after twenty-plus years of sitting on the sidelines. "I keep wondering," he had said sorrowfully, "what I forfeited—what blessings I missed giving and receiving—because I was too afraid to trust Doug to take care of my kids."

Would she have similar regrets if she turned Doug down now?

🏃 🏃 🏃 🏃 🏃

Jané returned to her post in Los Angeles just as Susana was closing up the clinic. Doúg had given her leave to meet her nephew, and she was immensely grateful. He was truly a remarkable child whom she had loved instantly.

Yet, remarkable or not, he was still only a child, and one who was suffering terribly after the events of the day before. Although he tried very hard to hide it, she could see the pain in his eyes. She could even empathize to some degree. She had lost one brother and her only sister—her best friend and business partner—to the rebellion. Still, she had been a mature 2,000-year-old adult at the time, and she was blessed with three supportive brothers besides. Poor Stanley had barely completed a decade of life, and his merciless upbringing had deprived him of the skills required to negotiate such a difficulty. He didn't even know how to accept comfort.

Still, she was hopeful. Doúg himself had chosen Stanley's new parents, and the Striders would be able to reach him, she was certain. Lessons they had learned while struggling through their own personal agonies would enable them to guide him through his grief. And they knew how to connect with children.

The question was: Would they accept the assignment?

At Jané's first glimpse of Susana in her office, something tightened within the guard's chest, and she knew fear on her nephew's behalf. Susana's indecision was written in large letters on every feature. Her customary smile had been replaced by a deeply furrowed brow. Her usually bubbly demeanor had wilted. Her lively step slogged as if she carried the entire weight of the earth. And, in a sense, she was, for she was once again insisting on bearing a load that only Doúg had the strength to bear.

Jané shook her head sadly. "Poor humans."

Truthfully, she didn't understand outlanders' struggle at times like these, even though she had watched them wrestle with such decisions for centuries. For her, obeying Doúg's commands and choosing to do his will was a wonderful blessing, even privilege. As a member of the Royal Guard, she was sometimes entrusted with duties that made her cringe—such as that moment on the cliff when she had to sit by and watch Susana risk her life. Yet even at those times, she was acutely aware of the honor her king extended in allowing her to participate in his astounding operation to rescue mankind. She never considered disobeying him; she knew beyond doubting that only her full compliance would be beneficial in the eternal sense. Most humans never seemed to trust him to that degree, and their vacillation caused them terrible suffering—even as Susana was suffering now.

"What can I do, Doúg?" Jané asked. "Isn't there something I can do to help her?"

"The decision is hers alone, little dove. But a reminder of my faithfulness would do her good. So would a nice run."

Jané broke into a grin. "Thank you, *Adu.*"

Dashing to Susana's car, the guard let herself in and quickly altered the audio programming. She slipped away, diving behind some bushes just as Susana came around the corner of the clinic's parking lot. Once her charge drove away, Jané stripped down to the running gear that she always wore beneath her street clothes. Then, lacing on her tennis shoes, she jogged away, taking the same route that Susana would take to pick up the children.

🏃 🏃 🏃 🏃 🏃

When Susana buckled herself into the driver's seat and turned on the ignition, the audio version of *The Runner's Manual* started up automatically, drawing a slight frown from her. She often listened to the *Manual* while driving, but she didn't remember doing so that morning. With a shrug, she decided she'd just forgotten.

Even before she turned out of the parking lot, she heard: "I know whom I have believed. And I am convinced that he's able to guard what I've entrusted to him."

She hit the brakes and stared at the machine. How perfectly appropriate to her situation. Of course, she knew Paul's declaration to be true intellectually. Doug was trustworthy, and she had entrusted her children to his keeping. But accepting these truths in her heart and incorporating them into her life—well, that was harder, wasn't it? Especially where her children were concerned.

She rewound and replayed that brief section twice, searing it into her brain before continuing home. The route she followed passed through several traffic lights. At the first one, a woman jogged through the crosswalk in front of the car. As Susana's gaze followed her, her feet felt a bit itchy—how liberating a good run would be right now. But she couldn't go, of course; she'd have to make dinner, feed the kids, give them their baths, and—

An impatient horn reminded her of her present duty, and she cruised through the intersection, passing the same runner as she progressed down the street. At the next light, the woman jogged past the car again, and they continued to leapfrog past one another until Susana turned into her parents' home to pick up the kids. Each time she passed her, her feet got a little itchier.

When she arrived at home, she was greeted with a most pleasant surprise: Chris had finished work early and already had dinner waiting. When she mentioned that she'd love a good run, he said, "Go for it—I've got this covered."

Susana changed into running gear and jogged toward the neighborhood park. Usually when she ran, she also chatted with Doug—a big part of why running was so therapeutic. But tonight she was reluctant to activate her transmitter.

As she approached the park, she was only slightly surprised to find Debora waiting on a bench. Her coach fell into step beside her, and soon Susana was just thinking out loud, summarizing the pros and cons of the question before her. When she finished, Debora said simply, "What does your gut tell you, my dear?"

"Well," Susana said thoughtfully, "that we should do as Doug asks."

"Then the problem is that you don't wish to do this?"

Susana hesitated. "I know I should want to do what Doug asks. I even *want* to want to do that. I'm just—afraid, I guess."

"Afraid of what?"

"That something will happen to the kids."

"To the children whom you have previously surrendered to Doug?"

Susana's ears burned. "Yes," she admitted softly. "Those children."

They ran in silence for a few moments before Susana spoke again. "Ben Strider once told me that he'd wasted much of his life because of that same fear."

"Even good things, if held too tightly, become idols that will lead you astray."

Stopping suddenly, Susana pled, "*Ami*, please help me. I don't want that to happen. I don't want to waste my life because of my worries. And I don't want my worries to limit what Doug can do through me and my family. I want to trust him with the kids. I just don't know how."

Debora smiled sweetly. "I will be happy to help you, dear one."

Clasping Susana's hands, Debora opened her mouth and exhaled slowly. Susana closed her eyes and let the sweet atmosphere envelop her. A gentle tingling spread through her, infusing her with confidence and strength. Her worry drained away, and she suddenly realized how heavy she had felt all day, as if she'd been carrying around a hundred-pound backpack. What a relief to set that burden down.

🏃 🏃 🏃 🏃 🏃

After the couple gave Doug their decision, Susana slept peacefully and awoke with no qualms, her fears having been supplanted by a sense of eager anticipation. Still, Chris insisted that they take their time with the *Manual* the next morning, saying they would likely need extra fortification in the days ahead. They ended up spending an extra hour in their joint study.

When Susana woke up Bethany, the seven-year-old looked at the clock and exclaimed, "*Mami*, you woke me up too late."

"We thought we'd take the day off school to go to the zoo. How's that sound?"

"*Sí, Mami, sí!*" Bethany jumped up and down, clapping her hands.

Five-year-old Andy was equally enthusiastic, and the family soon set out. Susana carried only her purse. Chris's backpack contained four sack lunches, their *Manuals*, and Juan Misi's necklace. They left everything else behind. Doug's instructions were very clear: they must look like they were going to the zoo for the day—and that's all.

They visited various animals at the Los Angeles Zoo before arriving at the bears' exhibit at exactly 11:30 a.m. A zookeeper approached them almost immediately. Her nametag identified her as Georgia, the one Doug had said to expect.

"Hi, kids. Would you like to come in the back and help me feed the bears?" she asked.

The children bubbled with excitement. "Please can we, *Mami*? Please?"

"Of course," Susana said. "That sounds like fun."

Georgia led them to an employees-only area where the children helped her prepare some treats for the bears. As they worked, she told the children, "We're sending one of our bears to the San Diego Zoo today. Would you like to go with him and see his new home?"

The kids burst into joyous pleas for their parents' consent, and Chris and Susana laughed as they granted it. When Georgia explained that they would have to pretend to be bears and ride in some big crates, the kids thought that made the game all the more intriguing. They giggled while crawling into the big wooden boxes, and Georgia soon had them crated up—Chris and Andy in one, Susana and Bethany in another. Shortly thereafter, their crates were loaded into a truck.

CHAPTER 39

ILLUSORY COMFORT

"The comfort they offer is illusory … But Israel's strength
will be in the Lord."
Zechariah 10:2–12 REB.

1 April 8020 M.E.

Camille stormed into Stan's office and slammed the door behind her. "Guess who called last night."

Her brother looked up from his desk with a scowl. He hadn't been home since Stanley's disappearance, and, between his fatigue and general bad humor, he was obviously in no mood for guessing games. Undaunted, Camille answered her own question: "Gabriel."

"Oh?" Stan intoned sardonically. "Is he offering to return the child?"

"He called to advise me of Max's danger."

Stan shrugged impatiently. "Who's Max?"

"Saxon's parrot. Apparently you threatened to eat the creature if he squawks?"

"It was a promise, not a threat. What's that to Gabriel?"

"Stanley was concerned that, in his absence, Saxon would forget to cover Max's cage when you get home. Can you believe the gall?"

"Certainly Gabriel didn't just call about a bird."

"Oh, yes—he did. That was the only topic of conversation. He did it merely to irk me, Stan, I'm sure of it."

"Then I'd say it worked. Did you trace the call?"

"He had it patched through the island."

"Figures. So did you storm in here just to irk me?"

"No, I did not." She jammed a fist onto her hip, and he stood up, his scar reddening.

"What was that?"

She paused to assume a more respectful tone of voice. "I apologize, Stan. You wanted a report on the failures in the entity management system."

He dropped back into his chair. "Proceed."

Taking a seat in front of the desk, Camille began, "The first loophole was obvious. Since we all believed the offspring couldn't defect, we've had them operating under the same procedures as Paradisians, with no precautions against subterfuge. And, since Stanley was charged with entering the names of the races' entrants into the computer, he simply omitted his own. No one was the wiser."

"Fix it."

"We already have. And Patric is establishing new procedures regarding the offspring generally."

Stan grunted. "And the Jenkins loophole?"

Camille drew a deep breath. Stan wasn't going to like this anymore than she did. "That one was more difficult to identify," she said carefully.

Stan's gaze sharpened.

"Patric finally discovered it," she continued, "by manually comparing the electronic record of runners with the microfiche made of the old paper files before they were destroyed. So far, he's found three cases, including Jenkins, where someone failed to convert the paper record into an electronic file. These, of course, are all older individuals who ran the race before we were fully computerized. However, the other cases were caught when they attended a RAB."

"Are you telling me Jenkins never joined a RAB? Whoever heard of a runner who doesn't attend a RAB?"

"It's possible she attended under a pseudonym."

Stan's chair creaked as he leaned forward, his brow furrowing in concern. "But that implies decades of preparation."

"I'm afraid so. No matter how we look at this, the inevitable conclusion is that Doú—" Camille coughed and rolled her eyes. "—that *he* arranged matters, over a period of at least fifty years, to keep this specific woman invisible to our system. It's as though—" She broke off, shaking her head.

"Go ahead. Say it."

She studied him. "You've already reached the same conclusion, haven't you?"

"Let's find out. Say it."

She drew a deep breath. "It appears that he knew we would raise human children before we ever considered the possibility. It appears that he devised a means of secreting a runner into our home specifically to proselytize those offspring. And it appears that he carried out this plan over a period of at least a half century."

Stan held her gaze for a moment and then abruptly swiveled his chair to stare out the window. Camille sensed his uneasiness and understood it completely, for she shared it. They had done everything possible to ensure that their children had no access to Doúg's version of truth. They had gone to great lengths, even establishing their own school, to assure that the offspring knew his "rescue" was unavailable to them. Indeed, they had truly believed it themselves.

Yet Doúg was apparently determined to offer their children the same opportunity open to other humans. So determined, in fact, that he had even assumed personal responsibility for assuring that those children knew of it. And, in truth, this one measly child would surely achieve that end, for news of Stanley's defection had already spread through the schoolyard. Every child in the organization would now question what their parents told them about the Damours. Even Saxon had made subtle queries.

But perhaps most disturbing of all was this: In order to accomplish this objective, Doúg had penetrated their most secretive, most secure systems. He had even managed to plant an enemy right in their very home—and he had kept her there, undetected, for over a decade. If he could do that, was anything beyond his reach? Was anywhere—or anyone—safe from his influence?

"We need to change our basic assumptions," Stan said.

"Agreed."

He swiveled back to face her. "We'll separate the business from the war effort. Offspring will have no access to confidential information pertaining to the war until we *know* they're on our side."

"And no access to sensitive intelligence until they've proven their loyalty for—what, a quarter century?"

He rubbed his chin. "And some terminations."

"Excellent. Once they've murdered, they'll need our protection from the law."

He nodded and fell silent. Sensing his disappointment over their spoiled plans, she said softly, "Stanley is only one child. Now that we know these offspring are vulnerable to Damour's propaganda, we'll tighten our program. We'll limit their exposure to outside influences so that no outlander has access to the children. We'll monitor every phone call and every keystroke. Perhaps we'll not have the 100 percent success rate with them that we had assumed, but they will still be a valuable source of manpower."

"I'm sure you're right," Stan said tentatively. Then, more firmly, "Of course you're right. It's only logical. This defection stings because we weren't expecting it. But we won't repeat that mistake. For one thing, the next child who defects won't have any information to share with Damour. And once he figures out that we're not giving them access to valuable intel, he won't have any interest in them."

Madelyn's voice came over the intercom: "Dr. Moden? Patric's here, sir. He says he needs to talk to Dr. Desmon urgently and thinks you'll be interested too."

"Send him in," Stan said.

"Howdy-do," Patric said as he bounced in. "Adlai's on the phone. He says he has urgent news." He motioned to Stan's phone. "May I?"

Stan grunted permission, and Patric punched a button on the phone. "Okay, Adlai. You're on speakerphone in Dr. Moden's office. The bosses are both here."

"Thanks, Patric," Adlai said. "Sirs, I'm calling—" He stopped and cleared his throat. "I'm calling to report that Strider and family—have disappeared."

"What?" Camille shrieked, jumping up. "So you're the cause of Stanley's defection!"

"Ma'am," said Adlai. "I swear to you, I watched that kid every minute. I never left him alone with Strider."

"Hold on, Adlai." Stan jabbed the hold button and glared at Camille. "Knock it off."

She returned his glare. "Don't you see what's happened? This family just happens to disappear at the same time as Stanley? Obviously Damour has picked them to raise the child. And why? Because Strider's the one who corrupted him—right under Adlai's very nose."

"There's no evidence to support that conclusion. Garrick himself combed through Stanley's correspondence. The child was not in touch with Strider or any other runner. This is entirely Jenkins's doing."

"Oh? Then it's mere coincidence that Damour's using the Striders as Stanley's foster family?"

"He could be doing that to spite us. He knows how much we hate Strider."

"I don't believe that for an instant," she insisted. "Adlai will pay for this. He will pay dearly."

A deep frown creased Stan's brow. Rising, he circled the desk. "I can't believe I'm doing this. I'm the one who's hardly slept in three days. You should be transfusing me." He held his hands out to her.

"I don't want it." Camille plunked onto the chair and crossed her arms. "I have every reason to be angry."

"Take my hands, *Kamíl*," he snarled. "Your eyes are too gray. We can't afford to have you abusing our best agent."

She eyed him. He wasn't going to be deterred, and she wasn't in the mood for a physical altercation.

"Oh, all right. Have it your way." She sulkily plopped her hands into his.

Patric had gradually slunk away as the siblings argued. Now he eased back to where he could watch Camille's eyes, which often changed color in response to a transfusion. After a few moments he let out an awed, "Whoa."

"That's enough." Camille snatched her hands from Stan's grasp.

"That is so cool." Patric sounded like a child who had just found a new toy. "Can you do that too, Dr. Desmon? Is it part of your link?"

"Yes," Camille said shortly.

"How does it work?"

"We don't know," Stan snapped.

"Can you do it with other people—like me maybe?" Patric persisted.

"No!" Stan and Camille exclaimed in unison, and both turned irritated looks on him.

"Oh." Looking properly chastised, Patric again slunk away from them.

Stan returned to the phone, but stopped to address Patric in a cautionary tone. "There are precisely three other people in this organization who have seen what you just saw, and I know who they all are."

"Got it," he said hoarsely. He pulled an imaginary zipper across his mouth. "My lips are sealed."

Stan turned back to Camille. "And you remember this: Adlai's health isn't what it used to be. Abusing him will accomplish nothing useful. If Strider's gone, Adlai's in the best position to help us find him."

She frowned but nodded her agreement.

Stan reconnected the call. "Adlai, give me the details."

"Yes, sir," Adlai said hesitantly. "Well, I realized there was a problem this morning. I went to Strider's office to drop off some documents for signature, and the place was all abuzz. It seems he failed to show for work, and I've never known him to do that. He hates inconveniencing his patients. Anyway, I got suspicious. I called the wife's office, and she was also a no-show, as were the kids at school. So I let myself into their house. The first thing I saw were their cell phones sitting on the counter. I immediately suspected an NMH operation, since they'd only be caught without those phones if Damour had instructed them to leave them behind. Taylor stayed in the house to search for clues while I went searching for the Striders. She says there's no indication of their plans. The computers indicate that they were making future appointments until yesterday."

"Any idea where they went?" Stan asked.

"I've had GPS trackers on their cars for years, so I had no trouble finding one of them in the parking lot at the zoo. I enlisted several of our New-RAB supporters to help me search for them, and some tourists did report seeing the family earlier, but they're nowhere to be found now."

"Check shipments."

"I did, sir, but this is the LA Zoo—it's big. They've had a slew of trucks in and out, some to places around the country. If I may make a couple of suggestions, sirs?"

"Go ahead."

"First, the quickest way to disappear from here would be into Mexico. Could we get their pictures to our resources along the border, as well as the local train and bus stations and the airports?"

Camille nodded to Patric, who bounded for the door. "On it."

"What else?" Stan asked.

"Strider has mentioned that he'd like to visit the village where his grandmother came from—Juan Misi's village in the Copper Canyon. That would be a great place to hide. It's so remote."

"I'll send Tony Fiden," Camille told Stan. "He already knows the language, and, after his momentous failure with Strider, I wouldn't mind chastising him further by burying him in such a secluded place."

"I also thought I'd call both of their families," Adlai said. "As a friend, I can claim concern over their disappearance. Of course, knowing the Striders, they probably followed Damour's instructions and didn't contact anyone, but maybe I'll be surprised."

"Try it," Stan ordered. "Keep us posted."

✲ ✲ ✲ ✲ ✲

During their two-hour ride from the Los Angeles Zoo to the San Diego Zoo, Chris and Susana explained to the children that they were on a secret adventure that would end with them getting a new brother. The kids were ecstatic. In fact, they were so excited that Susana was afraid they would stop the first person they saw and tell him all about their trip. In Susana's imagination, that person would, of course, be one of Stan's agents. So she reminded Bethany multiple times that it was a *secret* adventure and that the secret part was very important. In the other crate, she could hear Chris repeatedly reminding Andy of the same thing.

Once the initial ecstasy subsided, the children wanted to know all about their new brother. Although Chris and Susana had met Stanley as "Jared," the children had not. So they told them the little they knew, how he was doing an important work for Doug, and how he especially needed them to love him because his parents never had. Bethany almost cried at that. The idea of her new brother not being loved by his real parents was too much for her empathetic heart.

After they arrived at the San Diego Zoo, a zookeeper named Ron uncrated them, just as Doug had said. They watched Ron uncrate their bear friend, made a quick stop at the petting zoo, and had dinner at one of the food stands, all per Doug's instructions. Then they hailed a taxicab to take them to the border, where they were to cross on foot and find a specific money-changing booth as a particular clerk ended her shift.

However, while en route to the border, Susana got a puzzling case of the creeps from their driver. When she noticed his transmitter, one of the bulky ones from the New-RABs, her uneasiness worsened. What if George and Vanessa had already discovered they were gone? Would they guess their plans? Surely the news of Stanley's defection would have reached them; they might connect the two disappearances. If they did, wouldn't they enlist Stan's supporters in the New-RABs to find them?

She nudged Chris and quietly whispered her concern. Since she had her transmitter on in privacy mode, she was simultaneously relaying the information to Doug.

Dusk was deepening around them when the driver pulled off the freeway in Imperial Beach. Susana nervously leaned forward. "Why are we exiting here?" she asked over the *ranchera* music.

"I need some gas," the driver answered. "The traffic's heavier than I expected, so I'm using more gas than I planned. Sorry for the inconvenience, but it won't take long."

Susana directed Chris's attention to the gas gauge, which registered over a half-tank. She also whispered this fact to Doug.

"I'm already on it, little filly," Doug said. "Gather your things to change cars at my signal."

When the driver pulled up to a pump and disappeared into the gas station, Doug instructed, "Transfer to the tan sedan that's pulling up behind you. The driver's expecting you."

With sweaty palms, Susana grabbed Bethany's hand and dashed to the car behind them.

"What's wrong, *Mami*?" Bethany asked, her voice quavering.

"Just a little change of plans, *chiquita*. But Doug has everything under control."

Before the taxi driver returned, their new driver darted away from the gas station. "Howdy, kids," the jovial man greeted them. "My good friend Doug tells me you're on a real, honest-to-goodness adventure." He made his handlebar mustache dance for them, and then grinned as the children laughed.

He continued to make faces in the rearview mirror, tell jokes, and otherwise lighten the mood until both children relaxed, apparently forgetting their scare. He even managed to distract Susana with his antics. It wasn't until she noticed Chris staring fixedly into the headlights out the back window that she realized they were dodging the other driver.

They didn't completely lose their pursuer until they crossed the border. In a brilliant coincidence (which Susana would never believe was mere coincidence), the taxi driver hit the randomized red light that singled him out for a complete inspection at the crossing. Shouts of victory broke out in the tan sedan as they sped away from the border, leaving the taxi driver in the dust.

Even then, their new driver didn't lessen his vigilance. Still telling jokes and stories, he expertly wove through the streets of Tijuana for some time. When he was convinced they weren't being followed, he deposited the Strider family directly in front of their next contact's money-changing booth.

Carmen, the teller at the booth, closed up the establishment and took the family to her one-bedroom apartment. There they visited over a light supper and then bedded down on the floor of the small living room.

"I am so tired," Susana said as she lay down beside Chris.

"Yeah," Chris agreed. "The kids are already out cold. It's been some kind of day, hasn't it?"

"Mm-hmm." She laid her head on his chest. "I don't know when I've been so grateful just to have a safe place to stretch out and sleep. At least, I hope it's a safe place. That incident with the taxi was really scary."

" 'I will lie down in peace and sleep, for Doug will keep me safe,' " Chris quoted from the *Manual*. He kissed the top of her head. "If Doug says we're safe, we're safe."

She smiled and patted his chest. "I'm also really grateful for you. Your strength, your faith—just you."

She dropped off to sleep quickly and slept soundly. It seemed only seconds later that she awoke to pounding on the door. A quick glance at the wall clock told her it was 11:05 p.m., and a wave of fear shot through her. Doug's itinerary had said nothing of a brusque midnight awakening.

Chris was already on his feet and reaching for the baseball bat next to the door. "Get the kids' shoes on," he whispered. They had all slept in their clothes, just in case.

Carmen came hurrying from her bedroom, tying her robe. *"Quien es?"* she asked through the door. (Spanish: Who is it?)

"Soy yo, Miguel García," came the hushed reply. (Spanish: It's me, Miguel García.) That was the man who was to take them to their rendezvous point, but they hadn't expected him until morning.

"Is that his voice?" Chris whispered.

Carmen nodded. "But something must have happened." She opened the door while Chris stood to the side, bat raised.

Miguel entered, explaining quickly that Doug had sent him early because Stan's men had picked up the Striders' trail. Chris quickly confirmed the change in plans with Doug, and the family headed out the door. As they left, Susana overheard Miguel whisper to Carmen, "Make sure you clean up right away. Stan's people are coming."

Until that moment, Susana hadn't realized what Carmen was risking by helping them. She now imagined the worse. Would Stan's men track them to Carmen's apartment and beat her up while searching for them?

"Is she going to be all right?" she asked Miguel nervously.

"Don't worry, *mi hija*." Quoting the *Manual*, he added confidently, " 'Doug keeps constant watch over the whole earth so he can strengthen his runners.' We are, all of us, safe in his care."

At precisely 2:32 a.m., Camille was startled awake by a deep sense of anguish—sense, not feeling. That is to say, the emotion was not her own, but that of her linkmate. Nevertheless, it drew her with an urgency she could not ignore. She rose, donned her robe, and glided silently down the hallway, following the "tug" that would lead her to Stan.

As she neared the living room, the perception worsened, mushrooming into an overwhelming, tear-wrenching heartache by the time she entered the room. She could just make out her brother sitting on the sofa in the darkness. His back to her, he faced the unlit fireplace. Although he sat as still as stone, a multitude of emotions raged within him, including loss, worry, and apprehension. But above all else, she sensed loneliness, even homesickness.

Camille had not been close to her brother since his betrayal years before. Nevertheless, his anxiety merited her concern. His wholehearted participation in the war effort was essential to their overthrowing Damour. And, since such a funk was by no means common for him, she could not easily dismiss it.

With more impatience at having her sleep disturbed than true sympathy, she shuffled toward him, purposely making some noise to alert him of her presence. His link-sense did not include the locator ability that hers did.

His head jerked toward her in surprise, but anger played no part in his emotional response—a bad sign. "You're awake," he said flatly, returning his gaze to the cold fireplace.

"Actually, you woke me."

He grunted.

She rounded the sofa and lit a fire before sitting in the overstuffed chair adjacent to him.

"We missed them," he said.

"The Striders?"

"They slipped right through our fingers again in Tijuana."

Camille nodded. Bad luck, but no worse than she had expected. Certainly not an explanation for Stan's current despondency.

They lapsed into a long silence, which was broken only by the crackling and popping of the logs. The light of the flames cast flickering shadows over Stan's face as he stared into them, but his expression remained impassive. Still, Camille discerned his roiling emotions, and she knew from experience that, if he had not demanded her exodus, he would talk to her when ready. Furthermore, it was of utmost importance that she be available to listen and support him through whatever crisis this might represent.

At last he spoke, his voice low. "We may have just lost this war."

She carefully considered her options for approaching the problem. They had not discussed the ramifications of Stanley's defection since the initial exchange in her office. Indeed, she had been so busy that she hadn't considered that aspect of the problem again. Nor did she wish to. The obvious conclusion, which Stan had just stated with excruciating accuracy, was too unpleasant.

Ultimately she decided the best course would be to admit the truth: "I know."

Stan grimaced, which made her wonder if some remnant of big-brother protectiveness still existed in his cold heart. She watched him stare unseeing into the fire as several more moments passed in silence. Although his battle was not evident in his face, her link-sense informed her that he was struggling to maintain his composure.

"Our lives are going to end. We're going to—" He broke off to heave a deep sigh.

Camille couldn't say the word either, so it was left unsaid.

"Soon it will all be over. We'll be gone." He paused before whispering, "Forever."

These same thoughts had been chasing Camille. And, though she had been resolutely dodging them, she conceded that she could no longer escape the confrontation. She must face the monster stalking her. As she turned to look death in the eye, one overwhelming reaction surfaced: She didn't want to die alone. In fact, that possibility frankly scared her.

This admission reawakened within her that long-suppressed yearning for love, and she reflexively thought of the *lashani* she had once known in the Damours' presence. Then she felt disgusted with herself. Even if the Damours' love was still available to her—assuming she could somehow put aside her loathing of them—would she accept it? Could she agree that she had been wrong in questioning their Law? Could she admit that the last six thousand years of her life had been a mistake? And even if she could somehow manage that, would she lower herself to their standard of "love"? Never. Such a commitment required far too much of her.

Still, she had to admit, love did offer a certain measure of comfort. Not *lashani*, of course. But the support of a companion who could buoy her spirits— that could be most helpful. And a relationship based on mutual back-scratching required far less of her.

Her gaze wandered to her brother. He had once been an excellent companion. They had shared many interests—still did, in fact. They understood one another. They liked each other—or had in the past.

She sighed regretfully. But that was many years and one very large betrayal ago.

Stan turned toward her. "I don't want to die alone, Camille."

Even with her ability to sense his despair, his admission surprised her. And his frankness encouraged her to reciprocate. "Nor I."

"Do you think—?" He paused, studying her intently, and then continued in an uncharacteristically halting manner. "Kami, I may have done some things in the past—that I now wish—I had done—differently."

Camille could scarcely believe her ears. Though not an apology in the traditional sense, it was certainly the closest Stan had ever come to uttering one. He probably wasn't even capable of a clearer statement of regret.

She did not respond except to shift her gaze to the fire. She had once said she would consider reconciling if her brother apologized. Now she did exactly that—she considered it, methodically reviewing the pros and cons of restoring their relationship: the comfort of having someone with whom to share the vicissitudes of life versus the risk of placing her confidence in the man her brother had become.

She could not trust Stan. She knew this. He had betrayed her before; he would do so again if it served his purposes. But Camille lived in a difficult world. Her position of authority had required that she make some hard decisions through the centuries, and these had gradually robbed her of her once plentiful friends. She no longer had a real friend—not one. In truth, she was very lonely. She hated to admit that—especially now, with the end so near. To die alone seemed tantamount to admitting that her life had been worth nothing, that she had made a horrendous mistake in rebelling against Doúg.

Grief surged through her with the thought. Although she preached the danger of becoming vulnerable through love, she pined for it nonetheless. She wanted it so desperately that she was willing to accept a corrupted version of it. She longed for the acceptance of someone who truly knew her, even if his regard was capricious. She coveted the shielding arms of a protector, even if his protection was erratic. She yearned for an affectionate embrace, even if such demonstration was fickle.

In short, she craved her brother's love. Yes, his definition of "love" had changed through the years. But then, so had hers. And, unpredictable and imperfect though it now was, Stan's love was the best her world could offer. So it came down to one question: Was she willing to lay aside her pride in exchange for a love as uncertain as his?

A voice within her clamored, *No, not after what he did!*

But, even as the voice cried out, she knew she had already rejected that line of reasoning. She couldn't make Stan pay for his treachery without also punishing herself. And she hated the idea of spending the last few years of her life alone more than she hated the idea of accepting Stan's clumsy apology.

So, she would be the survivor she had learned to be. She would take what she could get and make the best of it. She would lay aside her pride and resentment if, by so doing, she could purchase companionship. She was just so very tired of being alone.

"I couldn't bear to be betrayed again," she murmured, still gazing into the fire.

"I've paid for that. I've paid dearly. I lost the love of the only person whose love matters to me at all, and just at the time when I needed it most." He paused until she met his gaze. "Return to me, Kami, and I will never betray you again. I promise you that."

She didn't believe him—she was no fool. But, in the end, it didn't matter. She simply couldn't bear the idea of facing the coming events by herself.

She eased onto the sofa next to him and tucked her hand into his arm. Relief flowed from him like a wave. He put his arm around her and drew her near, kissing her temple.

They sat together for some time. Although they spoke no further, the comfort of companionship gradually soothed their uncertainties. Camille perceived the release in Stan's emotions as clearly as she felt the spring of her own inner turmoil unwind. At last, she drifted into sleep, her head resting on his shoulder. She was dreamily aware of his head coming to rest against hers when sleep overtook him as well.

Stan always awoke at four o'clock without an alarm clock. That morning was no exception. She felt him shift on the sofa and roll his head as he tried to work a crick out of his neck. She lifted her head to look at the mantel clock, which confirmed the hour.

"Off to the gym?" she asked.

"Not today. I'd rather sit here with you." He drew her head back to his shoulder. "Go back to sleep."

She smiled as she snuggled into his broad shoulder and again surrendered to sleep. When she awoke at her usual time an hour later, Stan was jotting notes on the back of a magazine.

"Good morning," he said.

"Good morning. Did you get a bit of restorative sleep, at least?"

"Actually, I slept better than I have in some time."

"I'm glad to hear it."

"We have a couple of problems to solve," he said matter-of-factly. "The most urgent is that I need a new apprentice for the presidency of the company."

She nodded. "Saxon is perfectly suited to take over my position, but he's not well suited for yours. And Sheridan? Well …"

He nodded. "I know. Neither of us is sure we can trust him yet. On the other hand, if things do work out with him, he'll be an excellent military commander."

"Yet that still leaves us with a gap at the top."

"I don't have to tell you my first choice for solving the problem." He paused, and his next words surprised her. "But I'll leave it up to you. You know the advantages of having the top three administrators bound by both training and family ties. But I can make other arrangements."

She could sense his resentment at having to discuss this with her rather than order her to accept it. Yet he was choosing to place the decision in her hands. How long would their new accord last if she refused his wish?

She decided not to find out. "We've already agreed to work together in raising the youngsters to fill the top three positions. I see no reason to amend that agreement."

He broke into a smile. "You're a great partner, *zali*. The best."

Taking in his jotted notes, she read, "Dinner … park … lessons? Ideas for solving the second problem you mentioned?"

"Yes, we do need to make some changes around here. No more human nannies, of course. Even if we can block the holes that allowed a runner to slip through our system, who knows what other nonsense an outlander may plant in impressionable minds. Obviously our control over these kids isn't as complete as we thought. We'll have to be more careful."

She nodded as she finished his thought. "And spend more time with them for the manipulation to succeed."

"Mm-hmm. It's not really that bad. When they get annoying, we'll turn them back over to the nanny. But they're fairly well behaved and occasionally even entertaining. Sometimes they remind me—" His voice grew so soft as to be almost inaudible. "Remember Sashi?"

Camille nodded, a smile lifting her lips. "The goat that followed Jané everywhere. We had many good laughs from that animal's antics. Remember when Jané trained her to clean up the crumpled sketches she'd tossed to the floor?"

Stan laughed. "And then she had to un-train her when the animal ate one she'd discarded by mistake? I remember." He grew quiet. "Those were good times."

"They were indeed." Adding more confidence to her voice than she felt, she continued. "But this will be over one day, Stan. Once we overthrow Damour, we can settle into an easier life again."

She no longer truly believed in their victory, and Stan would know that if he chose to look her in the eye and evaluate her emotions. However, she wanted to believe the assertion. More important, she needed to believe it so she could continue working. If nothing more, she wanted the satisfaction of making Damour's life as difficult as possible for as long as possible.

Stan didn't choose to meet her eyes. No doubt, he knew her words didn't reflect her honest opinion, but he, too, wanted to believe them. "I admire your optimism," he said. "It's carried us through some difficult times."

With this encouragement, she continued in the same vein. "Losing Stanley was unfortunate. But we will recover. We'll do it because we have to."

"We'll brush ourselves off, learn from our misfortunes, and move forward. *Together.*"

"With even greater momentum than before."

He chucked her under the chin. "I do love your optimism."

CHAPTER 40
SHELTER

" 'He who sits on the throne will shelter them with his presence.' "
Revelation 7:15, NIV.

Having already had two close calls with Stan's minions, Chris had no trouble remaining vigilant as they drove through hundreds of miles of desert. Clearly, Miguel had done this before, for he was well prepared. He had stocked his SUV with food, water, and extra gasoline so they didn't have to risk being seen by stopping in populated areas. He also had pillows and blankets, as well as toys and games, which helped to minimize the cries of "Are we there yet?"

They arrived at a high-walled hacienda late that afternoon. The place certainly lay in no man's land—Chris could see no other sign of human existence in any direction. When they drove up to the gate, they were greeted by two Dobermans and a sentry in the casual uniform of the Paradisian Royal Guard. The guard instructed the travelers to activate their transmitters so that Doug personally approved their admittance into the compound. As they drove in, Chris craned his neck to assess the security and was initially overwhelmed at the size of the place. Adequately securing the whole estate—including sprawling gardens, a three-story mansion, a large stable, and a smaller house—would surely be a major undertaking. But when he noted armed guards roving throughout the grounds, plus more manning the thick wall's corner towers, he relaxed. Doug had things under control.

They arrived at the main house where Lanse greeted them warmly and showed them to their new quarters. Susana herded the children upstairs to freshen up, but Chris, anxious to greet their new son, headed straight for the pool, where Lanse said Stanley was swimming laps under Gabriel's watchful eye.

As Chris approached, a large smile lit Gabriel's face. "Chris, how wonderful to see you. I'm so pleased you accepted this assignment." He kissed him on the cheek in the Paradisian fashion and then nearly crushed him in a bear hug.

Once he'd caught his breath, Chris said, "I didn't expect to see you here."

"Well, I couldn't pass up the chance to meet my nephew." Gabriel motioned to the boy diligently swimming laps.

"Ah, yes, I'd forgotten about that relationship. So, what do you think?"

"He's a remarkable child—well-mannered, intelligent, and terribly brave, particularly considering his age. But Stan and Camille have been harsh and exacting, teaching him to despise weakness and value strength above all else. He believes love, hugs, and tears are all signs of weakness, and he considers outlanders to be feeble and daft."

To Chris's surprised expression, Gabriel added, "I do beg pardon for being so blunt, but you'll see it soon enough. He has much to learn—or unlearn, I should say. Yet his commitment to Doug is firm. He shows unreserved willingness to accept Doug's way once he understands it."

"That's promising," Chris said hopefully.

A sad expression came over Gabriel as he watched the young swimmer. "You can imagine what confusion and loneliness the poor boy must be feeling. He's separated from everyone he ever cared about. His nanny's death haunts his dreams, although he refuses to speak of it. He talks as an adult—reasons as an adult, in many ways—but he has all the emotional needs of a child without the slightest idea of how to handle them." Clapping Chris on the back, he added, "You've certainly got your work cut out for you."

"It sounds challenging," Chris admitted.

"You may not know this, but it was your interest that drew Stanley to running."

"Really? I hardly talked to him."

"Still, he perceived the concern in your eyes and the love in your touch. Even in a home where love is denounced as weak, it cannot fail to attract. It was enough to set him thinking."

"I never would have guessed that such a small thing could affect someone so deeply."

"I daresay that no action, when undertaken in love, is a small one."

"I guess not," Chris said. And to think, it was only through George that he'd had the privilege of touching Stanley's life at all.

They fell into a few moments of silence, during which Chris's attention was drawn to Stanley's powerful stroke. "I've never seen a child's body so well developed," he observed.

"Part of that is his physical training. He worked out for ninety minutes a day in addition to lessons in the martial arts—he holds black belts in karate and Muay Thai."

"Note to self—don't cross him," Chris said. "But what's the rest? Stan wouldn't put his own kid on performance enhancers, would he?"

"I believe my brother's now capable of doing anything that serves his purpose. However, in this case, the disadvantages outweigh the benefits—the drug's side effects would decrease Stanley's overall usefulness to him. No, most of what you see has to do with the neutralized consequences of *kanuf*."

Frowning, Chris admitted, "I'm not following the connection."

"*Kanuf's* effects are not simply emotional or intellectual, but physical as well. It even brings about actual genetic changes. Outlanders living today are the products of hundreds of generations of progressively weakened DNA. Your bodies simply don't have the same potential that Adam's did."

"And Stanley's DNA is less corrupted because it's only one generation removed from creation?"

"Perhaps even less than that. Doug has said little on the subject, but, from what I've gleaned, these children are apparently being generated in vitro—some type of cloning, I assume."

"Wow. Well, that would answer one of my questions—about siblings marrying. Does Stanley know his parents are brother and sister?"

"No, and Doug asked that I not tell him. He's a bright boy, but not immune to societal stigma—particularly as he has so many other confusing changes to process just now." He grinned. "So you will have the honor of explaining it to him at some future time."

Chris chuckled. "Got it."

Gabriel's expression turned reflective as he again watched his nephew. "Chris, that poor child has known nothing but heavy burdens and unending demands. He's been treated as though he's nothing more than a living tool. Literally since birth, every moment of his life has been invested in developing him into the instrument that Stan wanted him to be. Those who should have protected and nurtured him have belittled and terrorized him."

Shaking his head, Chris noted, "I can't imagine being raised by Stan *or* Camille, let alone both." Then, realizing that he'd just insulted Gabriel's family, he grimaced. "I'm sorry. I didn't mean—"

"No offense taken, my friend. You're quite right. From Stanley's accounts, I've learned that Camille callously demonstrates obvious favoritism toward the second boy. However, she does, at least, praise the boys when they've done well. Stan, on the other hand—" He expelled a harsh sigh. "The loving elder brother I knew is now consistently severe and fearsome. He even threatened to eat the boys' pet, if you can believe that. And I'm certain it was no mere threat. That's a particularly detestable tactic since Stan, to maintain his body in optimal condition, observes a rather strict vegan diet. Yet he was willing to make an exception merely to intimidate the youngsters. I'm horrified that he could be so heartless, especially to his children." Gabriel's jaw clenched balefully. "To own the truth, I'm furious with him."

Having been on the receiving end of Stan's anger, Chris held his tongue, unwilling to contribute to Gabriel's admitted fury. But, unlike his twin, the general seemed able to quickly shake off his rage. When Stanley stopped for a breather, Gabriel easily broke into a smile and called to him.

The boy swept back his dark brown hair, hoisted himself out of the pool, and obediently jogged toward them. Then he suddenly stopped, his eyes growing wide, and snapped to attention. "Dr. Christian Strider, son of Juan Misi—sir." Stepping forward, he formally extended his hand. *"Kuira, keni amígowa."* (Rarámuri: Hello, my friend.)

Chris was momentarily struck speechless. Doug had warned him that Stanley knew thirty-two languages, but why would one of them be the obscure Native tongue of Chris's ancestors?

Composing himself, he stepped forward to grasp Stanley's hand. *"Kuirabá, keni no."* (Rarámuri: Hello to you, my son.)

Stanley's eyes grew even wider. "Really? I'm to join *your* family?"

"If you'll have us."

"If I'll have you?" the boy exclaimed. "Why, this is better than anything I hoped for, although I dreamed about it and learned everything about you and your family, and even learned some Tarahumara or I guess you would call it Rarámuri because it was fun to pretend, but to actually be part of your family is more than I'd ever really hoped for—"

Hiding a grin behind his hand, Gabriel leaned over to whisper, "He does tend to rattle on when excited."

Stanley stopped abruptly and flushed. Returning to attention, he said, "My apologies, sir."

Chris bent down to Stanley's level. "No apology necessary. I'm happy to know you're as excited as I am."

"Are you, sir?" Amazement filled the boy's voice.

"I am. I'm looking forward to getting to know you."

"Wow," Stanley breathed. "Thank you, sir."

They returned to the house and, after Stanley changed clothes, gathered in the dining room for dinner. Chris introduced the new family member to Andy and reintroduced him to Susana. Stanley politely shook their hands and offered a "Pleased to meet you" to each.

When Bethany entered the room, things turned a bit peculiar. As soon as their eyes met, she and Stanley became obviously puzzled. His training kicked in first, and he extended his hand. When they shook, both of them seemed transfixed, staring first at their enfolded hands and then back at each other while still holding the handshake.

Finally Bethany said, "I know you."

"I know you too," Stanley replied.

"You've met before?" Susana asked. "Where—at the RAB in LA?"

Stanley shook his head, still holding the handshake and focused on Bethany. "No, ma'am. We've never met. We just know each other." The confidence with which Stanley spoke for his daughter unnerved Chris a little, and he moved behind her protectively.

"What do you mean?" Susana asked. "How long have you known each other?"

With the same assurance that Stanley had shown, Bethany answered, "Since always."

Chris looked to Gabriel, hoping he might have some light to shed on this strange meeting, but he looked as confounded as everyone else.

Chapter 41
New Things

"He who sat on the throne said, 'Behold, I make all things new.' "
Revelation 21:5, NKJV.

The next morning Chris was alone in the library studying the *Manual* when Gabriel entered. "Your new identities just arrived. Doug wants you to start calling each other by these names right away so you can get used to them."

Reaching for the packet Gabriel offered, Chris asked, "How long do we have to learn them?"

"You'll stay here until you become accustomed to them. It will also give you an opportunity to learn how to function together as a normal family. Debora will call on you in about a month to see how things are progressing. She'll determine if you need more time."

"I'm concerned about the 'normal family' part," Chris said. "Normal families don't have a bunch of guards around all the time."

"We'll be backing off now. Most of the men will leave today. Lanse will remain with several guards, but they'll move to the other house. And while we'll continue to post guards outside, they shan't be inside the house any longer. If you need assistance, you may signal the guards using the panic buttons located above the light switches."

"Oh, that's what those are. But what about you? I know you only met recently, but you're the only real family Stanley has now. I think it might be good if you're able to stick around for a while."

"I'm pleased you feel that way. Doug believes it would prove helpful with Stanley's transition if I remained nearby for a week, or perhaps a fortnight, but I don't wish to interfere."

"We'd welcome your help. Please do stay—as Stanley's uncle rather than as his guard."

After lunch Chris gathered his family and introduced their new names. He also warned that they could no longer speak the language that he had taught his children to love. "We can only talk English or Spanish," he concluded.

"For how long, *Onó*?" Bethany asked.

"I don't know, sweet pea. Maybe the rest of our lives."

"But why?" she asked plaintively.

"It's because of me," Stanley said, his voice tremulous. "My father's men will investigate anyone they hear speaking Rarámuri to find us. I'm really sorry." Unusually affected by Bethany's distress, his voice cracked as he finished. It was the strongest emotion they'd seen him express.

Chris exchanged a bewildered glance with Susana and then looked to Gabriel, who was studying the two children intently. But his bewildered expression promised no enlightenment.

"Okay," Chris said, changing the subject. "Would you like to know who you are?"

They all did, of course, so Chris introduced them to their new identities. He was pleased to discover he would still be able to practice medicine while working in a small village that had a clinic but no doctor. Susana would teach in the same village. When Gabriel hefted a file box onto the table with everything she needed to teach the six grades at the school, she laughed. "It looks like I've got a lot of homework to do before school starts."

Chris knew she was disappointed at not practicing physical therapy, but she didn't show it to the children. Wrapping his arm around her shoulder, he planted an appreciative kiss on the side of her head. He noticed Stanley, sitting on her other side, turn quickly away.

To help them learn their new identities, Susana organized a game that involved bouncing a ball back and forth while naming the person you wanted to catch it. Stanley had no difficulty picking up his new name; he said he was accustomed to using "covers." The others weren't so quick, and Bethany and Andy thought it was especially funny when their parents forgot their new names. Whenever this happened, they joined forces to chase the offending parent around the yard and smother them in "sloppy" kisses. Stanley stood apart and watched with a baffled expression.

Once when Susana was the object of such a chase, Chris said to him, "This looks pretty funny to you, huh?"

"No, sir—strange. I can't imagine my parents allowing such disrespect."

"Oh, it's not disrespect," Chris said, surprised. "Quite the opposite—it encourages respect."

Stanley turned a confused face up to him. "How, sir?"

"Well, how do you define respect?"

"It is treating a superior as a superior."

"Ah. Then I understand your confusion." Calling a quick explanation to Susana, Chris turned toward the house and led Stanley into the well-stocked library. There he found an English dictionary and handed it to him. "Please look up the word 'respect.' "

Stanley flipped through the book and read, "High regard, honor, esteem."

"Note: it's talking about attitude, not behavior. Now, when you defer to a superior even though you don't think well of him, is that based on 'high regard'? Or is it to avoid the consequences if you don't?"

"I do it so I don't get in trouble. It doesn't matter what I think of him."

"According to the dictionary, is that respect?"

"Well, no, but ..."

When Stanley went silent, Chris prompted, "But what?"

"I don't know, sir. It's not what I've been taught."

"Is it possible you've been taught a distorted idea of respect?"

Stanley silently looked first at the dictionary and then back at Chris.

"Here's how I understand it," Chris said. "Respect is thinking well of someone because of who they are. That means getting to know them, and that

means seeing them in a variety of situations. As our children get to know us as
people—not just disciplinarians, but people who work and play, laugh and cry,
even argue—they learn to know us better. And, if we're people worthy of respect,
that will help them respect us more, not less. Does that make sense to you?"

"Yes, sir, it does."

"Powerful people can force others to behave as if they respect them when
they aren't actually worthy of it. But, at least to me, that isn't real respect."

"No, sir, I guess it isn't." He looked at the dictionary and mused aloud,
"Then what I've been taught is respect is really intimidation."

🏃 🏃 🏃 🏃 🏃

The next afternoon, Chris walked into the kitchen where Susana was
working at the counter and, slipping up behind her, embraced her to kiss her
neck. Susana smiled and gave him a quick kiss. When Chris looked up, he noticed
Stanley sitting at the nearby table, his eyes wide.

Jumping to attention, the boy said, "My apologies, sir."

Chris joined him at the table. "Stanley, we're a family, not a military
outfit. You don't have to snap to attention or call me 'sir.' Doing that in front of
other people will draw attention to us and could be dangerous."

"I understand, si— I mean, okay."

"Good. Now, what are you apologizing for?"

Stanley's brow furrowed. "Because I was in the room when you kissed
your wife."

"I see," Chris said, swallowing a chuckle.

From what Gabriel had said, Stanley's birth family was very different
from their own, which meant the boy would need to make considerable adjustments. But what might that entail? What kind of family was he used to? Now
seemed like a good time to find out.

"Stanley, tell me a bit about your home. Where did you live? Who lived
with you? Who took care of you?"

"We lived in a penthouse apartment in Manhattan. I have two brothers—
Saxon is seven and Sheridan is five. Our nanny, Mrs. Jenkins, took care of us, and
the housekeeper, Mrs. Morrison, did too sometimes. Mother had another house
on the North Shore, but I never went there. She only stayed there when she was
tired of us or very angry at Father."

Tired of them? Did she actually tell the children that?

"And you never saw your parents show any affection for each other?"

Stanley hesitated before admitting reluctantly, "I did once."

"Can you tell me about it?"

"It was my fault. They have a special time together before going to bed.
They drink tea in front of the fireplace and listen to music and talk. I wasn't
supposed to watch. But one time I stayed awake and snuck into the living room
to see what they were doing. I—I saw them, well, holding hands." Stanley flushed
crimson as he finished.

Perplexed, Chris looked to Susana. What was he missing? Why would
Stanley be so embarrassed by his parents holding hands?

Susana asked softly, "And then what happened?"

"They heard me and got mad."

"What did your father say?" Chris asked, now understanding. The answer to Stanley's embarrassment lay not in what he had seen but in how he was treated for seeing it.

"He said, si—" Stanley glanced up. "Begging your pardon, but what should I call you?"

"*Papá* or *Papi*, or Dad or Daddy."

"Just like your own children?"

"Yes. That may be strange for you, but maybe you can think of it as a cover for now. Someday I hope you'll come to feel like you really are one of my children."

Stanley seemed moved. "Thank you," he whispered.

"So what did your father do?"

"He hit me and said I shouldn't invade his privacy."

Susana gasped, and Stanley glanced at her uncertainly. "What'd I say?"

Chris leaned forward. "Stanley, that—" He bit his lip. Stan and Camille's treatment had been reprehensible, but children's self-esteem was bound up with their parents. He would have to tread gently and avoid criticizing them directly. "It's that, as Doug's followers, we believe in treating people more kindly, especially family members. Even society at large has instituted laws making such actions illegal."

"Yes, I know. That's why we had to be careful Mrs. Morrison and Mrs. Jenkins never found out. Father said he would have to kill them rather than risk them telling outlander authorities. So we never told anyone, and we were careful they never saw our bruises. But in the end it didn't matter because Father had Mrs. Jenkins ki—"

Stanley stopped abruptly and his face went blank. After a moment, he said shortly, "Those are just outlander laws. We can break them if we don't get caught."

It took Chris a moment to get over his shock. Stan had told his sons he would kill their nanny and housekeeper if they found out about his abuse? What a heavy, horrible burden to place on a child.

When Chris found his tongue, he said gently, "I understand that's how you've been taught, Stanley, but it's not Doug's way. He teaches us to respect all laws, unless they conflict with his."

"Understood, sir—I mean, Dad," Stanley said, although he looked perplexed.

Chris gazed at him sympathetically. "There's a lot coming at you awfully fast, isn't there?"

Stanley's bearing relaxed some. "Yes, Dad. I'm learning a great deal."

"You're a brave and strong young man. If your father understood what true strength is, he'd be very proud. But please finish telling me about this. What was your mother's reaction?"

"Mother said holding hands had nothing to do with love, that the music just sounded better that way, and that love was a weak emotion to which only fools succumb. But—" He hesitated, his brows drawn together.

"But what?" Chris prompted.

"Well, Doug and Debora and Josh love people. They love me, you know," he added, his eyes lighting up. "And they're all very strong. The files indicate that

Josh has won every fight between him and Father. They're not worded that way, but that's what they mean."

His face again went blank and he continued in a monotone. "Mrs. Jenkins loved me too, and Lanse called her a strong woman. She died protecting me."

Chris watched in amazement as the ten-year-old child maintained an expressionless face while recounting the recent death of the woman who had been dearer to him than his own mother.

Placing a hand on the boy's shoulder, he drew him closer. "Did you love Mrs. Jenkins?"

"Love is weakness." Stanley stared straight ahead, his demeanor stony, and Chris suddenly understood. This was the poor boy's method of hiding emotions he considered "weak." He probably wanted to cry like a baby. What he needed was permission to do so.

Quietly, Chris said, "It makes me very sad to hear about Mrs. Jenkins." Extending his arms, he added, "I really need a hug."

Stanley looked at him in utter astonishment. "You, sir?"

Chris nodded. "Would you do me the favor?"

The boy hesitated, his internal conflict clear. Chris simply waited, trying to sympathize with the confusion and pain he must be feeling. He found himself comparing Stanley's harsh upbringing to his own, where love and hugs were given freely. A deep ache gnawed at his gut—an overwhelming desire to help him, to provide him with the fatherly love he'd been denied.

And then, something miraculous happened. Gasping, Stanley pointed at Chris's eyes. "That's it. And you're looking at me!" With that, he flung himself into Chris's arms.

Chris didn't know what "it" was, but he knew he'd won a major victory. Now he hoped to build on it. Still holding the boy, he said, "When I lose people I love, I cry a lot for a while. It's okay to do that, you know. It can even help us heal. Like hugs."

"It can?" Stanley's grip tightened.

"Yes, it can. Some people call crying 'weak.' But my father used to quote a man named Washington Irving. Have you ever heard of him?"

"Of course." Stanley's muffled response sounded vaguely offended. "The nineteenth-century author who wrote 'Rip Van Wrinkle.' "

"That's right. Well, Washington Irving said, 'There is a sacredness in tears. They are not the mark of weakness, but of power. They speak more eloquently than ten thousand tongues. They are the messengers of overwhelming grief, of deep contrition, and of unspeakable love.' "

Stanley was quiet for a moment before asking in a quavering voice, "And—and you cry sometimes?"

"Yes, I do."

The boy buried his face in Chris's shoulder. He seemed to be holding his breath at first—his last-ditch effort not to cry, as it turned out. Then his body heaved in great sobs, and tears soaked into Chris's shirt. Although Chris didn't know Mrs. Jenkins, he found himself deeply affected by the agony he heard in the child's keening.

Stanley's tears eventually ran out, but he continued to rest on Chris's shoulder. Just as Chris was wondering if he'd fallen asleep, Stanley murmured, "Thank you"—he paused before whispering tentatively—"Daddy."

Chris gave him a squeeze. "Thank you for the hug, son."

Slowly the boy drew back, wiping his face. "I've never cried before. I started to once, but Mother hi—" He glanced at Susana, approaching with a tissue. "Um, she told me never to do it again. She taught me to concentrate on relaxing the muscles in my face instead, so I wouldn't think about what I wanted to cry about. But you're right, Daddy. It feels better to cry." He bowed his head. "And I like hugs, even though Father says they're weakness."

"Around here, we like hugs too—and anything else that communicates how much we care for each other. Feel free to assault us with a hug anytime."

Stanley smiled. "May I ask, what did you mean when you said Father would be proud of me if he understood what strength really is?"

"Strength is a resource, like a talent, that can be used toward any goal. Your father seems to value power above everything else, and he focuses his strength toward that end. He probably believes love to be a 'weak' emotion because it would hinder his ruthlessness in seeking power. Josh, on the other hand, values *lashani* most highly and uses his strength to benefit others. But that kind of love means risking something of yourself, like Mrs. Jenkins risked herself for you. It requires a great deal of strength to love that much. You see, real love is more than an emotion. In its purer, better forms, especially *lashani*, it's a principle."

"What does that mean?"

"Well, take, for example, when Susana and I have a disagreement. I may be mad at her, but I still love her because I've made a decision to love her. I don't feel all warm and fuzzy right then, but the principle of love keeps me from treating her violently or disrespecting her no matter what my momentary emotional state may be. In fact, as far as hitting goes, it can take more strength not to hit someone than to hit them."

Stanley frowned as he asked dubiously, "How?"

"Because not giving in to an emotional urge requires the inner strength to control yourself. That's the greatest strength of all and the hardest one to develop."

Stanley bowed his head. "I have much to learn."

"We all do." Tousling Stanley's hair, Chris added, "But you're doing an amazing job."

CHAPTER 42

COMFORT

"I will turn their mourning to joy, will comfort them,
And make them rejoice rather than sorrow."
Jeremiah 31:13, NKJV.

Stanley and Andy had really taken to riding. Chris preferred self-propelled means of transport, but spending time with the boys was worth a few sore muscles. So today he found himself, as he often had during the last week, on horseback in the middle of a wide, open expanse of desert dotted by mesquite trees and cactus. Andy rode ahead with Lanse, who was instructing him in the differences between canters and gallops and who-knew-what-else. Stanley and another guard were behind, having stopped briefly to examine a cactus. That left Chris and Gabriel riding together, both having ended up with lazy mounts that required persistent urging to maintain anything above a leisurely walk.

As they progressed through the barren wasteland, Gabriel had grown quiet. Finally he shook his head and muttered, "Behold, your magnificent hand-iwork, brother."

Baffled by such a statement, and half wondering if he'd heard right, Chris said, "Excuse me?"

"All this bounty," Gabriel explained, not so very helpfully, as his arm swept the desolate scene before them.

"Bounty?"

The general glanced at him and burst into self-abasing laughter. "I'm not expressing myself very clearly, am I?" When Chris agreed, Gabriel said, "You should have seen this place fresh from the creator's hand. It was a beautiful garden—green, verdant, bursting with flowers and fruit."

Chris surveyed the bleak countryside with a fresh eye. "Hard to imagine now. What happened?"

"Lustanli Lanáj became Stanley Moden," Gabriel answered soberly.

The general fell silent, seemingly lost in old memories. But Chris knew that Gabriel was a willing fount of information, even when the topic became uncomfortably personal. So he allowed himself to pursue the conversation.

"How could anyone in such a blissful, peaceful world become so—well, evil?"

"Jealousy indulged," Gabriel answered sorrowfully. "Pride nurtured. I didn't even see it happening at first. When I did, I couldn't believe it."

"How did it start?"

Gabriel paused to draw in a large breath, as if preparing for a protracted explanation. "In many ways, Joshua was like one of us—or more precisely, he behaved like one of us. He still does. He takes his orders from Doug and obeys his commands. He interacts with us and works among us as though we were his equals. Stan, allowing a spark of doubt to ignite in his heart, misconstrued the prince's approachability. He interpreted his submission to Doug as a sign of weakness. He actually came to the point of thinking himself equal to Joshua."

Turning to Chris, he exclaimed, "Can you imagine—us, mere mortals, equal to the creator? Stan could never generate life—none of us could. But because Doug, in his generosity, called each of us 'son,' just as he did Joshua, my brother convinced himself that he had as much right to His Highness' place as Joshua did. He actually came to believe that Joshua was not as fully Deón as is Doug."

He met Chris's eye with sudden sternness. "But he is. Never forget that."

"I won't," Chris promised.

Gabriel nodded, apparently mollified, and returned to his account. "After that, the rest was an inevitable slide. Lustanli's pride fed that spark of doubt, fanning it into the roaring, consuming fire of envy. Self-exaltation was the natural consequence. He tried to seize Joshua's position—the creator's very throne."

Now understanding, Chris spread one arm to sweep the wilderness. "And this is the result. *Kanuf* played out in nature."

"Indeed—the glorious outcome of Stan's attempt at displacing his creator."

"Couldn't Doug have stopped it?"

"Yes, but the Deón gifted their children with freedom. They gave us hearts capable of choosing how we would respond to their generosity. Up until that time, our response had ever been love and joy." He paused, swallowing hard. "Lusu made a different choice."

"You mentioned the Deón—that's the Damours' middle name, isn't it?"

"Yes. Until the rebellion, it was their surname. It's still their real name—the name that *is* them rather than who they have chosen to be."

"What does it mean?"

Gabriel studied him for a moment. Then, guiding his horse closer until they were knee-to-knee, he answered in a reverential tone, "The eternal one."

Chris caught his breath. "What? Are you serious?"

"Never more so." Gabriel searched his face. "Have I—what's that colorful American expression?—fried your brain?"

Chris was indeed struggling with the immensity of the idea. "But—How—? I thought they lived forever because of the Viv fruit like the rest of Paradisians."

Gabriel shook his head. "No. They have always been, and they will always be. The *Viv Zabé* exists and its fruit gives life because they put that life in it."

"But wait—you said 'the eternal *one*.' So is Doug that one? What about Debora and Josh?"

"No, no—you don't understand their nature. They aren't three separate individuals but one individual with the ability to separate into three forms. When they unite—" A faraway smile spread across his face. "It's quite spectacular, my friend—the most magnificent fireworks show you'll ever see. The experience truly defies words."

"But if they're three parts of the same individual, how can Josh be Doug and Debora's son?"

"Joshua is the son because he accepted that role, not because he was born in the human sense. He took on the role of the son to be an example to us, to demonstrate how we should relate to Doug. They use language we understand, but our experiences are not adequate to describe all truth."

Chris nodded. He had seen Josh do that—express things in language that would make sense to his listener, even though it was an imperfect metaphor.

"What's more astounding is that Joshua accepted further limitations to answer Stan's accusation that it is impossible for an outlander to keep Doug's Law. For instance, he no longer has Doug and Debora's ability to talk to many people at once. And he doesn't possess Debora's ability to replicate herself so that she can literally be in millions of places at once."

"Is that why she always seems to be right around the corner?"

"Indeed, she probably is. Her nearest self simply replicates. But my point is that Joshua no longer enjoys these capacities because he chose to give them up. Not that he is any less Deón—never that."

"I think I understand. It's like donating a kidney—it doesn't make you less human."

"Just so."

Chris shook his head in amazement. "I knew Josh had given up many things for us. I didn't realize he'd actually given up part of himself."

"It is astonishing," Gabriel agreed. "Even after thousands of years, I still find new reasons to be awed as I learn more of the Deón nature."

Chris opened his mouth to pursue the topic further when the sound of a galloping horse drew his attention. Turning in the saddle, he saw Stanley racing to catch up.

"Let's go, *Papi*," he called. He seemed to especially enjoy calling his new parents *Papi* and *Mami*, or the English equivalents, Daddy and Mommy. Apparently he'd never been allowed to use such informal titles at home.

"Let's go," Stanley repeated as he neared them. "I'm hungry for cookies."

Gabriel pulled his mount to a sudden stop and exclaimed, "I beg your pardon?"

Chris stopped too, his interest piqued by Gabriel's reaction. Stanley halted between the two men. "Let's hurry home. I'm hungry for cookies."

Gabriel stared at Stanley as if seeing him for the first time. Then he threw his head back and roared with delighted laughter.

Not understanding the joke, Chris asked, "What makes you think *Mami's* making cookies?"

"No, *Papi*—Bethany. Bethany's making cookies. Probably oatmeal. They're my favorite."

On Stanley's other side, Gabriel grinned. "Ask him how he knows."

Chris regarded them both suspiciously. "How do you know Bethany's making cookies? Did she say she would?"

"No, *Papi*." Stanley paused as if considering the question and then shrugged. Behind him, Gabriel shadowed his shrug. "I just know," Stanley said while Gabriel mouthed the words. Prodding his mount into a trot, the boy called over his shoulder, "Let's hurry."

"You go ahead," Chris said. "I think I need to speak with your uncle."

As Stanley rode off to catch up with Andy and Lanse, Chris turned his attention to Gabriel. "What's this about? Something I should know about Paradisians?"

Gabriel nudged his horse into a walk. "If he's right about Bethany, it's apparently no longer limited to Paradisians. It certainly would explain the strange interactions I've seen between them over the last week. I'm surprised I didn't think of it before."

"What 'it' are we talking about?"

"It's called a link." Gabriel's mind seemed to wander, and he shook his head. "Such great potential—wasted, ruined."

"On Stanley?" Chris felt completely lost, and Gabriel's musings weren't helping any.

"No, no—I was referring to Stan and Camille. But I fear I'm making little sense. Let me explain."

"That would be helpful," Chris agreed.

Gabriel flashed a smile. "The link is a very rare gift, another sense that allows an individual a keener knowledge of his linkmate. There's only one linked pair in every 2.5 million Paradisians, and I've never heard of it occurring in out-landers before. It's also a very powerful gift. In fact, on the island every major accomplishment, in every field from art to zoology, has been made by linked individuals."

Chris frowned. "You don't mean something like ESP, do you?"

"Oh, no," Gabriel said with a laugh. "This is not a paranormal phenom-enon. It's a proven biologic ability, just like vision or hearing. Specialized nerve cells have been identified in linked individuals. Conceptually, it's perhaps closest to electroreception—are you familiar with that ability?"

"A little. I know that some animals have another sense—mostly marine life, I think—that allows them to detect electrical stimuli."

"Just so. A link is similar in many respects to that. Fluctuations in chemi-cals and electrical energy result from emotions or strong sensory experiences, like smell, and linkmates can sense these changes in their partners. You might think of it as a radio tuned to a specific frequency. Under certain conditions, a linked individual can even transfer some types of energy to his partner. And their ability to detect subtle responses enables them to work together in remarkable ways. By combining their talents, they can accomplish things the rest of us couldn't even envision."

"And Stan and Camille share this link?"

"Yes. Stanley's reference to cookies allowed it to fall into place for me because that happened with some regularity with Stan. He has a particular fond-ness for cookies. He and I would be working intently when he'd suddenly decide to make for home because Camille was baking cookies, and he wanted them hot from the oven. When I asked how he knew, he would always give me that precise shoulder shrug and say, '*Ut tsa'nui,*' 'I just know it.' And he was always right."

"You mean he could sense electrical changes in Camille when she wasn't even around?"

"Sensitivity does decline with distance. However, since it's a complex sense, one that combines multiple stimuli, some information is preserved even from a distance."

"I see. Because some chemicals—pheromones, for example—can be detected miles away."

"Precisely."

Chris watched Stanley, now trotting ahead of Andy and Lanse. "So you think Stanley shares a link with Bethany? She's not even Paradisian."

"Yes, that raises questions …" Gabriel lapsed into silence and then shook his head. "But his look, his confidence, reflects Stan's precisely. And their interactions have been of a most peculiar sort. Remember how Stanley reacted when Bethany was upset about not being able to speak Rarámuri? Although he's been trained to school his own emotions carefully, he reacted rather fervently to hers. Dealing with her emotions would be different, you see, a skill he's not learned. And remember when they first met? They both claimed they'd always known the other."

"Yeah, that was bizarre," Chris conceded. "But sometimes you meet people like that, someone you have a lot in common with, and it just seems you've always known them. What makes you think this is anything more than that?"

"Perhaps it isn't. Yet, if they were linked, they would feel as though they had always known one another, even when first meeting." He shrugged. "In any case, let's see whether Stanley's prediction proves accurate. If it does, watch for such events in the future. It will soon be obvious if a link truly exists."

"And what would be the purpose of such a relationship?"

"When I asked Joshua that question, he said the purpose of a link is twofold. First, it's a special gift given to help certain people accomplish something important. Debora endows gifts on all her children—teaching, healing, hospitality, and so forth—that help them fulfill specific roles within the assemblies of runners. The link is simply another such gift. However, it also has another purpose. It's an object lesson of the relationship shared by the Deón. They are so intimately linked that they think each other's thoughts and feel each other's feelings."

"That's hard to imagine."

"Precisely. As the *Manual* puts it, 'As the heavens are higher than the earth, so are his ways higher than our ways and his thoughts than our thoughts.' Yet, while it's difficult for us to understand the Deón, they seek our friendship and invite us to know them. Thus they give us object lessons to propel us toward more comprehensive understanding. The link has been such an object lesson for Paradisians. Outlanders have marriage and children. In each of these relationships, we learn something of the relationship between the Deón, and between them and us."

Susana frowned at Chris's reaction when he walked into the house. *"Cookies?"* he exclaimed, as though they'd never baked cookies before. *"Oatmeal* cookies?"

"Why?" she asked. "Have you taken a dislike to oatmeal cookies?"

"No, it's just that—" He looked to Gabriel, who burst into laughter.

Clearly, something was going on, but Susana wasn't to discover what it was until after dinner. Once the kids hit the pool to play volleyball with some guards, things settled down, and Chris asked her to have a seat on the sofa.

She sat there in amazed silence as Gabriel described his theory about a "link" between Stanley and Bethany. As he outlined the relationship, she realized it would account for all the odd things she'd noticed between the two children—how Bethany sometimes seemed to react for the inexpressive Stanley, how he so easily translated her feelings into adult lingo, and how he increasingly looked first to her to explain things he didn't understand.

As Gabriel finished, Chris asked, "What do you think, Suze?"

"I think it might explain a lot of things, including something odd that happened today." Crossing over to the sliding glass door, she called, "Stanley, please come here." He obediently hopped out of the pool and, as he approached, she noticed a large black-and-blue scrape on his right shin. "Uh-huh," she said.

"What?" Chris joined her at the door.

"That bruise on his leg. It must have happened today."

Reaching the door, Stanley asked, "Yes, *Mami*?"

"When did you hurt your leg?"

Stanley looked at his shin. "This? It's nothing, *Mami*. I just stumbled over some rocks this afternoon."

"I remember when he fell," Chris said. "But he didn't show any sign that he was hurt. He didn't even lift his jeans to look at his leg. Son, why did you tell me you were fine when I asked if you'd hurt yourself?"

The boy looked mystified. "I am fine, *Papi*. The injury is superficial."

Behind them, Gabriel whispered, "He was viewed as a tool. He would have been trained to bear injuries without complaint unless they were disabling."

Chris bent down to put himself at the boy's level. "Stanley," he said gently, "when we ask if you're hurt, it's because we want to know if you're in pain."

Stanley's puzzled frown deepened.

"It's because we care about you," Susana elaborated. "How you feel, your pain, your enjoyment, these are all important to us because we're interested in you as a person, not just in what you can do."

Stanley's expression turned to astonishment. "Oh. Thank you."

"What time did this happen?" Susana asked.

"I'm not sure, *Mami*. After lunch—maybe one-thirty?"

Susana nodded, grinning. "Thank you. You can go back to the pool." Reseating herself on the sofa, she said, "One thirty-eight, to be exact. I chanced to look at the clock."

Sitting down beside her, Chris asked, "Why? What happened?"

"Bethany was sitting right here next to me when all of a sudden she yelled 'Ow' and grabbed her right shin. When I asked her what had happened, she couldn't tell me. 'It just hurt for no reason, but it's gone now,' she said. That's when she asked if we could make cookies."

"Fascinating," Gabriel said. "So she felt his injury. I wasn't aware of that link-related ability. I suppose there would be little opportunity for it to manifest itself on the island."

"Do you think that's what it was?" Chris asked. "Not just some strange coincidence?"

"Coincidence is becoming less likely, wouldn't you say? With— Hello! I believe I know how we might set the matter to rest right now." Gabriel returned to the door and called both Stanley and Bethany. "I do beg your pardon for interrupting your game," he told them. "But I wonder if you'll humor me by playing another. Let's begin by having you grasp each other's hands. No, pile your hands together in one heap."

Excited to learn a new game, the children did as he instructed.

"Very good. Now, Bethany, you see that Stanley has injured his leg?"

"Yes."

"Uncle, it's only a minor injury," Stanley objected.

"But it does hurt, does it not?"

"Not really, sir."

"It's not nice to lie," Bethany scolded, and Stanley scowled at her.

Gabriel chuckled. "Well, let's make an experiment of that pain, whether large or small, shall we?"

Stanley shrugged.

"Now," Gabriel said. "I should like you both to concentrate on your hands. Bethany, you're also to wish that Stanley's leg will be better."

"Okay," she agreed. "I was wishing it anyway." Both children focused on their joined hands, but quickly jerked them away.

"What?" the adults exclaimed.

"Like when I stuck my finger in the plug," Bethany said.

"It hurt?" Gabriel asked.

"No," she said uncertainly. "Just crawly."

"It tingles," Stanley clarified.

"Might you ignore it and keep trying?" Gabriel asked.

They both nodded and tried again. After a minute or so, a scab began forming on Stanley's leg, right before their very eyes. Furthermore, the bruise changed in color from blue to green to yellow.

Gabriel turned to Chris, eyebrows raised. "Can you explain that, doctor?"

"No," Chris said, shaking his head. "It's—well, impossible."

"Very good, children," Gabriel said. "You may stop whenever you care to."

The children dropped their hands. "Thank you," Stanley said. "Did it hurt?"

"No, I just feel a little tired," Bethany answered, but her weariness seemed to disappear when she looked at his leg. She jumped up and down, clapping her hands. "Look, it's better!"

"Yes," Stanley said. "How come?"

"Through a special gift of Doug's called a link," Gabriel said.

"Like Mother and Father?" Stanley asked.

"Ah, so you do know of it. Then perhaps you've seen them do something similar? Perhaps when one of them is tired or hurt or—"

"Angry," Stanley said firmly. "They hold hands sometimes when Father's mad. 'So he doesn't do something ill-advised,' Mother says. Then he gets calmer. But they don't do it in front of other people, even though everyone knows they're linked. Mother says it's a better weapon if it's a secret."

"Interesting viewpoint," Gabriel said with a twitch of his eyebrows.

"What else does the link do, Uncle? Mother and Father wouldn't talk about it."

Gabriel moved toward the CD player. "There's much to tell, but I shall show you one fascinating ability now. The rest I'll explain to your mum and dad. They'll share the details as appropriate."

Gabriel selected a recording of Handel's *Messiah* and played a portion. Then he had the two children join hands as he replayed the same section.

"Oh, it's bigger!" Bethany squealed. "Happier!"

"The music is fuller," Stanley explained. "Richer."

Gabriel nodded. "You both experience more of the music because you're experiencing it through one another's senses as well as your own. You'll find similar benefits with other artistic pursuits, such as visiting an art museum or even watching a sunset."

When the excited children returned to the pool, they were holding hands and pointing at different sights with amazed exclamations. The adults returned to the sofas, where Chris pumped Gabriel for more information. "So what else should we know about this phenomenon? How else will it show up?"

"I can't be certain since the precise manifestations vary between individuals," Gabriel said. "Stan, for instance, had no capacity for locating Camille, even though she could always find him. Nevertheless, I'll tell you what I'm able. The most common manifestation is the ability to share experiences, especially joy, as what you just saw with the music. I observed that countless times between Stan and Camille. Only once did I witness the ability to share healing energies. It was during the war when I had seriously wounded Stan here." He drew his hand along his left side and then seemed to have trouble continuing.

When he spoke again, his voice was strained. "Stan was severely injured. Camille took his hands and, right in front of me, the bleeding stopped, Stan became stronger, and his color returned. Within minutes, he was on his feet and fighting again."

"Wow," Chris said. "What an amazing gift."

"Yes. I've long suspected that their ability to continue functioning at peak capacity in the grossly depraved world they've spawned is due to their ability to share strength. When the energy or determination of one flags, the other would be able to buoy him up."

"How kind of Doug to provide this advantage for Stanley," Susana said. "He's still just a little boy, but his whole world has been turned upside down and emptied of everyone who ever meant anything to him. His link with Bethany would be extremely comforting and help him feel more secure. It would help him adjust better, too, because she would know how to explain things in a way that would be easier for him to understand."

As she said it, Susana remembered her own reluctance to accept this assignment. If she had refused, she would have withheld from Stanley—and Bethany—this wonderful blessing.

Then she also recalled Josh's prediction about Bethany—that she *and her husband* would "do a work unprecedented in both type and importance." He had spoken of them as a unit—a linked unit, perhaps? She gazed at the children playing in the pool. Were they raising Bethany's future husband?

Meanwhile Chris asked, "Are there other abilities?"

"These are the main ones that I'm aware of," Gabriel answered. "However, it's possible that other abilities will manifest in your world which aren't seen on the island because the circumstances to spotlight the ability simply aren't present there. Bethany's ability to sense Stanley's injury, for instance. Also, I wonder at her scolding him for lying. She seemed so certain of her assessment. Detecting deceit may be another linked ability."

Susana giggled. "That could certainly be useful."

"Gabriel," Chris said thoughtfully, "earlier you mentioned that the existence of a link in an outlander raises questions. What was that about?"

Gabriel rubbed his chin. "Please understand; I am not Deón. I have over 8,000 years of experience on which to draw, but I'm not omniscient, so I can only speculate. Nevertheless, I once asked Joshua why links didn't exist among outlanders. He told me it would be cruel."

"Cruel?" Chris exclaimed, his protective fatherly hackles rising. "Why?"

"Because of death. Imagine the pain you would feel if Susana were to die. For a linked individual, that pain would be exponentially greater. It's commonly believed that a linked individual could not survive the death of his linkmate. So if Doug has linked Stanley and Bethany, I can only surmise that he knows one of two things will happen to them. Either they will die at the same time, or—"

Susana gasped. "They won't die at all! Could we really be that close to the end, Gabriel?"

He nodded. "Yes. Frankly, I believe that's the more likely possibility."

Chapter 43

TRAINING

"Keep yourself in training for the practice of religion."
1 Timothy 4:7, REB.

A wave of gratitude swept over Chris as he approached the hacienda after his solitary run. Out on the trail, it was just Doug and him. He could savor his adopted father's presence and bask in his mind-boggling love—unhurried, undistracted, and unburdened by the press of life's concerns. Alone time was difficult to find these days, but he had gotten a special dispensation from Doug to leave the guard behind this evening. The emotional respite had been priceless. When he left the house, he felt crushed beneath the weight of seemingly insurmountable burdens. How was he to provide for his family? How could he keep them safe from a filthy rich magnate with worldwide influence? How was he supposed to guide a lonely and confused super-genius like Stanley?

But in one run, Doug had corrected his outlook, swept away his anxieties, and lifted his spirit. And now, having released his cares, Chris found himself humming the little song Bethany had learned: *Doug is on his throne; there's no need to worry.*

He knew from past experience that such attitude adjustments wouldn't last forever. In fact, the older he got, the more he understood Josh's admonition at the race's finish line to keep running. He needed this kind of dedicated quality time with Doug regularly or the world perverted by Stan's lies would impose its distorted attitudes on him. Only through consistent training and continual resistance to Stan's efforts could he remain physically strong and mentally balanced enough to withstand his enemy's attacks.

"Good run?" Susana called as he passed through the kitchen.

"Great run!" he answered.

He hit the shower and changed, and then headed back to help Susana with dinner. When he came down the stairs, he saw her through the kitchen doorway, rubbing her temple. "You will eat at the table with the rest of the family," she was telling Andy resolutely.

"No, I wanna eat in the living room." Andy stomped his foot for emphasis.

As Josh had forewarned, Andy could be quite stubborn. And, as Chris had learned, conflict of any sort was particularly difficult for his tenderhearted wife. It appeared that their beloved son had, once again, given his mother a nice headache.

Wanting to provide her a little respite, Chris entered the room and assumed control of the problem. "Apologize to your mother for disrespecting her," he ordered calmly.

"No."

Stepping beside his son, Chris gripped Andy's shoulder in a way that would be painful only if he resisted. "Then come with me."

"No," Andy said as he tried to pull away. "Ouch."

"Come with me," Chris repeated evenly.

Andy peered up at him, his defiant expression giving way to resignation. "Okay."

Chris knew Andy would require time alone before he would be amenable to reason, so he guided him to his room and sat him in the chair. Returning to the doorway, he said, "When you're ready to apologize to your mother and obey the rules of our family, you may leave your room and come find me. I'll be eating dinner at the table with the rest of the family. That's how we *all* eat dinner in the Strider household."

Returning to the kitchen, he drew Susana into his arms. "Thank you," she said, her voice muffled against his chest. "He's been a little stinker all day."

"I know, and I'm sorry."

"It's not your fault."

"Yes it is. I'm the one with the 'persistent' gene."

She giggled. "I stand corrected. It is your fault."

"Go sit down," he said with a kiss to the top of her head. "I'll finish getting stuff on the table."

By the time Andy reappeared, they were almost finished eating. Chris excused himself and took the boy into the living room. Sitting on the sofa, he placed his hands on Andy's shoulders and drew him close. "Are you ready to apologize to your mother?"

Andy nodded.

"What are you going to apologize for?"

"For disrespecting her."

"How did you disrespect her?"

"I yelled. And stomped."

"And what's wrong with disrespecting her?"

"The *Manual* says I should honor my mother."

"Why?"

Glancing up at him, Andy shrugged. "Dunno."

"Let's see what it says, then." Chris grabbed his *Runner's Manual* off the end table and opened it. Lifting Andy onto the sofa beside him, he followed the text with his finger as he read: " 'You must keep the commands I give you today so all will be well with you.' "

Looking at Andy, he asked, "Do you understand what that means?"

Andy blinked at him.

"It means that Doug wants us to be happy and have a good life. So he explained how our bodies and minds function in his Laws. That way, by working with these laws, we can be happy. Do you feel happy when you're yelling at *Mami*?"

Andy hesitated and then shook his head.

"That's because you were disobeying one of the basic laws of your mind. And you don't just make yourself sad when you disobey. You made *Mami* unhappy, too. You even made her head hurt. Whenever you disobey Doug's Laws, you hurt yourself. Often you hurt someone else too."

"I didn't mean to hurt *Mami*," Andy admitted regretfully.

"But it happens anyway when we disobey Doug's Laws."

Andy considered that briefly before objecting, "But why do we have to eat dinner at the table? Stanley's family doesn't eat together."

"You might ask Stanley if that was a good thing or not. His parents do lots of things that we don't do. But in our family, we eat dinner together. And we eat it at the table with no TV or other distractions so we can talk to each other."

"But—"

"That's the rule in our home, Andy. You may have different rules when you grow up and have your own family, but that's the rule here. Disobeying it won't change the rule. It will only make people unhappy—the way you made yourself and *Mami* unhappy today."

Andy bowed his head, his defiance gone.

"Do you understand?"

His son nodded.

"Are you ready to obey this rule?"

He nodded again.

"Then let's talk to Doug. He can help you obey, and he can even help you want to obey."

After Andy chatted with Doug, Chris called Susana into the living room, and Andy apologized to her, his dark, tearful eyes expressing genuine sorrow. They ended with a hug all around, and then they sat down to finish their meal.

Not long thereafter, Gabriel left the table to take a call and returned saying he would have to leave in the morning. Stanley's head jerked up and, for just an instant, a disappointed, doleful look came over his features. Then his face went blank, and he finished eating in silence.

After dinner Stanley sat alone with his sketchpad while the rest of the family played charades. Bethany, unusually subdued, looked over at him several times. Finally she sat on the sofa next to him and reached for his hands. They sat together for a few moments, and then Stanley released Bethany's hands with a small smile. She beamed and returned to the game while Chris puzzled over what had just happened—that energy-sharing thing, perhaps?

Gabriel left the next morning, making his way around the group with handshakes, hugs, and cheek-kisses. When he got to his nephew, a blank-faced Stanley offered his hand. "I've enjoyed getting to know you, Uncle. I hope to see you again soon. Thank you for your assistance, and please extend my gratitude to my aunt as well. May you have a pleasant journey."

Gabriel hesitated. He wanted a hug—Chris could feel it. But he didn't push. Grasping the hand firmly, Gabriel said simply, "I will always love you, Stanley."

Stanley blinked a few times before turning away, and Gabriel continued with his goodbyes. When he came to Chris, he glanced at Stanley, now drawing at the table in the kitchen, and sighed.

Chris followed him outside. "Don't be discouraged, Gabriel. He's very fond of you, but it's going to be especially hard for him to express himself with you. After all, you do bear a resemblance to the man who's demanded stoicism of him while abusing him."

"Indeed I do," Gabriel said with a wry smile.

"Did you notice what he's drawing in his sketchpad?"

"Sketches of local zoological specimens when last I looked."

Chris shook his head. "Several days ago, he confided to me that he was afraid he would forget how Mrs. Jenkins looked. So I suggested he draw some pictures of her and jot down some stories. When you announced you'd be leaving last night, he started doing the same thing for you."

"Did he indeed? He's so hard to read, I didn't realize ..." Gabriel bowed his head for a moment, and then pulled out his wallet and excused himself. Returning to the kitchen, he placed a picture of himself with his family on Stanley's open sketchbook. "It occurred to me that you might care to have this." He dropped a kiss on Stanley's head and left.

Stanley's appreciation was obvious. He carried the picture with him everywhere throughout the day, pulling it out to stare at it with every opportunity. When he went to bed, Stanley carefully placed the picture on the bedside table where he could see it as he fell asleep.

The picture turned out to be the first installment in a larger gift. Shortly after lunch the next day, a Paradisian army courier delivered a small packet to Stanley from Gabriel. Inside were several surveillance-type photos of his birth family. There was even one of Mrs. Jenkins with Stanley.

The boy looked through the photos with an impassive expression. But Bethany, though unaware of the delivery, gasped from the other side of the room. She turned toward him, her eyes filling with tears, and Stanley met her gaze, still wearing that blank expression. Bethany was full out crying now, and rushed onto Chris's lap for consolation. That's when he realized that the link was useful not only in providing support for Stanley, but also in helping his parents understand him. Although Stanley now betrayed no emotion, Chris recognized his grief in Bethany's reaction.

Still holding his daughter, Chris held out a hand to Stanley. For a moment, the boy simply watched Bethany, but then he began blinking rapidly. Finally relenting, he accepted Chris's invitation, and was soon weeping with Bethany.

When their sobs subsided, Stanley whispered, "Will it always hurt this much?"

Chris hesitated, thinking back to those he'd lost: his brother Eddie, his grandmother, his father, little Petey. "It gets better with time. You start focusing on the good things you shared instead of on how much you miss them. But it will all be different when we live on the island. The *Manual* says, 'There will be no more death or mourning or crying or pain.' "

"My parents order people killed regularly, and they laugh about it. They like making people feel sad like this."

" 'Since they didn't think it was worthwhile to retain Doug's knowledge,' " Chris quoted, " 'he gave them over to their depraved minds, to do what shouldn't be done. So they have become full of every kind of wickedness.' "

"I—" Stanley paused for a long time. "I—helped them, Daddy. Planning, organizing, lab work on the poisons, stuff like that."

It took Chris longer to answer that. Had Stanley helped to develop the poison that killed Pete? Is that why he was around during the crisis?

He looked at the boy beside him, a youngster who had been used and abused all his life. How could Chris, whose home had been a place of love, presume to judge this boy's actions? No—he would leave that to the Damours.

He gave Stanley's shoulder a squeeze. " 'He will tread our sins underfoot and throw them all into the deepest sea.' "

The three sat together silently for a few moments.

"I'm really glad to have the pictures," Stanley said. "It was very good of Uncle Gabriel to take the trouble of sending them to me. Father would never do something like that."

" 'Be imitators of him, then. Live a life of love,' " Chris quoted.

Stanley sat up. "Do you answer everything by quoting the *Manual*?"

"Yea, verily," Chris said with a straight face. Stanley smiled and Bethany giggled, which made Stanley giggle, which made Bethany laugh. The effect continued to snowball until all three were sharing tears of laughter.

After dinner that evening, Stanley was again working in his sketchbook at the table when Chris approached. "Your uncle said you were sketching local animal life. Can I see what you've done?"

Stanley showed Chris his work, which not only contained remarkably detailed sketches, but meticulous observations on diet and habitat, as well as defensive, predatory, and social behaviors. Chris felt as though he were reading a textbook in zoology.

"I felt so inadequate," he told Susana after they'd gone to bed. "I'm looking through these field notes made by a ten-year-old kid and realizing his general scientific knowledge already approaches my own."

"Aren't you the guy who always says Doug won't give us a job we can't handle?" Susana teased.

"Yeah, but this kid's phenomenal, Suze. What can we possibly teach him?"

She leaned up on one elbow. "Doug didn't give us the job of teaching him science, did he? What he needs is good parenting and a moral education. He needs to learn to value people for who they are instead of for their usefulness. He needs to understand Doug's way of doing things, to see the world from his perspective. And he particularly needs to see *lashani* in action—especially in a man, so he has a real, flesh-and-blood role model, someone he can emulate."

Chris looked away. "You're not making me feel any better here. You of all people know how imperfect I am."

Her soft fingers caressed his cheek. "You can see that because your focus is on Josh, *mi amor*. The more of his righteousness you see, the more you recognize your own deficiencies. And you realize that, if not for Doug's grace, you could never reach such perfection."

"You've got that right."

"But something else happens. When you focus on him, you 'become more and more like him and reflect his glory even more.' Then other people can stand back and be wowed by Doug's *lashani* as it comes through you. That's what Stanley sees. He sees what it looks like and feels like when a real, imperfect human being allows Doug's grace to work itself out in his everyday life."

"I hope he can see that in me."

"He does. He already trusts you, and he's only trusted one other person in his life. He's even accepting lessons from you. You've helped him cope with the most painful loss he may ever experience. As a matter of fact, he saw that *lashani* before he ever met you."

"How?"

"Remember when Andy was being stubborn the other day?"

Chris laughed. "Which time? Andy's always stubborn."

Susana giggled. "When he didn't want to eat at the table with us."

"Yeah, I remember."

"I overheard Stanley talking to him later. He told Andy how lucky he was to have parents who liked to be with their children, how his father mostly ignored him except to discuss work. Then he said that he used to admire your picture before he even met you. He said you looked kind."

Chris shook his head. "The poor kid. The more I hear of how he was raised, the worse I feel for him. And to think, there are two other little guys still there, just as starved for love."

"Yes, but what I meant to point out was that Stanley recognized Doug's love in you before he even knew us. And he'll continue to see it—not because we're such good people, but because Doug's so amazing that he can make even us into great mirrors to reflect his *lashani* to Stanley. As long as we stay close to Doug, we don't have to worry about being good enough to raise Stanley, because Doug will handle that part."

"You're right. Thank you, *mi tesoro*." He drew her face toward him and kissed her on the cheek. "What would I do without you to keep me focused on the right picture?"

"I don't know. But it sounds like a service that deserves more remuneration than a kiss on the cheek."

"Really? Well, I'm open to negotiation. What's your idea of fair compensation?"

She unbuttoned the top button of his pajama top and kissed his chest. "H'mm. Let me think about it for a minute."

"Mmm. Take all the minutes you want. Shouldn't rush these high-level negotiations …"

CHAPTER 44

DISTRESS

*"Pure and genuine religion in the sight of God the Father means
caring for orphans and widows in their distress and refusing
to let the world corrupt you."*
James 1:27, NLT.

"Gracias, Rafael," Chris said as he placed a few coins in the vendor's hand. He really meant it, too. They'd been in the small village of Santa María for a month before they realized that Rafael, who lived in the nearest city about two hours away, drove through their village selling water every week. For a small fee—a pittance in Chris's eyes, but still too expensive for many of the villagers—Rafael filled the empty drums stored behind their house with clean water.

Before they discovered Rafael, Chris and the boys had made two trips a day to the village's small reservoir, carrying back several buckets of water on wooden poles across their shoulders. The villagers had thought Chris strange for fetching water—a woman's job—but he couldn't bear to see Susana and Bethany struggling with such heavy work. In any case, since finding Rafael, Chris's water-carrying days were blessedly rare.

As the vendor drove off, Chris filled a large bucket with water and strolled into what had been their home for six months. The three-bedroom cement block structure with a tile roof, electricity, and a telephone was hands-down the nicest house in the village. This, together with the fact that they had the luxury of an outhouse, put them in the upper echelon of village society.

Overall, Chris liked his life in Santa María. Naturally, he missed the folks back home; they hadn't had any contact with their families for over seven months. The absence of conveniences like plumbing could be trying too. And he often became frustrated with the limited medical facilities he had available at the clinic.

Still, the simple, unhurried life of this rural *ranchito* in the arid wilderness of central Mexico had its attractions. He liked waking to the crowing of roosters and braying of burros. He liked the evening hours spent on the roof telling his children stories and teaching them about the stars. He even liked the homey atmosphere of the kerosene lanterns they used when the electricity went out—which it did with some regularity. Most of all, he liked having time to spend with his kids, teaching them of Doug's values and principles as they ran together through country unspoiled by civilization.

Chris set the pail of water on the table in the kitchen. *"Aquí tienes, querida."* (Spanish: Here you go, dear.) He reached for the bottle of bleach and poured a few drops in. The water Rafael brought was much cleaner than the reservoir water, so they didn't need to strain it before use, but they still needed to treat it with chlorine before it was safe for washing dishes.

"*Gracias, mi amor.*" Susana sat at the table sorting out two piles: a larger pile of black beans, and a fist-sized pile of twigs, rocks, and dead beetles. "I'll need another bucketful to boil for drinking water. Cesar didn't come today." Cesar was another blessing. He came from the same city as Rafael to sell bottles of purified drinking water. But, like everything else in this country, he wasn't necessarily reliable.

"Okay, I'll get it." Chris picked up an empty pail from under the table and headed for the door. "Black beans for tomorrow, huh?" With a wink, he added, "What a treat."

Susana giggled. Chris found the diet of a *ranchito*—beans and tortillas three times a day, with rice, eggs, or canned tuna thrown in for variety—frankly boring. When the small village store got in a supply of black or pink beans instead of the usual pintos, he often teased Susana about her "gourmet" cooking.

When the phone rang, Chris set down the empty pail and headed toward the living room. "I'll get it."

The caller was the proprietor of the village store, who placed or received phone calls for villagers who didn't have phones. Tonight she was calling with a message that Laura, the lay midwife who delivered most of the villagers' babies, needed Chris's help at the Corona's home.

Instantly switching into emergency medical mode, Chris said, "*Ahora voy.*" (Spanish: Be right there.) He grabbed his medical bag and hurried through the kitchen. "Gotta go, Suze—a problem with María Corona's delivery."

Laura was a good lay midwife. Although she lacked formal medical training, she had excellent instincts and plenty of experience. Since she'd been delivering the villagers' babies for forty years, most of the women called her instead of Chris for their deliveries. He had made a point of maintaining a friendly relationship with her, so she didn't hesitate to call him when things turned bad. Unfortunately, though, when things went bad in obstetrics, they could go very bad very quickly. Chris, of all people, knew that.

The Corona's one-room, thatched-roof house was on the far side of the village. Chris drove over the rough dirt road as quickly as he could, kicking up great clouds of dust behind him. He arrived within a few minutes and found the husband, Juan, sitting out front with a beer in hand and several empty cans on the ground. He already had the bulbous red nose and spider-veined cheeks of a long-time alcoholic. When Chris approached, Juan wordlessly waved his permission for him to enter. Once inside, Chris smelled the problem at once: too much blood.

Laura was sitting at the foot of the bed in one corner of the room. She looked up when Chris came in, but said nothing. She didn't have to. The grief in her eyes said it all.

María, the wife, lay very still on the bed—her face too white, the sheets and towels too red. Chris quickly approached and felt for a carotid pulse.

Nothing.

He put his stethoscope to his ears and listened at María's chest.

Nothing.

He flashed his penlight at her pupils.

No reaction.

He gravely stowed the stethoscope and penlight back in his medical bag—a bag he kept stocked with methergine, which would probably have saved this young mother's life … if only he'd been called in time … if only there'd been a phone nearby. Who knew how many precious minutes had passed before Laura's SOS even got to him.

He moved to Laura's side and laid a hand gently on her shoulder. "It happened too fast," she murmured. "And they don't have a telephone."

"I know you did everything you could." This sort of thing shouldn't happen, and it made Chris angry that it did, but he didn't blame Laura. She did the best she could. Just like Chris.

Drawing alongside the sleeping bundle in a nearby cradle, he asked, "How's the baby?"

Laura rose. "Very big—four kilos, I'd say. María called him Jorge."

Chris unwrapped the pudgy baby and did a quick examination. The infant's large size made him suspicious that María had had undiagnosed diabetes, which would put the newborn at risk for problems too. Pulling a glucose meter from his bag, he checked the baby's blood. "His blood sugar is already too low. He needs to eat right away and be watched closely."

"Pancha lives next door," Laura said. "Her baby's still nursing. I'll go get her."

"Good. Then I'll get some formula and take him home with me until he's stable." Thankfully, the village store regularly stocked powdered infant formula.

As Laura headed toward the door, Chris asked, "Does Juan know yet?"

She bowed her head, and Chris drew the short, plump woman into a gentle embrace. "I'll tell him."

When Laura returned with Pancha, Chris turned to the unpleasant task of telling Juan of his wife's demise. As he did, he couldn't help but feel a renewed sense of gratitude that Susana had survived a similar catastrophe.

At first, Juan said nothing in response. He simply took another gulp of beer. Then he dissolved suddenly into great, heaving sobs of grief. Chris remained with him as night fell. Juan spent much of the time crying and slobbering onto Chris's shoulder. When he finally did go home, his shirt smelled so heavily of alcohol that Susana raised an eyebrow at him.

They kept Jorge with them for a couple of days until the baby was out of danger. When Chris returned him to Juan, he felt uneasy about it. The whole village knew Juan Corona drank away more money than he had given María for food. Chris had trouble picturing him as an attentive father. But maybe the responsibility of a baby who depended on him would help him straighten out. One could always hope. Besides, Laura promised she'd keep an eye on them and teach Juan what to do, and Chris knew she was reliable.

Things went well for about a month. Juan worked irregularly and brought Jorge to Laura to babysit when he did. Although he never brought the baby to the clinic, he let Chris come to the house to give Jorge his vaccinations, and Chris got frequent reports from Laura.

But one afternoon Laura came to the clinic, concerned. Juan hadn't brought the baby over for three days, so she'd gone to check on him. She found the house locked with Jorge inside and Juan gone. She could just hear the baby's weak cry from outside.

Grabbing a crowbar, Chris sprinted over to Juan's house. He'd have no qualms about breaking in if that's what it took to save a baby. Laura followed him as quickly as she was able. As Chris approached, he saw that Juan was now home, so he dropped the crowbar and slowed to a fast walk.

"Hola, doctor," Juan greeted amiably. He occupied his usual seat in front of the house, beer in hand.

"Hi," Chris said. "How are you?"

"Fine."

"How's the baby doing?"

Juan shrugged. *"No me importa."* (Spanish: It doesn't matter to me.)

This seemed strange, even for Juan. "No? Why not?"

"He's not mine."

Chris's eyebrows shot up. Although he hadn't been well acquainted with María, he'd never heard the slightest question of her reputation—a rumor that would certainly have made its way around the small village.

Meanwhile, Laura had arrived in time to hear this claim and exclaimed indignantly, "What? That's not true."

"The baby doesn't look anything like me," Juan responded, his speech slurred.

"Babies' looks change a lot in the first few months," Chris said. "He may not look like anyone for a while."

Juan shrugged.

"Can I check on him?" Chris asked politely, although nothing would have stopped him from going in.

"No me importa," Juan repeated.

Laura stayed outside to talk to Juan while Chris examined the baby. Jorge was asleep, but that didn't make Chris feel better. His trained eye quickly registered the infant's sunken eyes, dry tongue, and poor skin turgor. He had to work to rouse the babe at all, and when he did, Jorge's cry was weak and he produced no tears. Chris quickly wrapped him up and carried him outside.

"I need to take the baby to the clinic," he said in a tone that brooked no argument.

Juan shrugged. *"No me importa."*

As Chris strode back to the clinic, Laura hurried to keep up. "Is he bad?"

"Yes. He's very dehydrated. But he should be okay once I get some fluids into him. It's good you went to check on him. He may not have lived through the night."

"Taking care of a baby is too much work for Juan. He knows the baby's his, but he thinks if he says he's not, he won't have to take care of him."

"Then who does he think will take care of him?"

"I don't know. If there were someone in the village who wanted a baby, they'd raise him. But there's no one able to take him right now. I don't know what will happen to him."

Arriving at the clinic, Chris tackled the urgent need of getting some life-saving fluids into the baby. This ordinarily simple task turned out to be quite difficult. Jorge was so dehydrated that Chris had to do a cut-down—a minor surgical procedure to dissect down to the vein to insert a catheter directly into it. He initially planned to take Jorge to the hospital two hours away, but when the baby improved quickly with the IV fluids, Chris decided he could care for him there.

The only other problem he seemed to have was a very angry diaper rash—his diaper looked like it hadn't been changed in days.

As Chris looked into the baby's sunken eyes, he realized he could never bring himself to send Jorge back to Juan. He couldn't even trust him to give the boy water! But what could he do instead? In the States, he could call in Child Protective Services. But here? He had no resources available at all.

He stroked the baby's cheek. "What are we going to do with you, *pobrecito*?" (Spanish: poor little guy) "I'd take you in a heartbeat. Susana probably would too. But running from Stan may be more dangerous than living with your dad."

Since Chris would have to spend the night at the clinic with his little patient, Susana and the children brought him dinner. Bethany spent much of the time at Jorge's bedside, holding his hand and cooing encouragements to him. Stanley and Andy also crowded around, trying to make the little fellow laugh. And Jorge, despite his weakened condition, seemed enthralled with all the attention.

After dinner Chris sent all three children to the village store to buy some baby formula and diapers, giving him a chance to talk to Susana alone.

"Juan won't take care of the baby." Chris sat down at the table where Susana was gathering up the dishes. "He says he's not his."

"Oh, that's ridiculous," Susana exploded.

"Yeah, that's what Laura told him, but he won't budge. Laura says he doesn't truly question the baby's parentage, but taking care of him is too much work for him."

Susana frowned. "Taking care of his own son is too much work?" She stood beside the table, her entire focus on Chris. She seemed to have forgotten about clearing the dinner dishes.

"Apparently." Chris stacked the dirty cups and set them in the basket.

"Then who does he think is going to take care of him?"

Chris shrugged. "Laura says that when something like this happens, there's usually someone else in the village who wants a baby and they'll raise him. But she doesn't know of anyone who's able to."

"We could," Susana answered without hesitation.

Chris smiled and pulled her onto his lap. "Have I told you lately how much I love you?"

She laughed. "That's what you want to do, isn't it?"

"Yeah, it is. My only concern is whether it's wise for us to bring another child into our situation. It may not be any safer for him than staying with his father."

"We need to talk to Doug about that. Why don't we do it now?"

Chris activated his transmitter and filled Doug in on the situation, and Doug approved their idea of adopting him. That, however, brought up the issue of adoption paperwork and how to do it under their assumed names.

"These things are usually done without paperwork in those villages," Doug said. "The couple who wants the child simply takes him into their home and raises him with the birth parent's verbal approval. If paperwork is required later on, I'll handle it through your Paradisian papers, just like Stanley's."

"We have Paradisian papers?" Susana asked.

"Of course you do," Doug said. "All my heirs have Paradisian citizenship."

Juan never even came by the clinic to check on his sick son. Once Jorge was better, Chris and Susana paid the errant father a visit and talked to him about adopting the baby. Chris prefaced the conversation with a diplomatic acknowledgment of how difficult it would be for a single, working father to care for a baby. Although that could never be true for Chris, he knew it was true for Juan.

Juan nodded his head sagely as Chris spoke and easily accepted the proposed arrangement. Chris was glad there was no further tarnishing of María's character, either then or later. Afterward, whenever Juan spoke of the subject to someone else, he said he'd done the doctor and his wife the great favor of giving them his son, a strong, healthy boy who would grow up to be a good worker. Chris chuckled to himself the first time he heard the line, but said nothing to contradict it.

The other children took to Jorge easily. It wasn't unusual to find Bethany or Stanley changing a diaper before one of the adults could get there or Andy leaning against the crib, waiting for Jorge to wake up and "play."

On one particularly memorable occasion, Chris awoke at two o'clock in the morning to the sound of children whispering in the kitchen. He padded along the cool cement floor in his bare feet and stood at the doorway unseen. Stanley was heating a baby bottle on the stove while Bethany sat rocking the fussing Jorge. *"Ya mero, muchachón,"* (Spanish: Almost ready, big boy,) she cooed, using the nickname Chris had started calling him. *"Ya mero."*

Chris went back to wake Susana. "Sorry to wake you, Suze. But you've got to see this for yourself." She joined him at the kitchen door and they both watched the production until Susana's giggling gave them away.

Stanley turned, fist on his hip. "What's so funny? I'm used to mixing chemicals in a lab. I think I can heat a baby bottle." With that, he tested the milk on the inside of his wrist as he had seen the adults do and handed it to Bethany. "Just right." And when Chris double-checked it, it was.

CHAPTER 45
SUCCESS

"There is no wisdom, no insight, no plan that can succeed against the LORD."

Proverbs 21:30, NIV.

26 May 8021 M.E.

Camille sat in the living room of her office suite feeding three-month-old Sadira. Stan had finally received the daughter of Juan Misi he wanted so badly. Why he wanted the girl was still a mystery to Camille. Apparently he simply felt it would be more offensive to the Striders for him to have a "daughter" when they had such trouble generating one.

Nevertheless, Camille had to admit that she rather liked the child, who was both cute and good-natured. And, after three boys, the idea of having a daughter to take shopping and educate in the finer points of fashion was not at all unwelcome.

Things had changed a good deal around the Moden household once Stan and Camille realized that their manipulation of the offspring needed to be improved. In addition to spending more time with the youngsters, Camille occasionally hugged them and made a point of praising them frequently. Stan couldn't bring himself to hug the boys, but he did offer occasional positive comments to them. He also spent more time at home and usually ate dinner with the family. Furthermore, since Stan and Camille were on friendly terms again, they often spent their free time together with the children at museums or other educational venues. They even allowed the youngsters to share breakfast with them.

Sometimes Camille resented the changes they had been forced to make to accommodate the children. But usually she felt that, on balance, the benefits they would reap from them were worth the trouble. And the deeper relationship with her brother made many of the inconveniences less onerous.

"Dr. Desmon?" Madelyn's voice came through the intercom in the office.

Camille lifted Sadira to her shoulder to burp her as she made her way to her office phone. "Yes?"

"Dr. Moden would like you to join him and Dr. Sondem in his office."

"I'll be there in a few minutes." She took Sadira into the nursery and handed her off to the nanny. On her way back through her office, she looked over the shoulder of eight-year-old Saxon, who was working at a small desk next to hers. "That's excellent work, Saxon."

He looked up, beaming. "Thank you, Mommy."

She lifted a disapproving eyebrow. "You, and only you, may call me Mom if you wish, but never Mommy."

"Yes, ma'am, Mom."

"All right, then. I'll be in your father's office."

When she entered Stan's office, she immediately sensed his excitement. "We have a present for you," he teased.

"Oh?" She came to stand in front of his desk.

He looked to Garrick, standing beside him. "Go ahead. It was your work. You can do the honors."

Garrick's black eyes danced. "I think we've found Strider. And Stanley. They're together, as we expected. One of my men finally got a hit on the pictures we've been circulating. A traveling vendor in the state of San Luis Potosí, Mexico, says there's a tall doctor who looks like Strider in one of the villages. He also says there's a son Stanley's age."

"This is wonderful!" Camille exclaimed in a most unusual display of emotion. It was the first bit of good news they'd received since Stanley disappeared over a year before.

Garrick chuckled at Camille's effervescence. "I'm off to Mexico to investigate it for myself," he said as he strode to the door. "I'll bring Strider back alive for you, Camille. And the boy for you, Stan."

CHAPTER 46

SIFTING

" 'Satan has asked for you, that he may sift you as wheat.
But I have prayed for you, that your faith should not fail.' "
Luke 22:31, 32, NKJV.

"Hola, *Lupita,*" Susana said into the phone. "How's Dr. Strider doing? Will he be able to come home soon?"

"He just finished with his last patient," answered the nurse at Chris's clinic. "He should be home in plenty of time for Stanley's party."

"Oh, good. Then we'll see you both shortly."

Susana finished sorting through the rice and moved to the sink to wash it. "How's the homework coming?" she asked over her shoulder.

"Fine," chorused Stanley, Bethany, and Andy, all seated at the Formica table in the large kitchen. "I'll be done before the party," added Bethany.

"Me too," Andy said.

"Good work." Susana shot a glance at the three children before turning to the stove to toast the rice. Bethany was doing math, her tongue peeking through one side of her mouth in a moue of concentration. Stanley stood next to Andy, murmuring prompts and corrections as the younger boy worked on his reading. He frequently broke into grins and patted his little brother on the back when he did well, which reminded her of how dramatically he had changed. At his birthday party exactly one year ago, he had stiffly blown out candles and formally thanked Susana for his cake as if fulfilling a duty rather than enjoying his first ever birthday bash. She'd wondered then if he'd ever be able to enjoy life, or if his harsh upbringing had forever ruined that possibility.

But he had tremendous respect for his new parents—especially Chris, whom he adored—and this had helped him adjust on a mental level. Nevertheless, it had really been Doug's gift of the link, together with Bethany's generous spirit, that had helped him approach emotional normalcy in such a short time. He was now able to interact and play with children his own age almost like any other kid would. Smiles regularly graced his face, and that scary blank expression rarely made an appearance.

As if to underscore her thoughts, Stanley broke into a hearty laugh. "No, not 'come.' This is Spanish, remember? It's *'come.' "* (He eats) He comically mimed eating from a bowl.

All three children laughed, and Susana's face lifted into a gentle smile. How she loved these children. And to think, she had once believed she would never have a family of her own. Now she not only had a family, but she had an amazing family. In fact, she'd ended up with the "ideal" family of her childhood dreams—one daughter, three sons, and an incredible husband—just like in the picture Aedan had insisted she burn. How very, very blessed she was.

She added water and seasoning to the rice and left it simmering on the stove while she made salsa. Everything was nearly ready when Doug's voice burst through her receiver: "Susana!" The urgency in his voice also caught Stanley's attention, and his head snapped up.

Susana activated her transmitter. "Yes, Doug?"

"Evacuation Code Green," he ordered.

A bolt of alarm shot through her. "But Chris isn't here."

"Evacuation Code Green, little filly. Immediately."

Stanley pulled out Andy's chair and instructed calmly but firmly, "Come with me, Andy. Bethany, get the backpack."

No! Susana thought, her heart pounding. "Is this a drill, Doug?"

"Evacuation Code Green, Susana," Doug said, his voice becoming stern. "Immediately."

The children had already burst into action to take up their assigned places. Andy called, "Meet you there, *Mami*" as he and Stanley stepped outside, hand in hand. His excited tone said he believed this to be another drill.

Bethany ran to the coat rack and grabbed the backpack they kept stocked with their few irreplaceable items: Juan Misi's necklace and Stanley's memorabilia. "Aren't you going to get the *muchachón, Mami*?"

But Susana stood immobile. They had always done the drills as a family. Always. And something in Doug's voice told her this wasn't a drill. How could she leave Chris behind?

On the other hand, she couldn't threaten her children's lives either. She especially needed to compose herself if Chris wasn't here. Taking a deep breath, she hurried into the next room, scooped up the napping baby, and quickly settled him into a backpack infant carrier.

When she returned to the door with Jorge, Bethany peered up at her. "What about *Papi*?"

Susana swallowed the lump in her throat and said with an assurance she didn't feel, "Doug can take care of *Papi, chiquita*."

The two headed down the well-worn path that led behind the house, past the garden and chicken coop, and to the outhouse. They carried no possessions except for Bethany's backpack. Susana couldn't see the boys now, which was as it should be. This escape route was meant to get them all out of the house in a way that would look natural to any neighbors or passersby—as if a parent or older child was taking a younger child to the bathroom.

Their house was situated at the edge of town where houses were spread out, and the outhouse, some distance from the road, was hidden behind cactus and mesquite trees. This made it an excellent place to meet a member of the Royal Guard, who would lead them to safety.

Unless this was a drill. In that case, no guard would meet them, Doug would say, "Well done, children," and they would all go back home, laughing and congratulating themselves.

As Susana rounded the outhouse with Bethany, she drew in a sharp breath. The first person she saw was a big, burly man dressed in desert fatigues. The shirt pocket was embroidered with "LM" for *Lejani Mejad*—"Royal Guard."

This was no drill.

Stanley and Andy waited quietly at the guard's side. Having lost his excitement, Andy grasped Stanley's hand tightly, his expression tense. He had great respect for his big brother, who had an uncanny ability to make the unusually "persistent" boy see reason when no one else could.

Susana forced a smile and bent down to give Andy a reassuring peck on the cheek. "Well done, Andy." Knowing that Stanley hated to be treated like a child in front of outsiders, especially soldiers, she laid a hand on his shoulder. "Good work, Stanley. Thank you for your help."

He returned a quick, businesslike nod, his face as immovable as granite. "Our escort is Major Serji Meshon, General Lanse Meshon's brother."

"A pleasure to officially meet you," Serji said. "I'm sorry we've no time to become better acquainted at the moment. We must leave at once. Shall I carry Jorge for you?"

Leave? Another wave of fear swept through her. "But my husband's not here."

"General Meshon is aware of the situation," Serji said in a firm, though not unkind, tone. "He has dispatched another team to recover Chris. We are to meet them at the rendezvous point outside town. Please allow me to carry the baby for you. We can move faster that way." This time he reinforced his request by stabilizing the carrier for her to unfasten it.

"We're leaving on foot?" she asked as she transferred the baby to him.

"For now. Travel by car is impossible—Stan's men have roadblocks just outside the town in both directions."

A small cry of alarm escaped her. Chris's clinic was only a short distance from the opposite edge of town.

"My brother is doing everything possible," Serji said gently. "But we really must proceed, and rapidly."

She pressed her lips together, determined not to frighten the children by bursting into tears. With a nod, she managed to whisper, "Let's go."

Serji led them quickly through cactus, brush, and mesquite trees. They jogged some distance through the rugged terrain, with Serji also carrying Andy much of the way. As the sounds of the village faded behind, those of the arid wilderness engulfed them. Susana didn't know much about the various sounds made by birds and insects, but they had grown so familiar that she paid them little mind.

However, Stanley was, as usual, paying attention to everything. As they crested a small ridge, he suddenly crouched and fell back, his arms going out protectively to pull Andy and Bethany back with him. "Major Meshon, sir," he called in a hoarse whisper. "There are no blackbirds in this area."

"You're correct," Serji said. "But that's no enemy, merely my teammate's signal."

Serji returned a birdlike whistle, and a tall brunette in desert fatigues appeared from behind a cactus to motion them toward a stealth helicopter hidden under a camouflage tarp. From a distance, Susana almost thought she was seeing Camille with darker hair. As they drew closer, she noticed other differences, including a squarer face and a cleft in her chin. Still, the woman was strikingly beautiful, and Susana was not surprised when Stanley introduced her as his aunt.

The woman did seem to be surprised, or at least disappointed, at Stanley's reaction to her. Susana couldn't blame her, either. When the woman smiled broadly and greeted him enthusiastically, he responded with a terse nod. "Aunt Jané, I am very happy to see you," he said in a businesslike tone that conveyed no pleasure whatever. "Please allow me to introduce Dr. Susana Strider, Bethany, Andy, and Jorge." Turning to Susana, he continued, "This is my father's sister, Colonel Jané Lanáj."

Although Stanley's cool reception brought a trace of disappointment to the woman's eyes, her manner didn't alter. Instead, she urged them toward the helicopter saying, "We've been ordered to leave at once."

"But we have to wait for the team with Chris," Susana objected.

Jané turned back, her expression both sympathetic and unyielding. "We cannot wait any longer."

"But what about my husband?" Susana cried, panic rising within her. "We can't just leave him!"

Grasping her upper arm firmly, Jané insisted kindly, "I'm sorry, Susana. I don't know what has happened. But we've been ordered to get you and the children out of harm's way immediately." She paused, lowering her voice. "Further delay will risk all of your lives."

Susana searched the guard's eyes and knew instinctively that this woman understood her fears and wanted only to help. Waiting longer wouldn't help Chris, but it would jeopardize the lives of the children. Bobbing a shaky nod, she whispered, "Let's go, then."

They quickly boarded the helicopter and rose into the falling darkness. The reason for their urgent departure became apparent when Susana perceived several army-type jeeps parked outside their house and the school. Soldiers swarmed the buildings and spread out into the surrounding countryside. Some were following the fugitives' trail, already nearing the site where they had boarded the helicopter. She pressed her face to the window, desperately looking for any sign of Chris or his SUV. Maybe Doug had warned him and sent him driving off in another direction. Maybe they would meet him—

Her heart stopped in her chest as the opposite side of the village came into view. She could clearly see Chris's SUV parked beside the clinic and, at its side, an army jeep. Two large men in green shirts stood outside the still-lit clinic.

"Is Chris still there?" she asked, even though she knew the answer.

Jané hesitated. "It seems so. He's not in the care of any of our teams."

"But those men—are they *Lejani Mejad?*"

"They are wearing the casual uniforms of my father's men," Stanley said evenly.

Susana gasped and clamped both hands over her mouth. They had him! Camille had Chris, and he would suffer unspeakable torture and death at her hands. After all these years—her worst fear had become reality.

She was nearly suffocating herself in her attempt to maintain some degree of composure for the children's sake. Still, she couldn't stifle her sobs.

Having just noticed what was playing out below, Bethany wailed, "There's bad men outside *Papi's* clinic. Do they have him, *Mami*? Do they?"

Susana couldn't have spoken, even if she knew what to say. But Bethany didn't need an answer. She'd already burst into tears, with Andy and Jorge joining in as well. In fact, as the little *ranchito* of Santa María faded into the distance, the whole family surrendered to uncontrollable weeping.

Everyone, that is, except Stanley. He sat, stone-faced and mute, staring into the night.

🏃 🏃 🏃 🏃 🏃

Chris was whistling "Happy Birthday" as he walked into his small office within the clinic. He had already sent Lupita home and was just leaving himself. As he bent over to gather some packages of peanuts and candy for Stanley's birthday piñata, an odd noise caught his attention. He stopped whistling to listen.

The noise came again. It didn't sound exactly like a knock at the clinic door, but what else could it be? Probably another patient wanting to be seen. Setting the piñata stuffers down, he stepped into the hallway.

Oomph! A large fist slammed into his gut.

He stumbled, groping at the wall for support. Someone yanked the hand back and locked it in an iron clasp behind him. A blow to the back of his knees threw him to the ground. A boot landed on his neck and mashed his face against the cold tile. In a matter of two heartbeats, he was as thoroughly subdued as the calves at last week's rodeo.

Straining against the boot, he managed to snatch glimpses of his attackers—four brawny men in black slacks and green polo shirts. The colors of Stan's army.

The men made no sound. In the preternatural silence, Chris's heartbeat drummed loudly in his ears: *Suze—the kids—are they safe?*

One man, shrouded in shadows, nodded down the hallway. Someone jerked Chris to his feet and shoved him into the clinic's lab. He struggled—futilely. The men were gigantic and, like all Paradisians, superhumanly strong. The room itself shrank in their presence. In no time, they had him stripped shirtless and bound to a chair.

So this was it—the meeting he'd dreaded for so long. Could he hold out? Could he resist telling these goons anything important?

The man who had been in the shadows, the one who seemed to be in charge, wordlessly pointed one finger toward the clinic's front door. Two men snapped their fists to their chests and marched toward the lobby.

The dark-skinned, fine-featured leader stepped forward—slowly, deliberately. Huge muscles strained the bounds of his shirt and bulged at his thighs. He addressed Chris in a soft, calm baritone—chillingly calm, considering his obvious threat.

"Strider, we just want Stanley. There's no reason for you or your family to get hurt. Dr. Moden simply wants his son back. So tell me where your wife's taken him, and we'll be on our way."

Chris couldn't help the silly grin that came to his face. This man had just divulged the only thing he really cared about: Stan's men didn't have his family.

"I don't know where they are," he said.

The man smiled. "After all I've heard of you, I would have been disappointed if you'd said anything else. Besides, I'll enjoy an evening's entertainment."

The other soldier still in the lab chuckled ominously. Also a large, dark-skinned man with fine features, he looked like he could be the leader's brother.

And he seemed to anticipate his superior's intentions. The leader had only to nod and the second man reached into a medical bag to withdraw a vial and syringe.

"What's that?" Chris asked.

"Would you like the scientific name or the common name?" the leader asked conversationally.

"I'm not a pharmacologist."

The leader flashed a menacing grin. "Unhappily for you, I am." He drew up some of the medication, tapped the syringe, and squirted out some of the cloudy liquid to clear the air bubbles—all as though he'd done it a zillion times. "This little treasure is my special concoction. My men call it *rat-kulín*. In simple terms, it sensitizes the nocioceptors, which are more commonly known as—"

"Pain receptors," Chris said with a sigh. In other words, it made pain worse. "Sounds delightful."

"Oh, it is, I assure you." The man injected the solution into Chris's arm and then pulled on the black leather gloves that the second man offered. As Chris watched, the hair on his neck stood on end. Those gloves were special. They were fighting gloves—padded, like mufflers, to protect the user's hands. But the right one also had stuff on it: a serrated blade, strips of metal, sandpaper...

The man finished donning the gloves and held his hands up, flexing them meaningfully in front of Chris's face. Then he bent down, his nose inches away. As their gaze met, a chill passed through Chris. His captor's eyes were as dark as midnight and just as cold.

"So, where did you say Stanley was?"

"I don't know," Chris answered.

Wham! The leader punched Chris on the right cheek with the unadorned glove. "Wrong answer. Want to try again? I'll give you a hint. We know your wife called the clinic just before they disappeared. What did she say?"

Chris answered honestly: "I never got the message if she did."

This time the punch came to the left with the other glove. It ended with a quick, expert twist that drew the blade along Chris's cheekbone, and he cried out with the unexpected, searing pain.

The man stood back and cocked his head, as if evaluating a work of art in progress. "What do you think, Errol? A little longer?"

"H'mm." Errol rubbed his chin. "Yes. A half centimeter more toward the nose, I'd say."

Chris gritted his teeth as the man deliberately extended the gash. Standing back, he said, "Yes, that's about right. That one's for your great-grandfather from Dr. Moden."

More questions came, questions about contingency plans, evacuation routes, and contact people. Chris evaded them all, each time earning more punches and more creative uses of the right glove's ornaments.

When the electricity went out, Chris got a short break. By that time, his bruised and lacerated skin throbbed, his head ached, and his mind was growing slow. He was seriously questioning whether he could hold out. It seemed only a matter of time before he caved.

"Be strong, *towí ke akemi*." (Rarámuri: Runs-Barefoot) Doug spoke over the receiver, his voice inaudible to the intruders. "I haven't forgotten you. And you are aiding your family's escape by keeping the men distracted."

Because the transmitter component of his device wasn't activated, Chris couldn't speak back to Doug, but the message was just what he needed. Doug deemed him—the relentless, determined *towí ke akemi*—able to persevere. He could have received no better fortification. Digging deep within himself, he determinedly mined all hidden reserves of strength and resolved to see this thing through.

The respite provided by the power outage was short-lived. The clinic kept kerosene lamps handy for these frequent occurrences, and it didn't take the soldiers long to find a couple of them. Errol cursed the country's unreliable power system as he lit them, and then the leader again bore down menacingly upon Chris.

Suddenly his tormentor jerked upright and spun to Errol. "Colonel?"

Having received the impression that the man had heard something he didn't like, Chris strained to hear anything unusual in the stillness of the blacked-out town. A gentle thudding directly above them caught his attention, but he didn't immediately recognize it. When he did, his heart jumped with excitement: the blades of a stealth helicopter—Doug's rescue for his family.

Errol spoke quietly into a headset, and then with a tiny, almost imperceptible shake of his head, he murmured, *"M'ailashtu,"* into the leader's ear. (Paradisian: We're pursuing them.)

The leader turned back to Chris, his eyes now sparked with anger. Yet his icy calm was unchanged. "Well, maybe that little break gave you a chance to reconsider. Are you ready to cooperate?"

Chris stared into the inky depths of the man's eyes and glimpsed a great abyss filled with loathing. He perceived not a speck of mercy to offset it. Not an ounce of justice to tame it.

In that moment, Chris knew: He was going to die—tonight, if he was lucky. If not, he would be taken to Camille, where he would be her "entertainment." Either way, he would never see his family again.

A wave of suffocating disappointment welled up in him. He'd never see his kids graduate, never walk Bethany up an aisle, never bounce grandchildren on his knee.

Fear followed—not for himself, but for Susana and the children. What would become of them? Would they escape Stan's men? If they did, how would she raise four kids alone while running from Stan? He'd never meant to place her in such a difficult position.

But he had no time to indulge these concerns now. Doug had given him a mission. He needed to help his family by keeping these guys occupied for as long as possible. And, he decided, that would be a while. He might not have the brute strength of the men who'd captured him, but he had taken Josh's admonition to keep running seriously, thereby maintaining both his physical and mental endurance.

Towí ke akemi lifted his chin and summoned every ounce of his natural stubbornness to glower into the blackness of the man's eyes. *"Me* cooperate? Fat chance!"

CHAPTER 47
DEATH

"They have defeated him by the blood of the Lamb
and by their testimony.
And they did not love their lives so much
that they were afraid to die."
Revelation 12:11, NLT.

The helicopter landed at a place Serji called *La Concha de Mar,* "the seashell,"
although Susana had no idea why it merited such a name. The small cement
block house had no electricity, phone, or plumbing. An outhouse, a well-tended
garden, and a little pen with goats and chickens all sat nearby. The entire area
was under camouflage tarps and completely isolated, being probably a hundred
miles from the nearest city of any size. And they certainly weren't near a beach.
Concha de mar indeed.

But then, deciphering the guards' code wasn't her first priority at that
moment. Having simply no tears left to shed, she and the children had stopped
crying. Jorge, utterly exhausted from wailing, had fallen asleep in her arms.
Bethany sat hugging Andy, who still clasped Stanley's hand. Stanley hadn't moved
from the window, hadn't spoken, hadn't shed a tear.

One part of Susana registered this as a problem. He hadn't been this
incommunicative since they left the hacienda. When he had occasionally started
to return to this silent state during the past year, Chris was the one who had
helped him through it. She certainly had no energy for tackling that hurdle just
now.

The blades of the helicopter whirred to a stop. Serji opened the door,
helped the children down, and reached for Jorge. Susana wordlessly handed the
baby to the gentle giant. She saw then that several others of the Royal Guard
were waiting for them. Hope sprang up within her—maybe they were from the
team sent to rescue Chris.

"Is Chris here?" she asked.

Lanse stepped forward to help her down. "I'm sorry, Susana," he said
kindly. "We were unable to reach him."

"Do they—?" She knew what the answer to her question had to be, yet
she couldn't help asking it anyway, hoping against hope. "Does Stan have him?"

He nodded. "Yes. I'm afraid Stan's men have him."

Somehow her overworked tear ducts managed to power up again, and
tears poured silently down her cheeks. Lanse tenderly enfolded her in his arms.
As she wept, another voice made its way into her consciousness—a familiar
female voice, low and calm and reassuring. She looked up to see Debora gathering the children around her. Her mere presence granted Susana a measure of

comfort, and she joined the children in subdued greetings as they made their way to the house.

The warm, homey smells of *champurrado* and freshly baked cookies met them, reminding Susana of long ago afternoons at her *abuelita's* house. But the cozy memory only served to underscore the wretchedness of this situation. She collapsed rather than sat at the large table while the children nibbled on the refreshments.

All except Stanley, that is. He insisted on scouting out the new home. He returned to report that the house had two bedrooms. The larger bedroom, where the two shifts of guards bunked, looked like a barracks, containing five sets of bunk beds and some lockers. The smaller bedroom contained a double bed, a bunk bed, and a playpen, where Debora was, even now, soothing little Jorge and putting him back to sleep.

"The most logical arrangement," Stanley concluded, "would be that I sleep in the barracks since there is an empty bed in there and I am the oldest child." It was the kind of unimpassioned, pragmatic comment so typical of Stanley's stoic persona—and so very out of place in this setting.

"Thank you for your thoughtfulness, Stanley," she said. "But Bethany can share the double bed with me. That way, you and Andy can sleep in the bunk bed in the family's bedroom." He stiffened as she laid a hand on his shoulder, so she withdrew it. "If you want to, that is."

"I shall sleep in the barracks. That will leave sleeping arrangements for—your husband."

She frowned slightly. "All right." Perhaps he needed to know there was a space for Chris if he did return. But why did he call him "your husband" instead of Papi? It sounded like he was withdrawing from the family. Why would he do that?

"Have some *champurrado*," she said. "It's very good. And Debora made oatmeal cookies, too—your favorite."

"Thank you, ma'am, but I am not hungry at present."

Ma'am—not *Mami*?

"Well, at least sit down with us. Here, sit by Bethany." Maybe the link would help Bethany figure out what was happening. Maybe she could do that energy-transfer thing that always seemed to comfort him.

"Yes, ma'am." He obediently sat beside Bethany, but when the girl laid a hand on his bare arm, he roughly shook it off.

Debora returned after putting Jorge to sleep and reached for Andy, who was sitting on Susana's lap, halfheartedly nibbling at a cookie. After taking him for a walk, she settled the sleeping boy into a bunk bed. She then repeated the same routine with Bethany. Finally she returned to the table for Stanley.

"You may see to the others, Your Majesty," Stanley said. "I am fine."

"You don't appear fine," Debora said gently.

Stanley's frown aptly conveyed his offense.

"Yes, it's true that you've shown no emotion, dearest," she said. "But that isn't normal in this situation."

Staring straight ahead, he said, "With respect, ma'am, I show no emotion because I do not require your assistance at this time. Please see to my—" He stopped himself and swallowed. "To Dr. Strider's needs, ma'am. This is a devastating development for her."

Susana watched the interaction in astonishment. She had thought Stanley had truly become part of their family, loving them as they did him. But, in Chris's absence, he seemed to be severing himself from them, as if he wanted no part of the family unless Chris was there. Could his cruel upbringing have truly robbed him of all feeling?

"Very well, dearest. I can only help you if you will allow it." Debora stroked Stanley's head a few times, but neither his rigid expression nor posture changed.

Finally she turned to Susana and extended her hand in invitation. The two proceeded outside, but were barely out of earshot when Susana cried, "What's going on with him, *Ami*? Why is he pulling away from us? What have we done to deserve his treating us like this?"

"You believe he's punishing you, then, rather than himself?"

Susana stopped short. "Himself? Why would he punish himself?"

"You should know the answer to that, dear one. You have a great gift for empathy. 'Tis only your resentment that thwarts your understanding of this poor child's pain."

Susana opened her mouth to point out that she was in pain too, but Debora continued without pause. "Your own pain is normal, yes. But it is the resentment that stymies you in this matter, and that's something you may relinquish if you choose." With a sidelong glance, she noted, "You have never surrendered Chris to Doug, you know."

"He's my husband!" she cried, the heat of anger rising within her chest. "How can I give him to Doug?"

"You know the answer to that as well. You have already done it with your children."

Susana turned away, chewing on her lip.

Laying a comforting arm across her shoulders, Debora said, "Do you remember when you were so terribly scarred that you believed no man would ever marry you? You released to Doug the 'right,' as you saw it, to know the special joy of companionship with a like-minded man. You told me then that you would gladly accept the life of a single woman committed to honoring Doug and serving her fellow man. And that surrender allowed you to open your heart to the needs of others in an unrestrained manner. Do you remember this?"

Susana nodded mutely.

"Yet Doug saw fit to bring a remarkable young man into your life and to grant you the very privilege you had renounced. Why, then, do you cling so tightly to the gift you once voluntarily forfeited? Can you not be thankful for what you have enjoyed these many years rather than aggrieved at its removal?"

"Removal?" Susana asked weakly and choked on a sob. "He's really gone, then?"

"I cannot say, dear. Nor is the answer relevant to my question. The point is that, unless you yield everything, your greatest talents will be forever withheld from those you love most." Her tone grew warmer, sympathy permeating each word. "You must release Chris to Doug—not piece by piece, as you have been wont to do these many years, but freely and unconditionally. Until you do so, your resentment will remain a barricade between you and those you would most like to serve, including Stanley."

"But I can't!" Her anger returning, Susana stomped a few steps away and turned to face her coach. "I can't let Doug have Chris—he'll take him from me if I do!"

The words that slid from her mouth stunned her. Yet, though she'd never put the feeling into words before, she knew at once that's exactly what she'd always feared.

"Is that what you believe of Doug, then? That *he* is responsible for killing his children?"

"N-no," Susana intoned, confused. Then she clarified, "No, I don't mean that he would harm Chris, but maybe he won't protect him. Maybe he'll let Camille have him."

"So you believe that Doug deliberately wrenches from his children that which they most love, simply because he can? That's not characteristic of any love with which I'm familiar. Do you behave thus with your children?"

"Of course not!"

"Yet this is what you accuse Doug of doing."

Susana didn't know how to answer.

"And do you believe that your withholding Chris will in some way affect what is happening to him tonight? I assure you, it will not. Your choice can affect only your response to tonight's events, whatever those events may be. As matters stand, I fear for you. The path you've chosen leads into the dark valley of anger and bitterness. Furthermore, it will influence others, particularly your children. Do you wish to see them follow you down such a wretched pathway?"

"No." Susana shook her head, all her anger gone. Now that her underlying motivations were exposed, she understood how faulty they were. "No, I don't want that."

Taking Susana's face tenderly in her hands, Debora said, "My dear, dear daughter, for years you have asked us to move upon the hearts of our runners, to inspire them toward revival and reformation."

Susana frowned, baffled by Debora's shift in focus. "What does that have to do with this?"

"Don't you see? I have been working, child—on you."

"Me?"

"You have sought revival for a nebulous, worldwide group of individuals, but it cannot come in that form. Each runner must embrace it individually. It must begin with you."

Susana caught her breath. Could it really be that her holding back had resulted in such a delay? Immediately a picture sprang to mind. She stood in the War Room with Josh—dragging her feet, *trying* to obstruct Josh's object.

Standing in the purity and majesty of Debora's presence, Susana saw herself—really saw herself—for the first time in a very long time. It was as though she'd been wearing dark sunglasses that Debora had now removed. She'd thought she lived a pretty good life; now she saw how her resistance had limited what she might have accomplished.

Tears flooded her eyes. "I'm sorry, *Ami*. I'm so sorry."

"Do you want to surrender everything to Doug, then, my dear? Will you give Chris to him?"

Now painfully aware of her failings, of how thoroughly *kanuf* had tainted every action and attitude, she doubted her own ability to make such a commitment. "I—I want to, *Ami*. But I need your help."

Debora smiled, opened her mouth, and breathed on her. Susana closed her eyes, willingly, gratefully, breathing in the sweet-smelling air, redolent of peace and contentment, that flowed into her. As she did, she felt her resentment melt away and the tightness in her stomach relax.

Then, as if standing on a station platform while one train departed and another arrived, she heard the sounds of cicadas and wild burros fade into the distance while blaring alarms and the low hum of an air conditioner grew louder. When she opened her eyes, she was in the War Room. Josh stood before her, studying her closely, and her own last thought echoed in her mind: *Josh is just asking too much of me.*

She didn't know how she had come to be there, but there was no question of it being a dream—she knew it was not. In fact, she wondered how she could ever have believed it to be a mere dream. If anything, this place was more real than what she called the "real" world.

In a voice that was at once soft and resolute, Josh said simply, "May I have the red rose, Susana?"

Her gaze dipped toward the bouquet in her hands, but it caught at the markings on Josh's shirt pocket. Like the others in the room, he wore the casual uniform of the Paradisian army. And like the other uniforms, his pocket was embroidered with the gold initials "EMP" and a symbol representing his rank. But she now noticed that that insignia was unique.

Bedazzled by its significance, she reached forward and traced the symbol with her finger: a lamb. No, not *a* lamb—*the* lamb. The one who had renounced everything to rescue her from Stan's grip. The one who had shed his own blood to secure the right to refute all Stan's accusations against her. Hadn't she seen him do exactly that for the pitiable man on her first visit?

And then the meaning of the red rose became clear. She had remembered that blood was somehow related to its significance, but she now understood whose blood. Josh himself had purchased her freedom with his very life, so even the love she shared with Chris was a privilege made possible through Josh's sacrifice.

He was asking too much? Never.

With tears blurring her vision, she looked again at the flowers in her hands. How pathetic her offering. And how reluctantly bestowed. She had made Josh extract each flower from her bouquet as though it were a king's ransom—when all the time, the King's Ransom had patiently stood before her, asking politely for her little gift.

Thrusting what remained of her bouquet into his arms, she fell to her knees, unable to bear the weight of his gaze. "Josh, I'm so sorry. I'm so sorry. I'm such a failure."

"Failure?" he echoed, his hand resting tenderly on her head. "No, you're not. It's true that you made your course more difficult than it needed to be by clinging to your bouquet of worries. But you never stopped running. We count none a failure who continues to run with us."

"But have I waited too long? Have I ruined everything?"

He drew her gently to her feet and wrapped his arms around her. "No, dear one," he murmured against her ear—with a touch of amusement, she thought. "All is not ruined. But if you wouldn't mind taking this card to Chris, I'd sure appreciate it. It is getting late."

"Oh, yes. Yes, of course." She took the access card and hurried toward the door where Chris waited. She noticed the clock still counting down: 23:45:29—30, 31, 32 …

Less than 15 minutes. Oh, why had she waited so long? She'd probably only made Chris's job harder.

The door slid open with a swish and then closed behind her. Her appearance obviously startled Chris, who looked up with tired, bloodshot eyes and a harried expression. "Suze?"

"Hi," she said with a grin. "Looking for this?"

Relief washed over his face. "I sure am. You have no idea how long I've been searching for it."

"Oh, I think I have a notion."

As she handed the key card to him, she realized that she'd probably never see her husband again until the Awakening. Grief poured over her like a wave but, strangely, brought no regret for the decision she'd made. Swallowing a sudden sob, she reached up to give him a kiss and whispered, "I love you, Christian Strider—so very much."

He smiled tenderly and stroked her hair back. "I love you, *mi tesoro*. But I have to go."

She forced a smile. "I know. Josh is waiting for you." She stepped aside while he held the card to a scanner. The door swished open and then closed behind him.

Closing her eyes, Susana drew a deep breath and exhaled it slowly. She felt sad at losing her husband, but she wasn't upset or afraid as she'd once thought she would be. What's more, she had the paradoxical sensation of lightness—as though she'd finally relinquished a burden that had always been too heavy for her to carry.

She opened her eyes to find herself back in the Mexican desert with Debora. Placing a kiss gently on her forehead, her coach whispered, "Well done, *ve nela*." (Paradisian: my daughter)

They spoke for a few more minutes before Debora boarded the helicopter and departed. Returning to the house, Susana found Stanley sitting at the table. As she entered, he straightened his posture, his eyes flicking to her quickly before he looked away again.

In that instant, she saw—she felt—his pain, and she understood. How could she have missed it before? Stanley felt this whole thing was his fault. He was withdrawing from the family, not because he wished to, but because he didn't think he deserved their love.

Knowing he would never reveal "weak" emotions in front of strangers, much less soldiers, she asked the two guards who were then in the room to allow them a few minutes alone. When they stepped outside, she crossed behind her son and wrapped her arms around him, ignoring his stiffening when she did.

"I love you so very much, Stanley," she whispered. "I'm really glad you're a part of our family. I love being your *mami*."

He swallowed hard and squeezed his eyes shut.

Kissing him on the head, she continued. "I want you to know that none of this is your fault, sweetie. You know, even better than I do, how long *Papi* has been on your parents' lists. You know how much they hate him. You are not responsible for what they do to him. Doug will strengthen *Papi*—and us—to endure whatever we must. And part of that strength will come from the love we each have for one another."

Giving up his tough-guy pretense, Stanley sprang up, threw his arms around his *mami*, and surrendered to sobs.

🏃 🏃 🏃 🏃 🏃

The beating went on and on. Chris hadn't given up any information yet—not one hint about their various escape routes or hiding places. But he wasn't sure how much longer he could hold out. He'd grown nauseated from the pain. His head pounded. Every agonizing breath he drew stabbed like a knife in his ribs. The ruthless blows and unremitting pain tested the limits of even *towí ke akemi's* natural obstinacy.

I wish he'd just kill me and get it over with.

The thought jolted through him like an electric shock. He couldn't think like that. He had a wife and four children depending on him. He had to do his utmost to survive as long as possible, to give them more time to outrun Stan's—

Another clout to the head overwhelmed him with dizziness, and then he must have blacked out. When he came to himself, he was mumbling "Cactus" over and over.

"That's fine, Strider," the leader said. "A good try. And I'd like to give you points for that, I really would. But, you see, it doesn't actually help me very much. In case you hadn't noticed, there's more than one cactus around your sorry little excuse for a house."

A measure of relief—at least he hadn't given them anything useful—was swallowed by the terrifying understanding that he'd given them anything at all. How could he prevent it from happening again?

"Call on my name when you need strength," came Doug's voice through the receiver.

The instruction made no sense. Since the transmitter wasn't activated, Doug wouldn't be able to hear Chris's voice. Still, his logical mind had little energy to object, so habit won. Doug had said to call on his name; Chris obeyed, whether it made sense or not.

"Help me, Doug," he mumbled, the utterance scarcely more than a breath.

A gentle tingling emanated from the transmitter, and he received a little burst of energy, enough to clear his mind a bit. Josh had once told him that the transmitter had Viv properties built into it. Was that the source of his help—some kind of emergency program triggered by Doug's name?

The idea recalled a saying: *All of his biddings are enablings.* He didn't remember where he'd heard that phrase, but after getting the unexpected lift, it suddenly held incredible promise. He wasn't strong enough to hang tough until the end—he'd already proven that. But Doug had ways of fulfilling his promises that Chris knew nothing about, even when those promises didn't seem to make sense.

This insight focused his attention wholly on Doug. An inexplicable sense of peace descended on him, even as his tormentor landed another punch to his exquisitely tender ribs. He petitioned Doug's help again with the same result. This time an image also flashed into his mind, as if Doug had text-messaged it directly to his brain: his trophy ring.

Since his hands were tied behind him, he fumbled for his wedding ring. Forcing himself to concentrate, he focused on the stories represented by the jewels his trembling fingers encountered. First, a large, smooth oval. That would be the ruby, memorializing the time Josh gave up his life in Chris's place. How long ago was that? His brain was still too muddled to recall the specifics, but he knew it was a long time ago—years. Years during which he'd cherished the love of an incredible woman, worked in a profession he enjoyed, and knew the wonder of being called "Daddy." Good years. Bonus years—years he shouldn't have lived, but did live because of Josh's love for him.

Gratitude surged through him, granting him another boost of strength. He continued to explore his ring, and he came to the multifaceted surfaces of two equal-sized circles—the emeralds representing his fights with Stan. Both of those battles were eventually won in Josh's strength.

In Josh's strength.

The message was reiterated over and over as he progressed around the trophy ring, and each repetition undergirded his determination to persevere. Now he understood why Doug emphasized running rather than strength-training. Doug knew Chris could never be strong enough to resist Stan or this beefy fellow beating on him now. He could only win if, thanks to the habit of endurance he'd developed through running, he persisted in tapping into Josh's strength.

His coach had brought him through many difficult situations. Some had been frankly impossible to Chris's way of thinking. Yet that passage from the *Manual* had always proven true: *I can do all things through Josh, who strengthens me.* And it would be true again today, in this very situation—as long as he held on to Josh's strength.

He repeated that passage aloud—"I can do all things through Josh, who strengthens me,"—and he received an energy boost at Josh's name. But the next punch fell with more force and landed squarely on Chris's lips. When blood flowed from his mouth, a tooth dribbled out with it. Apparently his interrogator didn't enjoy hearing the *Manual* quoted—which only made the mulish Chris more likely to do it again.

With gratitude still surging through his veins—a profound, though perhaps incongruent, sense of what an amazing life Doug had blessed him with, of how many incredible gifts he'd granted him—Chris voiced the first passage that came to mind: " 'I will exalt you and praise your name, Doug, for you have done marvelous things.' "

A soft blue luminescence suddenly lit the room. Dazed as he was, it took Chris a few moments to realize that it emanated from the *tsuma* chain around his neck. The light soothed him, but the two soldiers stumbled back and lifted their arms to shield their eyes from it. Garrick immediately recovered and braved the circle of blue light to clout Chris on the jaw—a punch intended to break his jaw, Chris was certain. However, the blow failed in that aim, being noticeably weaker than its predecessors.

Chris grinned feebly as his sluggish mind remembered his Paradisian vocabulary and put the pieces together. *Tsuma*—Paradisian for "praise"—had a strengthening effect on him but drove the enemy back and robbed him of power. With as great a sense of victory as he could muster, Chris breathed, "Great is the Lord, and greatly to be praised; his greatness is unsearchable."

The waning blue light surged forth again, and the leader fell back, out of its reach. But this *tsuma* problem apparently wasn't a new one to the soldiers, for they both seemed to know what to do. The leader had only to wordlessly hold out a hand, and Errol reached into another bag to hand him a whip. Lashings to Chris's chest and abdomen followed, but even the whip's effect was weakened by the blue radiance of *tsuma*.

Still, Chris's body grew weaker under the continued onslaught. Finally the leader said quietly, "How much longer do you think you can take this, Strider? You wield the enemy's defenses well, I'll give you that. But men throughout history—much greater men then you, believe me—have given in and told me what I wanted to know. You'd already be dead if I didn't know my job so well. Is protecting your enemy's son really more important than living to raise your own children?"

Already be dead?

The words struck Chris like a physical blow, for he realized suddenly that the guy had been avoiding injury to vital areas like the liver or spleen. And he must have been modifying his shots to Chris's head too, or he would have been unconscious by now. Obviously, this man was very knowledgeable and experienced—and he was intentionally prolonging the punishment to make it last as long as possible.

A wave of despair coursed through him. Could he do it? Could he hold out and not tell them anything useful?

"Help me, Doug," he pled, his words barely audible, and he received another boost in strength.

" 'Doug will not let you be tempted beyond what you can bear,' " Chris breathed. " 'But when you are tempted, he will also provide a way out—' "

"*Zuule*," Errol hissed as he suddenly snapped to attention and saluted. (Paradisian: elder brother)

A shadow darkened the doorway, but in the dim light of the kerosene lanterns, Chris couldn't identify the newcomer. He could only see that he was a very large man.

The leader turned and drew back in surprise. "What are you doing here?"

Crossing his arms, the stranger asked quietly, "Since when do you question me, Garrick?"

Chris immediately recognized Stan's voice. His British accent momentarily confused him, but then he remembered that Stan's accent reverted to British when he was angry.

"I apologize, sir," Garrick said quickly. "I was just surprised to see you."

Stan flicked his chin toward Chris. "What are you doing?"

"I know he's on Camille's List—I've been careful not to injure him."

Chris snorted at that. Uninjured, did he call it?

Stan ignored Chris. "No fractures, then?"

"None of any consequence. Just his nose and a couple of ribs on the right."

Stan grunted. "What have you gotten from him?"

"Nothing," Garrick grumbled and then swore. "Only praise and passages from that accursed *Manual.*"

"Then I should like a turn with him." Stan started rolling up his sleeves. "Be gone with you."

"Yes, sir." Garrick pulled the nasty gloves off as Errol gathered up their gear. "We'll continue following up clues from the subject's home. I have another squad on the way. Shall I leave some men with you?"

"Are you calling me a weakling? I think I can manage a pitiful outlander who can't even hold up his head."

"Yes, sir." Garrick saluted and strode out with Errol on his heels. Stan accompanied them while issuing more orders. "Check in with Camille at 0700 if you don't hear from me before then. And keep your men out of my way ..."

As soon as they left the room, Chris mumbled desperately, "Help me, Doug." But he must have been in pretty bad shape because the shot of strength he received wasn't even enough to help him sit up, much less figure out how to escape before Stan returned.

"I suppose you've seen better days," Stan said as he strode back into the room. "How do you feel?"

Chris didn't respond, being too slow to think up a pert rejoinder.

Stan brought the kerosene lamp closer and bent over, his brow furrowed. He lifted Chris's chin and aimed the light in each of his eyes, checking his pupils. This gave Chris a chance to examine Stan's face too, and he realized there was something strange about him. His eyes looked different, not hard and ruthless. And his face was missing something—what was it?

The answer came to him suddenly, and, in the way that unfunny things become hilarious when you're exhausted, he dissolved into a delirious sort of laughter that even the pain in his ribs couldn't check. The man's concern intensified, and he quickly released the ropes binding the prisoner. Too feeble to do otherwise, Chris slid down the chair. The man caught him and lowered him to the floor, where he checked several reflexes before Chris could contain his amusement. Finally he managed to murmur, "You're Gabriel" and started laughing again.

Rumbling laughter began deep within the big man's chest and culminated in a belly laugh as he joined Chris's mirth. Then, as suddenly as it had started, the funniness wore off and Chris whispered urgently, "Susana?"

"She's well," Gabriel said, sobering. "They're all well."

A relief beyond any Chris had ever known engulfed him and swept away any notions of machismo he might have nursed. Streams of tears rushed unbidden from his eyes. His family was alive—even well.

"Thank you," he choked out. "Thank you."

"Thank Josh. He got Lanse's men to them in record time. They extracted her and all four children minutes before Garrick's men invaded your home." As he spoke, Gabriel was doing a swift, but quite expert, examination of Chris's abdomen. "I received an urgent call from my *Mikaél*—that's Prince Joshua. He ordered me to proceed to this location alone and in street clothes. I must admit, I puzzled over the order, although I've far too much experience with his wisdom to question it. Now I see that the power failure led Garrick and his men to a most convenient, albeit inaccurate, conclusion that they wouldn't have entertained if I had come with any of my own men. I daresay Garrick will have difficulty explaining his error to Stan in the morning." (Paradisian: Commander-in-Chief)

He pulled a stethoscope from his jacket and listened to Chris's chest and abdomen. "You appear to have no mortal injuries. For that we must thank Garrick's skill. By the by, you've just been tortured by the world's foremost authority in the field."

"I'm honored."

Gabriel flashed a wry smile before his expression turned apologetic. "We have a long and difficult journey ahead of us this evening, and it will be none too comfortable for you, my friend. I daren't take the time to tend to your wounds properly here, nor would I wish to mask any symptoms of potentially dangerous injuries with pain medication. I am sorry."

"I understand completely. And I'm not sorry—I'm just grateful to be alive. I really mean that."

Gabriel nodded. "Well, let's bind those fractured ribs, at the least. That will reduce some of the pain. I can also reverse that contemptible *rat-kulín*." He pulled out a pre-filled syringe and sank the needle into his patient's thigh as he spoke. Then he set to work and, in an amazingly efficient and expert manner, soon had Chris's chest bound. Carrying him outside to a waiting SUV, he laid him on a stretcher in the back and repeated the abdominal exam. Chris kept waiting for Stan's men to show up, but they had apparently taken Gabriel's order seriously—they were staying well out of his way.

Between the poor roads and the periodic stops for Gabriel to reassess his patient's condition, their journey did not progress rapidly. But at least they didn't encounter any more of Stan's men. After bumping along the rough dirt roads for some time, they came to a helicopter, and Gabriel and the pilot loaded Chris's stretcher. Just before dawn they touched down again.

As the noise of the chopper blades died away, Chris heard Susana call, "Gabriel, do you know anything of Chris?" Despite the obvious worry in her voice, it was wonderful music to his ears.

"He's here," Gabriel called. "I have him."

She released a cry of surprise and relief. "How is he? Is he alive? Is he—?"

As she arrived at the helicopter door, their eyes met. Chris thought he'd never seen anything as beautiful as her red-rimmed, velvety brown eyes. *"Hola, mi tesoro,"* he whispered. "Sorry I'm late for Stanley's party."

She swallowed hard, tears streaming down her face. "Oh, *mi amor*," she breathed. She seemed afraid to touch him, but finally grasped his hand. "I'm so glad to see you. We thought—we thought you were dead."

"I thought so too."

Gabriel carried Chris into the house and settled him on a double bed in one room. After giving him a shot of painkiller, he cleaned his wounds, set his broken nose, and sutured the larger gashes on his face and chest. His movements were so deft and sure, Chris asked if he was a physician.

The general flashed a rueful smile. "If by 'physician' you mean, do I have an MD? No. I've just had too much experience cleaning up my brother's messes."

Since the house had no electricity and, consequently, no ice, Susana sat beside him with a pail of cold water and applied cool compresses to his wounds while relating the story of how Lanse's men had rescued them. As she spoke, a fog of wooziness crept over him. His medical mind told him this was probably from the pain medicine and his exhaustion, but, for a moment, he was afraid he was dreaming—or even hallucinating.

Reaching up, he stroked Susana's cheek and was instantly reassured by how solid she felt. "I can't believe it—you're real. I honestly thought I was going to die."

She looked his face over and bent down to plant a gentle kiss on his forehead. "I think that's the only spot I can kiss without hurting you."

"I don't care if it hurts. I want a real kiss."

She hesitated and then bent to brush his lips lightly with hers.

"I know you can do better than that," he said with a weak grin.

She smiled, hesitated, and finally kissed him. Ignoring the pain and the stitches in his lip, he kissed her again, grateful beyond words. Cradling her face against his, he whispered. "I love you, *mi tesoro*. I am so glad to be alive."

"I love you, Chris. I really thought—" She hid her face in his shoulder and sobbed what he knew to be great sobs of relief.

Soon after she returned to applying the cool compresses, the children started awakening. Six-month-old Jorge was first, fussing until Susana laid him on the bed next to Chris. Bethany and Andy woke up next. Bethany burst into tears when she saw Chris, and then Andy and Jorge started bawling too. Soon all three of them were on the bed caterwauling.

The ruckus woke Stanley and the off-duty guards in the other bedroom. Rounding the corner, Stanley approached hesitantly, his face blank. His eyes traveled methodically over Chris's face and chest, left to right, top to bottom, as if reading a book. Then he asked simply, "Garrick?"

Chris nodded.

Unshed tears glistened in the boy's eyes—eyes that were much, much too old for their age. "I'm sorry, sir."

Chris reached out and drew him close. "This is not your fault, son. You didn't turn them into bad people. And that's 'Daddy' to you, if you don't mind."

Stanley buried his face into Chris's chest, and great rivers of tears tracked down his bare skin, stinging the wounds they found on the way. But the discomfort meant little to Chris. He couldn't imagine the combined pain from worry and fear, guilt and shame, that the poor child must be feeling. He was only thankful that he was here to comfort him.

After weeping uncontrollably for some time, Stanley rested in Chris's embrace, his breaths coming in ragged gasps. "I love you, Daddy," he whispered at last. "I really do."

"I know you do, son. And I love you, too."

When Stanley carefully joined the other children on the bed, he promptly put himself in charge of making sure nobody bounced. "It'll hurt *Papi*," he warned the others.

About that time, Gabriel, who had been unloading supplies, appeared in the doorway. When Stanley saw him, he drew up as if ready for a fight.

"No, Stanley," Chris said. "He's not your—"

"Uncle Gabriel!" Stanley took a running leap off the bed, forgetting all about not bouncing, and landed in his uncle's arms. "I missed you."

Gabriel spun Stanley around, laughing. "I missed you, too, Stanley. How wonderful to see you." When he set the boy down, Gabriel looked to Chris and mouthed, "Thank you."

🏃 🏃 🏃 🏃 🏃

Tears of joy moistened Jané's eyes as she watched Stanley hug Gabriel. A year ago, she and Gabriel had wondered if their nephew, so cruelly treated by their own siblings, could ever enjoy normal emotions. But Doúg's *lashani*, as manifested through this special couple, had been able to work the magic that Doúg had promised was possible.

And more magic had been worked tonight as well—Susana had finally, truly surrendered everything and everyone to Doúg. It was a decision years in the making, but all the more precious because of it. Jané guessed that even Chris would rejoice in his ordeal if he knew how significant it had been in bringing about Susana's long-delayed decision. Her burdens would be so much lighter from this day forward. Even her relationship with Chris, though already good, would improve.

Yes, this was a magical night.

Stanley looked up, a little dizzy from the ride Gabriel had just given him, and his eyes fell on her. "Oh, Aunt Jané," he cried. "Did you see? My daddy's back, and he's going to be okay." He charged at her full force, arms wide open.

She received his embrace with all the joy she'd been saving up for a year. "Yes, I saw, *nulu*," she choked out, using the Paradisian endearment for "son" since her native tongue knew no word for "nephew." Through her own tears of joy she added, "I'm so *very* happy."

CHAPTER 48

WARNING

> *"If anyone does not heed the warning and is overtaken by the sword,*
> *his fate be on his own head!"*
> Ezekiel 33:4, REB.

28 May 8021 M.E.

C amille was just settling in at her desk when Iona's voice came over the inter-com. "Dr. Sondem on line three for you, ma'am."

A smile pulled at Camille's lips as she reached for the phone. Garrick generally reported to Stan; if he was calling her, it must be because he had a gift for her.

"Good morning, Garrick. Does this mean you have Strider?"

"No, but Stan does. Surprised he hasn't told you." Garrick sounded tired. No doubt, he'd been up all night. "I'm just reporting in to you as he directed when he took charge of Strider here last night. Has he called in yet?"

What?

"Please hold for a moment, Garrick." Camille put the call on hold and stalked down the hallway toward Stan's office. Charging through his door, she announced, "You need to hear this." She went straight to his desk and engaged the speakerphone. "Garrick, please repeat what you just told me."

Garrick sucked on his teeth, one of the few outward shows of impatience that he allowed himself. Speaking with exaggerated slowness, as if to a child, he replied, "I said, I'm reporting in to you as Stan directed when he took charge of Strider here last night."

Jumping up, Stan demanded, "What do you mean when I took charge of Strider?"

"Stan?" Garrick's surprise was obvious. "You're back in New York already? Did you find Stanley, then? Why didn't you tell me—"

"You're talking nonsense!" Stan shouted. "I haven't left New York!"

Silence answered him.

Glancing at Camille, Stan said warily, "What's this about? Explain."

"I think we have a problem," Garrick said and then mumbled a curse. "And it must involve Gabriel."

"Go on."

"When we got to Strider's house last night, we found no one there or at the school where the wife teaches. But we did find Strider at the clinic. While I was interviewing him, someone who looked, spoke, and behaved exactly like you came in and assumed charge of the interview."

"So you were duped! Didn't you notice he didn't have my scars?"

Garrick heaved a sigh. In a voice that spoke of both fatigue and frustration, he said, "It was nighttime, and the electricity was out. You know how unreliable the power is down here."

"Apparently that's not the only thing that's unreliable!"

"You're right, sir. But who would expect an unarmed enemy to walk into a contingent of fully armed soldiers all by himself? And, in my defense, allow me to point out that, if it had been you, and you were angry enough to be speaking with a British accent, you wouldn't have allowed me to get close enough to check you for scars."

"How dare you speak to me like that! I'll—"

"Excuse us for a moment, Garrick," Camille interjected. Putting the call on hold, she turned to Stan. "I'm as upset about this loss as you are, but we need to keep our long-term goals in focus. We certainly cannot afford to antagonize Garrick, particularly not at this critical point in our history. And you know how rarely he errs." Softening her tone, she added, "Besides, he's right, Lusu. You would not have allowed an examination in that situation."

He scowled and reengaged the line. "All right. What happened after he took over with Strider?"

"We staked out the house and followed a few clues we found there, but they were all dead ends. He ordered me to report in to Camille this morning, which gave him a whole night's head start." He muttered an oath. "So, I'll call in more men and get started—again."

"Very well," Stan agreed. "Keep us informed."

Stan hung up, peppering the air with epithets before roaring, "We've lost that boy again!"

"Yes," Camille agreed reluctantly. "Even when Gabriel had a mere half-hour head start, we couldn't find any trace of him."

Madelyn interrupted on the intercom. "Mr. Damour on line three, sir. I'm sorry."

As Stan put the call on speakerphone, his hand trembled—and not with anger. "What is it, Damour?" he bellowed, no doubt to hide a tremor in his voice as well.

"I thought you'd like to know that little Stanley is safe once again," Doúg said. "I'm sure you were worried, what with all the criminals after him."

"Did you call just to taunt us?" Camille spat.

"Actually, I called to formally issue a warning. The following runners are now and will remain hands-off: Stanley Moden Jr., hereafter known as Stanley Strider—"

"You can't give our son away," Stan objected.

"Your son, is it?" Doúg challenged. "Do you really believe that I'm unaware of his true origins? Would you rather have me expose to the world the genetic research you've been doing on humans?"

Stan grunted.

"Very well. Then, to continue, Stanley Strider is under my protection, as is Christian Strider, Bethany Strider, Andrew Strider, and Jorge Corona Strider."

With the last name, Stan cast a questioning glance at Camille, and she shrugged. She'd never heard of him either.

Doúg continued. "Again, these are all lifetime orders. I will also take the liberty of reminding you that a lifetime order is already in place for Susana López Strider. Unless any of these individuals commits some evil whose consequences you can legitimately maneuver into bringing them serious harm, they are under my protection."

"Understood," Stan grumbled.

"Do we need to review the terms, or are we clear as to the result of a breach in our agreement?"

"Don't insult my intelligence," Stan snarled. "I'm not one of your little human pets."

"We're clear, then?"

"We're clear. I won't be giving you an excuse to call the Final Battle. I'll honor your *request*."

"Very well. Good day."

When Stan hung up and paused to draw a calming breath, Camille surreptitiously did the same. Although she pretended fearlessness—indeed she truly feared little—these compulsory chats with Doúg wholly unnerved her. It brought her some little consolation to know that even Stan himself suffered trepidation in the tyrant's presence.

Lifting the phone, Stan dialed Garrick. "Abort the mission. We just got a hands-off order … No, the order's for all of them … Excellent idea. Here she is."

Stan handed the phone to Camille. "Confirm for him that I'm me and not Gabriel."

She took the phone. "Hello, Garrick. You were just speaking to Stan, and I will confirm that we've received a hands-off order on the entire family. For *life*." She heaved a frustrated sigh.

Garrick sucked on his teeth. "Great."

"Garrick," Camille said, "Have you any information about another child, one Jorge Corona Strider?"

"No, but there was a crib and other baby supplies in the house. I'll find out what I can about him before returning."

"Very good." After Camille hung up, she stared at the phone for several moments. But her disappointment at being denied Strider suddenly dissipated when she realized that Stan was unusually quiet. Turning, she saw him staring silently out the window, arms crossed. It wasn't like him to be so calm after a call from Doúg. It rather worried her.

"Lusu, what is it?"

He rubbed his chin. "Two things. First, why did he wait to issue that order? We've been after that child since he disappeared, yet he put him in the NMH instead of issuing a hands-off. Why go to the extra trouble?"

"I see what you mean. He must have used this time to some advantage."

"That other child, perhaps? Someone else they influenced while in hiding? Something they did there?"

"Perhaps. We'll need to investigate all possibilities."

Stan didn't respond.

"And what's the other thing?" she prompted.

He turned to face her. "We've been operating on the assumption that more time is better, trying to put ourselves on the best footing possible. But we've done a lot in the last few years. The offspring have already lightened our load and allowed us to work more efficiently. The organization's never been as coordinated or strong as it is at this moment."

Camille nodded thoughtfully. "You're thinking it may be better to trigger the Final Battle ourselves, at a time that suits us best."

"Yes—instead of letting Damour pick the time."

"We're certainly not organized yet. We could only actually set up our own states in one, perhaps two, areas just now."

"Yes, that's true—we're not yet ready. But we're getting close."

"I like the idea of triggering the Final Battle. Why should we allow him to choose the time he finds most advantageous?"

"Precisely."

A slow smile spread over her face. "*Zuulu*?"

He chuckled. "Yes, *zali*, with pleasure. I can think of no hands-off order I would rather violate than that of the man who stole Stanley from us. When the time's right, we'll use Strider as the trigger."

CHAPTER 49

RETURN

"The ransomed of the Lord shall return, and come to Zion with singing, With everlasting joy on their heads."
Isaiah 35:10, NKJV.

The rooster's crowing awoke Susana just as the sun's first rays began to light the sky. The family had been in their primitive hideaway for nearly two months. To her, *La Concha de Mar* now seemed almost like their own little piece of paradise. So much healing had occurred here. She had come to understand that's what the name referred to—a protected place of growth and healing.

She propped herself up on one elbow to gaze at her sleeping spouse. His physical wounds had healed quickly. Except for some new scars and the addition of a little bump to the profile of his nose—all of which only made him more ruggedly handsome—he was as fit as ever. Not surprisingly, he'd had some nightmares from which he'd awake mumbling something about "cold eyes." But their little retreat, removed from both the conveniences and distractions of the modern world, had turned out to be exactly what he needed. The labor required to feed everyone and keep them reasonably clean demanded an unceasing round of physical chores—drawing water, milking goats, hoeing the garden, and more. It was good therapy for all concerned.

Each of the children had also shown evidence of the family's trauma. Jorge had been unable to sleep for the first month unless Chris put him to bed. Andy kept crawling into bed with his parents. Bethany had awakened frequently with nightmares. And Susana often awoke in the middle of the night to find Stanley standing beside the bed, simply watching his daddy—as though he might disappear if not kept in view.

Debora had helped solve most of these problems by suggesting that Stanley and Andy share a bed, their heads at opposite ends of the lower bunk. Andy felt more secure with his big brother nearby; Stanley could keep an eye on Chris; and Bethany felt more settled with her linkmate in the room. It made for a crowded room, but everyone slept more soundly.

Debora also dropped by to see them frequently. Her unhurried visits brought her special kind of tranquility. She ran with each of them individually, even taking little Jorge on private walks, and spent as much time with them as they wanted.

Susana had borne her evidence of trauma, too. Mostly, she couldn't sleep unless she was touching Chris in some way. And if he happened to roll away from her in the middle of the night, she awoke in a panic. But, like the others, she was now feeling safer—more at peace.

In fact, peace swathed her entire life like a comforting blanket. She hadn't realized how much mental energy she'd been expending in worrying about her family. How silly that seemed now; she finally understood she could never protect them absolutely. Of course, she would do whatever she could to keep them safe and happy. But there were so many things beyond her control. Strangely, accepting that truth was incredibly liberating. She just refused to worry over what she couldn't control, relegating the unknown to Doug's loving care.

When the rooster crowed again, Chris awoke. He stretched and murmured, "Another beautiful day in the Mexican desert."

She giggled and bent down to kiss him. "I love you, *mi amor*."

"I love you."

Maybe someday their mutual appreciation for being alive together would wear off. For now, they voiced those words as often as possible.

They rose and dressed quietly so as not to wake the children. Greeting the ever-vigilant Jané as they exited the house, they embarked on their usual morning stroll to chat with Doug. The day would soon turn hot, but the early morning breeze was cool and refreshing. They ambled into the yard, their leisurely footsteps sending up puffs of dust from the parched ground. The chickens that provided them with eggs ran toward them clucking, but soon wandered off again when they realized they had no scraps to share. The goats likewise bleated for a few moments, settling down only after Chris and Susana sat by the well.

Chris activated his transmitter, and, after the usual greetings, Doug asked, "How would y'all like to go home?"

"To Santa María?" Chris asked.

"To California," Doug said.

Susana let out a whoop and a yell. "Really, Doug? Really?"

Doug laughed. "Yes, little filly, really. I had a little chat with Stan after their latest show of interest, and I've been watching 'em close-like ever since. They've recalled all their men and have been behavin' just fine. Y'all will be safe from their mischief."

The three older children, awakened by Susana's joyful cry, came running out of the house in their pajamas. "What is it, *Mami*? What is it?"

"We're going home," Susana exclaimed, hugging them. "We'll get to see your *abuelitos, y tíos, y primos, y—y todos!*" (Spanish: Your grandparents, and aunts and uncles, and cousins, and—and everyone!)

Stanley activated his transmitter. "Did you issue a hands-off order, *Ada*?"

"Yes, buddy. Lifetime orders on the whole family," Doug answered. "And they're honoring it."

"Lifetime orders on *all* of us?" Stanley laughed. "I'll bet they're going nuts 'cause when they got the lifetime order on *Mami*, Father and Garrick holed up in Father's office for days, and Father never even came home until Mother got back from Washington and figured out the solution to the problem Father and Garrick were having, which was ..."

As Stanley babbled excitedly, Bethany jumped up and down beside him, squealing with delight while Andy ran circles around them both, yelping and hooting. The rambunctious display sent the guards into fits of laughter.

When things settled down again, Chris asked, "What about George and Vanessa?"

"They were recalled shortly after your disappearance. George was quietly helping Stan in his lab until a month ago, when he disappeared again. He'll show up in another guise to be around if y'all slip up and commit some evil whose consequences he can toy with. Otherwise, he'll keep his hands off you. You'll be able to move back into your old house and rejoin your practices."

"We still have a house?" Chris asked. "I mean, it's been over a year."

"I've been sending Benny the money to cover your mortgage, property taxes, and all that. Knowin' your families, I'm sure the house will be clean as a whistle and waitin' for y'all when you get there."

"Wow, Doug," Chris said. "Thanks. What a great surprise."

"You're welcome, pardner. Your Paradisian passports and papers will arrive tomorrow, and then y'all can be off." Doug hesitated before adding in a teasing tone, "Although there is one little side trip I was thinkin' of askin' y'all to make. But, nah, I doubt it would interest you much."

Chris chuckled. "What did you have in mind, Doug?"

"Well, there's this village I know of in the Sierra Madres," Doug began, and Chris's eyes popped. "Tony's been hangin' out there, hopin' you'd show up. When he cleared out, he left behind a mess. It sure would be a help if I could find a pediatrician and a physical therapist who wouldn't mind spendin' a few months up there. 'Course the chances of finding a team like that, especially one that speaks the language, is pretty slim."

"Doug," Chris said with a mixture of disbelief and exhilaration. "Are you sending us to Juan Misi's village?"

"Well, not if it's too much bother," Doug teased. "I wouldn't want to put y'all out any."

Chris looked to Susana, excitement on every feature. He'd wanted to visit the village of his ancestors ever since she'd known him. She eagerly nodded her approval. With a whoop, he lifted her and twirled her around. The children likewise twirled each other around, hugged their parents, chattered excitedly in bits of Rarámuri and—

Well, it was generally another happy mess, with Doug laughing through it all.

Finally Chris said, "Doug, this is amazing. I've wanted to go there since I was a kid. Thanks so much."

"Happy to do it, pardner. There will be some work involved, but mostly y'all will just be restin' up some more before goin' back to LA."

Back to LA. The words filled Susana with gratitude. They were going home!

CHAPTER 50

DREAMS

> " 'I will pour out My Spirit on all flesh ...
> Your old men shall dream dreams,
> Your young men shall see visions.' "
> Joel 2:28, NKJV.

A door opened with a swoosh, granting Chris entrance to a room buzzing with activity. Several members of the Paradisian army bent over different consoles and spoke into headsets while alarms blared. Other officers gestured energetically as they conferred around a large holographic globe in one corner. Josh and Gabriel conversed in urgent tones at a big-screen projection of a battle plan.

He'd stepped into a war room. Probably the one from which Josh was directing the war with Stan.

At Chris's entrance, the multiple conversations ceased. Turning toward him, Josh broke into a great smile. "Welcome."

"Josh. How great to see you!" Chris grasped his old coach's outstretched hand and found himself in a hug.

"And you, my dear, dear boní. Welcome to my little hideaway."

As yet another alarm blared, Chris observed, "Not a peaceful one, it seems. What's all the excitement about?"

"There's not much time left." Josh motioned toward a digital clock on the wall behind Chris.

Noting that the red numbers were counting steadily forward from 23:46:15, Chris asked, "What's the countdown for—the Final Battle?"

"Exactly right. But there's still much to do."

"Then put me to work," Chris said as he pushed up his shirtsleeves. "What can I do to help?"

"I do love you," Josh said with a tender smile. "And, as a matter of fact, I have a very important job for you."

"Name it."

"I want you to help Stanley raise an army."

... army ... army ... army ... army ... army ...

As Josh's words echoed into the distance, Chris's eyes fluttered open to meet the dimness of the humble one-room dwelling they had called home for the last several months. His family slept peacefully in the predawn darkness, their rhythmic breathing providing a decided contrast to the noise of the dream.

No, that didn't seem like the right word for what he'd just experienced. It had been too vivid, too urgent. A vision, maybe? Yet the commission seemed so far-fetched. He knew nothing about raising an army.

With the dream's urgency still weighing on him, propelling him into action, he couldn't possibly return to sleep. So he arose, ducked through the hut's low doorway, and strode restlessly to a ridge overlooking the canyon below.

There was no way that experience—so vivid, so compelling—was a mere dream. But it must have some symbolic meaning. He was a doctor, not a soldier. How could he possibly help Josh raise a literal army? And Stanley—what could a twelve-year-old know about military organization? No, there must be some other meaning that he was missing.

"*Papi*?" Stanley called softly. "Is that you?"

"Yes, son, it's me." Chris moved toward him. "What are you doing up so early?"

"I had a dream," the boy said, rubbing his eyes.

Chris groaned inwardly. He'd hoped the nightmares were behind them. Putting an arm around Stanley's shoulders, he drew him close. "It's all right, son. We're all under Doug's protection. Nothing will happen to any of us that we can't handle with his help."

"No, *Papi*, not a bad dream. A message dream."

"Oh?" If that description hadn't so perfectly expressed his own experience, Chris might have contested Stanley's claim. But now he merely asked, "What was the message?"

Stanley gazed up at him, his eyes lit with supernatural intensity. "Josh wants me to raise an Outlander Division for his army," he said deliberately. "He said you would help."

Chris stared at him, unbelieving. It almost sounded as if Stanley had been listening in on his dream. "Stanley, tell me about this dream you had."

When Stanley did, Chris exclaimed, "That's incredible. It's almost exactly the one I had. But I don't think it's meant to be literal. I don't know anything about running an army."

"Oh, no—it's only a division of an army, *Papi*."

"*Only* a division? Stanley, I don't know anything about running any part of an army."

"But Prince Joshua said I was supposed to run it, and I can do that part."

"You?"

"Of course. My education has included military history and organization—"

"But there's a big difference between studying military history and directing a real outfit."

"My education was not merely academic," Stanley said with the exaggerated patience of a parent instructing a child. "I was also trained to assume full control of the army should Father and Garrick be temporarily unavailable. I was provided with practical training in all aspects of military supervision."

Of course he was, Chris thought with combined outrage and pride. Was there no end to Stan's exploitation of this poor child? Yet, no matter what Stan had required of him, Stanley had risen to the challenge.

"I have participated in military operations since age seven," Stanley continued. "I was placed in control—"

"Stop." Chris laid a hand on his son's shoulder, feeling a bit weak in the knees. Perhaps he shouldn't be surprised at such revelations. But by now, Stanley had become fully integrated into their family, and Chris preferred to think of him as his normal twelve-year-old son. He would rather expunge all mental images of the cruel world his child had been forced to enter so prematurely.

"I get the idea," Chris continued sadly. "You can run a division."

"Yes, *Papi*. However, I'm not certain about the recruitment aspect. I have no experience with that."

"I guess that's where I'm supposed to come in. In my dream, Josh said I was to help you *raise* an army. But the truth is, I have no idea how to do that either."

"But of course you do," Stanley exclaimed. "You've already done it."

Chris squinted at the boy. "I've raised an army?"

"Yes. You raised—" A look of sudden comprehension came over him. "Oh, this is what they meant."

"What who meant?"

"Mother, Father, and Garrick. They talked about it not being 'engaged' yet, that the Activator—that's you—hadn't yet understood its purpose."

If this was meant as an explanation, it wasn't working—Chris was only more confused. "The purpose of what?"

"The Kids' Klub, of course. Its true purpose is to prepare youth to join Doug's army."

"No, its true purpose is to help kids develop a relationship with Doug. Josh told me that himself."

"Really?" Stanley's face crinkled into a puzzled frown. "Well," he said slowly, "can it have two purposes?"

As Chris considered the question, a series of experiences came back to him: Stan's sustained interest in the Kids' Klub; Josh's warning that Stan saw another purpose for it; Aedan saying that Stan could see potentials beyond the immediate future …

Chris didn't believe Doug intended to use the Kids' Klub itself as a recruiting tool. That smacked too much of Stan—of groups like the Hitler Youth and the organization Stan himself used to "educate" kids in third-world countries. It was just too sneaky for Doug. Yet, the organizing, recruiting, and public relations skills that Chris had learned while establishing the Kids' Klub were exactly those he'd need to recruit for Doug's army. The contacts he'd cultivated and the network he'd built up for the one could also be used for the other. He thought he was unprepared for the job? Doug had been preparing him for thirteen years.

Stanley was right: With Doug's help, Chris had raised an army of sorts. And if he had done it once, he could do it again—easier and faster and with fewer kinks to work out.

Chris chuckled, a great sense of relief washing over him. "You know what? I think it—I think we—can do anything Doug wants us to do. Come on; let's wake the family and go home. We have work to do."

As they started back to the hut, he noticed Stanley cast a regretful glance behind them. "Something wrong?" he asked.

"No. It's just such a pretty sunrise. *Papi*, do you think we have time for a run?"

Chris tousled Stanley's hair. "Son, there's always time for a good run. Come on—I'll beat you to that ridge."

FOREIGN WORDS AND PHRASES

P = Paradisian: Spoken in the fictional country of Paradise Island. (More information on the rules and grammar of this invented language is available at www.DellaLoredo.com)

R = Rarámuri (Tarahumara): Native American language that has no written alphabet. It has been transcribed phonetically using various alphabets, which results in different spellings for the same word (e.g., the word for "hello" may be spelled kuira, cuira, and even quira). I chose the spellings that seemed easiest for an English speaker.

S = Spanish: as spoken in Mexico

abuelita (S): grandmother (endearment)
Áchimi tamí bichíima? (R): Will you trust me?
ada *(AH-dah)* **(P):** dad; **adu** *(AH-doo)*: daddy
Ahora te digo lo que hiciste (S): (Right now) I'll tell you what you did
ama *(AH-mah)* **(P):** mom; **ami** *(AH-mee)*: mommy
amoúr *(ah-moe-OOR)* **(P):** I moan
anát *(ah-NAHT)* **(P):** a hormone produced in the tonsils of Paradisians and vital to the regulation of their immune systems
ayena abi (R): yes
bachí (R): older brother
boní (R): younger brother
champurrado (S): a traditional hot beverage made with cornmeal and chocolate
chiquita (S): little one (endearment)
d'alasház *(dah-lah-SHAZ)* **(P):** I love you
d'amoúr *(dah-moe-OOR)* **(P):** I moan (yearn, long) for you; **Anglicized:** Damour *(duh-MORE)*
Deón *(day-OWN)* **(P):** eternal one (always capitalized; is both singular and plural)
desmón *(days-MOAN)* **(P):** one who inspires awe; **Anglicized:** Desmon *(DEHZ-men)*
Ekanu Mejad Paladisi *(eh-KAH-noo MAY-zhad pah-lah-DEE-see)* **(P):** Paradisian Royal Army

fidén *(fee-DANE)* **(P):** one of unusual cunning; **Anglicized:** Fiden *(FIE-den)*
fuj *(foozh)* **(P):** faith
inje *(EEN-zhay)* **(P):** a quantity too large to express in words; tremendously
jishana *(jee-SHAH-nah)* **(P):** righteousness
kanuf *(KAH-noof)* **(P):** selfishness, evil, sin
kuira **(R):** hello; **kuirabá:** hello (in return)
Kuira, keni amígowa **(R):** Hello, my friend
Kuirabá, keni no **(R):** Hello to you, my son
la concha de mar **(S):** the seashell
lakviv *(LOCK-veev)* **(P):** degenerative condition caused by a lack of Viv fruit
lanáj *(lah-NAZH)* **(P):** to help or serve
lashani *(lah-SHAH-nee)* **(P):** selfless love
Lejani Mejad *(lay-ZHAH-nee MAY-zhad)* **(P):** Royal Guard
lok *(loke)* **(P):** to stand ready
m'ailashtu *(ma-ee-LASH-too)* **(P):** We are pursuing them
mami **(S):** mommy
menod *(MAY-node)* **(P):** to complete a task to perfection; **Anglicized:** Menod
    (Mee-nahd)
meshon *(MAY-shone)* **(P):** one who shows compassion
mi amor **(S):** my love (endearment)
mij dinósh *(meezh dee-NOSH)* **(P):** restoring enzyme
mikaél *(mee-kie-EL)* **(P):** commander-in-chief
misi **(R):** cat
mi tesoro **(S):** my treasure (endearment)
modén *(moe-DANE)* **(P):** exalted one; his/your highness: **Anglicized:** Moden
    (MOE-den)
Modén Eshí (M.E.) *(moe-DANE eh-SHEE)* **(P):** Moden Years (a dating sys-
    tem in which the year 0 is the year of Stan's birth; instituted by Stan, it is
    used within Moden Industries.)
muchachón **(S):** big boy (Chris uses as an endearment)
natérarabá **(R):** thank you
Nij Mashil Halini *(neezh MA-sheel ha-LEE-nee)* **(P):** Program to Shelter
    Runners
No me importa **(S):** It doesn't matter to me
nulo *(NOO-low)* **(P):** son; also used for nephew; **nulu** *(NOO-loo)*: son
    (endearment)
onó **(R):** father
pad'amoúr *(pah-dah-moe-OOR)* **(P):** I ached from missing you
papi **(S):** daddy
pobrecito **(S):** poor little guy
poli *(POE-lee)* **(P):** a birthmark of particular significance
Que es? **(S):** What is it?
Quien es? **(S):** Who is it?
rat-kulín *(raht koo-LEEN)* **(P):** pain-enhancer
sin hablar conmigo **(S):** without talking to me
sondem *(SONE-dame)* **(P):** ally; **Anglicized:** Sondem *(SAHN-dem)*
Soy yo **(S):** It's me
towí ke akemi **(R):** lad who runs barefoot

tsuma *(TSOO-mah)* **(P):** praise

Ut tsa'nui *(oot tsah-NOO-ee)* **(P):** I just know it

ve nela *(vay NAY-lah)* **(P):** my daughter

viv zabé *(veev zah-BAY)* **(P):** life-tree

y tú ni pensaste en mi **(S):** And you didn't even think about me

yushún *(yoo-SHOON)* **(P):** family of siblings; **yushuni** *(yoo-SHOO-nee)*:
   families

zala *(ZAH-lah)* **(P):** sister; **zali** *(ZAH-lee)*: sister (endearment)

zule *(ZOO-lay)* **(P):** brother; **zulu** *(ZOO-loo)*: brother (endearment)

zuule *(zoo-OO-lay)* **(P):** elder brother; **zuulu** *(zoo-OO-loo)*: elder brother
   (endearment)

SNEAK PEEK AT THE LAST BOOK IN THE TRILOGY:
FIGHTING THE GOOD FIGHT

HELP!

"Oh, please help us against our enemies,
for all human help is useless."
Psalm 60:11, NLT.

Captain Jorge Strider hiked quickly along the mountain trail, his night vision goggles granting him easy passage through the moonless night. His black body suit made him virtually invisible; his training as a member of the Special Operations Forces of the Paradisian army's Outlander Division made him virtually soundless. Were he alone, his pursuers would never detect him, even with the unconscious child he carried on his back.

However, he was not alone, and the four prisoners he had freed from the enemy's detention facility in Peru had none of these advantages. The three ambulatory prisoners—a twelve-year-old boy and his parents—followed Jorge closely but clumsily. To his trained ears, their progress was just plain noisy. Yet they couldn't slow down to go more quietly. With every passing minute, their well-trained, well-equipped pursuers were closing on them. At the last bend, he'd even glimpsed the leader. His only hope now was to reach the river over the next rise before their pursuers caught them. The boat he kept hidden there would carry them to safety.

This escape route was not his preferred course. In fact, it was Plan D of four getaway options. Although he kept himself familiar with the trail, he had never been forced to use it on a mission. The fact that the enemy had foiled all three of his alternative routes was only one of the several problems he'd encountered during this operation, and the series of mishaps gnawed at him. Rescuing prisoners from Stanley L. Moden, President of the Allied States of Desmoden, was never easy. Once he had someone in his iron grasp, he held on with the tenacity of a wolverine. Still, Jorge had rescued prisoners from that detention facility numerous times and had never run into so many obstacles. Why had this mission gone so wrong? Could there be a mole in the Outlander Division? Or had he gotten overconfident and lax in his procedures?

The labored breathing of the five-year-old girl strapped to his back drove home the latter possibility with excruciating force. When he had attempted to implement Plan C, she'd been mauled by guard dogs patrolling an area that had never been patrolled by dogs before. He'd cleaned and dressed the nasty wounds on her legs, but infection had still set in. She was now unconscious, and, with her little body tied to his, he could feel her fever rising.

When a curve in the trail revealed the graveyard that topped the mountain, Jorge surged forward with new energy. Maybe they would get out of this mess yet.

His superiors and family probably already thought he was dead—or worse, captured. He'd dropped off their radar three days ago, three long days of hiding and trekking. But soon he could relieve their minds. Deliverance was just through that cemetery and down the hill.

The family also seemed to catch a second wind. Jorge could sense their relief as they followed him through an opening in the stone wall. Still following the trail, they quickly weaved between the graves to the far side of the cemetery. However, as he approached the other opening, he stopped abruptly. The boy grunted as he collided into his back.

"Wait here," Jorge whispered. Spinning around, he rapidly retraced his steps toward the other opening. As the gap in the wall came into view, he saw that their pursuers had already reached it. Sprinting back to the far end of the graveyard, he examined that opening to assure himself that what he'd seen through the goggles was accurate. Picking up a rock, he tossed it into the wire mesh blocking their exit—a fence that had never been there before. A loud ZAP! testified to the electricity running through it.

They were trapped.

"There's no way out," a soldier called triumphantly in Spanish. "You've pestered us long enough, Phantom—now you're mine!"

Whispering instructions to the family, Jorge quickly unstrapped the makeshift harness and secured the unresponsive girl to her father's back. Then he transferred his night vision goggles and last remaining handgun to him as well. He had one more plan, although he recognized it as an act of desperation.

They could not all escape—this he knew. But he hoped to draw the soldiers to the back of the graveyard and, between the darkness and the confusion of the hunt, give the family a chance to sneak out the front. They would still have to find a path around the cemetery and make their way down to the hidden boat. Yet if he could keep the pursuers distracted long enough, the family just might make it.

At his signal, the family crept away. Dashing from the cover of one tombstone to the next, they moved toward the other opening until Jorge could no longer see them. He stayed near the fenced-off opening at the back, darting in different directions and tossing rocks here and there to create the impression of several fugitives scattering to different hiding places.

When he heard two enemy troops drawing near, he dove behind a tombstone. There he crouched in absolute silence, even holding his breath. Only the heartbeat drumming loudly in his ears broke the stillness. Nevertheless, the muzzles of two rifles poked around either side of the tombstone.

He would have liked to watch the twenty-two years of his life pass before his eyes in that moment. But he could not be so optimistic. His death would not be a quick one. Even if Stan Moden knew the meaning of the word "mercy," he wouldn't grant Jorge any. He had been a pest for too long. He knew too much. And, perhaps most important, he was the son of Dr. Christian Strider, son of Juan Misi.

We invite you to view the complete
selection of titles we publish at:

www.TEACHServices.com

Scan with your mobile
device to go directly
to our website.

Please write or email us your praises, reactions, or
thoughts about this or any other book we publish at:

TEACH Services, Inc.
P U B L I S H I N G
www.TEACHServices.com • (800) 367-1844

P.O. Box 954
Ringgold, GA 30736

info@TEACHServices.com

TEACH Services, Inc., titles may be purchased in bulk for
educational, business, fund-raising, or sales promotional use.
For information, please e-mail:

BulkSales@TEACHServices.com

Finally, if you are interested in seeing
your own book in print, please contact us at

publishing@TEACHServices.com

We would be happy to review your manuscript for free.

CPSIA information can be obtained
at www.ICGtesting.com
Printed in the USA
BVHW062022280122
627332BV00006B/111